AF560769

TIME IN INDIA
CONCEPTS AND PRACTICES

STUDIES IN ORISSAN SOCIETY, CULTURE AND HISTORY

Editors: HERMANN KULKE and BURKHARD SCHNEPEL

Vol. 1: Jagannath Revisited: Studying Society, Religion and the State in Orissa, edited by Hermann Kulke and Burkhard Schnepel

Vol. 2: The Jungle Kings: Ethnohistorical Aspects of Politics and Ritual in Orissa, by Burkhard Schnepel

Vol. 3: Text and Context in the History, Literature and Religion of Orissa, edited by Angelika Malinar, Johannes Beltz and Heiko Frese

Vol. 4: Altar of Power: The Temple and the State in the Land of Jagannatha, by Yaaminey Mubayi

Vol. 5: The Aghria: A Peasant Caste on a Tribal Frontier, by Uwe Skoda

Vol. 6: Time in India: Concepts and Practices, edited by Angelika Malinar

Vol. 7: Periphery and Centre: Studies in Orissan History, Religion and Anthropology, edited by Georg Pfeffer

TIME IN INDIA

Concepts and Practices

Edited by
ANGELIKA MALINAR

MANOHAR
2007

First published 2007

ISBN 81-7304-713-8

Published by
Ajay Kumar Jain for
Manohar Publishers & Distributors
4753/23, Ansari Road, Daryaganj
New Delhi 110 002

Printed at
Lordson Publishers Pvt. Ltd
Delhi 110 007

Distributed in South Asia by

4381/4, Ansari Road
Daryaganj, New Delhi 110 002
and its branches at Mumbai, Hyderabad,
Bangalore, Chennai, Kolkata

Contents

COPING WITH MODERN HISTORIOGRAPHY: TIME AND THE PROBLEM OF IDENTITY

Acknowledgements

On behalf of the Orissa Research Programme I wish to express our thanks to the Government and research institutions of India, scholars and friends in Orissa for supporting our research.

In stoic composure, Robert Parkin, University of Oxford, carefully copy-edited the manuscript and made many valuable suggestions. I am grateful to him and to Sebastian Dreyer, Free University of Berlin, for his patience and engagement in formatting the final version of the manuscript. Tim Schwabedissen, University of Kiel, deserves my thanks for creating the electronic version of the index, and Nicole Pohland for her work on an earlier version of the manuscript. Hermann Kulke, University of Kiel, cheerfully supported the finalization of the volume and ensured its safe arrival in India. Many thanks to him and to Ramesh Jain and Siddharth Chaudhury, Manohar Publishers, for their support and co-operation.

Since this volume is the outcome of the annual International Conference of the Orissa Research Programme in Salzau 2002, I am grateful to Nils Aulike and Jörg Heinke for helping to organise this Conference. We all owe our thanks to the German Research Council (DFG) for the generous grant which made the Salzau Conference 2002 possible.

ANGELIKA MALINAR

List of Contributors

FRÉDÉRIQUE APFFEL-MARGLIN is Professor of Anthropology at Smith College, Boston (Mass.).

GEORG BERKEMER is Research Fellow at the South Asia Institute of the University of Heidelberg.

G. N. DASH is Professor emeritus of Linguistics at Berhampur University.

ULRICH DEMMER is Outside Lecturer at the Department of Anthropology, University of Munich.

LIDIA J. GUZY is Research Fellow at the Institute of Religious Studies, Free University Berlin.

BARBARA LOTZ is Lecturer in Hindi at the Institute of Indology, University of Würzburg.

ANGELIKA MALINAR is Lecturer in Hinduism at the School of Oriental and African Studies, University of London.

CORNELIA MALLEBREIN is Senior Research Fellow at the Seminar for Indology and the Comparative Studies of Religion, University of Tübingen.

TINA OTTEN is Research Fellow at the Institute of Ethnology, Free University Berlin.

JAYANTA SENGUPTA is Reader in History at Yadavpur University, Kolkata.

UWE SKODA is Research Fellow at the Institute of Ethnology, Free University Berlin.

HEINRICH VON STIETENCRON is Professor emeritus of Indology and the Comparative Study of Religion at the University of Tübingen.

ROMILA THAPAR is Professor of History at the Jawarhalal Nehru University, New Delhi.

Introduction: Time in India

Angelika Malinar

For many, Indian notions of time may evoke images of circles and wheels, of collective and individual histories vanishing into the endless, repetitious movement of cosmic death and rebirth. However, time is perceived in India in as many different ways as in other parts of the world. In India too, experiences relating to time have stimulated a wide spectrum of philosophical interpretations and speculations, theological doctrines and arguments, mythological narratives and ritual performances. Seen from the perspective of cultural studies, these can all be regarded as 'cultural constructions' and varieties of 'social time'[1] that mirror different natural, historical or social contexts. Usually these constructions are nourished by what, in any given culture, are defined as manifestations of 'real' time. According to Leach most societies cope with two different kinds of experience: '(a) that certain phenomena in nature repeat themselves [and] (b) that life change is irreversible.'[2]

Thus, dealing with time means considering the passage of moments, the difference between 'before' and 'after', or the repetition of events and the return of the similar. Notions of time not only emphasise the continuity of a movement, but also discontinuity and destruction. They address the ambiguity ingrained in the experience of time as something that not only sustains life in the unstoppable and thus relatively certain movement from one moment to the other, but also disrupts it in experiences of change, loss or peak moments like initiation, revelation or ecstasy. Cultures have found different ways to relate to such experiences and to use them as elements of social order or markers of their internal and external boundaries. By drawing and reflecting on these different experiences, humans 'create time by creating intervals in social life',[3] thus integrating certain rhythms into the social order while excluding others.

---

[1] This concept can be traced back to Durkheim 1915 and Sorokin and Merton 1937. In this perspective, time intervals acquire a specific quality due to their relationship to certain social activities. For critical comments, see Bergmann 1981, 1983; Gell 1992, Ch.1.

[2] Leach 1961, 125.

[3] Ibid.,135.

These rhythms of social order become manifest in both mythological and historical narratives, and ritual and artistic practices or methods of healing.

Social time is thus rarely uniform, but multi-layered and complex. One aspect of this complexity consists in the necessity of dealing with time in terms of quantity and quality. Events and moments are both counted and evaluated by referring to social values and natural rhythms.[4] Accordingly, different concepts of time can be distinguished, such as linear, cyclical, periodic or oscillating time, all of which serve to establish and classify relationships between events. These are not only regarded as being related in and through time, but rather their very relationship is regarded *as* time. Thus communicating about time is all about establishing relationships and memorizing them in a specific socio-cultural context. The relational quality of time serves as the basis of its many different interpretations. 'Relational' here means that time emerges as the relationship between two events, which is established by providing a third point of reference which serves to define the relationship.[5] This is the case, for example, with 'oscillating' time: not only are there day and night, but these are also said to succeed each other and even to alternate, because they are regarded as 'repeated contrasts'.[6]

Seen from a more philosophical perspective, there are two fundamental ways of interpreting 'time' as a relationship between events, which have been coined the 'A- and B- series' views of time respectively. Recently, this distinction has entered fruitfully into discussions about time in different disciplines, and it can also be used as a referential framework for dealing with Indian notions of time.[7] According to the A-series view, events are classified according 'to their being at any one time past, present

[4] Thus Evans-Pritchard 1939, 189ff., distinguishes between 'oecological time', which refers to the annual cycle, and 'structural' time, which refers to the moral norms of social life.

[5] Mecke 2000, 20ff.

[6] According to Leach, 'oscillation' means that recurrent alternations of time intervals are turned into parts of a sequence: 'the sequence of things is discontinuous; time is a succession of alternations and full stops. Intervals are distinguished, not as the sequential markings on a tape measure, but as repeated opposites ... day-night day-night ... time is a "discontinuity of repeated contrasts".' Leach 1961, 133-4.

[7] This terminology was employed by the analytical philosopher McTaggert 1927 and has been accepted by major sociological and anthropological studies, such as Bergmann 1981 and Gell 1992.

or future events'.[8] Such a classification must be regarded as 'a structure of human time-consciousness, and thus a subjective-intersubjective structure, not a real one.' [9] Therefore it depends on agents and social contexts. In contrast to this, the B-series view categorizes events 'temporally according to whether they occur before or after another. Events do not change with respect to this criterion in the way that they do with respect to the criterion of pastness, presentness and futurity.' This distinction allows us to clarify the use of two different perspectives on time. The B-series view stresses the reality and irreversibility of events because of their position in a fixed sequence of events, as in physics or in establishing a historical chronology. The A-series view highlights the role of time-consciousness, thus permitting events to be qualified as past, present or future, irrespective of their position in any 'real' or 'probable' sequence. The A-series view takes account of change and development, but also of the freezing of time intervals in relation to the 'present', as in certain patterns of kinship.[10] This view seems to be fundamental for all social usages of time, as it allows both quantitative and qualitative aspects of time to be described. In this way, life can be regarded as dynamic, as a process of 'becoming' and a sequence of passages through and in time. It also allows the present to be the axis of movement and to draw together all the relevant events, whether past or future, for example, when marriage alliances are being planned. However, there is an intrinsic relationship to the B-series view in that societies invariably regard themselves as being dependent on some insurmountable experience of a fixed, external or, in modern terms, 'objective' sequence of 'before' and 'after'. This shows that the two views are by no means mutually exclusive. Rather, their

---

[8] Gell 1992, 151.

[9] Bergmann 1981, 31.

[10] Such as the so-called 'age-set system' of the Nuer described by Evans-Pritchard. This system enables the Nuer 'to state when events took place, not in number of years, but in relation to groups of people' (Evans-Pritchard 1939, 210). Since these relations remain stable, the distance from, nearness to or 'intervals' between the groups is not subject to time and thus remain constant, irrespective of how many years have actually passed. 'European time is a continuum. Whatever point we start at, each succeeding generation increases the distance from that point. Our grandfathers were nearer to 1066 than our fathers and our fathers were nearer to 1066 than we are. The Nuer system of lineages, on the other hand, seems to be a fixed system having a constant number of steps between living persons and the founder of their clan' (ibid., 212-13).

interconnection helps the self-perception of a society *vis-à-vis* some 'outside' or 'other', whether natural or social, to be analysed.

The actual boundaries and corresponding notions of time depend on what a society regards as the natural or social 'other'.[11] For example, it is well known that in some cultures (as in India), mountains are regarded as important parts of the cosmos, even as divinities, which allow entry into the heavenly regions, while in others they are seen as 'mistakes' of creation, as in medieval Europe.[12] The cultural differences in the exclusion or inclusion of other beings and thus their times and rhythms results in a variety of time concepts. The distinction between the so-called A- and B-series permits a more complex referential framework for individual cultural contexts and their comparative study. The different notions of time are not so much clues for a better understanding of time as such, but they are important as markers of a specific cultural construction or collective representation of the world.[13]

Scholars have not only described the various constructions of time, they have also connected them with different historical contexts and types of society.[14] Today, these different types not only co-exist on a global scale, but also in one and the same cultural sphere. This is also true for contemporary India, given that it is characterised by the co-existence of different social structures and corresponding world views, by what historian Reinhard Koselleck has called the 'simultaneity of the non-simultaneous'.[15] In India nowadays we find structures of modernity,

---

[11] Time concepts are also used in order to construct or even devalue other cultures, as in the encounter between modern Western and pre-modern societies; cf. Fabian 1983 for a critical study. With regard to India, for example, the alleged dominance of a cyclical view of time has nourished perceptions of backwardness (see below).

[12] The scientific discoveries that mountains were older than mankind and that they can be read as documents of the planet's 'history' contributed in Europe to the crumbling of the former Christian world view and to the increasing relevance of a historical, or more precisely here geological view of nature. Cf. Gould 1991.

[13] Gell 1992, 36: 'The relevant distinction does not lie between different "concepts of time", but different conceptions of the world and its workings.'

[14] For example, Lévi-Strauss' distinction between 'hot' and 'cold' societies. See also the classifications proposed by Luhmann 1975, Bergmann 1981 and Gell 1992.

[15] 'Gleichzeitigkeit des Ungleichzeitigen' in the original (Kosellek 1979). Following Fabian's discussion (1983, 31f.) of the merits of 'coevalness' as a

characterised by market liberalization and social mobility, that exist side by side with social life ordered by the older, 'traditional' values of hierarchy and purity, both, in their turn, interacting further with the segmentary structures of the so-called tribal societies. The interplay between all these social formations produces complexity of various kinds, such as different time regimes.[16] These include world ages, eras, astronomical calculations and genealogical patterns of alternation which can be used in order to mark an event or confer a social position on an individual. We find combinations of different eras with other methods of time reckoning, such as the digital clock, side by side with lunar calendars when it comes to dating certain events. These calculations can again be related to notions of 'auspiciousness' or 'danger'. We come across life-cycle rituals that mirror the view that the very passing of time results in a change in the quality of an individual's life because it is intrinsically connected with time regimes enacted in other cosmic spheres. The interplay between time as quality and quantity persists in many aspects of social life in India, and modern standardisation has not yet completely succeeded in separating them. Thus time is not regarded as homogenous and equally available for everybody; rather, it is not only experienced differently by different people in different places, but also reckoned differently. These differences were and are used to mark social boundaries. However, this did not preclude the introduction of overarching time frames and methods of reckoning in pre-modern India also. In calculating and evaluating time, one had not only to account for differences between regions and social groups, but also to coordinate and integrate them. Therefore, the (mostly) brahmanical elites in India sought to establish unifying notions of time that would serve to connect the different time regimes. These notions can be regarded as the functional equivalent of modern 'world time', though they are not operated by mechanical or digital devices, but managed by specialists and thus embedded in social communication. One example of overarching concepts of time can be found in the construction of Indian cosmic time according to world ages[17] that allow dynastic histories of both pan-Indian and

---

translation of the German 'Gleichzeitigkeit' in studying concepts of time, an alternative rendering of this passage might be 'coevalness of the uncoeval'.

[16] For a study of the co-existence of religious and scientific notions of time in the modern USA, see Finzsch and Hampf 2000.

[17] On the doctrine of *yuga* and *kalpa* in the epics and Purāṇas, see Scheftelowitz 1929, González-Reimann 2002, and Trautmann 1995.

regional relevance to be accommodated. This 'cosmic time' served as a medium of communication not only down the centuries, but also across different regions, local communities and social strata. Thus, in India too time appears as a 'moving multiplicity'[18] that shows different faces in different mirrors.

The present volume is an attempt to highlight this multiplicity by studying both notions and practices of time in relation to the different contexts in which they are enacted. The papers collected in this volume are the proceedings of a conference that took place in 2002 on 'Identities in Time' in Salzau (Germany). The conference was planned and organized by Angelika Malinar, Heinrich von Stietencron and Cornelia Mallebrein in the context of the Orissa Research Programme,[19] and brought together scholars from such different fields such as history, religious studies, anthropology, literary studies and indology. Since most of these scholars work in Orissa, the essays present case studies from this region and thus contribute to the now well-established field of Orissan studies. However, although the essays by and large concentrate on Indian traditions located in Orissa, the 'red thread' that connects them is not confined to what may be regarded 'regional' cultural constructions. While there are some distinct features that relate to Orissa in particular, it is clear that many regional and local traditions are deeply embedded in pan-Indian notions. However, these are interpreted and used in unique ways. The studies not only show the diversity of Indian notions of time, but also of the interplay of pan-Indian and regional traditions. Furthermore, the essays address a thematic spectrum that has rarely been covered in this way, because the issue of time has so far been studied with regard to such different fields as history, religion, time-reckoning, festivals, rituals, kinship and the life-cycle, and they even include further the consequences of the encounter between older forms of interpreting time and western historiography for the creation of social and individual identities. The connections between these different fields will be delineated below by pointing to some wider contexts of with the treatment of time in Indian cultures.

---

[18] Cf. Dimock and Stewart 1999, 116.

[19] This research project was granted by the German Research Council and conducted from 1999 to 2005. For general information on the project see the webpage and the other volumes of the Orissa Studies series.

Irreversibility and Repetition: Historical Constructions and Religious Discourse

For more than a century, Indian cultures have been perceived as basically structured by religious values and a strict demarcation of social boundaries. This view arose in the early nineteenth century in Europe, when the increasing recognition of cultural diversity resulted in new classifications of cultures. Modern historiography and the newly established discipline of 'the history of religion'[20] were academic fields which contributed heavily to this endeavour. A favourite and widely used distinction permitting a contrast to be established between Europe and India was that between linear and cyclical time.[21] While European cultures use linear notions of time, are aware of their history and open to progress, Indian cultures regard time as moving in circles and do not know of history, but only of the stability of a religious universe. Such juxtapositions have nowadays been given up as an over-simplification.[22] However, especially with regard to Hinduism cyclical time is still regarded as characteristic of the 'Indian world-view'. Its corollary is the argument that, due to the dominance of cyclicity, individuality and uniqueness are denied. However, scholars have since demonstrated that Indian cultures made ample use of linear concepts of time too. At least when it comes to dealing with historical and archaeological sources, the presence of a degree of historical consciousness is not longer disputed. The existence in India of methods and devices for astronomical and even mechanical time-reckoning[23] that are based on the meticulous observation of planetary movements and the counting of time units have also been widely acknowledged.[24] Epigraphic evidence shows the widespread

---

[20] Cf. Kippenberg 1997.

[21] For a discussion of the emergence of this view in nineteenth century colonial contexts see Trautmann 1995. This view has entered the text-books with Mircea Eliade's studies. Qualifications of the concept, such as Balslev 1983, 140-50, have remained rather unnoticed.

[22] Moreover, they are much too common and cannot serve as analytical categories: As Goody remarks (1968, 21): ' ... cyclical and linear patterns, and systems of time reckoning occur in all human societies, but the emphasis differs' (1968, 31).

[23] Cf. Falk 2000, Schopen 1998.

[24] On methods of time-reckoning and astronomical calculation see Jacobi 1920, Pingree 1981 and Falk 2000.

attempts by kings and other imperial rulers to create an era in their name and make the reckoning of regnant years the overarching paradigm of social time.[25] The establishment of royal time regimes marks the importance of dynastic power-structures which go along with hereditary forms of kingship and supporting concepts of kinship that substantiate the legitimacy of succession. Counting and naming regnant years became an instrument of claiming and maintaining power. Some eras, such as the Vikrama and Śaka, survived the disappearance of the royal families with which they were originally identified and succeeded in becoming an overarching time-frame, something like an ancient pan-Indian era that allowed eras in other parts of the subcontinent to be synchronized and coordinated.

The rise of hereditary kingship resulted in the creation of dynastic genealogies that were traced back to the beginning of the world. In this way linear time served as a means to substantiate legitimacy and claims of hegemony.[26] However, the presence of dynastic chronologies did not result in wiping out other ways of interpreting time in terms of cosmic history as related in myths and re-enacted in ritual performances. These dealt with creation as the beginning of time and laid the foundations for anchoring social life in an ever-lasting temporal and spatial order, a specific cosmology and cosmography. In this way, India or Bhāratavarṣa became one region of the cosmos, and everything that happened there was placed in the framework of cosmic time. In consequence, dynastic histories, epic narratives and myths, origins of rituals and festivals became part of this overarching framework.

More often than not, historical events that were sometimes recorded in inscriptions or other documents were embedded in this cosmic time-reckoning and thus gained a trans-historical quality. In the eyes of modern western historians (those fond of the B-series view of time; see above), this embeddedness spoiled, or at least seriously placed into question, the historical value and reliability of later dynastic genealogies and chronicles, thus confirming the assumption that linear time and historical consciousness are lacking. However, this embeddedness is not so much the result of lack of a linear time concept, but of the dispersal of history in regional and local histories of dynasties and temples that sought to establish their importance by using cosmic paradigms. In synchronizing

---

[25] On the introduction of regnant years and eras in India, see Falk 2002.

[26] This seems to be a world-wide pattern; cf. Bergmann 1981, 188. For India, see Thapar 2000.

these different histories, the focus was rarely an epoch or a central imperial kingdom,[27] but rather the region or a king in relation to mythic paradigms of divine incarnations and of lunar and solar dynasties (and later also Agnivamśa dynasties) that were found to reappear in many different places in the form of smaller or greater kings, and sometimes also queens. The intention behind these constructions was not history as such, but memorizing and proving the highest possible descent of the present ruling class by placing it in the framework of cosmic time. Perhaps no other scholar has studied this intersection between cosmic and historical time in early India as intensively as Romila Thapar, who has analysed the function of the combination of myth and history in the epics and Purāṇas.[28] In her contribution to this volume, she analyses the importance of both linear and cyclical time for the formation of social identity in early India. She highlights especially the function of the era as an interface between both notions. Often rooted in 'local events and systems of time reckoning ... the era became a link between local perceptions and the more exact measurements required in urban centers and royal courts'. This continuum between linear and cosmic time implies a hierarchy of descent and a process of decay that leads straight down into the *kaliyuga*, in which each and every local or regional history takes place.

This insight opens the path for studies of regional and local records and constructions of history that show the multi-layered structure of the construction of dynastic histories.[29] The actual use of such notions in constructions of social identity has been studied by anthropologists in different Indian contexts. The application of theories of cultural memory to such local forms of memorizing the past and narrating the history of a kingdom, or even a caste, have proved useful. Major anthropological studies deal with the importance of historical memory and its role in power struggles and contested social relationships.[30] Another example that exemplifies the role of time concepts in establishing hegemony is presented in Georg Berkemer's essay in this volume, which describes a unique system of reckoning regnant years in Orissa, the so-called *aṅka* system. This method was introduced by the imperial Gangas in the eleventh century and was used by the subsequent Gajapatis and the Rajas

---

[27] The existence as well as the rarity of a chronicle like the Kashmirian *Rājataraṅginī* confirms this observation.

[28] Cf. Thapar 2000.

[29] See, for example, Kulke 2004.

[30] Cf. Basu 2004.

of Khurda. This system creates for the king his 'own time', which serves to demonstrate his dominance over all the other little kings and vassals of Orissa. In this way the king himself is put 'at the centre of time-reckoning'.

Not only kings or other dominant groups, but also religious communities in India tend to create their own time frames that include in varying degrees the temporal parameters of their social context. Thus in religious discourse too we find multilayered conceptions of time that often, like dynastic histories, used the framework of Indian cosmic time. However, the interplay between linear and cyclical concepts of time highlighted by historians has only rarely been taken up as a topic in studies of Hindu religious traditions. The otherwise relativized notion of cyclical time is still widely applied to Hinduism in general. However, studies of individual religious traditions demonstrate that the situation is no less complex than in the case of the constructions of history discussed earlier. In the different religious traditions and philosophical schools, we find a wide spectrum of interpretations of time as an everlasting element of existence.[31] In religious discourse, time is interpreted as a transcendent or at least eternal and all-pervading reality that is the cause of its empirical manifestations, being regarded by some as a quality of the creative power of the divine. Such religious notions are usually mediated with extant cosmic, historical, calendrical and ritual time frames, and last but not least with the schedules of daily life that structure the lives of the members, be they lay followers or religious specialists. Angelika Malinar's chapter in this volume examines the use of these different time frames using a case study of the Caitanya tradition of Hinduism. This is pursued against the background of a discussion of Eliade's interpretation of Indian cosmic time as cyclical. She suggests that we distinguish between two different understandings of cyclical time; first, cyclicity in the sense of a 'recurrence of counted time-units'; and secondly, cyclicity as the 'return of the same'. Both notions are applicable in the Caitanya tradition. This helps to qualify the view that Hindu religion only recognises cyclical time and thus to open up the analysis to a more complex and varying picture.

The relationship between temporal frameworks created in a religious context and the social time of its environment is a relevant topic for any study that places a religious tradition in its cultural context. The boundaries that separate a religious community from its environment are

---

[31] On the concept of *kāla* (time, moment, death) and its interpretation in Indian philosophical traditions, see Silburn 1955, Balslev 1983 and Prasad 1992.

not only doctrinal and practical, but also spatial and temporal. The latter often includes specific time regimes that regulate the religious life of the followers, not only in the case of festivals or rituals, but also when they interact in monastic institutions. Both time-reckoning and the (mechanical) devices used for it are important in order to regulate and coordinate the activities in such a religious space.[32] Time reserved for religious activities varies according to the position of individual adept. In the case of ascetic renouncers, their whole life is oriented by the religious quest, and their renunciation actually separates them from 'social time', as it literally implies their 'social death'. Nevertheless ascetics interact with their environment, be it in terms of certain times of pilgrimage or seclusion. The norms and practices of Hindu asceticism have been studied intensively,[33] for example by Patrick Olivelle on the basis of texts, and the interaction of monastic institutions with their lay followers has also attracted attention.[34] The effects of a religious doctrine in two different social settings are highlighted in the essay by Lidia Guzy with regard to the Mahima Dharma tradition of Orissa. She shows how ascetic monks and converts in a tribal setting respectively practice their religion in relation to specific 'sacred' times. While in the case of the monastic community this time is structured by ascetic practices and the performance of fire rituals, religious practice by the tribal converts converges with former notions of ecstatic contacts with the divine that take place at night.

The temporal frameworks established in Hindu religious contexts point in two different directions. On the one hand, in religious discourse time is constructed against the background of social time and is thus part of it. On the other hand, religious time provides opportunities for interactions between the spheres of the human and the divine, which are otherwise spatially and temporally separated. The effects of this temporary opening up of boundaries are manifold. Most important perhaps is that it allows for the manifestation of the divine in the human

---

[32] It is well-known that a strong impulse to use mechanical devices for measuring time in ancient Europe came from clerical and monastic circles (cf. Le Goff 1960). In India too we find that the idea of a mechanized time regime supports monastic discipline, as has been shown by Schopen 1998 with regard to Buddhism. On the possible connection between Puranic concepts of time and scientific instruments, see Kloetzli 1985.

[33] For example, Olivelle 1986.

[34] For example, Sawai 1992

world, whether as an embodiment or as a doctrinal revelation. This not only opens up a path to salvation, it also creates new changes to improve one's present life, as the power of the divine can manifest itself repeatedly, for example in ecstatic moments, the healing of diseases and many other blessings. In addition to daily ritual activities and those that are scheduled according to the calculation of 'auspicious' or 'inauspicious' moments, many religious communities open up a wide spectrum to individual practice on the assumption that the divine is an ever-present reality and thus can be approached at any time if one knows the right method.

Ritual Time and Life-Cycle: Collective Representations, Individual Needs

The dominant field of interplay between religious notions and social practices is ritual. Not only in the context of the numerous religious traditions and communities, but also generally in India, social life is structured by ritual time and thus deserves special consideration. Ritual time means both time that is reserved for daily ritual activities and time that interrupts daily routine, as is the case with festivals or life-cycle rituals. The special feature of ritual time consists in relating a fixed schedule of recurrent activities to a pattern of alternating qualities of time. In this respect it resembles Leach's notion of 'oscillating' time,[35] in that we are dealing here with a sequence of a 'repeated contrast' between auspicious and inauspicious moments, of right or wrong time. Ritual time is not homogenous, as for example modern time, but is time qualified. It is based on the idea of different, coexisting cosmic realms, each marked by different temporal rhythms. Therefore, ritual time is calculated in relation to the rulers of the planets, the gods, demons and ancestors, who all prefer one moment to another. In order to select the right time for a ritual, one has to know these preferences. Ritual timing depends on this knowledge auspiciousness or inauspiciousness of a moment, which is prescriptive of individual activities. This is the case with the date of a marriage, which in many parts of India is not a matter of individual choice, but rather depends on the 'marriage season'. Thousands of young people and their parents each year strive to marry 'on time', otherwise they have to wait until the auspicious season returns. In her contribution to this volume, Frederique

[35] See above, note 6.

Apffel-Marglin deals with the fundamental difference between ritual and more abstract notions of modern time by analysing the Raja Parba or festival of the menses in Orissa. The ritual enacts the relationship of Oriya villagers to 'the alternating rhythms of the more-than-human world'. Being part of a cosmic whole means that one has to contribute to its continuity. Moreover it is through ritual that time is regenerated; in fact, 'ritual is the making of time'.

However, such a vision is embedded in the social order that validates it, which in its turn is based on establishing proper relationships between its parts and with adjacent social realms. Therefore, ritual is necessary in order to maintain relationships with the other spheres of the cosmos. Indian traditions do not only consider gods, demons and ancestors as the addressees of ritual communication, but also the planets and stars, which are both objects of worship and of astronomical calculation and astrological evaluation. The 'science of the stars' (*jyotiṣa*) has a long history on the subcontinent, and the determination of the right times for rituals has been a field of priestly specialization since Vedic times. The observation of both solar and lunar times led to the creation of a unique lunar-solar calendar, the so-called *pañjī*, which is used all over India for ritual timing. In his contribution to this volume, Heinrich von Stietencron studies this calendrical version of ritual time by dealing with two *pañjī*s used in many parts of Orissa, from Puri and Jajpur respectively. The significance of sun and moon stems from their ancient connection to ideas of the after-world, that is, to the lunar region of the ancestors and the solar world of the gods. Ritual thus had the function of upholding the connection between the spheres or, in the case of demons, to preserve the boundaries between them and the human world. Accordingly, what is included in the calendar as an occasion for ritual activity varies, which explains regional and local variations of the *pañjī*.

This system of calculation is not only used for public rituals or communal festivals, but also in calculating the performance of life-cycle rituals. The alternation of 'right' and 'wrong' times is said to influence the quality of an individual's life. The 'right moment' relates to the continuation of life as much as it serves to advert its risks and dangers. The performance of life-cycle rituals marks the stages that are necessary for everyone to become a social being. In contrast to the alternations of rituals, life-cycle rituals are regarded as a sequence of passages. This sequence is not just linear movement, but a trajectory. The movement is predictable and implies familiarity with the next stage; it is a journey to well-known places. Although the passages are felt to be dangerous, each stage is safe and well established, a slot the individual has to fill in order to preserve social order. Evans-Pritchard regarded this fixed sequence as 'structural time': 'A man's structural future is ... already fixed and is broken into different periods, so that a boy standing at the threshold of life can foresee the total changes in status he will undergo if he lives long enough.'[36] In her contribution to the volume, Tina Otten studies the temporal framework of the life-cycle rituals of women in the Rona community of southern Orissa. The quality of a woman's life, her *bhāgya*, depends on the timely performance of all life-cycle rituals, starting with the birth rituals. The moment of her birth connects her irrevocably to the rulers of the day and month at that time, and this necessitates specific ritual activities. Therefore life-cycle rituals establish positive relationships with the gods, who also protect the girl from dangers brought by demons and others who wish her ill. Ritual time is thus also an opportunity for preventative health.

In the context of ritual time, nothing is caused by time itself. In this regard it stands in striking contrast to notions of fate and fatality, which also have a long history in India.[37] Rather, the agency is conferred on those gods or demons who rule over certain times. Thus life-cycle and other rituals aim at averting danger by appeasing these powers or establishing alliances with other powerful and protective beings. However, the time between life-cycle rituals can also pose a threat. In his contribution to this volume Uwe Skoda deals with a specific form of 'risk management' practised in the Aghria community in northwest Orissa. Here, children are 'sold' or 'thrown away' in order to save their lives from being endangered by weakness or disease. In reversing the parameters of social ranking, danger is averted by deliberately making children impure by 'selling' them to low-status families. The aim is therefore to hide the vulnerable child in a social space that is otherwise considered dangerous. In this way, the child is made to survive a period in its life in which it is considered to be 'unripe' by transferring it temporarily to a grey zone of indeterminacy. Nonetheless these ritual strategies cannot alter the fact that

---

[36] Evans-Pritchard 1939, 190.

[37] Indian traditions have also accepted notions of fate and fatality, as can be seen in the *Mahābhārata* and in the differentiated vocabulary for different forms of fate (*daiva, diṣṭa, bhāga,* etc.); cf. Schrader 1902.

one's temporal existence is finite, that life is lethal.[38] Yet, rituals allow death to be qualified as either auspicious or inauspicious. This is based on the idea that it is a passage to another region. Therefore. the death ritual is included among the life-cycle rituals. Extensive research has been dedicated to notions and rituals of death. In his essay in this volume, Ulrich Demmer highlights an aspect that has received less attention, the memorization of the deceased during the ritual. The performance of death rituals among the Koya of south Orissa implies both the memorization of kinship ties, in the sense of the 'performance of affinity', and of the life of the deceased person. This allows for a double movement in establishing a boundary between the living and the dead and in integrating the deceased into the social realm by conferring on him the status of an ancestor, which allows him to remain a member of Koya society. In this way the past is included in the present.

Ritual time is based on the recognition that social life is established not only by internal rules, but also by the various relationships in which the group stands with other social formations of the cosmos and the temporal rhythms that mark their existence. In this regard, ritual time establishes a referential framework which can be compared with the function of cosmic time in dynastic chronologies or religious texts, which also allows for the participation of gods, demons and ancestors in earthly (hi)stories. However, neither the ritual co-existence of gods, demons, ancestors and humans, nor the idea that history relates the present to cosmic rhythms, was accepted by modern historians as meaningful, since historical research aims to establish the 'true' or 'real' sequence of events. Seen against the background of the previous discussion, the impetus of modern historiography can be regarded as a quest to establish the B-series view of time and to provide a reliable temporal order of 'before' and 'after' against the fluidity, presentness and inter-subjectivity of the A-series view.

Coping with Modern Historiography: Time and the Problem of Identity

The consequences of the advent of modern historicism in nineteenth-century India have been studied extensively.[39] This has resulted not only

[38] This insight is conveyed by the Sanskrit term *kāla*, which already in its earliest usages can be translated as both 'time' and 'death'.

[39] For example, Chatterjee 1993, Sharma 2003

in a devaluation of those very ideas that were discussed before, but also in the adoption of this view in Indian constructions of the past and in the formation of present social and individual identities. Accordingly, in historical discourse identity itself became historical. It was no longer regarded as being primarily constituted through commonly remembered events or genealogies or ritual performances, but as resulting from a sequence of incidents, decisions and events starting from some verifiable origin. Thus, 'true' origins can no longer be mythical, but must be historical. However, connecting identity with history is nothing neutral or 'objective', because in practice it means rather to turn sequence into consequence and to connect the 'chain of events' in a historical narrative. This opens up all the possibilities of turning history into a narrative, whether didactic or other. Conversely, history can be seen as something which can be made and changed.[40] As a consequence, social formations and individual lives have become 'identities in time' that are subject to various changes, historical circumstances and contingencies, while also being open to choice and decision. This new openness with regard to the future results in new strategies of self-ascertainment through constructions and discoveries of the past. In this way, historical reconstruction goes hand in glove with historical imagination and inventions of traditions.[41]

In Orissa too, the methods of modern historiography have been regarded as legitimate instruments in claiming and establishing identities in academic, political, economic, educational and artistic arenas. In this way, identity has become a contested area in which it is no longer only the traditional elites who have the final say, but many other, including so-called 'subaltern' voices can be heard. No less than in the context of ritual, theology and dynastic history discussed earlier, here too we come across multi-layered concepts of time. One reason for this can be seen in the intimate connection between historiography and story-telling. The temporal structures that provide a story with a rhythm, a logic and a message can also be detected in historical writing.[42] Therefore, history not only deals with events in time, but also uses certain notions of time in establishing and interpreting their sequence. In this way history regains mythic dimensions, as with ideas of history as the recovery of a 'golden

---

[40] This process has become the topic of many studies, in which it has become connected with the discovery of the future as a category of history and of social life. See, for example, Koselleck 1979.

[41] Cf., for example, Anderson 1991.

[42] Cf. White 1978.

age' or as a process of decay. Such ideas were used in creating the historical identity not only of groups, but also of regions. Of special importance for Orissa is the encounter between tribal communities and Hindu caste society which, from the nineteenth-century onwards, came to be perceived and interpreted in terms of history.

The well-known issue of the historical relationship between tribal communities and Hindu kings[43] is taken up in Cornelia Mallebrein's essay on the changing perceptions of two tribal goddesses in the course of their transformation into the iconically represented family deities of Hindu royal families. Members of both the tribal communities and the royal families cope with this change not only ritually, but also in terms of narratives that are transmitted in oral traditions, written legends and dynastic histories. For the members of the tribal community, the fact that the Goddess has settled with the royal family represents a confirmation of the mythical ties between the king and the tribe. Conversely, the legends circulating in the circles of the royal families see in the advent of the Goddess powerful proof of the legitimacy of their rule after their migration into new settlements. The different accounts point to the conundrum implied in the historicising view of change, in that it connects notions of an unchangeable origin with experiences of change such as migration or power struggles.

This can also be seen in the direct encounters between tribal communities and modern western historiography, which have created new arenas for claiming and negotiating identities. A pertinent issue in this encounter is the western attempt to 'historise time and extract scientific facts out of orally transmitted time concepts', as Barbara Lotz puts it in her essay on the reconstruction of the 'golden past' of the Santal community. The major innovation consisted in the transformation of oral traditions into written documents that would then be used as sources of history. This was accompanied by the creation or 're-discovery' of a specific Santali script, which was regarded as the marker of another, past time, in which the Santals were a community of literati. This new mode of viewing quickly became an instrument for putting forward demands for social uplift and recognition in the larger public space of colonial India. While the emphasis on language and script emulated strategies of identity formation that were also used in the Oriya movement, its sacralization became a special feature that in turn was taken up by other tribal communities, in which other tribal scripts were also rediscovered. Thus,

[43] Cf. Kulke 2002.

all over India the new consciousness about identity, history and locality was deeply linked with questions of language. Having a history implies having a language of one's own. This assumption resulted in claiming a separate identity for different language communities. However, it also resulted in new social formations and, in Anderson's words, 'imagined communities',[44] for example, the construction of Orissa as the region of Oriya speakers, irrespective of their social status. The success of the Oriya movement and the creation of Orissa as a separate province became the model for sub-regional movements also to claim their own culture, history and political independence. In this volume, G.N. Dash analyses this processes with regard to the Sambalpuri movement, showing that intellectuals and politicians from Sambalpur first took sides with the Oriya movement when it protested successfully against the introduction of Hindi as the official language of Orissa at the end of the nineteenth century. At that time the differences between the varieties of standard Oriya were not seen as significant. From the 1960s a movement started that claimed Sambalpuri or Koshli as a separate language on the basis of the results of historical language studies. Dash views this movement as the struggle of the Sambalpur people against their being neglected and discriminated against by coastal Oriyas.

This self-perception is connected to a wider topic of Orissan historiography since the *topoi* of 'loss', 'neglect' and 'discrimination' have become markers of identity in many text books. It can be regarded as one of the results of the increasing perception of history as a field of opportunities and choices. Rather than putting up with neglect or suppression there was a shift to viewing oneself as having become the victims of history and of hostile power constellations. In the case of Orissa, it even became a means of claiming for the region and its people a fate that is different from the rest of India. In his contribution to the volume, Jayanta Sengupta shows that in almost all accounts of the ebb and flow of Orissan history, the reference to neglect and deprivation is the 'red thread' that runs through time and that creates the impression of 'standstill'. Curiously, it is the very notion of modern history in terms of change and progress that provokes the idea of time having stood still. The timeless quality ascribed to one's identity, according to Sengupta, 'serves a specific function ... of claiming and demanding resources and "special status" from the colonial as well as the postcolonial Indian state.' Thus not only in cosmic, ritual and religious notions of time, but also in historical

[44] Anderson 1991.

accounts based on documented sources, time is not only recorded but also evaluated.

The chapters collected in this volume show that time in India is as diverse as in other cultures. Not only do we find older notions of cosmic or ritual time still active in the modern times of globalization and of a unified digital world time, but also the coexistence of different types of society and of different cultural constructions of time.

References

Anderson, B. 1991. *Imagined Communities: Reflections on the Origins and Spread of Nationalism*, London: Verso.

Balslev, A.N. 1983. *A Study of Time in Indian Philosophy*, Wiesbaden: Harrassowitz.

Basu, H. 2004. *Von Barden und Königen: Ethnologische Studien zum Gedächtnis und zur Göttin in Kacch*, New York, Bern: Peter Lang.

Bergmann, W. 1981. *Die Zeitstrukturen sozialer Systeme: Eine systemtheoretische Analyse*, Berlin: Duncker und Humblodt.

— 1983. 'Das Problem der Zeit in der Soziologie: Ein Literaturüberblick zum Stand der 'zeitsoziologischen' Theorie und Forschung', in *Kölner Zeitschrift für Soziologie und Sozialpsychologie* 35, 462-504.

Chatterjee, P. 1973. *The Nation and its Fragments: Colonial and Postcolonial Histories*, Princeton: Princeton University Press.

Eliade, M. 1957. Time and Eternity in Indian Thought, in J. Campbell (ed.), *Man and Time Papers from the Eranos Yearbooks*, New York: Pantheon Books, 173-200.

Evans-Pritchard, E.E. 1939. 'Nuer Time Reckoning', in *Africa* 12, 189-216.

Dimock, E.C. Jr. and Stewart, T. 1999. *Caitanya Caritāmṛta of Kṛṣṇadāsa Kavirāja: A Translation and Commentary*, Cambridge (Mass.), London: Harvard University Press.

Fabian, J. 1983. *Time and the Other: How Anthropology Makes its Object*, New York: Columbia University Press.

Falk, H. 2000. Measuring Time in Mesopotamia and Ancient India, in *Zeitschrift der Deutschen Morgenländischen Gesellschaft* 150, 107-32.

— 2002. Frühe Zeitrechnung in Indien, in H. Falk (ed.) *Vom Herrscher zur Dynastie: Zum Wesen kontinuierlicher Zeitrechnung in Antike und Gegenwart*, 77-105.

Finzsch, N. and Hampf, M. 2000. 'Y2K-Madness und andere Millenarianismen: Eine historische Betrachtung zum Ende des Jahrtausends', in A. Simonis and L. Simonis (eds.), *Zeitwahrnehmung und Zeitbewußtsein der Moderne*, Bielefeld: Aisthesis, 153-96.

Gell, A. 1992. *The Anthropology of Time: Cultural Constructions of Temporal Maps and Images*, Oxford: Berg.

González-Reimann, L. 2002. *The Mahābhārata and the Yugas: India's Great Epic Poem and the Hindu System of World Ages*, New York, Frankfurt: Lang.

Goody, J. 1968. Time. Social Organization, in D.L. Sills (ed.), *International Encyclopedia of the Social Sciences*, Vol. 16, New York: Macmillan, 30-42.

Jacobi, H. 1920. 'Einteilung des Tages und Zeitmessung im alten Indien', in *Zeitschrift der Deutschen Morgenländischen Gesellschaft* 74, 247-63.

Kippenberg, H.G. 1997. *Die Entdeckung der Religionsgeschichte: Religionswissenschaft und Moderne*, München: Beck.

Kloetzli, W.R. 1985. 'Maps of Time: Mythologies of Descent: Scientific Instruments and the Purāṇic cosmograph', in *History of Religions 25 (2)*, 116-47.

Koselleck, R. 1979. *Vergangene Zukunft: Zur Semantik geschichtlicher Zeiten*, Frankfurt: Suhrkamp.

Kulke, H. 2002. *Kings and Cults: State Formation and Legitimation in Indian and Southeast Asia*, New Delhi: Manohar.

— 2004. 'The Making of a Local Chronicle', in A. Malinar, J. Beltz and H. Frese (eds.), *Text and Context in the History, Literature and Religion of Orissa*, New Delhi: Manohar, 43-66.

Leach, E. 1961. Two Essays Concerning the Symbolic Representation of Time, in Leach, E. *Rethinking Anthropology*, London: Athlone Press, 124-136.

LeGoff, J. 1960. 'Temps de l'église et temps du marchand', in *Annales (ESC)* 15, 417-33.

Luhmann, N. 1975. Weltzeit und Systemgeschichte, in *Soziologische Aufklärung* 2, 103-33.

McTaggert, J.E. 1968. *The Nature of Existence*, Cambridge: Cambridge University Press (1st edn. 1927).

Mecke, J. 2000. 'Zeittheorie, Zeit-Medien und Medien-Zeit', in Ulrich G. Leinsle and J. Mecke (eds.), *Zeit - Zeitenwechsel -Endzeit. Zeit im Wandel der Zeiten, Kulturen, Techniken und Disziplinen*, Regensburg, Universitätsverlag, 17-35.

Olivelle, P. 1986. *Renunciation in Hinduism: A Medieval Debate*, 2 vols. Wien: Institut für Indologie der Universität Wien.

Pingree, D. 1981. *Jyotiḥśāstra. Astral and Mathematical Literature*, Wiesbaden: Harrassowitz (*History of Indian Literature*, Vol. 6, 4).

Prasad, H.S. (ed.) 1992. *Time in Indian Philosophy: A Collection of Essays*, Delhi: Sri Satguru Publications.

Sawai, Y. 1992. *The faith of ascetics and lay smārtas: a study of the Śaṅkaran tradition in Śṛṅgeri*, Vienna: University of Vienna (Publications of the de Nobili Research Library 19).

Scheftelowitz, J. 1929. *Die Zeit als Schicksalsgottheit in der indischen und iranischen Religion*, Stuttgart: Kohlhammer.

Schopen, Gregory. 1998. 'Marking Time in Buddhist Monasteries: On Calendars, Clocks, and Some Liturgical Practices', in P. Harrison, P. and G. Schopen (eds.), *Sūryacandrāya: Essays in Honour of Akira Yumira on the Occasion of his 65th Birthday*, Swisttal-Odendorf: Indica-et-Tibetica, 157-79.

Schrader, F.O. 1902. *Über den Stand der indischen Philosophie zur Zeit Mahāvīras und Buddhas*, Leipzig: G. Kreysing.

Sharma, A. 2003. *Hinduism and its sense of history*, Oxford: Oxford University Press.

Silburn, L. 1955. *Instant et Cause : Le discontinu dans la pensée philosophique de l'Inde*, Paris: Vrin.

Sorokin, P.A. and Merton, R.K. 1937. 'Social Time: A Methodological and Functional Analysis', in *American Journal of Sociology* 42, 615-29.

Thapar, R. 1997. 'Linear Time in Historical Texts of Early India', in *India and Beyond. Aspects of Literature, Meaning, Ritual and Thought: Essays in Honour of Frits Staal*, London: Routledge & Kegan Paul, 562-73.

— 2000. *History and Beyond*, Delhi: Oxford University Press.

Trautmann, Thomas R. 1995. Indian Time, European Time, in D.O. Huhghes (ed.) *Time: Histories and Ethnologies*, Ann Arbor: University of Michigan, 167-97.

White, H. 1978. *Tropics of Discourse: Essays in Cultural Criticism*, Baltimore: John Hopkins University Press.

1

Time Concepts, Social Identities and Historical Consciousness in Early India

Romila Thapar

For many decades now, it has been argued that a single, cyclical concept of time characterized Indian civilization. This view was so firmly held that the argument was extended to maintain that cyclical time prevented the evolution of a sense of history. This became a distinguishing feature of Indian perceptions of the past, which were therefore said to be ahistorical. Among the more recent and influential proponents of this view was Mircea Eliade, who wrote of the Indian myth of eternal return.[1] But the argument had an ancestry that goes back to the early Orientalists, as is evident from the introduction to the *Viṣṇu-Purāṇa* by Horace Hyman Wilson.[2] The repeated mention of cyclical time in the sources was doubtless one of the reasons for this argument.

Some scholars did suggest that there was a strand of linear time in certain texts, but the prevailing view was that time was seen as cyclical, with no firm beginning or termination. This was thought to obstruct differentiation between history and myth. It was contrasted with the Judeo-Christian eschatology of the Garden of Eden at the start of time and Judgement Day at the end. Repeating cycles repeated events and thus minimized the centrality of human action.

I have argued that in addition to cyclical time there was also a linear concept, not necessarily described as such, but implicit in a variety of forms.[3] Many of these were more pertinent to records that were viewed as reflecting a historical consciousness. Linear time had a different function from cyclical time, but the two did intersect on occasion, and this intersection has an interest of its own. The use of time as a marker of identity is less precise in the cyclical form but is strongly imprinted in linear forms. The notion of cyclical time is essentially cosmological, and one of its functions was to provide an imagined time context to myth. Linear time is foundational to a perceived historical rendering of the past

[1] Cf. Eliade 1955.

[2] Wilson 1972b.

[3] Thapar 1997.

that is dependent on human activity. Questions relating to memory and identity can perhaps be seen as part of the intersection of the two concepts.

'Cyclical' and 'linear' are qualifiers, derived from the way time is presented, particularly if it is represented as a form. There are, of course, many more categories of time than these two. The categorization is largely, although not solely, dependent on the function of time. Thus social groups often differentiate and identify themselves by adopting varying categories of time for varying functions. But forms of time determining historical interests have largely been restricted to these two, and cyclical time was the one associated with India. I would like to consider both forms in juxtaposition. The first has already been discussed at length by scholars, while the second has entered the discussion more recently.

The earliest unit mentioned in the texts was the *yuga*, which marked a particular conjuncture. Initially the most convenient conjuncture was settled as a period of five years. The repetition of this pattern within a time period suggested a cycle, and this was seminal to cosmic time. But the cycle of time associated with calculations in astronomy was to grow to an immense size, as required for the calculations. This conditioned notions of cyclical time.

The notion of time moving in a cycle probably derived from the cycle of the seasons and the recurring rituals of the year. It is measured by natural changes in climate and landscape and the observance of rituals relating to these. It is therefore projected as a time frame that is natural, and to that extent is cosmic. Linear time, by contrast, is a measurement of time controlled by human decision. It is easier to manipulate linear time in the ordering of society. The construction of cyclical time was also of human authorship, but unlike linear time it extended beyond the human dimension into imagined time. Measurements of the cycles expanded and became complex. Cyclical time can encompass linear time and to that extent they can flow together. But the two are also on occasion in contradiction, since repetition breaks linearity.

Concepts of time are reflected in calendars, even when not explicitly formulated as such. The earlier forms had a variety of markers of time, many that were common to virtually every society in the ancient world. What were predictable were the movements of the sun and the moon. Natural catastrophes, such as floods and wars, although unpredictable, nevertheless overwhelmed society. The movement of the sun was reflected in the solstices, namely the *uttarāyaṇa* or summer solstice and the *dakṣiṇāyana* or winter solstice. A counterpoint to these was the demarcation of the equinox, perhaps also inspired by the central ritual in a sacrifice. It was easier to keep track of the movements of the moon in its phases and in relation to the constellations – the month or *māsa* – and the phases of the moon, with the neat division of the two lunar fortnights of *śuklapakṣa* and *kṛṣṇapakṣa*, could be further subdivided into days or *tithi*, and the day into smaller measurements such as the *muhūrta* (a moment or eighteen minutes).

The lunar and solar calendars were not necessarily maintained as distinct demarcations of time, even though their functions might differ. Attempts were made to chart points where the two coincided, attempts that sometimes involved intercalation. The calendar of rituals was often easier to track if lunar measurements were used, and agricultural activities related more closely to the solar. A lunar-solar calendar seemed to provide the answer. The time cycle was called the *yuga* and was the unit of cosmological and astronomical time.

The relatively simple time-reckoning of the *yuga* gradually evolved into a grandiose plan of immensely longer cycles. The structure for the framework of the *yuga*s is described in texts such as the later sections of the *Mahābhārata,* the *Mānava Dharmaśāstra*, and the *Viṣṇu-Purāṇa.* These descriptions assume a form that had been absent in earlier texts. It is interesting that the change occurs early in the Christian era and may have been associated with other changes. This was the period that was seminal to Purāṇic Hinduism, in many ways a departure from Vedic Brahmanism. Presumably it required a different kind of cosmology, especially in relation to time-reckoning. There were also at this time exchanges of knowledge between India and the Hellenistic world. Among these were knowledge of astronomy and medicine. With the migration into India of large numbers of peoples from central Asia – the Śakas, Parthians and Kuṣāṇas, doubtless bringing divergent mythologies – there would have been an interest in the firming up of a cosmology of time.

In setting out cyclical time, the largest cycle was the *kalpa*, infinite and immeasurable. It is said to begin with creation and to continue until the cataclysmic termination of the universe. As part of cosmology the *kalpa* is often represented spatially, but in such a manner that it could not be measured in temporal terms. For instance, a Buddhist description of the *kalpa* reads as follows: if there is a cube-shaped mountain measuring approximately three miles on each side and if every hundred years the mountain is brushed with a silk scarf – and according to some this was held in the beak of an eagle flying over the mountain – then the time taken for the mountain to be eroded is a *kalpa*.[4] A description from an Ājīvika text[5] states that if there is a river that is 117,649 times the size of the Ganges, and if every hundred years one grain of sand is removed from its bed, then the time required for the removal of all the sand would be one unit of measure; and it takes three thousand of these units to make one *kalpa*. Although the fact that the action took place every hundred years introduces a temporal dimension of humanly manageable real time, the image is essentially spatial. The length of the *kalpa* is a deliberate transgression of time, and the silk scarf would have quickly disintegrated. And who could remove the grains of sand from the bed of a flowing river?

The notion of the temporal length of the *kalpa* provided in some Brahmanical texts may have come from contemporary astronomy, where the length of the *kalpa* was reckoned as 4,320,000 years.[6] The figure had to be enormous so as to be large enough for calculations in astronomy. The same figure was used in cosmology for the *mahāyuga*, the great cycle. But the *mahāyuga* was divided into four lesser cycles of unequal length. Some astronomers, such as Āryabhaṭṭa, maintained that the divisions were of equal length, while other, later astronomers used different figures. It is likely that there was a dialogue between osmologists and astronomers, although it remains unclear as to who borrowed from whom. Perhaps cosmology was seeking legitimacy by borrowıng the figures used by the astronomers.[7]

There appear to have been two systems of calculating the cycles, that of the *mahāyuga*s and that of the *manvantara*s.[8] Attempts are sometimes made to reconcile the two, but the fit is not sufficiently close. Here I shall confine myself to the first, which appears to have been more commonly used. Each *mahāyuga* consisted of four lesser cycles or ages sandwiched within twilight periods. The four were perceived as the *kṛta* or *satya*, the first, consisting of four thousand divine years, then came the *tretā* of three thousand years, followed by the *dvāpara* of two thousand years, and finally the *kaliyuga* of a thousand years. The figures for the twilight periods also follow a descending arithmetical progression, from

[4] Cf. Kloetzli 1983.

[5] Cf. Basham 1951.

[6] Cf. Thibaut 1899.

[7] However, in saying this I may be indulging in my twentieth-century positivist view of the data!

[8] Cf. Mitchiner 1982.

eight hundred to two hundred. Altogether these make twelve thousand divine years and are multiplied by 360 to convert them into 4,320,000 years.

Apart from the first, the names of the ages were taken from throws of the dice, thus introducing an element of chance into the flow of time. The present age has been called 'the age of the losing throw'. The start of the *kaliyuga* begins by describing the position of the constellations. This has been calculated as equivalent to 3102 *BC*. In contrast to the immensity of the cycle, we are told that the length of a human life is that of a dewdrop on the tip of a blade of grass at sunrise.

The descending arithmetical progression in the length of the four cycles points to a concern with mathematical orderliness and pattern, even if the figures are imagined. There is a play on numbers such as 7, 12 and 432, which were regarded as magical in India, as well as in Mesopotamian and Hellenistic sources. Since the length of the cycles is not identical there was a difference from one cycle to another and some unique events were possible.

The mathematical pattern underlined the scheme of the social and sacred ordering of society as formulated in Brahmanical normative texts. The first and longest age, the *kṛtayuga*, encapsulated an initial utopia. Subsequently there was a decline in each of the succeeding ages, until finally the *kaliyuga* was associated with degeneration. The symbols of decline are easily recognizable and are common to many cultures: the human body becomes smaller, the lifespan shorter; marriage becomes necessary to procreation since men and women are no longer born as adult couples; and above all, human beings have to labour in order to live. There is also an abundance of heretics and unrighteous people. In one text it is said that *dharma* – the essential social and sacred duty – is like a bull that stands on four legs at the start, but with each age it drops one leg. This is a picturesque way of stating that there was a substantial change from one age to the next, and that the *kaliyuga* is unstable.

The change is particularly pertinent to the increasing distancing of people from the norms of a society based on caste as envisaged in *varṇa*. In predicting the future, it is said that the status and functions of the upper castes will be usurped by the lower castes. Rituals that had hitherto been guarded as a Brahmin preserve would now be performed indiscriminately by any caste. An even greater disaster will be the liberation of women, as this will undermine caste society, which required the subordination of women and their acquiescence in patriarchy. This was a description of a distopia as seen from the Brahmanical perspective, but implicitly it was also the utopia of the lower castes. It has been argued[9] that this description of the *kaliyuga* mirrored the changes that were taking place in northern India in the early centuries *AD*. The influx of migrant populations and the dynasties of the degenerate or *vrātya kṣatriya*s introduced many social changes. Such societies did not maintain the social norms of the Dharmaśāstras. This was said despite the endorsing of Dharmaśāstra norms in the earliest Sanskrit inscription issued by a Śaka king, Rudradāman, in the second century *AD*. However, it can equally well be argued that these statements need not have referred to actual changes but to the fear that they might come about. Theoretically some non-Brahmanical sects supported such ideas. Any dominant group unable to sustain an unchallenged dominance would have feared a loss of dominance. There is also the logic of cycles, namely, that an upswing has to be complemented by a downswing.

The decline of *dharma* and the transgression of caste norms associated with the *kaliyuga* suggests that cyclical time was closely associated with a preference for Brahmanical norms. The function of cyclical time is to perpetuate the norms, to which a return is made with each new *mahāyuga*. The recitation at, and performance of, rituals associated with cyclical regeneration enacted the myths of cyclical time, and such rituals drew upon Brahmin ritual specialists. The nature of time-markers such as the cataclysmic end to the great cycle or the messianic coming of Kalkin underlines an element of permanence in the cycle of time. However, the transgression of social norms was associated with the end of time.

The logic of events in the *kaliyuga* is that conditions will deteriorate to such an extent that those faithful to the norms will flee to the hills and await the coming of the last incarnation of Vishnu in the form of the Brahmin Kalkin. He will restore the norms of caste society. The concept of Kalkin echoes, although it is not identical with, the large number of saviour figures that emerged as part of the expectations of various religious sects of the eastern Mediterranean and western Asia. In each case they were seen as coming to save the true doctrine from extinction and to re-establish the original teachings. Thus we have the Buddha Maitreya, Saoshyant among the Zoroastrians and John of the Revelations among the Christians. The coming of Kalkin was an alternative to the

---

[9] Sharma 1966, 1982.

cataclysmic end of the *mahāyuga*. Kalkin initiates another golden age. History does not end; time does not cease.

These changes in the cycle were also linked to an increase or decrease in *dharma*, or sacred and social obligations. The utopia is placed at the start of the cycle. But the cycle does not necessarily return to it if a new cycle is inaugurated by the coming of Kalkin, although his coming initiates utopian conditions. The four cycles within the *mahāyuga* do not return to their beginnings but move into the next and smaller cycles. Such continuity hints at a different form than just a cycle, perhaps a helix or spiral, which if stretched might form a wave or even perhaps a not very straight line.

The start of the *kaliyuga* has been calculated to a precise point in cyclical time, which also marks the start of linear time. Even though linear time forms part of the cycle, it was perceived as different. This is highlighted in relation to the current cycle, and the former three cycles can be seen as the prehistory, as it were, of the present. Unlike cyclical time, which is described in a variety of texts, linear time is most evident in the Purāṇas, in particular the *Viṣṇu-* and *Matsya-Puraṇa* among the earlier texts of this category. Interestingly both concepts of time are to be found in the same *Viṣṇu-Purāṇa*.[10] The earlier chapters describe the *mahāyuga* and its components, and a chapter towards the end – the *vaṃśānucarita* section – describes the events that form part of linear time. It is curious that H.H. Wilson[11] recognized only the presence of cyclical time when he was editing the *Viṣṇu-Purāṇa* and missed the obvious pattern of linear time.

The *vaṃśānucarita* section is concerned with the flow of historical succession and encapsulates the start of linear time. This is calculated on a different set of premises from cyclical time, being based on human activity, the notion of causation being implicit, even if it is not clearly stated. This is a contrast to cyclical time, where human intervention is negated and even the coming of Kalkin is a preordained incarnation of Vishnu. At most it can be said that Kalkin comes when the norms of society are subverted. But the narration is in the future tense, and Kalkin is inevitable and predictable.

The *vaṃśānucarita* narrative becomes foundational to a perspective of the past in a range of texts purporting to be concerned with *itihāsa*, and it can, in a manner of speaking, be detached from the cycle. The historical

[10] Wilson 1972, *Viṣṇu-Purāṇa* 1.3-5; 2.8 and 4.

[11] Wilson 1972.

consciousness that is implicit in *itihāsa* has a linear form.[12] Not all these sources were necessarily historical or accurate – in fact few were – but the time framework was linear. Social demarcations are noticeable, less in the events and more in the change of authorship. Tradition has it that what was believed to be the record of historical succession was initially preserved by the *sūta* or bard. But when control over the past became an important mechanism in legitimizing kings, as from the early centuries *AD*, the record was often compiled, edited, and appropriated by the Brahmin, portions of it being incorporated into some Purāṇa, or later into chronicles.

The *vaṃśānucarita* section begins with the age of the Manus. The first time-marker is the Great Flood. A deluge clears away the past and prepares for the future. Vishnu in his *matsya-avatāra* or fish incarnation helps Manu to survive. After the Flood, therefore, Manu becomes the progenitor of succeeding generations. In the Vaiṣṇava reading, the *matsya* incarnation of Viṣṇu at the beginning and Kalkin at the end are the two termini of the time frame and suggest an eschatology.

The succession of heroes that emerged when the Flood receded were allotted an identity in one of two distinct descent groups, the Sūryavaṃśa and the Candravaṃśa.[13] This evoked a symbolism not unconnected with calendars and time – the sun and the moon. But these were also symbols of social dichotomies because although the status of the heroes was that of *kṣatriyas*, the pattern of their genealogies marked a social differentiation. The solar line practised primogeniture and therefore claimed to record descent only from eldest son to eldest son. The *Rāmāyaṇa* was the narrative of the descendants of Ikṣvāku, who was ancestral to the Sūryavaṃśa. This epic became the foundation text of the solar lineage. The other descent group, the Candravaṃśa or lunar lineage, had a pattern of segmentary clans, primarily the Yādavas and the Purus. The pattern therefore kept fanning out since all the sons and their sons were recorded, not just the eldest. This is also a system by which unrelated clans can be incorporated into the genealogies. These lineages were theoretically, at least, the progenitors of the protagonists in the *Mahābhārata.* This text became the source for narratives of the *Candravaṃśa*. There were marginal overlaps between the two epics, but at a broad level they were distinctive.

---

[12] Pargiter 1922.

[13] Thapar 1978.

Such lineage patterns were not to be taken literally as history. They were perceptions of the past and were ways of indicating variation in the societies of the past. The genealogies were constructed on what was presumed to be the succession of ruling clans, and in later times these provided links with ruling dynasties. The lists cover over a hundred generations and are in large part fabricated. Nevertheless they can be analysed not as authentic history, but as reflections of a consciousness of history. Time measured by generations, as in genealogies, is essentially linear. The word used for succession, *vaṃśa*, that is, bamboo or cane, is a visual demonstration of a node and of succession. There are also various lesser time-markers and genealogical patterns in the *vaṃśānucarita* section, which underline sequential, linear time.

The presence of more than one form of time measurement in the same text is perhaps intended to point us towards different statements being made about each. Genealogical time or the counting of generations is at the start of the record, whether in the Purāṇas or the chronicles, and precedes what we recognize as conventional history. Genealogies were important in societies where status was based on birth, lineage, and kinship, and could be manipulated by being stretched or telescoped. This was less easy to do with dynastic descent but by no means impossible. Genealogies could also be manipulated in favour of those being inducted into the society, as happened in the post-Gupta period. A link with the descent group could be established at a particular point in the genealogy. Some dynasties claimed descent from Lava and Kuśa, the sons of Rāma, while others claimed connections within the large network of descent groups of the Yādavas or the Pauravas. Manipulating genealogies is also indicative of the relative openness of political power.

The supposed history of the early heroes was then tied together, as it were, in another time-marker, the battle at Kurukṣetra. Virtually all the clans were involved, and the war ended their glory. The focus of the text then changed to recording dynasties rather than descent groups. The list of successive rulers and their regnal years, as given in some Purāṇas, highlighted linear time. The dynasties were not related to each other, as were the *kṣatriya rājā*s. Kings were of diverse castes – frequently Brāhmaṇa or Śūdra – not to mention what were called the *vrātya* or degenerate *kṣatriyas*. After the battle at Kurukṣetra, which marks the start of the *kaliyuga*, the story is narrated in the future tense. This is a significant way of indicating change.

This point in time is also an intersection of cyclical and linear time. In the cyclical reckoning, the *kaliyuga* is associated with a particular stellar pattern, a point in time over which there is no human control, nor is the date marked by any particular human activity. In the linear reckoning, the start of the *kaliyuga* is linked to events created and controlled by human activity, namely, the period subsequent to the Kurukṣetra war.

In using the future tense and pretending to predict historical change, the narrative also invoked astrology. The political importance of astrology becomes more evident in inscriptions from the first millennium *AD*. This was when competition, contestation, and insecurity increased, and prediction was doubtless seen as an attempt to control the present by prophesying the future. Astrology requires an auspicious moment, which may have coincided with the political need to mark status by celebrating a moment in time. In addition, linear time encouraged the use of yet another form of measuring historical time, namely, the creation of eras.

The historical era or *samvatsara* became a symbol of political power and the royal court. The earliest inscriptions, those of the Mauryan emperor, Aśoka, are dated in regnal years. This is parallel to the regnal years associated with dynasties in some of the Purāṇas. But the recording of regnal years is not the same as using an era. The latter highlights a point in time and makes a claim to exalted status.

An early era used in historical sources was the *kṛta* of 58 *BC*, later to be called the Malava era and more frequently the Vikrama era. There has been an ongoing debate on what this era commemorates. It is now suggested that it marks the accession of Azes I, who was not, however, the most important of early rulers. A calculation in astronomy as the basis of this era cannot altogether be ruled out. '*Kṛta*' means established, the Malava peoples are associated with Ujjain, and Ujjain was the meridian and location for calculations in astronomy. This era, which continues to be used today, was familiar over an extensive geographical area.

Subsequent to this there was an outbreak of new eras. The rationale for these is linked to historical events, although sometimes the date or the association or both are controversial. As time-markers they shift from highlighting an event to becoming measurements of time, but they use time to link events.

The Śaka era of *AD* 78 is thought by some to mark the accession of Kaniṣka. The Gupta era of *AD* 319-20 records the establishment of Gupta power. This fashion continues, and among others we have the Harṣa era of *AD* 606, the Cedi era of *AD* 248-9, and the Cāḷukya -Vikrama era of *AD* 1075, symbolizing the supremacy of the Cāḷukya king, Vikramāditya VI.

Establishing an era was a sign of political supremacy. It could, however, have been a supremacy arising by resolving conflicting claims to the throne, as happened clearly in the case of Vikramāditya and is also hinted at in the case of Harṣa. Eras are time-markers, yet eras in the form of dates indicate a different social concern from the use of the Flood and the Kurukṣetra war as time-markers. Eras are based on small measurements of time and reflect an attitude to time that is closely tied to historical events.

The association of identity with an era is more clearly demonstrated in the adoption of the date of the Buddha's *mahāparinirvāṇa* as an era, specific to Buddhist sources and concerns. A date was decided which became the starting point of the chronology, irrespective of its actual historical accuracy, although it was projected as accurate. The use of such an era was meant to emphasize the historicity of the religion. The use of multiple eras points to interesting complexities in the societies of the time. Some of these eras would have originated in local events and systems of time-reckoning, in tandem with the growth of regional kingdoms. The era became a link between local perceptions and the more exact measurements required in urban centres and royal courts. Different social groups used eras to record different events. This then becomes another interface between cyclical and linear time. Apart from measuring time, the linear form is often identified as encapsulating regional or local concerns. Cosmological time is the more generalized form of time-reckoning, which is drawn from what might be called the civilizational context and which envelopes the regional forms. This could be seen as yet another aspect of the interface in the separation and mingling of the *mārga* and the *deśi* – the mainstream in contrast to the more localized cultural form. The perspective from the cyclical to the linear must sometimes be seen not as a dichotomy but as a continuum. The question worth pursuing is, when in the history of a region do both forms of time-reckoning become evident?

One function of these historical eras is their attempt to demarcate historical time from cosmological time. They occur most frequently in association with royal inscriptions, which are now regarded as the annals of Indian history. A document is judged as more authentic and authoritative if it is accompanied by a date. Inscriptions recording grants of land would have required dates in order to prove the legality of the document. This would be an even more necessary requirement where the grant of land was a reward for predicting an eclipse or for what was believed to be the warding off of a disaster. The time of the eclipse would have to be meticulously dated. Such time-reckoning could draw on both cosmological and historical time.

From about the mid-first millennium *AD* onwards, inscriptions recording the official version of the events of a reign began to be issued as a normal procedure by a range of ruling families. Many began with narratives of the origins of the family that involved recounting the past and making connections. This took them from mythological origins to more recent events. Where actual social origins were obscure or low, it became necessary to envelop them into fancy claims. Perceptions of the past were therefore important to these texts.

The legitimation of power included a range of activities, including the making of grants of land to individuals, religious beneficiaries, and institutions such as monasteries and temples. These would then act as a network of support for the ruling family and the royal court. The inscription recording the grant was a legal document and required to be dated with great precision. In a society increasingly given to astrology as was the post-Gupta elite, there was also the question of making the grant at the most auspicious moment – and that moment had to be recorded. This was the occasion for obscure families who had risen to rule to claim a status equivalent to that of the established ruling families, a claim that the beneficiaries of the grants were ready to substantiate. The document accompanying the grant had to be inscribed on imperishable material – copper or stone – so that its permanence could be ensured should anyone decide to challenge one's ownership of land or property. Grants, often bestowed in return for legitimation, had to be impressive in their generosity, and there was much honour involved in being regarded as the most munificent ruler. A continuity of time even longer than that of the *kalpa* is assumed in the inscriptions, which carry the formulaic phrase that the grant should last as long as the moon and sun endure.

A further category of texts reflecting linear time were the *vaṃśāvalī*s, literally 'the path of succession'. These were chronicles of dynasties or regions in various parts of the subcontinent and were written from about the eleventh century onwards. The *Rājātaraṅginī* of Kalhana, a history of Kashmir written in the twelfth century, is the most quoted *vaṃśāvalī* and is justifiably regarded as a remarkable example of historical writing. Texts in the same genre, but less incisive, are those similar to the chronicle of Chamba, written in the shadow of the *Rājātaraṅginī*. More distant places such as Kerala also had chronicles such as the *Musakavaṃśakāvya* of Atula pertaining to north Malabar. The *vaṃśāvalī* often beginning as an oral tradition, seems to assume visibility as a text at the point at which a regional political entity evolved into a state and was staking its claims to statehood. The records of the past were collated from various sources and a chronicle was put together, sometimes providing a coherent history, though not averse to a little mythology. The earlier sections of such chronicles often incorporate fragments of genealogical material from the Purāṇas as a way of legitimizing the status of the ruling family. These fragments formed a prelude to what was viewed as the history of the region.

In the chronicles and inscriptions, time is linear, the assumptions of cyclical time being possibly implicit but remaining distant. Cyclical time is not denied, but it forms part of a larger reckoning in which deities and incarnations play a major role rather than human heroes. Events relating to the human scale are more properly expressed as part of linear time, which was more functional. Yet it is in an inscription that there is the most precise and evident expression of the intersection of cyclical and linear time. A seventh-century inscription of Pulakeśin II in a temple at Aihole in the Deccan records an event in the Śaka era of *AD* 78 and includes a reference to the date calculated in terms of the *kaliyuga*. This enables us to crosscheck the date of the *kaliyuga* and calculate its equivalence in the modern calendar. What seems to have been essential was the historical date: the reference to the *kaliyuga* may have been an addition. Curiously the date is not given in figures but in words.

Linear time within the *kaliyuga* creates an intersection with cyclical time. It is almost as if a small segment of the cycle is stretched into a more linear form, or alternatively, that the linear forms a small arc of the large circle. The cyclical then encompasses the linear and becomes a temporal frame within which any past could be accommodated. The *vaṃśānucarita* section becomes part of the calculation of the *yuga*, yet it also retains a distinctiveness that separates it from the *yuga*. That there was simultaneous use of more than one measurement of time suggests a parallel with a more recent European discussion of historical time, namely that of Fernand Braudel. He argues that the historian has to handle three categories of time in terms of depth. The *long durée* goes back to geological time and incorporates a changing landscape. Less extensive is the period of the few centuries that determine social and economic history. Finally there is the momentary time of the event. The first encompasses the second and the third, and therefore each has a component of the others. This introduces the notion of simultaneous time measurements.

Time was tied into social and political functions. These can be seen either in the diverse authorship of historical traditions, or else in the use of time for diverse purposes, as in the genealogical records. The earlier ones were maintained by the *sūta* or bard and incorporated the worldview and social requirements of the ruling clans, where time was measured by generations and by kin relations. But when this record was taken over by Brahmin authors and re-compiled, the concern was less with measuring generations and more with establishing the social claims – whether actual or fictive – of the dynasties. The editing of the record therefore changed hands from the *sūta* to the Brahmins in accordance with the function that the record was supposed to perform. Neither editors nor patrons were consistently of the same social group. The past, seen as a qualifier of status, allows linear time to be treated as social time.

The capturing of the past is tied to the writing of history. The question then is the point at which history comes to be recorded. It would be used not just to legitimize a ruling family but also the system so represented. Possibly the most pertinent time was when multiple identities had to be converted into a few effective identities or, in the case of a dominant group, into a single identity. Does the consciousness of linear time coincide with the formation of an independent state system? And does it take its form from the parallel establishment of a dominant religion? Monastic chronicles attempt to capture this change. The simultaneous use of more than one form of time and its layered representation indicates some awareness that different segments of a society may view their past differently. For the legitimation to be acceptable, it had to be beyond question. Here the claims of linear time were easier to manipulate.

There is yet another aspect of time, which I can only mention in passing, namely, the relationship between time, memory, and history, restricted to the context of linear time. To locate events in the first three cycles of the *mahāyuga* that cannot come under human control is virtually to declare them as being outside history. What is projected as remembered is taken for granted, little effort being made to place it in the context of what may have been forgotten. History is viewed as a process of reaching into memory, and also of retrieving the forgotten. This has political and social dimensions and can be used as an infrastructure for ideology, even of earlier times. The manipulation of genealogies may not be an act of memory, but it becomes such an act through the historian selecting what is to be included and what discarded from the past, what the historian chooses to remember or prefers to forget. A retrieval can also involve the need to draw on multiple readings of an event over many centuries, gathered from a variety of sources. Comparative studies of variant versions and attempts to place these in their historical contexts is one way of trying to ascertain what has been chosen and what has been forgotten or discarded. In comparing variant versions of the same narrative written at different times, the historian must take into account what was suppressed and what was recalled in the narrative in changing from one version to another, and equally importantly, why was this done. If the changing historical context was a factor, then the link between time, history, and memory becomes a possible explanation.

This also raises a parallel concern relating to historical events as distinct from a fictional narrative. A historical narrative requires at least a minimum reflection on how memory is constructed in the period between the event and the historical interpretation of the event, whenever that happened. This is difficult to do for early periods, when the range of sources used in the construction of histories is not easily available. But possibly some creative extrapolation back to those periods would be helpful. Such an exercise becomes necessary because of the pretence of using memory in inventing historical traditions. A proneness to this is characteristic of all societies, but especially those that have a complex past demonstrated in their multiple cultures. The reconstruction of memory is also specific to histories and cultures, as Frances Yates has demonstrated.

Memory also has the ability to compress or expand time, thus reducing the accuracy of its time-reckoning. In looking back on the past, there is a distinction between time as recent and time as an expression of temporal distance. Cyclical time can impinge on linear time when the significance of events is negated by saying that they are happening in the *kaliyuga*, and since the *kaliyuga* is an age of decline and distopia there is little point in marking historical events. Such markings are of course available in sources that are conditioned by linear time. Where events are contemporary with the text, memory, or even the play on memory, would be of consequence. Time links events, and the causal connections must be explored.

It has been said that history overcomes time and memory. But before it can do so, history must investigate the making and marking of time in its social and historical dimensions.

References

Basham, A.L. 1951. *Histories and Doctrines of the Ājīvikas: A Vanished Indian Religion*, London: Luzac.

Braudel, F. 1981-4. *Civilisation and Capitalism 15th-18th Century*, Translated from the French by Sian Reynolds, 3 vols. London: Collins

Eliade, M. 1955. *The Myth of the Eternal Return*, London: Routledge & Kegan Paul.

Kloetzli, R. 1983. *Buddhist Cosmology: From Single World System to Pure Land. Science and Theology in the Images of Motion and Light*, Delhi: Motilal Banarsidass.

Mitchiner, J.E. 1982. *Traditions of the Seven Rishis*, Delhi: Motilal Banarsidass.

Pargiter, F.E. 1922. *Ancient Indian Historical Tradition*, London: Oxford University Press.

Sharma, R.S. 1966. *Light on Early Indian Society and Economy*, Bombay: Manaktalas.

— 1982. 'The Kali Age: A Period of Social Crisis', in S.N. Mukherjee (ed.), *India, History and Thought: Essays in Honour of A.L. Basham*, Calcutta: Subarnarekha, 186-203.

Thapar, R. 1978. 'Genealogy as a Source of Social History', in R. Thapar, *Ancient Indian Social History: Some Interpretations*, New Delhi: Orient Longman, 326-60.

— 1997. 'Linear Time in Historical Texts of Early India', in Dick van der Meij (ed.), *India and Beyond: Aspects of Literature, Meaning, Ritual and Thought: Essays in Honour of Frits Staal*, Leiden: International Institute for Asian Studies, 562-73.

Thibaut, G. 1899. *Astronomie, Astrologie und Mathematik*, Strassburg: Verlag von Karl J. Trübner (Grundriss der Indo-Arischen Philologie und Altertumskunde [Encyclopedia of Indo-Aryan Research] Band 3, Heft 9).

Wilson, H.H. 1972. *The Vishṇu Purāṇa: A System of Hindu Mythology and Tradition*, Translated from the Original Sanskrit and Illustrated by Notes Derived Chiefly from Other Purāṇas by H.H. Wilson with an Introduction by Dr. R. C. Hazra, Calcutta: Punthi Pustak.

Yates, Frances A. 1968. *The Art of Memory*, London: Routledge.

2

The King's Own Time: The Aṅka System of Orissa[1]

Georg Berkemer

The notion of time usually evokes pairs of opposite terms, such as circular *versus* linear, secular *versus* sacred, marked versus unmarked. More synthetic approaches discuss time in terms that try to integrate these opposites. Time can oscillate, as Edmund Leach writes, or be textured, as described in a recent book by Velcheru Narayana Rao, David Shulman and Sanjay Subrahmanyam.[2]

Talking about time also evokes the notion of the cultural patterns that structure it. Certain periods of time have their special meanings and cause people to behave in distinctive ways. As we all know, it is difficult to make a person sing a song which belongs to Siva Ratri at Dasahrā or a Christmas carol on Midsummer's Day. Does that mean that time really has power over people and their behaviour? We hear from philosophers and psychologists that humans cannot perceive time at all. We do not feel time in the same way as we feel thirst, pain or weight. The perception of time may be more closely related to such complex, culturally structured emotional states as pride, greed, or joy.

What humans perceive is not time, but variations such as movement and change. Some things change their location or appearance according to regular patterns, linear, circular, or otherwise. Others change in very unpredictable ways. Change can be observed and felt in one's own body, in one's immediate social environment, in natural rhythms and cosmic phenomena, in art, music, etc. All cultures provide means to articulate, create and interpret such more or less regular patterns of change. It seems to me that change is at the basis of all those expressions in whose semantic fields notions of time occur, in whatever form that may be.[3]

---

[1] The following abbreviations are used here and refer to collections of inscriptions listed in the bibliography under their editors: *IO* (Inscriptions of Orissa, see Rajaguru 1960, 1960a, 1961), *SII* (South Indian Inscriptions, see Krishna Sastri 1925 for vol. 5, Subrahmanya Aiyer 1928 for vol. 6), *TIAP* (Temple Inscriptions of Andhra Pradesh, see Mukunda Rao 1980).

[2] Leach 1966; Narayana Rao, Shulman, Subrahmanyam 2001.

[3] Examples from English would be the various connotations of 'time' itself, denoting the duration as well as the frequency of events in a temporal frame of

This means that time does not exist per se as a physical force like gravity. Instead it is a cultural construct, and whereas change can hardly be made undone or manipulated, time can. Time can be made visible in stone, reversed in plays and rituals, attributed with new meanings in stories, and re-created in history books. Clocks do not indicate time but measure movement with ever increasing preciseness. All this has to do with time, but it is not time. It shows us what was and what is now and gives us the means to compare stages in processes of change and refer to them in terms of 'earlier' or 'later'. Our languages and cultures provide us with rules to interpret such changes as 'time'. It seems to me that St. Augustine's famous dictum is still valid: 'When nobody asks me about it, I know it; yet if, when asked, I shall explain it, I do not know it.'[4]

In the following, a rather extreme case of the flexibility of socially constructed time will be discussed: the Orissan *aṅka* system. This is one of those systems of dynastic time reckoning[5] that are used to make a political statement. Ruling families, which maintained their own dynastic era or special way of counting regnal years together with other symbols used for the same purpose, openly claimed paramount royal authority in their region. Inferior rulers were expected to use the same reckoning as their overlords as a symbolic statement of their subordination.

Counting Time in Aṅka Years

In Orissa, the *aṅka* reckoning can be traced back to the eleventh century *AD*. In the epigraphic records of the Imperial Gaṅga dynasty (1077-1434) and their successors, the Sūryavaṃśa Gajapati dynas (1435-1568) and the rājas of Khurda, this special way of counting regnal years was and still is regularly used. This system can be recognized by the addition of the words *aṅka*, *aṅka-śrāhi* or *śrāhi*[6] to the number of regnal years. It is, therefore, in modern parlance called the '*Aṅka* system'.

---

reference, the quality of a situation ('having a good time', 'hard times'), 'tides', 'tidings' and related words, and space-time references such as 'deadline', 'trip down memory lane', or 'once in a blue moon'.

[4] Augustinus 1995, Book 11, XIV, 17.

[5] For a more general discussion of dynastic eras, see the articles in Falk 2002.

[6] *Aṅka* means here 'number, marking'. *Śrāhi,* however, is more difficult to interpret. A typical example of a statement of regnal years in Orissan *aṅka-śrāhi*, here just called '*śrāhi*', is the following: '*vijaya-rājya-saṃvatsarambulu 7 śrāhi*', quoted from a Telugu inscription in Śrīkūrmam, dated to the seventh *aṅka* in the 'years of the victorious reign' of Puruṣottama Gajapati. The date is 20 June 1471

Aṅka years are based on a circle of sixty numbers, from one to sixty. Any higher number cannot exist. A further rule specifies that certain numbers among the sixty have to be omitted. These are all numbers ending in either zero or six (6, 10, 16, 20 ...) There is one more number that is never counted, namely one. Year one of a new king is always also the last year of the old king, and this year of two kings is officially counted as the year of the old ruler. Consequently, the number for the first full year of the new king after New Year's Day (which in this case is in September) is already 'two'. In order to compensate for the missing 'one', the 'ten', which according to the general rule stated above should be dropped, is counted as a regular year. The numbers not used are therefore 1, 6, 16, 20, 26, 30, 36, 40, 46, 50, 56, 60. Thus, for every ten regnal years, there are twelve *aṅka* years (*aṅka* 12 r. 10), and when one arrives at *aṅka* fifty-nine, the calendric count shows eleven years less. This results in a condensation of sixty *aṅka* 'years' into forty-eight astronomical years. In other words, the king has command over sixty *aṅka*s in the same amount of time that a commoner needs to get to forty-eight years. The king's own time runs at a different speed than the commoners' time.

If a king reigns for more than forty-eight normal years, his *aṅka*s are expected to begin again. This consideration is academic in so far as no king after the routine establishment of this system under Coḍagaṅga Anantavarman (reigned 1077-1147) ever ruled for such a long time, and Codagaṅga continued to count his years in a linear fashion.

(Subrahmanyam 1986, 112, line 3). The word *aṅka* itself does not help to solve the problem because it occurs quite frequently in inscriptions just to indicate the repetition of a chronogram or symbolic 'number-word' in figures. It occurs in Gaṅga records for the first time in the *Ponduru* plates of Vajrahasta IV (Rajaguru 1960: *IO* 2, No. 39) where the year is given twice, in words and in numerals: *Gaṅgānvaya-pravarddhamāna-vijayarājya-saṃvatsara-śata 100 aṃkēṅāpi āṣāḍa-māsa-dina-ādityavāre* ('The year 100 – in numerals: 100 – of the prosperous and victorious rule of the Gaṅga family, on Sunday, the [first] day of the month Āṣāḍa ...'). In this early inscription the word '*aṅka*' clearly does not denote anything other than the original meaning 'number'. The problem here is not the meaning of *aṅka*, but the date of the inscription. The dating of the record to the year 100 of the Gaṅga era is surely wrong on paleographic and stylistic grounds and would wrongly suggest a very early occurrence of the term in Gaṅga inscriptions. D.C. Sircar suggests reading '500', which would date the inscription to the years AD 996 to 998, while Rajaguru (1960) offers no opinion (*IO* II, p. 185). Gaṅga Era 500 coincides with the time of Vajrahasta IV, the son of Kāmārṇava and successor of Vinayāditya mentioned above.

The year of the *aṅka* cycle has a fixed beginning on the twelfth day of the light half of the lunar month of Bhadra (*Bhadra śukla dvādaśī*; in 2002 this was September 18).[7] This day is counted as the twelfth day of the year in Orissa.[8] The day in question is called *suniā* (golden) in the Oriya calendar.[9] This date is the beginning of the fiscal year in Orissa and oscillates around the autumn equinox. This is also the time when the monsoon ends. It is the first of the autumn rituals that culminate in the Dasahrā and Vijayadaśamī festivals, when kings worship their weapons and traditionally set out for hunting and war. This sequence of festivals also starts the first full regnal year of the new king, which is counted as his second *aṅka*.

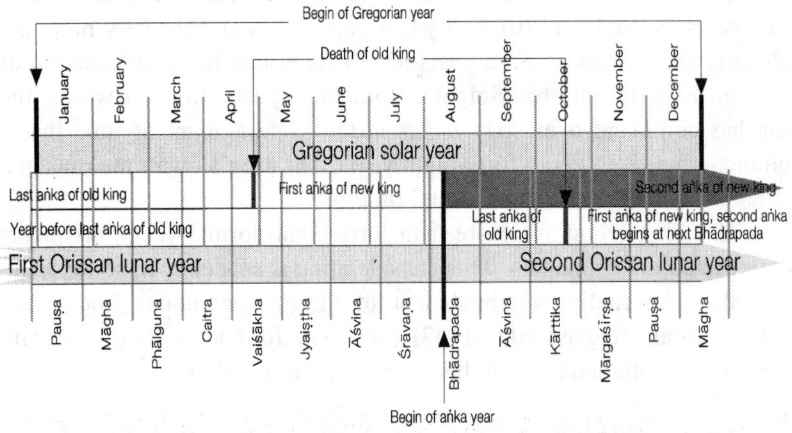

Fig. 1: Relation of *aṅka* year to Gregorian year. If a king dies before the beginning of the *aṅka* year, the last *aṅka* of the old king and the second *aṅka* of the new king fall into the same Gregorian year. If a king dies after the beginning of the *aṅka* year, the last two *aṅka*s of the old king fall into the same Gregorian year, but the second *aṅka* of the new king begins with Bhādrapada in the next Gregorian year.

---

[7] Cf. Subrahmanyam 1957, 9; Tripathi 1962, 388; Rajaguru 1968, 201; Geeta Devi 1998, 91; Acharya 2002, 29, fn. 14.

[8] Subrahmanyam 1986, xxxi.

[9] The name is derived from the minting ceremony performed on that day (Hardenberg 2000, 123). It is also the day for the celebrations of Vāmana Janma, Garuda Pārśvaparivartana and Indradhvaja Pūja. Since Viṣṇu conquers the world as Vāmana, the placement of festivals of the king's new year and the birth of Vāmana on the same day seems to be no coincidence (see *Record of Rights*, Part II, p. 116-8).

The (Gregorian) year in which the *aṅka* cycle of a new king begins depends on the day of his coronation. His first regnal year commences on the day of his coronation, at which time the last year of his predecessor is incomplete. Therefore, his first *aṅka* year and the last of his predecessor end at the same time, the twelfth day of the bright half of the lunar month of Bhādrapada (Bhadra śukla 12). The new king's first *aṅka* is therefore never a full year, which explains its irregular omission in counting *aṅka*s. If the coronation takes place before the beginning of the fiscal year in autumn at Bhadra śukla 12, three *aṅka*s fall within one year of the Gregorian calendar: the old king's last (defective) *aṅka*, the new king's first (defective) *aṅka* up to Bhadra śukla 11, and the new king's second (regular) *aṅka* from Bhadra śukla 12. If the coronation takes place after Bhadra śukla 12, there is only one *aṅka* count in that year. The first full *aṅka*, counted as the second year of the new king, begins on Bhadra śukla 12 in the following year. If the day of the death of the old king is unknown, it remains uncertain whether the second *aṅka* begins in the same Gregorian year or the year after.

Besides Vijayadaśamī, the tenth day of the Dasahrā festival in October, the annual ritual beginning of the king's own yearly cycle was the most important royal festival in Orissa. It was derived from the medieval royal ritual of the imperial Gajapatis. Its main event, the minting ceremony, has been described in detail and analysed by Roland Hardenberg for the contemporary Suniā festival in Puri.[10] It was also a major festival in the nineteenth century for the southern Gajapati of Parlakimedi. S.N. Rajaguru relates the following details:

> The introduction of this era indicates the overlordship of the Gaṅgas over a vast territory. Even today, we find that some Zamindars in Orissa who belong to this ancient family and observe the Aṅka perform the minting ceremony in the month of Bhādrapada Śudha Dvādaśī (Suniyā).[11]

---

[10] Hardenberg 2000, 123-54.

[11] Rajaguru 1968, 129; he assumes a connection between the establishment of the Ganga era and the celebration of Suniā, though there is no historical evidence for this.

On the Origin of *Aṅka-śrāhi*

The origin of this dating system is an enigma not only to the ordinary people of Orissa, whose knowledge of it is restricted to certain astrological usages, such as establishing a person's year of birth. Among experts, too, opinions differ widely, and many who write about eras and dating systems never touch the problem of the *aṅka-śrāhi*. It is particularly regrettable that D.C. Sircar's standard works on Indian epigraphy[12] do not discuss this question at all. K.N. Mahapatra states that both the origin of the *aṅka* system and its terminology are undetermined.[13] S.K. Acharya's recent book on numerals in Oriya Inscriptions mentions *aṅka* without any further explanation.[14] Rajaguru divides the problem into the following three parts, which permits him to clarify at least some aspects to the satisfaction of the reader: (1) the origin and date of the strange custom of omitting certain numbers; (2) the first occurrence of the names *aṅka* and *śrāhi*, whether in Orissa or elsewhere; and (3) the cultural and historical context in which the system has been developed.

In order to answer the first question, Rajaguru traces the *aṅka-śrāhi* tradition, especially the use of the term *śrāhi* in written sources,[15] back to the Gaṅga king Anantavarma Vajrahasta V (reigned 1038-69 *AD*).[16] This king is known as one of the greatest reformers in Kaliṅga.[17] In his reign occurred the first long genealogy in a Gaṅga copperplate inscription, the first inscriptions in the vernaculars of Kaliṅga (Oriya and Telugu), the first mention of officers called *nāyaka* in the service of the Gaṅgas, and the first record dated to the Śaka-era. Before Vajrahasta V, only Sanskrit inscriptions on copperplates dated in Gaṅga-*saṃvat* and lacking an elaborate genealogy are known.

---

[12] Sircar (1965, 328; 1966, 316) suggests nothing but a doubtful etymology.

[13] Mahapatra 1961, 145.

[14] Acharya 2002, 23.

[15] See fn. 7.

[16] According to his own, newly invented genealogy, he should be named Vajrahasta III (see Konow 1911). This genealogy lists more than three generations of kings for the first time in Gaṅga history. Vajrahasta's grandson Coḍagaṅga Anantavarman, however, introduced an even more elaborate and fictitious genealogy. He lists Vajrahasta as the fifth of this name. Coḍagaṅga's version of the genealogy remained the standard in the *praśasti* of the imperial Gaṅgas.

[17] Berkemer 1993, 128f, 145-51.

The very first temple inscription of the Gaṅgas, also dating from Vajrahasta V's time, contains the word *śrāhi*. This is also the first Telugu inscription of the Gaṅga dynasty. This fact is more than a mere coincidence, because the rare Oriya inscriptions are dated in accordance with normal regnal years. The Telugu record just mentioned was inscribed on a pillar in the Madhukesvara temple of Mukhalingam. It records the donation of a perpetual lamp by the wife of a Gaṅga official. The passage containing the date runs as follows: '*śakavarṣaṃbulu 98*[*0* (RG) / *8* (MR)][18] *śrīmad-anantavarmma-dēvara-prava*[*rddha*]*māna-saṃvatsarambulu* [*3*] *yagu śrāhi vriccikamāsa-śukla-pakṣa-*[*pañcamiyu* (RG) /-*paḍyemuyu* (MR)] *guruvāramunāṇḍu*' (In the year Śaka 980/8 in the prosperous *śrāhi* year 3, current, of Śrīmat Anantavarmadeva [Vajrahasta], on Thursday, the [fifth/eleventh] day of the light half of (the Month of) Vṛścika ⌊*scorpio*]).

The successor to this king, Rājarāja I (r. 1070-77), is not known to have used the system. Rājarāja's son, Coḍagaṅga Anantavarman, obviously used *aṅka-śrāhi* according to the rules of omission just stated, though continuing to count beyond fifty-nine, the last number of the cycle.[19] The 'regular' *aṅka-śrāhi* system was routinely used by the sons of Coḍagaṅga and their successors up to the present time, but whether any of the kings actually used *aṅka-śrāhi* in a circular fashion cannot be determined. Nobody after Coḍagaṅga Anantavarman ruled long enough to be faced with the decision of which rule to follow.

Due to the lack of historical evidence, Rajaguru cannot go back beyond the eleventh century. There is no clear indication of the use of any part of the *aṅka-śrāhi* system by the Gaṅgas before that time. Resorting to conjectures, Rajaguru assumes that the tradition started simultaneously

---

[18] MR: reading acc. to Mukunda Rao (1980, 1); RG: reading acc. to Rajaguru (1960, 5), who corrects the date to Śaka 988.

[19] Rajaguru 1961, Appendices II A-F. In Codagaṅga's case as in some others, many *aṅka* years are difficult to read or do not tally with the regnal years given in Śaka era. See Krishna Sastri 1925 (inscr. *SII* 5, No. 1125), also Rajaguru 1960 (*IO* 3/1, No. 21) and Mukunda Rao 1980 (*TIAP* 1, No. 13); *SII* 5, No. 1117 (also *IO* 3/1, No. 24 and *TIAP* 1, No. 14); *SII* 5, No. 1115 (also *IO* 3/1, No. 23 and *TIAP* 1, No. 17); *SII* 5, No. 1058 (also *IO* 3/1, No. 29 and *TIAP* 1, No. 15). N. Mukunda Rao 1991, 12 shows that in an inscription by the son and successor of Coḍagaṅga Anantavarman, Kāmārṇava (1147-57), that *aṅka-śrāhi* was actually used at that time (source: *SII* 5, No. 1148, also *IO* 3/2, No. 247 and *TIAP* 1, No. 127). His analysis supports the lists in Rajaguru's appendices (see Rajaguru 1961, Appendix II-C).

with the Gaṅga era on the day one of year one.[20] Using his way of reconstructing the era of the Gaṅgas of Kaliṅga, day one of the first *aṅka* year of the first Gaṅga king Indravarman would have been at the beginning of the seventh century, probably in *AD* 612.[21]

S.N. Rajaguru was certainly one of the most important authorities on the living royal traditions of Orissa. Moreover, due to his position as the *rājaguru* of Parlakimedi, he had detailed knowledge of the living *aṅka* system and its ritual connotations. The written sources of the pre-eleventh century Gaṅgas, however, reveal no details that corroborate his hypothesis of a simultaneous emergence of the Gaṅga-*saṃvat* and *aṅka-śrāhi* traditions. He never comes forward with circumstantial, let alone factual evidence highlighting the cultural atmosphere in which the system could have been developed in early medieval Kaliṅga.

There is also a logical argument against the identification of *aṅka-śrāhi* with the Gaṅga-*saṃvat*. In all Gaṅga inscriptions in which the *aṅka-śrāhi* system is used, the date is also given in the Śaka era. It is obvious that from the eleventh century onwards, when Śaka reckoning was introduced into the Gaṅga records, there were always two dating systems, one ritual and reserved for the kings, namely *aṅka-śrāhi*, and one for common usage among scribes, merchants, etc., namely the Śaka era.[22] Only with the dissociation of ritual and common time could the complexity of the apparently 'useless' system of counting royal time have developed.

As will be described in the following, the basic idea is indeed older than the eleventh century, and it can be demonstrated that it had nothing to do with the Gaṅgas, or Kaliṅga, or Orissa at that time. Rather, it is evident that there is a connection between the use of Telugu and the *aṅka-śrāhi* dating in the inscriptions of Mukhalingam. Vajrahasta's temple record is by no means the oldest inscription containing the terms *aṅka* or *śrāhi*, but it is the oldest in the cultural context of the mixed Oriya/Telugu language area of Madhyama Kaliṅga, the region of Gaṅga origin.

Older evidence comes from the 'Old Canarese Inscriptions' published by John F. Fleet in the *Indian Antiquary* and containing the

---

[20] Rajaguru 1968, 129.

[21] Rajaguru dates the era to the early seventh century. Most authorities, however, assume a date around *AD* 498.

[22] The Śaka or Scythian era of *AD* 78 survived for centuries after the decline of the Kuṣāṇas and the succeeding supremacy of the Gupta empire and the Gupta era as a non-royal era, mainly used by astrologers.

word *śrāhi*. Friedrich Kielhorn, whose attention was drawn to the problem by Fleet's publications, writes:

> The editor of these inscriptions considers the *srāhī* to be a technical word, which has no particular meaning in the context. I myself am unable to offer any explanation of it.[23]

Two years later he proposes a technical explanation for the word:

> This result, in my opinion clearly shows that the phrase *ē srāhi*, 'in this *srāhi*,' with which the date opens, takes the place of, and is synonymous with, the expressions *asminn=ēva saṁvatsarē* and *tasminn=ēva śakē* of other inscriptions; and I do not consider it doubtful that the mysterious word *srāhi* is used here in the sense of 'year'. This meaning would also suit the use of *srāhi* in the dates to which I have drawn attention ante....[24]

This has been the state of affairs for more than a hundred years, and even though the meaning of *śrāhi* is fairly clear, it seems that no one has as yet been able to offer a plausible etymology for the word.[25]

Coming back to the question of origins, one can trace the system back at least one step further. At least three centuries before its occurrence in Gaṅga records, it is already present in a rudimentary form in the Krishna-Godavari delta. The oldest inscription relevant in our context is a record from the Eastern Cāḷukya dynasty dated to the eighth century *AD*, to either 752 or 798.[26] As far as one can infer from this source and a few

---

[23] Kielhorn 1894, 224.

[24] Kielhorn 1896, 286, with reference to Kielhorn 1894, 224.

[25] According to Sircar (1965, 328; 1966, 316) the term *śrāhi* is derived from the locative *śaradi* of the Sanskrit word *śarad* via a assumed Prakrit form **sarahi*, both meaning 'in autumn' or figuratively 'in the year'. However, linguists (G.N. Dash, B. Kölver, S. Srinivasan, H. Falk, pers. comm.) do not accept this derivation. Radha Krishna (1971, 504) derives the word from *śrīḥ*, holy, via *śrīhi*, which occurs once in a Ganga inscription (Radha Krishna 1971, 135, No. 153; *SII* 5, No. 1117). Semantically, if not etymologically, a derivation from *śrāya* ('possessing', 'furnished with'; Monier-Williams 1976, 1096) is more convincing. *Aṅka-śrāhi* would then have a meaning close to 'having regnal years'.

[26] The dating depends on the fact that the inscription mentions a king 'Sarvalokāśraya' (a common Cāḷukya title, not a name) Viṣṇuvardhana who ruled for more than thirty years. There are two such candidates at that time, Viṣṇuvardhana III and Viṣṇuvardhana V (Berkemer 1993, 133, fn. 165). The date in this source is '*vijayarājya saṃvatsaramulu 30 yagu śrāhi*' (mentioned in Radha Krishna 1971, 37 and with fewer details in Rangacharya 1916, Vol. 2, 836, No. 772; text in *SII* 6, No. 250). This single source does not allow anything

other pre-eleventh century inscriptions, the *aṅka-śrāhi* system was brought to Kaliṅga and subsequently to Orissa in the wake of the wars of Kulottuṅga I against his relative and rival Codagaṅga Anantavarman.

So far nobody has used the Cāḷukya inscriptions to make a systematic search for occurrences of the word *śrāhi* or possible traces of the rule of omission. The inscriptions from Andhra have so far been overlooked in the literature on the Orissan *aṅka-śrāhi* system, despite the fact that their existence definitely excludes a folk explanation of *aṅka-śrāhi* which attributes it to Muslim influences.[27] The *terminus post quem* for such an influence in Andhra would be *c.* 1325 and in Orissa *c.* 1590. Only in Orissa did it survive long enough into the era of Muslim political dominance for a Muslim calendar to have conceivably had any impact on it. In Andhra, *aṅka-śrāhi* had already disappeared by around 1200, with the end of the imperial Cāḷukya-Cōḷā rule. All this reasoning, of course, does not exclude the possibility of an extension of the practical use of the *aṅka-śrāhi* system as the 'king's own time' after 1590, which means in practice its use for the reckoning of the fiscal year in the Mughal dominated part of Orissa. For the sake of argument one might postulate a common source for both the Muslim fiscal year and the *aṅka-śrāhi* system in the old Persian fiscal year, which was widely used in Muslim countries as a secular calendar. Its New Year's Day also fell in September, but so far there is no indication of any connection between the Muslim fiscal year and any Hindu calendrical system whose year begins in September.

Conclusion

It seems that from a practical point of view, only the combination of *aṅka-śrāhi* and a second era, here the Śaka era, could have been useful in the context of state ritual. In this combination of *aṅka* and Śaka, the dual functions of the previous Gaṅga era as an official device for time-reckoning and as a political tool for expressing sovereignty over the little kings of the area are being separated. It is probably also no coincidence that the introduction of both the *aṅka-śrāhi* and the Śaka eras in Kaliṅga happened in the eleventh century a time of crisis: the Śaka era was first introduced simultaneously with the emergence of inscriptions issued by the little kings of Kaliṅga using a different dynastic era. We encounter an

definite to be said about whether *śrāhi* was used to indicate the use of the omission rule.

[27] Hardenberg 2000, 123, fn. 82.

era called the 'Gaṅga-Kadamba-*saṃvat*',[28] and also several inscriptions dated in Śaka. As a rule, a king who introduces a new era and abandons that of his overlord does so in order to strengthen his claim to sovereign rule without having to acknowledge any great king. In the eleventh century *AD*, the little kings of Kaliṅga could freely imitate the great kings because the Gaṅga kingdom was in severe crisis. However, it seems that they were unable to innovate: they could not introduce their own features of chancery style or their own symbols of royalty, but merely took over what was already in fashion under the Ganga kings; alternatively they used the all-Indian Śaka reckoning. The great kings of Kaliṅga from Vajrahasta V to Coḍagaṅga Anantavarman were still one step ahead by imitating even greater kings, the Cōḷa and Cāḷukya rulers, in their adoption of *aṅka-śrāhi*.

The symbolic overlordship of the new line of imperial Gaṅga kings could be much more elaborately expressed without the hindrance of an era which must for practical purposes be attached to the calendrical system. Already in the time of the first kings who used *aṅka* as the king's own time, this co-occurred with the elaborate *praśasti* (eulogy) that links the king and all his ancestors with the remotest past of the Vedic sages, the time of the epics and the historic kings of the western Gaṅgas. While the *praśasti* becomes the repository of ordered knowledge about the dynasty's past, the king frees his own time from counting the generations of kings by adding years of dynastic time. He himself comes into the centre of time-reckoning: he 'makes' time anew every year in the minting ceremony of the *suniā* ritual, and it is his time that is counted by his Brahmans in a way that is arcane to all but his own experts.

The key to the issue of how *aṅka-śrāhi* became the imperial symbol of royal time in Orissa is the Cōḷa king Kulottuṅga I (1070-1120), who frequently used this dating system in his inscriptions.[29] He was followed in this by his younger relative and opponent, Coḍagaṅga Anantavarman of the Gaṅga dynasty of Kaliṅga. No other rulers are known to have used *aṅka-śrāhi* at that time. One can therefore assume that the well-known rivalry of the two kings for hegemony over the south-east coast of India also found its expression in the creation of a new idiom for the demonstration of royal greatness. Using a distinctive dynastic era was a common way of structuring time in a historical period without the

---

[28] *IO* 2, Inscr. No. 31.

[29] Radha Krishna 1971, Inscr. Nos. 143, 146, 147, 155, 163, 173, 174, 175, 178, 181, 182, 183, 184, 185.

technical and social means to create an institutionalized, overarching social time. Making one's own time by using *aṅka*, however, was so new that it could be used as a symbol of ritual sovereignty not only over space, but also over time.

In a recent paper Romila Thapar has once more offered reflections on the complexity of constructions of social time in various early Indian societies. As she says, it is the social meaning of time that enables us to understand that 'groups within a society visualise time in different ways'.[30] Time as a social phenomenon is connected with agency because complex social events need coordination. The more complex the events are, the more they are dependent on experts, among whom there may be experts of time-related phenomena, such as priests, spirit-media, bards and others who are in charge of past, present or future according to their social role. Some of them have the power to control the actions of other participants in the event, in some cases in a very severe and terminal way. One drastic example of the interconnectedness of social time and power is war, a state ritual in which the active participants are usually drafted into an army and are characterized by having a rather small amount of agency relative to their own social time. Another example is the Aztec sacrifice of the human heart to the sun and the priest's role in it, as an expert not only in human anatomy but also in cosmic time.

Of course, the usual way of encountering the connection between time and power is much less dramatic. Any complex society is based on rules according to which a certain amount of life time must be devoted to the benefit of those who are in positions of power. This is a rather roundabout way of saying that states depend on surpluses and other more or less voluntary contributions of their subjects' life-times to state activities.

Seen from the point of view of agency, the *aṅka-srāhi* system is a very elaborate way of expressing a simple fact: that the king is the lord of the earth and its existence in time. Subject only to cosmic forces, he displays his sovereignty over the temporal existence of his subjects by using a different time-scale that makes him rule 'longer': sixty *aṅka* years correspond to 'merely' forty-eight in the life of a commoner. *Aṅka* time is the king's own time. It has almost no practical usefulness besides demonstrating the uniqueness of the king in his role as the ruler not only of social space, but also of social time. His dominance over social space is symbolized in rituals and texts that proclaim him the ruler of the earth,

---

[30] Thapar 2001, 12.

and Rajaguru is probably right when he links the introduction of *aṅka-śrāhi* with the claim to overlordship of the Gaṅgas 'over a vast territory'.[31]

On the other hand, one could argue that *aṅka-śrāhi* is a statement proclaiming the power of the king – who, as *dharma-rāja*, can stop the evils of the *kaliyuga*, as is said many times in inscriptions – to slow down change in general too. He does this by putting his subjects' time into 'slow motion', as it were, thus emphasizing the uniqueness of his own time. This is the opposite of the generalized time of the mechanical clock, which subjects everybody to the same time regime. *Aṅka* is a display of patterned time, somewhat like in a *rāga*, in which different rhythmic patterns converge into one movement after some time. In our case, the time of convergence would be the end of the *aṅka* cycle after its fifty-ninth year, or the death and re-creation of the king, whichever comes first. The end of personal time through death is followed by the creation of a new royal time through the coronation of a new king, whose *aṅka* years begin in the rituals of the following month of Bhādrapada.

References

Acharya, S.K. 2002. *Numerals in Orissan Inscriptions*, Shimla: Indian Institute of Advanced Study.

Augustinus, A. 1995 (1886). *The Confessions and Letters of Augustin*, edited by Philip Schaff, Peabody, Mass.: Hendrickson.

Berkemer, G. 1993. *Little Kingdoms in Kalinga: Ideologie, Legitimation und Politik regionaler Eliten*, Stuttgart: Steiner.

Falk, H. (ed.) 2002. *Vom Herrscher zur Dynastie: zum Wesen kontinuierlicher Zeitrechnung in Antike und Gegenwart*, Bremen: Hempen.

Geeta Devi. 1998. 'Sunia': The Regnal Beginning of the Kingship in Orissa', in *Orissa Historical Research Journal* 42 (1-4), 91-7.

Hardenberg, R. 2000. *Ideologie eines Hindu-Königtums: Struktur und Bedeutung der Rituale des 'Königs von Puri'* (*Orissa/Indien*), Berlin: Das Arabische Buch.

Jagannātha-Sthala-Vṛttāmtamu n.d. *Jagannātha-Sthala-Vṛttāmtamu*, Translation. Manuscript No. 443 of the Orissa Research Project, Heidelberg: Orissa Archive, South Asia Institute, Heidelberg University, Call No. 265 mss 16/443.

Kielhorn, F. 1894. 'Srahi', in *Indian Antiquary* 23, 224.

— 1896. 'The Meaning of Srahi', in *Indian Antiquary* 25, 285-6.

Konow, S. 1911. 'Narasapatnam Plates of Vajrahasta III; Saka-Samvat 967, *Epigraphia Indica* 11, 147-53.

[31] Rajaguru 1968, 129; see also fn. 11.

Krishna Sastri, H. 1925. *South Indian Inscriptions,* Vol. V: *Miscellaneous Inscriptions from the Tamil, Telugu and Kannada Countries*, Madras: Government Press.

Leach, E.R. 1966 (1961). 'Two Essays Concerning the Symbolic Representation of Time', in Edmund R. Leach (ed.), *Rethinking Anthropology*, London: Athlone Press, 124-36.

Mahapatra, K.N. 1962. 'Reckoning of Chāturmāsī, Lunar and Solar Months and Different Eras in Orissa', in *Orissa Historical Research Journal* 11 (3), 135-46.

Monier-Williams, Sir M. 1976. *A Sanskrit-English Dictionary*, Delhi, Varanasi, Patna: Motilal Banarsidass (reprint).

Mukunda Rao, N. (ed.). 1980. *Temple Inscriptions of Andhra Pradesh,* Vol. 1: *Srikakulam District*, Hyderabad: Government of Andhra Pradesh.

— 1991. *Kaliṅga under the Eastern Gaṅgas, ca. 990 A.D.-1200 A.D*, Delhi: B.R. Publishing Corporation.

Narayana Rao, V.; Shulman, D.D.; Subrahmanyam, S. 2001. *Textures of Time: Writing History in South Asia, 1600-1800*, Delhi: Permanent Black.

Radha Krishna, B. 1971. *Early Telugu Inscriptions* (*Up to 1100 A.D.*), Hyderabad: Andhra Pradesh Sahitya Akademi.

Rajaguru, S. (ed.). 1960. *Inscriptions of Orissa* (*C. 600 - 1100 A.D.*)*,* Volume II, Bhubaneswar: Research and Museum, Government of Orissa.

— (ed.). 1960a. *Inscriptions of Orissa.* (*C. 1045 - 1190 A.D.*)*,* Volume III, Part I, Bhubaneswar: Research and Museum, Government of Orissa.

— (ed.). 1961. *Inscriptions of Orissa.* (*C. 1045 - 1190 A.D.*)*,* Volume III, Part II, Bhubaneswar: Research and Museum, Government of Orissa.

— 1968. *The History of the Gangas,* Vol. 1, Bhubaneswar: Orissa State Museum.

— 1972. *The History of the Gangas,* Vol. 2, Bhubaneswar: Orissa State Museum.

Rangacharya, V. 1985. *A Topographical List of the Inscriptions of the Madras Presidency* (*Collected till 1915*) *With Notes and References,* Vol. 2, New Delhi: Asian Educational Services (reprint).

Record of Rights on Jagannath Temple, n.d. Part II, Translation. Manuscript No. 83 of the Orissa Research Project, Heidelberg: Orissa Archive, South Asia Institute, Heidelberg University, Call No. 265, mss 16/21, 3.

Sircar, D.C. 1965. *Indian Epigraphy*, Delhi, Varanasi, Patna: Motilal Banarsidass.

— 1966. *Indian Epigraphical Glossary*, Delhi, Varanasi, Calcutta: Motilal Banarsidass.

Subrahmanya Aiyer, K.V. 1928. *South Indian Inscriptions,* Vol. VI: *Miscellaneous Inscriptions from the Tamil, Telugu and Kannada Countries*, Madras: Government Press.

Subrahmanyam, R. 1957. *The Sūryavaṃśi Gajapatis of Orissa*, Visakhapatnam: Andhra University Press.

— 1986. *Inscriptions of the Sūryavaṁśi Gajapatis of Orissa*, Delhi: Indian Council of Historical Research and Agam Prakasan.

Thapar, R. 2001. *History and Concepts of Time in Early India: S. C. Misra Memorial Lecture*, Calcutta: Indian History Congress.

Tripathi, K. 1962. *Evolution of Oriya Language and Script*, Cuttack: Utkal University.

3

Interconnecting Parallel Times: Notions of Time in the Caitanya Tradition

Angelika Malinar

In many religious traditions, time is perceived and interpreted in relation to a belief in a transcendent realm of timelessness or the eternal presence of a divine being. Religions claim that there is another sphere of existence beyond those structured by 'social time'.[1] Furthermore, religious teachers maintain that this sphere of timelessness is the ultimate cause of time and that it therefore gives meaning to all its manifestations. However, this function of a time-transcending sphere, that it confers meaning on temporality, only becomes operative when it is related to the existence and movement of time. Thus, in many religions the revelation of a time-transcending realm takes place in time and may be regarded as a singular and historically recorded event. Usually the revelation of the timeless truth of a religious teaching is dated by drawing on methods of time-reckoning used in the social environment in which the religious community is embedded. Sometimes religious movements even manage to make the date of the revelation of their religious truth or some important event in the life of their founder the beginning of new era or calendar (as in Christianity or Islam). Counting time and dating events according to a 'religious era' then becomes a sign of membership and belief, signalling that the members of the community concerned are living in a specific time, while being simultaneously aware of the common social time, in which one interacts with those who do not belong to the community.

In any case, for the religion's followers, the temporal and even historical revelation of the religious teaching is a unique event that serves as a point of departure for travelling on the path that ultimately leads out of time and into the transcendent sphere. This implies that the individual adept must be able to cope with the transitions between the temporal framework of daily life and the realms of trans-social time that one may

---

[1] On the concept of 'social' time in relation to different forms of experience of time and 'time-consciousness', see Bergmann 1981, Gell 1992, and the introduction to this volume.

temporarily reach through religious practice. Living in relation to transcendence while still being able to manage one's daily life plays an important role in the self-perception of members of religious communities. The ability to coordinate these parallel times on both the conceptual and practical levels and to be in control of the transitions is what distinguishes the adept. Religious practice and doctrine are concerned about establishing, organising and explaining these transitions. In doing so, religious traditions usually draw on the temporal frameworks of the surrounding society, which they interpret according to the doctrine. Notions of time in a religious tradition are therefore multi-layered, as one must deal with first, the time-frames that a religious community uses in order to relate the present (social) existence as a whole to the time-transcendent realm; and secondly the representation, interpretation and use of social time in the religious context. The religious aim of transcending socially constructed time while living in it necessitates ways being found of interconnecting these different levels of representing time in religious doctrine and practice.

However, when it comes to discussing notions of time in Hinduism, such distinctions are rarely drawn. One reason for this lies in the readily maintained assertion that Hindu religion(s) generally use 'cyclical time'. Its epitome is seen in the Purāṇic doctrine of repeated creations and destructions of the world that take place in the cosmic eras called *kalpa* and *yuga*. The endless repetition implied in Hindu 'cosmic time' has often been regarded as mirroring the 'cycle of death and rebirth' (*saṃsāra*) in which each and every living being is entangled, and which stimulates the desire to escape what is described as the 'wheel of existence'. This interpretation had an influential advocate in Mircea Eliade and was supported by those who see in the absence of historiography a characteristic feature of Indian civilisation. The latter no longer seems to be taken for granted, and historians especially regard the combination of cyclical and linear notions of time as a special feature of Purāṇic texts and later dynastic accounts.[2] Yet although Eliade's interpretation is still widely applied to Hindu religious traditions, a closer examination of his position and of the different religious traditions of Hinduism creates a more complex picture and certain clarifications with regard to the idea of 'cyclical time'. Therefore, I shall at first discuss Eliade's position and propose a conceptual distinction that will be applied in the subsequent analysis of the different time-frames used in the Caitanya tradition.

---

[2] Cf. Thapar 1997 and in this volume; Falk 2002.

Mircea Eliade and Indian Cosmic Time

Mircea Eliade has dealt with notions of time in ancient cultures in a comparative perspective in several publications. Fundamental here is his monograph, *The Myth of the Eternal Return*, published in 1949, which was followed by a major article on time and eternity in India.[3] In these works, he contrasts the linear, historical time of Western culture with the concept of cyclical time in archaic societies such as one finds in India. In these societies, he argues, the linear passage of time was felt to be unpleasant. As a result, attempts were made to replace this idea of an irreversible flow by transforming historical events into myths, that is, into repetitions of something that has already happened: 'In the traditional societies men endeavour consciously and voluntarily to abolish time at periodic intervals, to efface the past. [...] Myth tears man away from his own time, from his individual, chronological, 'historical' time [...]'.[4] This endeavour resulted in the invention of the widespread myth of a primordial time of creation, which Eliade calls *illud tempus*, 'that very time of beginning'. According to this myth, the time of creation is not seen as a unique event but as recurrent. Consequently, 'the life of archaic man...although it takes place in time, does not bear the burden of time, does not record time's irreversibility'.[5] This notion also implies the idea that time may be regenerated, a task that in many societies is accorded to rituals or made the topic of mythical narratives. In these contexts also arises the notion of an 'eternal return' and the image of a 'wheel of time', as they both signify regeneration brought about by repetition. According to Eliade, the notion of cyclical time documents the resistance of ancient societies to uniqueness and history. It shows the 'secondary character of human individuality as such',[6] a feature that stands in sharp contrast to the esteem of the individual in Western societies.

However, when one tries to make out what precisely is meant by 'cyclical time', Eliade's interpretation becomes ambiguous. Two different notions are referred to as 'cyclical time', first the repetition of the act of creation or its periodic recurrence, and secondly the cyclical return of the

[3] Eliade 1954 [1949], 1957.

[4] Eliade 1957, 174.

[5] Eliade 1954, 86.

[6] Ibid., 1954, 48.

past.[7] When considered on the conceptual level, these two notions do not have the same implications. Repetition in the sense of 'periodic recurrence' and the return of the past are not the same thing, nor do they necessarily imply cyclicity. On the contrary, in order to be distinguishable, the phenomena of repetition and periodic recurrence must be set in a sequence, allowing them to be identified and counted. Recurrence thus implies some sort of linear or at least indexed sequence.[8] The occurrence of a repetition can only be noticed if the first occurrence of an event can be distinguished from its repetition. For example, only if one knows of two New Year's celebrations does it make sense to say that the New Year is being celebrated again. Thus, the fact that something is happening again at a certain point of time neither necessarily nor logically implies any cyclical movement. Recurrence does not imply the identity of what recurs, but a distinction between the recurrent events or time-units, which makes is possible to identify the events in and as a sequence of countable repetitions or occurrences. For instance, although we find each year the thirty days of June listed in the calendar, it is not just the same June, and we would not call the recurrence of June cyclical time.

Only when it comes to the second notion, the cyclic return of the past, is time indeed conceived as moving in circles because identical actions and events will take place again and again. With respect to the 'sameness' implied in the notion of an 'eternal return', Eliade distinguishes two aspects: first the repetition of identical actions, such as the 'act of creation'; and secondly, 'archetypical sameness'; as in recurrent events like spring, harvest or the birth of a hero.[9] According to

---

[7] A distinction between two notions of cyclicity is also discussed by Balslev 1983, 140ff. The notions of recurrence is identified as 'Indian', the view of eternal return as 'Greek' and it is argued that the latter 'in India ... in nowhere to be found' (149). However, we also meet conceptions of 'eternal return' in India as will be shown below.

[8] Gell 1992, 35: 'The recurrence of events, as opposed to the simple occurrence of events, presupposes that repeated event-tokens of any event type can be temporally indexed. Repeated events form an ordered series; the occurrence of event e, followed in time by its first recurrence as event e', followed by its second recurrence as event e''...and so on, ad infinitum, or until the cycle is concluded for the last time. [...] it is only with respect to...a linear time-axis that any event could ever said to have "repeated" itself'.

[9] The notion of the recurrence of identical archetypes can be regarded as a parallel to the above-mentioned recurrence of time-units on a qualitative level because archetypal repetition includes recurrent, but often not individualized and thus

Eliade, the combination of both aspects results in the annihilation of the individual characteristics of an event, which would make it unique, non-repeatable and potentially 'historical'. In this way, 'the primitive, by conferring a cyclic direction upon time, annuls its irreversibility. Everything begins over again at its commencement every instant. The past is but a prefiguration of the future. No event is irreversible and no transformation is final. In a certain sense, it is even possible to say that nothing new ever happens in the world.'[10] In this situation, it is neither necessary nor desirable to record the return of the past chronologically, because chronology would not notice any difference. The revolutions of this wheel of time need no counting. Eliade draws on Purāṇic texts in order to demonstrate that Indian cosmic time generally corresponds to this understanding of cyclicity as a return of the past, perfect time.[11] The Indian construction of cosmic time testifies to 'a metaphysical depreciation of *human history*' and 'to a notion of the perfection of beginnings'.[12] However, according to Eliade the doctrine of the four ages also indicates a degree of historical consciousness, as it also describes catastrophe and decay. Therefore it has some consoling effect 'for man under the terror of history'[13] because the doctrine allows suffering and social crisis to be explained as transitory moments in an otherwise regulated and secure cosmos. This interpretation has been quite influential and is quite apt if one keeps in mind the distinction between recurrence and cyclical repetition. Unfortunately, Eliade sometimes confounds the two notions when he classifies Indian cosmic time generally as cyclic,[14] although the picture is more complex. The following analysis of notions of time in the Caitanya tradition will show that it is helpful to maintain the distinction between 'recurrence' and 'cyclicity'. The first consists in the

---

dated events, such as the killing of the demon in the case of a hero, the celebration of harvest festivals, etc.

[10] Eliade 1954, 89.

[11] Compare Eliade's description of the reckoning of yugas in the Purāṇas, which results in huge numbers of years, as an 'avalance' or 'orgy' of figures. He concludes: 'The essential element in this avalance of figures is the cyclical character of cosmic Time.' (1957, 179).

[12] Ibid., 180 (original emphasis).

[13] Ibid., 118.

[14] For example, Eliade speaks of the 'eternal repetition of the fundamental cosmic rhythm, the periodic destruction and re-creation of the universe' (ibid., 180), and calls this the Indian 'myth of eternal return' (ibid., 181), without making it clear that this is actually brought about by the sequential recurrence of time-units.

recurrence of time units, which implies counting and sequence, or in brief linearity; the second, conversely, is cyclicity that entails the eternal return of the same.

Notions of Time in the Caitanyacaritāmṛta

Against the background of this distinction between 'recurrence' and 'cyclicity', I shall now analyse as a case study the interconnection of different time-frames used in the Caitanya tradition, the so-called Madhva-Gaureśvara *sampradāya*.[15] As the textual basis I shall use the *Caitanyacaritāmṛta*, the sacred biography of Caitanya, an authoritative and widely used text, which is also regularly taught in major monastic communities of the *sampradāya*.[16] First, I shall consider how the appearance of the Caitanya is placed within the framework of Indian cosmic time and thus turned into an *avatāra*, a new embodiment of Kṛṣṇa. Then I shall deal with the relationship between Kṛṣṇa's eternal presence in his divine realm and his temporary manifestations.

Dating the founder

Several studies of 'founding' religious communities have shown that, although the religious teacher is often aware of a task or mission to be fulfilled, he rarely saw himself as the founder-to-be of a religious community that would bear his name. Rather, it seems that the impact of the charismatic personality on his companions and disciples led to reconstructions of his life that turned him into a founder and a divine or semi-divine being.[17] So-called 'hagiographies' and 'sacred biographies'

---

[15] On the name of the community, see Deadwhyler 1992. For a general outline of the religious doctrine, see Dimock 1966. For the history of the community, see Chakrabarty1985.

[16] In the interviews I conducted in the monastic institutions of the Caitanya tradition in Orissa, the *Caitanyacaritāmṛta* was almost always listed together with the *Bhāgavata-Purāṇa* as a highly important and authoritative text.

[17] The most discussed and renowned case of this in India is perhaps Śaṅkara, who has been turned from a philosopher into the founder of the Daśanāmi order. Cf. Lorenzen 1987, Malinar 2001a. Studies of a number of traditions are included in Callewaert and Snell (eds.) 1994.

play an important role in this process.[18] Sacred biographies usually relate those events in the life of the charismatic teacher or founder that confer religious meaning on his appearance on earth. Although they may contain historical data and refer to historical events, these texts do not primarily document historical or biographical truth. As a corollary, by constructing its origins in relation to a founding figure, the community extends itself back into the past. Thus, the process of writing and transmitting sacred biographies mirrors the debates of a community in the making. This process of textual production also provides the community with a temporal framework that serves to identify one's specific position with regard to the already established social and religious constructions of time. Sacred biographies become important means of orientation for followers, this being one of the reasons why they continue to be written today.[19] Such texts are not only narratives of the successful 'bridging' of parallel times through religious teachings leading to salvation, they also present the life-histories of exceptional individuals who have been turned into nodal points of different times and spheres. In this connection, the relationship between the founder and the divine being or the religious truth he preaches becomes an important topic. Subsequent theological discourse thus often has to deal with the question of how the eternal, a-temporal existence of God is connected to his temporal appearances and representations.

These general observations will be put into more concrete terms with regard to the interpretation and dating of Caitanya's (1486-1533) appearance on earth in what has become his most important, canonic sacred biography, the *Caitanyacaritāmṛta* of Kṛṣṇadāsa Kavirāja. According to Dimock and Stewart, the text was completed between *AD* 1600 and 1612.[20] As Stewart has shown, the text acquired this position because it offers a synthesis of important and divergent views of other texts.[21] One element in this synthesis is the acceptance of the doctrine that

[18] For a discussion of the term 'sacred biography' in contrast to 'hagiography', which uses the life of a saint in order to exemplify an already extant religious teaching, see Reynolds, Capps 1976, Keyes 1982.

[19] For a study of the sacred biography of a recent charismatic teacher in the Caitanya tradition, see Malinar 2001; of one in the Satyanārāyaṇa tradition, see Schreiner 2001.

[20] See the introduction to the translation of the *Caitanyacaritāmṛta* (*CC*), which is used in this paper unless otherwise indicated.

[21] Stewart 1985, 1992.

Caitanya should be regarded as the joint incarnation of both Lord Kṛṣṇa and his divine consort, the Goddess Rādhā.

In explaining this doctrine, the text draws on the following time-frames, which belong to different spheres of existence:

1. trans-cosmic, cyclical time (eternity) in Kṛṣṇa's eternal abode: Goloka / Vraja.
2. common cosmic time: Brahmā days, *manvantara*, *yuga*. Cosmic time corresponds to the spatial configuration of the cosmos called 'the world of Brahmā'.[22]
3. *yuga* sequence: the special time of Bhāratavarṣa (India) as a cosmic region in contrast to other cosmic regions.
4. Śaka era: the dates of the appearance and disappearance of Caitanya are reckoned according to Śaka, the era of the current *kaliyuga*. Months and days are counted on the basis of traditional astronomical-astrological reckoning, the lunar-solar calendar.

The author of the *Caitanyacaritāmṛta* (henceforth *CC*) uses these different time-frames, not only in order to 'date' the appearance of Caitanya by drawing on both cosmic time and the Śaka era, but also to answer the following questions: (1) how is Kṛṣṇa's eternal, a-temporal existence connected to its temporary and successive representations; and (2) why does Kṛṣṇa leave his eternal sphere of repetitive, cyclical time and enter a realm characterised by a sequence of time-units, whose counting allows for records and memories?

First of all, the relationship between Lord Kṛṣṇa and Caitanya is established by drawing on the framework of 'common cosmic time', that is, the days and nights of Brahmā, *manvantara*, etc. This is the framework used in most texts in locating the different incarnations or descents, the *avatāra*s of Hindu gods and goddesses. In order to 'date' and record Kṛṣṇa's descent as Caitanya, this must be distinguished from his previous incarnation. This is possible because Kṛṣṇa's descents are recorded according to cosmic time units as they operate in Bhāratavarṣa, the region of the god's appearance. This must be stressed because it often remains unnoticed that, according to the cosmographic accounts in the epics and Purāṇas, the sequence of the four *yuga*s, the so-called *yuga-avastha*, passes only in Bhāratavarṣa. The other cosmic regions (heavens, hells,

[22] Time-reckoning varies also within the cosmos according to different regions, which are codified in the cosmographic accounts of the Purāṇas, cf. Kirfel 1967.

continents) are described either as places characterised by the particular period of time that migrating souls spend there in order to enjoy or suffer the results of their *karma*, or as a spheres in which the condition of one of the *yugas* is preserved (in many cases, the *dvāpara yuga*). Consequently, Bhāratavarṣa is defined in the Purāṇas as *karmabhūmi*, the land of *karma*, that is, the cosmic region where people are responsible for their lives and determine their future by their deeds. In the other regions, one only experiences the consequences of one's *karma* (*bhogabhūmi*). Thus Bhāratavarṣa is the only place with a future, where change and unexpected turns of events are possible. Compared to the other cosmic regions, Bhāratavarṣa functions as a hub in that ascent or descent to other regions is only possible if one comes from Bhāratavarṣa. Conversely, souls return to this region when they have used up their *karma*. Furthermore, the residents of the other cosmic regions, including gods and godesses, descend upon Bhāratavarṣa when they have a task to fulfill or they just chose to do so. Stories and histories of gods usually take place in Bhāratavarṣa because only here does time make a difference.

Time in Bhāratavarṣa has to be seen, on the one hand, in relation to the extant time-frames of other cosmic spheres and, on the other hand, to the eternity which qualifies the heavenly realm of the highest god or goddess. As the sequence of the *yugas* runs in Bhāratavarṣa, the descent of a god or goddess takes place in a particular *yuga*. This is also true for Kṛṣṇa's descent as Caitanya in that it happens during a *kaliyuga*, the age and time-unit when he descended. This aspect is neglected when the sequence of *yugas* is represented as *the* Indian cosmic time and as a cyclical time at that, without making it clear that the *yugas* are also time-units. The sequence of *yugas* (*yuga-avasthā*) is the time-reckoning that is valid in Bhāratavarṣa and serves to record its internal history. Furthermore, from the perspective of the cosmic spheres, in which time is not reckoned in *yugas*, the *yuga* sequence is a parallel time, to which the inhabitants of these spheres are closely related. One of the reasons for this relationship is the fact that the god or goddess, who is regarded as the initiator of the creation of the cosmos, observes, or at least can be made to observe, what happens in Bhāratavarṣa. Vaiṣṇava traditions even assert that Viṣṇu and Kṛṣṇa respectively indicate and accompany the transition from one *yuga* to another by changing colour or by withdrawing or creating an *avatāra*.[23] With regard to the *kaliyuga*, the god is often allotted

[23] CC 2.20.279-83, quoting *Bhāgavata-Purāṇa* 10.8.13; cf. also 11.5.20-32. This concept is already applied to Kṛṣṇa in the Mahābhārata, cf. *Mbh* 3.187.31.

the task either to accelerate the process of decay (for example, by appearing as a teacher of heretic doctrines) or to counteract the hopelessness of the general situation by opening up paths to salvation, which are easier to pursue than those already available. Thus, the sequence of *yugas* is conceived as a specific time-span that is not only defined quantitatively, but also qualitatively. For instance, the *kaliyuga* is the shortest age, in which general decay goes along with greater possibilities for individual happiness.[24] The unique combination of decadence and the simultaneous increase of chances of salvation is often indicated by moments of divine intervention. Such interventions may aim at the revelation of a new religious doctrine or the renaissance of a forgotten one, but it does not stop the *yuga* sequence and thus prevent the final destruction. Nevertheless, it opens up what in the *CC* (1.3.89) is called the '*dharma* bridge' (*dharmasetu*), which interconnects the coexisting spheres of the created world and eternity. Accordingly, it is claimed that one can leave one's present time in order to enter another. The means of such 'crossings' and the contexts in which they take place depend on the actual, historical conditions which at that moment dominate social and religious life in Bhāratavarṣa. Caitanya, the incarnation of Lord Kṛṣṇa and his divine consort Rādhā, is no exception.

Two chapters of the *CC* (1.3-4) are dedicated to explaining the date and motif of Caitanya's appearance. At first it is declared that, although Kṛṣṇa enjoys eternal pleasures in his heavenly sphere of Vrajaloka, he decides to descend again on Bhāratavarṣa and in the *kaliyuga* out of compassion for those who miss and seek him. Kṛṣṇa's last appearance in Bhāratavarṣa is then dated as follows: 'The Satya, Tretā, Dvāpara, Kali – I know these four ages and these four ages are one *divya yuga*. Seventy-one of each of the four ages are one *manvantara* and there are fourteen *manvantaras* in one day of Brahmā. This is the seventh *manvantara*, named Vaivasvata. Twenty-seven four-age periods are within it. Twenty-eight four-age periods ago, at the end of the Dvāpara [age], Kṛṣṇa appeared within his companions in Vraja' (*CC* 1.3.3-5).

[24] This is also asserted in *CC* 2.20.287 by quoting *Bhāgavata-Purāṇa* 12.3.51: 'O king, though it is a storehouse of faults, the Kali age has one great quality; only by praising Kṛṣṇa may one reach the highest [abode of Kṛṣṇa] as one who is freed from attachment.' *kaler doṣanidhe rājann asti hy eko mahān guṇaḥ / kīrtanād eva kṛṣṇasya muktasaṅgaḥ paraṃ vrajet //*. On the function of the decay ascribed to the *kaliyuga*, see von Stietencron 1986.

In this passage, the life of Caitanya is not dated nor narrated by référring to a cyclical repetition of similar events or by interpreting it as a repetition of the past, but by placing it in a sequence of recurring time units that are counted and thus mark the irreversibility of time in Bhāratavarṣa. The largest time unit, which not only encompasses all the smaller ones but also consists of them,[25] is the day of Brahmā. The day of Brahmā is the largest cosmic time unit that contains all the other units and qualities of time and encompasses all the spheres of the created cosmos (*brahmaloka*). As a consequence, events happening in a Brahmā day can be dated because they are reckoned by identifiable time units.[26] By contrast, events in other days of Brahmā are not recorded because the number of days and nights of Brahmā is infinite. Also, the corresponding creations and destructions of the world of Brahmā are not counted because of their infinite number. Therefore, we do not know whether we are dealing with events in the seventh or the fiftieth day of Brahmā; in fact, this does not matter because we have no records, no sequence, no memory. This may indicate that Brahmā days are identical and that in any other day of Brahmā the same things just happen again as an 'eternal return'. However, such a return has no consequences for the perception of the events during the current day of Brahmā. Even if in each Brahmā day the same things would happen even, such a return cannot be detected: since the first occurrence of a Brahmā day is not distinguished from its repetition, we are just left with a day of Brahmā that can be any day.

Although the infinite number of Brahmā days may suggest that we are dealing here with a rather 'open' cosmic history that knows no beginning and no end, it actually results in the closure of the created world. In fact, one is dealing here only with the current time of a single Brahmā day and the corresponding Brahmā world. This closure stands in contrast with the effect that the phenomenon of the infinite number has in modern Western contexts, in which it resulted in the notion of an openness and uncertainty about the past and future, in the problem of contingency, unpredictable evolutions and lost histories. In the case of Indian cosmic time it becomes clear that there is always only one history,

---

[25] The notion that time consists of its units is quite old. It is explicitly stated in the *Maitrayaṇīya Upaniṣad* and distinguished from time as a cosmic entity. Cf. Malinar 2003, 34ff.

[26] Thus, for example, in *CC* 2.20.269-78 the *manvantaras* are also distinguished by the fourteen *manvantara-avatāras* of Viṣṇu.

that one always lives in the only time that counts and is counted.[27] Events happening in the world and day of Brahmā are unique because time units are counted and not regarded as repeatable events within a cyclical movement of time. They may be repeated in another day of Brahmā, but such a repetition literally does not count or influence the passing away of time during a day of Brahmā or the perception of events as being determined by time and place. Time moves in the passing of recurrent time units that revolve like a wheel. However, this is a wheel that does not just turn around itself and is otherwise at a standstill. Rather, it moves like a wheel that, with each revolution, actually brings about a movement in space, causing progress and pushing the wheel forward.[28] Thus, the wheel of time includes not only a revolution around its axis but also sequential movement, thus also implying a linear time-axis in that time moves on and on.[29]

Thus, in the wake of another descent as Caitanya, the uniqueness of Kṛṣṇa's past appearance as Kṛṣṇa is maintained in the following manner. First, Kṛṣṇa's previous appearance in Vraja is placed in the definite past of a previous *yuga*, that is, it is dated back to the *dvāpara yuga* of the current *yuga* sequence of the seventh *manvantara*. This distinguishes the past from narrated time in the *CC*, which deals with the *avatāra* Caitanya, who lives on earth in the 28th *kaliyuga* of the seventh *manvantara* called Vaivasvata. Secondly, both descents are declared to be unique with regard to what could possibly happen during a day of Brahmā. As already pointed out, since Brahmā days are not counted, similar events in other Brahmā days may take place, but cannot be dated or recorded. Thus Caitanya does not simply appear in the *kaliyuga*, but in the 28th *kaliyuga* of the seventh *manvantara* called Vaivasvata. I stress this point in order to make clear that we are dealing here with cosmic time in an Indian text, in which events are depicted as non-repeatable, because they are placed in the sequential succession of numbered cosmic time units. In brief, we are dealing with cosmic time which is not cyclical in the sense of an 'eternal

[27] Thus, Eliade's above-mentioned observation (cf. Eliade 1954, 118) is corroborated in a modified form.

[28] Malinar 2003, 30f.

[29] Gell points out that the difference between modern and traditional perceptions of time does not so much concern the concept of time as either linear or cyclical, 'but different conceptions of the world at its workings. [...] But is quite essential, both to the belief that "the world goes on and on being the same", and to the contrary belief that "the world goes on and on becoming different", that one believes that the world goes on and on' (1992, 36).

return', but rather operates as a counted sequence of recurrent time units. They function like the thirty days of June, which we find time and again in our calendar, but it is always a different June.

Therefore, an *avatāra* never appears twice in Bhāratavarṣa in order to fulfil his task. At least, I do not know of any text in which a story of the reappearance of an *avatāra* is recounted. An *avatāra* of one and same god is different in different times and places. Because of the irreversible and non-repeatable character of the events in Bhāratavarṣa, divine interference and religious revelation can happen more than once. Therefore, religious truth (*dharma*) declines and may even be lost, only to be rediscovered and revealed again. Conversely, when *avatāras* disappear from Bhāratavarṣa, they are often transferred to other regions of the cosmos, where they are worshipped by their devotees.[30] They can still be reached, but they do not return. Thus Kṛṣṇa can also appear only once as Kṛṣṇa in Vraja because this is bound to the sequence of counted time units and is dated. He may appear in other days of Brahmā, but this is not recorded, since days of Brahmā are not counted. Therefore Kṛṣṇa cannot again live in Bhāratavarṣa as Kṛṣṇa; he has to appear in a different shape and under a different name, living a different life in a different time. This uniqueness, and with it the irreversibility of time, is emphazised in the following statement about Kṛṣṇa's previous descent in Vraja: 'Only once in a day of Brahmā, he, having descended, makes manifest *vihāra* ["sojourn", AM]' (*CC* 1.3.4). This manifest *vihāra* or *līlā* (*prakaṭa līlā*) has already taken place in Vṛndāvana/Vraja as recorded in the *Bhāgavata-Purāṇa*.[31]

Having established the uniqueness and nature of Kṛṣṇa's descents in term of cosmic time, the Kṛṣṇadāsa Kavirāja places Kṛṣṇa's descent and Caitanya's birth in the temporal framework of the Śaka era, the current common era: 'Śrī Kṛṣṇa Caitanya descended at Navadvīpa, and for forty-eight years his sport was apparent. 1407 of the śaka era witnessed his birth, and in 1455 he disappeared' (*CC* 1.13.7-8). Even the date of Kṛṣṇa's descent into the bodies of Caitanya's parents is placed in this chronology: 'In 1486 [*sic*: read 1406] śaka, at the end of the month Māgha, Kṛṣṇa entered into the bodies of Jagannātha and Sacī. [...] In 1407 śaka, in the month of Phālguna, on the night of the full moon, in the evening, the auspicious moment came. It was at the sign of the Lion, the

[30] They may stay in temples as the presiding deities in the form of icons (*vigraha*, *mūrti*). However, these *vigrahas* do not act as *avatāras*.

[31] On the distinction between manifest and unmanifest *līlās*, cf. Entwistle 1987, 71ff.; *CC*, 177, note 4.

entrance of the sun into the sign of the Lion, and planets were on the ascendant, and in the sixth and eight houses, with all signs auspicious, the stainless Gaura, the golden moon, appeared ...' (*CC* 1.13.77; 89-90). The auspiciousness of the date shows the reliance on the common methods of reckoning and interpreting time, as it draws on two dates which Hindu astrologers regard to be of special importance and auspiciouness: the full-moon day in combination with a full lunar eclipse. The re-appearance of the full moon after the eclipse is related to Caitanya's 'birth' as the 'golden moon' (Gauracandra) of the present.[32]

The combination of cosmic time, common era and astrological qualifications of time in dating the appearance of Caitanya causes no difficulties, as there is no gap, logical or other, between two different notions of time, such as cyclical or linear. Rather, the Śaka era is the time-reckoning, which is valid in Bhāratavarṣa in the present age (28th *kaliyuga*, seventh *manvantara*) and is thus, on the one hand, embedded in the common temporal and spatial framework of the cosmos, being something like a 'close-up' of cosmic time as it moveṣ in Bhāratavarṣa. On the other hand, it is singled out as a time that is particular to this cosmic region and thus allows these various manifestations. In this way, the unique position of Bhāratavarṣa is again confirmed, as here time moves on and on, allowing living beings to appear and disappear, travel to other regions, progress or decline in the perfection of their condition. For the religious community, this date marks the beginning of its history and it is thus commemorated and celebrated in Orissa and elsewhere each year on Phālguna Pūrṇimā, according to the *pañjī*, the ritual, lunar-solar calendar. For the devotees, this date marks the beginning of a re-enactment of the 'timeless' events that have once taken place in Vraja and are ever-present in Kṛṣṇa's heavenly realm.

[32] Compare the detailed study of the accounts of Caitanya's birth by Stewart. He points to the symbolic transformation entailed by the birth date: 'Rahu, a demon head sans body ... swallows the moon, which in Indian mythology is associated with that elixir, with masculinity, and, by extension, fertility, specifically semen. The moon enters the womb of his mouth only to re-emerge from the end of his severed neck. Simultaneously, the child Gauracandra ... emerges from the womb of his mother, Śacī, the moon's immortality transferred ... from the heavens to the earth in form of Caitanya.' (1997, 232).

Something Left to Know: Kṛṣṇa's Descent as Caitanya

The irreversibility of time is not only acknowledged and commemorated with regard to the date of divine interventions and manifestations, but also when Kṛṣṇadāsa Kavirāja considers Kṛṣṇa's motives for descent. Two motives are given. The first is Kṛṣṇa's compassion with his devotees (*bhaktas*), as they presently have no opportunity to experience the devotional ecstasy that Kṛṣṇa's sojourn in Vraja once incited. Therefore, Kṛṣṇa decides to appear on earth in order to teach how the ecstasy of highest, divine love (*prema*) can be experienced by chanting the name of the Lord (*nāma-saṃkīrtana*). It is the function of the *avatāra* to provide this new teaching (*dharma*) and the means to follow it in the form of *mantras* and songs. This task is summarized in the statement that Kṛṣṇa's *avatāra* Caitanya is the *dharma* bridge (*dharmasetu*; *CC* 1.3.89). Caitanya differs from other *avatāras* in that he does not come with the sword, but with *mantra* and *kīrtana*.[33] It is emphasised that this *avatāra* descends as 'God himself' (*svayaṃ bhagavān*) and not, as in most other cases, as a partial manifestation (*aṃśa-avatāra*). Since Caitanya is a full *avatāra*, the powers and qualities of all other *avatāras* descend together with him, but do not become manifest (*CC* 1.4.9ff.). The stage for descent is carefully set, because Kṛṣṇa is about to perform a complete *līlā*, that is, he will spend a whole life on earth. In doing this, the god participates in the genealogical structure of human existence. Therefore Caitanya's mother and father have to descend first. The value implied in the chronology of the genealogical sequence, the principle of seniority, demands that the seniors be honoured. This makes it necessary that the elders descend first, as is stated in *CC* 1.3.73-4: 'When Kṛṣṇa makes an *avatāra* upon the earth, he first sends his group of elders. Father, mother, guru and the rest – all those to be honoured, he causes first to be born upon the earth.' As is usual in the Indian tradition, the genealogical principle is not restricted to the maternal and paternal ties of kinship, but also includes *gurus*. Advaita Ācārya, one of the most prominent companions of Caitanya, also belongs to the elders. He is said to have prayed each and every day to Kṛṣṇa in order to make him descend again. The immediate cause and motive for Kṛṣṇa's descent is thus the rewarding of Advaita Ācārya's devotion (*CC* 1.3.89), which has not been performed 'free from desire', as its ascetic version would have it, but in a state of urgent desire and longing.

---

[33] *CC* 1.4.33: 'In this way Caitanya Kṛṣṇa is *pūrṇa bhagavān* – the establishment of the *yuga-dharma* is not his task.'

However, this is not the whole story, but only what is qualified later in the text as the 'external motives'. Of at least equal importance is the second set of motives, which is called by Kṛṣṇadāsa Kavirāja 'internal'. These 'internal motives' turn Kṛṣṇa's previous descent as Kṛṣṇa in Vraja into something like the personal history of the god, which functions as a background story to his present descent as Caitanya. It is related (*CC* 1.4) that Kṛṣṇa muses over the course of his earthly sojourn and realizes that something is missing, that there is something left to know. This can only be known when he again descends to Bhāratavarṣa is the only place in the whole cosmos where something new can happen and thus differs from the stable and ever-repeated activities scheduled in the other cosmic spheres. Kṛṣṇa decides to descend in order to fulfil some unfulfilled desire that arose only in retrospect, while he was thinking about the past and about his companion and lover, Rādhā. Kṛṣṇa has come to envy her because she had an experience that he lacks. She has experienced the rapture of loving Kṛṣṇa, while he only experienced how it feels to be loved and desired. Thus Kṛṣṇa himself wants to become Rādhā and thus to be the 'container', the subject, not only the object of love (*prema*): 'My heart longs to gain that joy which the container of love gains. But [though I try] eagerly, I cannot taste it. Indeed, how could I? If I could be the container of this *prema*, I could experience the bliss of that *prema*.' Thinking thus, Kṛṣṇa remained full of eager desire' (*CC* 1.4.115-18). Therefore, he descends and takes a male body, whose disposition and 'state of being' (*bhāva*) is, however, female. This is the very definition of Caitanya's special mode of being as the joint incarnation of Rādhā and Kṛṣṇa; he is, indeed, a new form of Kṛṣṇa. Without going further into the details of its theological interpretation, it should be clear that the appearance of Caitanya as an *avatāra* is intimately related to Kṛṣṇa's past, which he had in a former and non-repeatable time in Bhāratavarṣa. His descent as Caitanya is represented as a manifestation of his divine being, which is almost regarded as a continuation of his personal history. However, this descent does not call into question his divine perfection and the completeness of his heavenly paradise, in which he and his companions continue to enjoy the pleasures of ecstatic rapture.

Trans-Cosmic Time and Cyclical Repetition

Kṛṣṇa appears as Caitanya and at the same time stays in his heavenly abode, Goloka. How is Kṛṣṇa's eternal presence in Goloka connected with his temporary existence as an *avatāra*? As is to be expected, it is asserted that both co-exist and happen simultaneously. The presence of eternal Goloka is that other, parallel time, on which the life of Caitanya and his followers is concentrated. Thus on the one hand, as a 'god on earth' Caitanya represents the continuous presence of the events in the transcendent, heavenly realm and reconfirms the 'timelessness' of Kṛṣṇa's being. On the other hand, he lives like a human devotee and can thus become a model of the ideal relationship with the divine while being himself a 'god'.[34] Caitanya's life cannot be understood without remembering the past history of Kṛṣṇa, that is, the theme of the 'eternal play' (*nitya-līlā*) of his past sojourn in Vraja, which is staged again and again in the heavenly region, but only fragmentarily in Caitanya's life. The interconnection between these time frames is established from both sides: first, by integrating Kṛṣṇa's previous incarnation into common cosmic time; and secondly, by presenting Caitanya as a '*dharma* bridge' through which one can reach trans-cosmic, eternal time and enter Kṛṣṇa's *nitya-līlā*. This is accomplished by mediating Kṛṣṇa's 'eternal play' and his many other descents (also called *līlā*) on earth with cosmic time. It is asserted that, although Kṛṣṇa's eternal play is staged in a trans-cosmic time and space, his other appearances (*līlās*) successively pervade the world created by Brahmā. The parallel times and spheres of existence can be interconnected because the *līlās* and *avatāras* of Kṛṣṇa are as infinite and innumerable as the days and nights of Brahmā.

The infinite number of Kṛṣṇa's appearances indicates that the god is regarded as being coextensive with the spatial and temporary manifestations of the cosmos created by Brahmā, which are also infinite. Thus, one cannot count Kṛṣṇa's appearances in the equally uncountable days and nights of Brahmā. The interconnection between the infinite number of *līlās* and the infinite number of worlds of Brahmā is explained in the *CC* as follows:

> As many *līlās* there are – the killing of Pūtanā and the rest – every moment he (Kṛṣṇa, AM) manifests progressively all these eternal *līlās*. Brahmā-worlds are infinite – there is no counting of them; and each līlā is

[34] As Stewart 1997, 226 puts it: 'The timeless paradigmatic pattern of Kṛṣṇa's acts lends meaning and intelligibility to the historically contingent acts of Caitanya.' Although I agree with Stewart's position that the paradigm of Kṛṣṇa's acts and the eternal presence makes Caitanya's acts 'replicas', this cannot be regarded as repetition in the sense pointed out above. Therefore I would not deny the uniqueness of each manifestation (Stewart 1997, 225) in the context of subsequent appearances.

> manifested in each Brahmā-world. In this way all the *līlā*s are manifested like the streams of the Gaṅgā. [...] All the śāstras speak of the eternal *līlā* of Kṛṣṇa; we cannot understand. How can the *līlā* be eternal? I give an example; then people will understand. The Kṛṣṇa *līlā* is eternal – and the proof of it is in the wheel of the planets. In the wheel of the planets the sun travels night and day, and crosses over the seven islands and seas and gradually returns. [...] One, two, three, and at the end of the fourth *prahāra,*[35] the suns set; and when four *prahāra*s of the night have passed, again the sun rises. Thus is the circle of the Kṛṣṇa *līlā* in the fourteen manvantaras; it returns gradually, pervading the circle of the Brahmā-worlds. A hundred and twenty-five years was the manifest *līlā* of Kṛṣṇa ... in Vrajapura. The wheel of that *līlā* returns like a wheel of fire; thus all līlās gradually take place in all the Brahmā-worlds. [...] There are locations for certain *līlā*s in certain Brahmā-worlds, and because of this the āgamas and purāṇas say 'eternal *līlā*'. The places Goloka and Gokula are all-pervasive like Kṛṣṇa; at the wish of Kṛṣṇa they appear in the Brahmā-worlds. Thus he has eternal activities in Goloka and he is progressively manifested in the Brahmā-worlds.' (*CC* 2.20.315-31)

This is why Kṛṣṇa may appear on earth time and time again. However, the sun-like progression and the variety of his manifestations do not imply that the light always reveals the same landscape or the same people. It is not time that moves like a wheel, it is an ever-present being, the god who appears in the created world like the sun, which moves through the circle of the planets. This movement through fixed spatial boundaries, which is measured in recurrent time-units of different quality, constitutes time. While the movement through one circle can be counted, the number of circuits and circles cannot be counted, as Brahmā worlds are of infinite number. It is therefore not because of a cyclical movement of time that events are not any longer dated and Kṛṣṇa's *līlā*s cannot be counted, but because of the phenomenon of the infinite number. Thus Caitanya's appearance is just a moment in the progressive manifestation of Kṛṣṇa in the world(s) of Brahmā. However, with regard to the current *kaliyuga*, he opens up a unique path to that very region that is beyond the Brahmā worlds. This path shows that 'sacred' timelessness and 'profane' time overlap, and this makes it possible 'that by participation in the earthly replica the *bhakta* also participates in the eternal *līlā*, for the temporal

[35] There are eight *prahāra*s, or watches, which serve to structure not only days and nights on earth, but also the love play of Rādhā and Kṛṣṇa in the so-called *aṣṭa-kālīya-līlā*. See below.

penetrates the atemporal'.[36] But it is also the other way round: Caitanya 'opens the profane to the infusion of the sacred'[37] and his followers are heading for the one eternal realm, Goloka, where the play of Kṛṣṇa's divinity is the daily activity. In this divine realm, time indeed moves in circles.

This implies that the eternity of this realm is not a state that is not structured by time, it is not a *nunc stans*, an ever-remaining present. Rather, it consists of the incessant repetition of the chronology of past events. It is this eternity that can be regarded as cyclical time *par excellence*: it is the 'ewige Wiederkehr des Gleichen', the eternal return of the same events, counted in the same time units, and enacted by the very same actors on the very same stage. What is enacted is a love story between Kṛṣṇa and his consort Rādhā, who embodies that very form of selfless love, *prema*, that is also the aim of religious practice. Its attraction lies in its many forms and contradictory qualities, which arouse the desire to taste (*rasa*) it again and again. Kṛṣṇa's beloved Rādhā is the epitome of this love and of the possibility of its ever-growing intensity, although this seems neither physically nor metaphysically possible. The paradoxical structure of *prema* is described as follows:

> Kṛṣṇa said: 'I am the fundamental truth, filled with full *cit* (consciousness AM) and full *ānanda* (bliss AM); but because of the *prema* of Rādhā I become as mad. I do not know how much power there is in the *prema* of Rādhā, but by that power I am continually overwhelmed. The *prema* of Rādhā is my *guru*, and I am her dancing pupil; [...] The *prema* of Rādhā is all-pervasive and eternal; though there is no room for growth, still it grows greater with every moment. Surely there is no more profound matter than this *prema*. It is the *dharma* of profundity, devoid of pride.' (*CC* 1.4.106ff.)

To practise this '*dharma* of profundity' and experience the cyclical, eternal return is the aim of religious practice: to participate in the cycle, not to escape from it. In this context, endless repetition is not equated with suffering and boredom, but rather with ecstasy brought about by intensive repetition. This notion also has consequences for religious practice.

[36] CC, introduction, 118.

[37] Ibid, 119.

Parallel Times and Religious Practice

This interpretation of divine time as eternal repetition is not only a cherished idea of theologians and philosophers, it is also important for the religious quest and daily schedule of the devotees. The key concept and the main practice for bringing about the transition between social and transcendent time is *smaraṇa*, that is, the memorization and realization of important events in the life of Caitanya and the *līlā* of Rādhā and Kṛṣṇa.[38] *Smaraṇa* is successful when one visualises these events and enters the transcendent realm, in which they are continually being staged. Meditative practices, ritual performances, *kīrtana* festivals, *bhajana*s, recitations of the sacred biographies etc., are different contexts for *smaraṇa*. Repetition is its mode of being: the repetition of *mantra*s, of *pūjā*, of narratives, of songs. Repetition is a self-enforcing practice, since the ability for *smaraṇa* is gained by *smaraṇa*. In the context of monastic life, this is also related to notions of ascetic power because the adept is supposed to acquire the strength to bear the results of *smaraṇa*. This is necessary because entry into another temporal frame has a liminal quality and is thus potentially dangerous, since it implies a bodily transformation. This becomes clear in many descriptions of ecstatic rapture, which indicates successful practice, in the canonic texts. Fainting, being unconscious for a long time, trembling, etc., are signs of ecstasy, which indicate that the devotee has entered another sphere of existence. However, this stage is normally only reached through a very controlled and scheduled practice, in which not only are the repetitions counted, but also *smaraṇa* is integrated within a fixed timetable. In this timetable, the current time in the heavenly region is mediated with the temporal framework that the monastic community has to cope with, such as the schedule for *pūjā*s in the shrine, office hours, cooking, cleaning etc.

The co-ordination of these frames is facilitated by a quite simple stipulation that connects the social time, in which the devotee usually lives, with the sequence of events in Goloka: in both spheres, time is structured according to the same time units, the so-called *prahāra*s or *yama*s. These are eight time units of varying length (from two-and-a-half to five hours), which indicate and measure different periods of the day and night. Thus, one *prahāra* starts at dawn, another at midday, etc. Not only is the sequence of events in the heavenly region of Goloka measured and structured by these units, but also the *pūjā* schedule in the monastery or

---

[38] For Caitanya, see McDaniel 1993; for Rādhā and Kṛṣṇa, see Entwistle 1987.

the use of certain melodies for *kīrtana*.[39] Yet, the *prahāra*s of the *pūjā* schedule do not coincide with what is happening in Goloka, because *pūjā* does not play a prominent role in the *līlā*. *Pūjā* and *smaraṇa* differ in another respect too. While one must usually enter a shrine in order to perform or attend a *pūjā*, the meditative practice of *smaraṇa* implies a certain independence with regard to time and place. Meditation can be conducted anywhere, and entered into at any point in time. If one is aiming to visualise the eternal abode, one only needs to know what is happening there during the respective *prahāra*. Orientation with regard to this is provided, for example, in the context of a practice called '*aṣṭa-kālīya-smaraṇa*'.[40] The practice is widespread, but not followed by all devotees. This *smaraṇa* can involve a rather elaborate ritual, whose details I cannot present here. In the daily practice of individual devotees, it is guided by different texts, such as the *Bhāgavata-Purāṇa*, the *Govindalīlāmṛta* ascribed to Kṛṣṇadāsa Kavirāja, the author of the *CC*, or the *Aṣṭakālīyalīlāsmaraṇamaṅgalastotra*.[41] The latter consists of eight verses, which refer to the eight *prahāra*s or *yama*s. The *smaraṇa* starts with the first *prahāra* or *yama*, the 'end of the night'. Nowadays the *prahāras* are also measured according to modern world-time, and the manuals of the ritual give the respective duration in hours and minutes, thus leaving aside the reckoning according to the actual dawn, etc., which may vary when measured with a watch.

1. *niśānte*	end of night (dawn) (3.36-6.00)[42]
2. *prātaḥ*	morning (6.00-8.24)
3. *pūrvāhna*	forenoon (8.24-10.48)
4. *madhyāhna*	midday (10.48-15.36)
5. *aparāhna*	afternoon (15.36-18.00)
6. *sāyāhna*	evening (18.00-20.24)
7. *pradoṣa*	nightfall (20.24-22.48)
8. *nakta*	night (22.48-3.36)

---

[39] Malinar 2004, 193f.

[40] On this practice, see also Haberman 1985; 1988, 125ff.

[41] This text is ascribed to either Kṛṣṇadāsa Kavirāja or Rūpa Gosvāmin (16th cent.).

[42] The times listed in brackets have been adduced in the edition of the *Aṣṭakālīya Stotra* by Advaitadāsa. In other manuals the times vary, for example, *niśānta* is from 3.22 to 5.46.

An example of what should be remembered is one of the eight verses of the *stotra*, the verse which belongs to the *smaraṇa* of the pastimes of the two lovers at nightfall, the *pradoṣa yama*:

> I remember Śrī Rādhā at nightfall, being dressed by Her girlfriends in white or in dark clothes according to the lunar fortnight, going out to meet Kṛṣṇa with Her messengers in the desire-tree grove in Vṛndāvana, on Vṛndā's indication. I also remember Kṛṣṇa, who witnesses artful games in the assembly of cowherds at that time, and is then carefully taken to His bedroom by His affectionate mother, from where He goes to the solitary grove to meet Rādhā.[43]

In the daily lives of resident monks and lay followers, this practice cannot be followed exclusively, but has to be coordinated with their current duties. Especially with regard to monastic institutions and to the sequence of *pūjā*s, this may result in the drawing up of rather complex schedules.[44] Seen from this perspective, monastic life is all about coordinating these different time frames. When a devotee is about to reach the spiritual goal, the time he spends in *smaraṇa* may increase heavily. The devotee enters the time of Kṛṣṇa's *līlā* more frequently, and this becomes visible in the appearance of certain physical states and signs that indicate this transition to the other realm. Often this transition has an ecstatic quality, as the feelings of devotion reach their highest point.[45] One finds many textual accounts of devotional ecstasy not only in theological discourses, but also in the sacred biographies, the *carita*s of teachers and devotees. The practice shows not only how these different times and spheres of existence should be connected, it also reminds the adept that, in the end, one must leave social time in order to enter the highest abode, the realm of the eternal return.

Final Remarks

The present analysis of the *CC* has shown that, in the interpretation of the life of the founder, an important role is played by notions of time that are already current in the socio-cultural context and subject to interpretation

---

[43] *rādhāṃ sālīgaṇāṃ tāmasitasitaniśāyogyaveśāṃ pradoṣe / dūtyā vṛndopadeśād abhisṛtā yamunātīrakalpāgakuñjāṃ / kṛṣṇaṃ gopaiḥ sabhāyāṃ vihitaguṇikalālokanaṃ snigdhamātrā / yatnādānīyasaṃśāyitam atha nibhṛtaṃ prāptakuñjam smarāmi //*

[44] Some of these schedules are listed and discussed by Cakrabarty 1985, 308-16.

[45] On ecstasy as a religious emotion, see Malinar and Basu (forthcoming).

by the religious tradition. The account of Caitanya's life not only furnishes the ideal of a successful religious life, but also explains the temporal frameworks in which it is embedded. These serve as a stable point of orientation, irrespective of the actual situation of the individual follower or the community as a whole. This relative independence from the contingency of historical circumstances results from the interpretation of a unique and significant past, one which is irretrievably lost in time, as divine time. This means that the past is turned into an everlasting presence located in a trans-cosmic sphere that encompasses all the other, created spheres of existence. Therefore, this ever-present past may be commemorated and represented in certain situations on an earthly plane, or else the realm of its eternal presence can be entered. On the other hand, Caitanya's life is dated and recorded according to the Śaka era, the current chronology of Bhāratavarṣa. This construction implies having to cope with different times and their respective spheres. Thus, an important part of the training of the adept consists of acquiring the ability to enter and exit the different time frames and to coordinate them with the schedule of the religious community and the surrounding social environment. The life of the charismatic teacher and founder demonstrates how these parallel times are to be connected.

The case of the Caitanya tradition shows that, in the Hindu religious context, notions of time cannot be understood by applying the favourite distinction between linear and cyclical time without qualification. This distinction has long served to put linear time on the side of history and progress as epitomized by Western civilisation, modern individuality and Christianity, with cyclical time being placed on the side of mythology as symbolized by Indian civilisation and Hinduism. As has been pointed out with regard to Eliade's interpretation, it is helpful to be precise about one's understanding of cyclical time and to distinguish between cyclicity and recurrence. This distinction helps us analyse how different concepts of time are used in Hindu religious traditions. The present case study of the Caitanya tradition shows that we find here a rather complex situation, in which linear time is established through the counting of time units and the memory of past events. Thus we were dealing with events that are regarded as unique and placed in a cosmic chronology, which operates with huge but nevertheless counted time units. Certainly we also come across a concept of cyclical time that closely matches the notion of the 'eternal return of the same'. However, this time is not the epitome of cosmic time, but of divine time: it marks the presence of God.

In the *CC*, Caitanya, the divine founder of the community, is made the model for the successful mediation and interconnection of these different temporal frameworks and for relating them to the religious goal of reaching the trans-cosmic realm of eternal repetition. His worldly appearance is dated according to common cosmic time. However, the counting and dating of events is also limited when it reaches the boundary of time-reckoning, that is, the day of Brahmā, since this unit is uncountable because of the problem of its infinite number. Seen from a sociological point of view, the common cosmic time can be regarded as the traditional Indian world-time (Weltzeit), allowing the mediation, communication and synchronization of the different time frames used in the different regions and the different religious communities in India. Another level of the mediation of different regions and localities are the ritual calendars (*pañjī*), which are based on the common lunar-solar time reckoning. Modern world time is measured by the clock and synchronized through time zones. Before its introduction, world time was different in different cultures, depending on their extension and range of diversity. Not only in Europe, but also in India, it permitted the adaptation and synchronization of events that happened in different spheres and regions. Within the framework of cosmic spheres, time is counted and events dated according to the common cosmic time, so that events in Bhāratavarṣa are encompassed and related to each other as being earlier, later or simultaneous, thus synchronizing specific local and regional calendars and chronologies.[46] Although this common time is not repetitive, cyclical time, Hindu religious traditions teach notions of the cyclical repetition of the same along side it, but this is regarded as divine time that is located beyond the cosmos, a trans-cosmic time signifying salvation. In the case of the Caitanya tradition, cyclical repetition is not something one tries to leave; on the contrary, it is a time that one desires to enter in order to escape the fact that, while being on earth, one is endlessly being pushed forward into another day, another year, another era.

References

Balslev, A.N. 1983. *A Study of Time in Indian Philosophy*, Wiesbaden: Harrassowitz.

---

[46] On the inclusion and insertion of (local) history in the over-arching time frames of cosmic and Indian history, see Thapar 1997, Kulke 2004, Basu 2004.

Basu, H. 2004. *Von Barden und Königen: Ethnologische Studien zum Gedächtnis und zur Göttin in Kacch*, New York, Bern: Peter Lang.

Bergmann, W. 1981. *Die Zeitstrukturen sozialer Systeme: Eine systemtheoretische Analyse*, Berlin: Duncker und Humblot.

Caitanyacaritāmṛta 1999. *Caitanya Caritāmṛta of Kṛṣṇadāsa Kavirāja*, A translation and commentary by Edward C. Dimock, Jr., with an introduction by Edward C. Dimock, Jr. and Tony K. Stewart, Edited by T.K. Stewart, Cambridge (Mass.), London: Harvard University Press.

Callewaert, R.; Snell R. (eds.) 1994. *According to Tradition: Hagiographical Writing in India*, Wiesbaden: Harrassowitz.

Chakrabarty, R. 1985. *Vaiṣṇavism in Bengal: A Historical Study, 1486-1900*, Calcutta: Sanskrit Pustak Bhandar.

Deadwhyler, W. 1992. 'The Sampradāya of Śrī Caitanya', in S.J. Rosen (ed.), *Vaiṣṇavism: Contemporary Scholars Discuss the Gauḍīya Tradition*, New York: Folk Books, 127-140.

Dimock, E.C. 1966. 'Doctrine and Practice Among the Vaiṣṇavas of Bengal', in M. Singer (ed.), *Krishna: Myths, Rites, and Attitudes*, Honolulu: East-West-Centre Press, 41-63.

Eliade, M. 1954. *The Myth of Eternal Return*, Translated from the French, New York: Pantheon.

— 1957 [1951]. 'Time and Eternity in Indian Thought', in J. Campbell (ed.), *Man and Time: Papers from the Eranos Yearbooks*, New York: Pantheon, 173-200.

Entwistle, A.W. 1987. *Braj: Centre of Krishna Pilgrimage*, Groningen: Forsten.

Falk, H. 2002. 'Frühe Zeitrechnung in Indien', in H. Falk (ed.), *Vom Herrscher zur Dynastie: Zum Wesen kontinuierlicher Zeitrechnung in Antike und Gegenwart*, Bremen: Hempen, 77-105.

Gell, A. 1992. *The Anthropology of Time: Cultural Constructions of Temporal Maps and Images*, Oxford: Berg.

Haberman, D.L. 1985. 'Entering the Cosmic Drama: Līlā-Smaraṇa Meditation and the Perfected Body', in *South Asia Research* 5 (1), 49-57.

— 1988. *Acting as a Way to Salvation: A Study of Rāgānugā Bhakti Sādhana*, New York: Oxford University Press.

Keyes, C.F. 1982. 'Introduction: Charisma: From Social Life to Sacred Biography', in M.A. Williams (ed.), *Charisma and Sacred Biography*, Missoula: Scholars Press, 1-22.

Kirfel, W. 1967. *Die Kosmographie der Inder nach den Quellen dargestellt*, Hildesheim: Olms.

Kulke, H. 2004. 'The Making of a Local Chronicle', in A. Malinar, J. Beltz and H. Frese (eds.), *Text and Context in the History, Literature and Religion of Orissa*, Delhi: Manohar, 43-66.

Lorenzen, D.N. 1987. 'The Social Ideologies of Hagiography: Sankara, Tukaram and Kabir', in M. Israel and N.K. Wagle (eds.), *Religion and Society in Maharashtra*, Toronto: Centre for South Asian Studies, University of Toronto, 92-114.

Mahābhārata 1933-59. *The Mahābhārata for the first time critically edited*, Vols. 1-18, Poona: Bhandarkar Oriental Research Institute.

Malinar, A. 2001. 'Rādhāramaṇa Caraṇa Das und die Caitanya-Nachfolge in Orissa: Zur Textualisierung von Charisma', in D. Lönne (ed.), *Tohfa-e-Dil. Festschrift für Helmuth Nespital*, Reinbek: Wezler, 295-313.

— 2001a. 'Śaṅkara as Jagadguru According to Śaṅkaradigvijaya', in V. Dalmia, A. Malinar and M. Christof (eds.), *Charisma and Canon: Essays on the Religious History of the Indian Subcontinent*, Oxford, Delhi: Oxford University Press, 93-112.

— 2003. 'Zeit und Zeitpunkt in den Upaniṣaden und im Epos', in W. Schweidler (ed.), *Zeit: Anfang und Ende*, St. Augustin: Academia Verlag, 33-50.

— 2004. 'Mantra-Recitation as a Religious Institution: Śrī Kalpataru Sevā Āśrama in Bhubaneshwar', in A. Malinar, J. Beltz and H. Frese (eds.), *Text and Context in the History, Literature and Religion of Orissa*, Delhi: Manohar, 175-202.

Malinar, A. and H. Basu. (forthcoming). 'Ecstasy', in J. Corrigan (ed.), *Oxford Handbook of Religion and Emotion*, Oxford: Oxford University Press.

McDaniel, J. 1993. 'Dancing in the Hidden Vṛndāvana: The Ritual Service of Caitanya', in *Journal of Vaiṣṇava Studies* 1 (3), 72-83.

Reynolds, F.E. and D. Capps. 1976. 'Introduction', in F.E. Reynolds and D. Capps (eds.), *The Biographical Process: Studies in the History and Psychology of Religion*, The Hague, Paris: Mouton, 1-33.

Schreiner, P. 2001. 'Institutionalization of Charisma: The Case of Sahajānanda', in V. Dalmia, A. Malinar and M. Christof (eds.), *Charisma and Canon: Essays on the Religious History of the Indian Subcontinent*, Oxford and Delhi: Oxford University Press, 155-70.

Stewart, Tony K. 1985. *The Biographical Images of Kṛṣṇa-Caitanya: A Study in the Perception of Divinity*, Chicago (unpublished Ph.D. thesis).

— 1992. 'The Biographies of Śrī-Caitanya and the Literature of the Gauḍīya Vaiṣṇavas', in S.J. Rosen (ed.), *Vaiṣnavism: Contemporary Scholars discuss the Gauḍīya Tradition*, New York: Folk Books, 101-25.

— 1997. 'When Rāhu Devours the Moon: The Myth of the Birth of Kṛṣṇa Caitanya', in *International Journal of Hindu Studies*, 1 (2), 221-64.

Stietencron, H. von. 1986. 'Kalkulierter Religionsverfall: Das Kaliyuga in Indien', in H. Zinser (ed.), *Der Untergang von Religionen*, Berlin: Reimer, 135-50.

Thapar, R. 1997. 'Linear Time in Historical Texts of Early India', in D. van der Meij (ed.), *India and Beyond: Aspects of Literature, Meaning, Ritual and Thought: Essays in Honour of Frits Staal*, London: Routledge, 562-73.

4

Babas and Alekhs: Notes on Concepts of Time and Social Change in a Contemporary Ascetic Doctrine

Lidia Guzy

In this paper, are presented some notes on concepts of time within the contemporary ascetic Mahima Dharma doctrine in two of its communities in Orissa.[1] Mahima Dharma is an ascetic tradition involving monks (*baba*s) and laymen (*bhakta*s). The main features of this religion are belief in the God *Alekh*, asceticism, a vegetarian diet, and the rejection of caste. While the monks are concentrated around Joranda in Dhenkanal, the monastic centre and holy city of the ascetic doctrine, the laymen are scattered throughout Orissa. The observations described in this paper are based on comparative fieldwork among ascetics (*baba*s) of central Orissa (Dhenkanal) and tribal converts (*alekh*s) in the south-west of this region (Koraput).[2] While followers of Mahima Dharma mainly originate from among the Hindu rural population, in recent times there have also been converts from the tribal population.[3] By comparing the various socio-cultural settings of Mahima Dharma, different concepts of time and their impact on religious identities will be described. The chapter will show how those belonging to the monastic tradition regard themselves as

---

[1] Since I have introduced the concepts and social structure of Mahima Dharma elsewhere, in this paper I shall concentrate solely on the issue of time. For further details, see Guzy 2001, 2002, 2006; also Beltz, 2006.

[2] I thank the Deutsche Forschungsgemeinschaft (DFG) for giving me a generous grant, without which this study could not have been carried out. In order to study the structure and forms of the Mahima Dharma ascetic tradition, I stayed for six months in Jaka, a *tirtha* of Mahima Dharma near Dhenkanal town. For their great help in the course of my research, I would like to thank Prof. Prasanna Kumar Nayak, the family of Jagmohan Sahu, and the respected Mahima Dharma ascetics, Promot Das and Vira Das from the Jaka *tirtha*, for their constant help and assistance. In order to study tribal conversions and the comparative situation, I stayed in a Rona village in Koraput district. For help necessary to this research, I thank Prof. Georg Pfeffer. For her aid as my research assistant I thank Miss Sunita Dolai. Lastly, for their reception of me and their friendliness towards me, I thank all my Rona friends.

[3] See Eschmann 1986, 386-7; T.R.B. 1968-9, 44-76.

members of a religious community with its own sacred time and how tribal converts conceive themselves as new voices of the traditional sacred time. I shall also demonstrate how religious change is strongly embedded in traditional time and social concepts while nevertheless indicating social change. This is especially noticeable in the changing ethic of the tribal converts, which is evolving from the tradition of temporary ascetic practices into the new permanence of an abstemious life.

For Mahima Dharma ascetics, the time of ascetic practice stands for the end of ordinary social time and for the beginning of a new life within a monastic community that is governed predominantly by Hindu rules of world renunciation. The social time of the ascetics creates a sacred society of holy men, symbolized in the monastic centre and structure of the doctrine.

For the tribal converts or *alekh*s, permanent ascetic practice is creating a new community of abstemious moralists with their own ritual specialists. Here, the ascetic path always leads to ecstatic eruptions of sacred time that are expressed through *alekh gurumai*, the *alekh*s' ecstatic ritual specialists. In the tribal context, the time of ecstasy reveals indigenous and traditional concepts of sacred time that differ from the other-worldly society of the *baba*s. Whereas sacred time for tribal converts is wild, crazy, and unrestrained, the sacred time of the *baba*s mainly consists in the strict exercise and discipline of body and mind. Ritual ecstasy as the sacred time of tribal *alekh* ritual specialists is two-fold, depicting traditional concepts of the wild sacred time while simultaneously indicating a change of social ethic. Traditionally, ritual ecstasy, as well as ascetic preparations for it, are temporary. For the new adherents of Mahima Dharma, short-term ascetic practice is changing into a permanent ascetic way of life. In the tribal context, this ascetic ethic can be seen as an indicator of social change, the result of a process of transformation from a temporary asceticism within a ritual (and transitory) framework into a permanent morality of abstinence within one's own life.

In both communities, in becoming the adherent or religious specialist of the ascetic doctrine, religious identities and with them concepts of time change. The *baba* community and the community of tribal converts show a diversity of ideas of time that evoke different ideas of the social and sacred worlds in one and the same religious doctrine.

The Time Concepts of the *Baba* Community: Mahima Dharma in Dhenkanal

In the context of the ascetic life of *babas*, the doctrine of Mahima Dharma, literally 'the glorious *dharma*',[4] implies a sacred time that differs from the social time of laymen (*bhakta*). For ascetics, the sacred society (*sammaj*) is represented by the monastic community in Joranda and its local monastic satellites, as well as by its ascetics (*babas*) themselves. The sacred time of the monastery and its local branches is orchestrated by rituals performed by ascetics. The main rituals are those of bodily discipline and of fire (*yagya*). In contrast to this, for ascetics the lay adherents (*bhakta*) represent the model of worldly time and its unsystematically structured communities, highly diversified and embedded in local contexts. Besides this local diversity, the common religious rules of the Mahima Dharma doctrine are strict celibacy for ascetics, a strong disciplined body and mind for both ascetics and devotees, a vegetarian diet, the rejection of caste, and belief in the almighty God, Mahima Alekh. Mahima Dharmis worship Mahima Alekh as the highest, unwritten (*a-lekh*[5]), indescribable God. Mahima Alekh is conceived to be *sunya* – the void – all and nothing. This God can only be approached through meditation, an ascetic lifestyle and ritual practices. The monastic doctrine permanently affirms the monotheistic concept of Mahima Alekh as the one and only God, although lay theological concepts may differ due to their specific local belief systems.

The concepts and values of Mahima Dharma *babas* go back to the founder of the religion, Mahima Gosvami, who lived at the beginning of the nineteenth century. His origins are unknown, but for his devotees he is considered the incarnation of Mahima Alekh. According to legend, Mahima Gosvami came from the Himalayas and appeared at Puri in 1826, from where he began his religious mission throughout Orissa. For the next twenty-four years, he is said to have meditated in the Kapilas Hills of Dhenkanal, where he lived for the first twelve years on fruits and roots of

---

[4] Dharma is a polysemic socio-religious concept of South Asia. In connection with Mahima Dharma it can be translated as a 'religious code'. For a discussion see O'Flaherty and Derrett (eds.) 1978.

[5] *A-lekha* in the sense of 'not to write/unwritten' refers to everyday usage. In Sanskrit, the term itself means 'without writing', 'illiterate', thus indicating a pejorative meaning.

the forest delivered to him daily by a Savara[6] chief. Over the following twelve years, Raja Bhagirati Mahindra Bahadur, the King of Dhenkanal, supplied Mahima Gosvami with a daily quantity of milk. After a long period of meditative preparation, Mahima Gosvami is said to have started his religious teachings in the Feudatory States of Orissa.[7]

Pioneering research conducted by Eschmann defined Mahima Dharma as 'an autochthonous Hindu reform movement' that derived 'its criticism of the Hindu tradition directly from the tradition itself'.[8] Eschmann's main interest was the dynamics of indigenous regional traditions in contact with pan-South Asian forms and ideas. Later investigations by Dube stressed the historical development of Mahima Dharma as a sect that contested dominant structures in the nineteenth century,[9] while also undergoing substantial changes through processes of institutionalization. Dube characterized Mahima Dharma as the 'transformation of a subaltern religiosity' into 'an institutionalized religious order'.[10]

My own research revealed the regional and socio-cultural diversity of a contemporary ascetic doctrine whose various parts are only kept together by the proper functioning of the monastic structure and administration. By issuing an identity card, for example, as official proof and a symbol that one is an adherent to the new ascetic doctrine,[11] the monastic administration is able to manage the diversity of different local settings by providing an official religious identity and identification.

Levels of Time Concepts

In this section, I shall describe how the Mahima Dharma doctrine in Dhenkanal shapes the ordinary lives of the *baba*s and their adherents. The

[6] The Savara, also referred to as the Soara/Saura or Sahara, are a Scheduled Tribe in Orissa. See Senapti and Tripathy 1972, 104. In Dhenkanal the Savara live especially in the neighbourhood of the Malaygiri Hill (ibid., 48). Together with the Khond and the Gond, they represent the aboriginal societies of the district of Dhenkanal (ibid., 422). Dhenkanal city, the capital of the district, is said to owe its name to a Savara chief called Dhenkanal (ibid., 427).

[7] For further information on the places connected with Mahima Gosvami's journeys in Orissa, see Senapati 1972, 443-8.

[8] Eschmann 1978, 375.

[9] Dube 2001, 149-78.

[10] Dube 1999, 98, 125

[11] For more details, see Guzy 2001, 61-70; 2002.

doctrine of Mahima Dharma influences notions of time on the following levels:

On the theological level, the monastic *baba* community transforms the 'social time' of rebirths into a 'godlike time' of ascetics and their sacred monastic society. By following the rules of ascetic conduct, the religious goal of transcending social time and the world can be achieved. In this way, sacred time and an other-worldly society can be entered. Monastic living symbolizes the permanence and eternity that can be achieved by following an ascetic way of life.

On the sociological level, the monastic tradition is creating its own social concepts and the social structure of a sacred society. The monastic community has its own ideas of authority, which are shaped by the principle of seniority. This age-related principle generates a hierarchy of its own based on old age.

On the lay level, the ascetic life-style offers temporary choices for religious experiences for laymen and thus illustrates the relationship between ascetics and laymen.

The Ritual Body of Ascetics: The Code of Conduct

Baba asceticism involves the strict discipline of body and mind. As such it represents the main path to deification. In sticking to the code of religious practice, ascetics extinguish the arbitrary nature of human time. Ascetic life becomes predictable and periodic through the strict obedience to the religious laws of Mahima Dharma. By incorporating the religion through an austere discipline of body and mind, ascetics and their bodies represent 'the temples of the god Alekh', which are gathered together in the great temple of the Joranda monastery and its branches. The temples of Joranda and other monastic sites have huge fire altars where fire rituals (*yagya*) are performed. *Baba*s perform the fire rituals at different altars and themselves become the representatives of the sacred fire.

Ascetics must obey the rules of conduct (*guruagya*) that Mahima Gosvami laid down for his followers. The religious duty of the ascetics prescribes no less than thirty-two rules of conduct.[12] The main principle of ascetic life in Mahima Dharma is the severe discipline. Discipline of mind, body, and action provides a framework for ethical and ritual life conduct. The *babas* worship the highest and only God, Mahima Alekh, without interference. They live in simplicity, without property, and are

---

[12] For detailed descriptions, see Eschmann 1986, 394-5; T.R.B. 1968-9, 50.

devoted to a deeply rooted trust in God. The rules include strict celibacy, no idol worship, a vegetarian diet, daily prayers seven times before sunrise and five times before sunset, no meal after sunset, one meal (*vikhya*) from one devotee a day, a strong prohibition on staying more than one night in any one village (and that always outside the house), and finally the ritual obligation to perform *yagya* (fire rituals) for the well-being of society.

Ascetic life conduct and ritual practice make it possible for *baba*s to reach their goal of *moksha*, the absolute death which liberates them from *karma*, the repetition of death and rebirth on earth. Due to their disciplined bodies and minds, even while they are alive *baba*s are enacting the absolute 'time of the gods', the sacred time of the ritual, which is orchestrated by the performance of fire rituals (*yagya, ghiopura*), as well as being incorporated into the spiritually exercised bodies of the ascetics, who belong to a sacred monastic society.

The idea of a sacred, other-worldly monastic society of Mahima Dharma *baba*s is grounded in the South Asian ideal of world renunciation that requires one to leave worldly relationships of family and caste (*jati*).[13] By transcending the social rules of life, ascetics sanctify their existence by spiritually exercising their bodies and minds. Being members of a monastic tradition, they belong to a sacred society.

World renunciation

Baba asceticism, in the sense of a technique of transforming the human body into a sacred one, is based on a long period of preparations and exercises. Ascetic practice has its special time and thus reflects the monastic hierarchy of Mahima Dharma, which is strongly grounded in the social principle of seniority. The stages of world renunciation begin with the role of a young wandering *tyagi*, which lasts for about ten to fifteen years. This role then leads to the status of a more senior ascetic or *das*, who, as a semi-itinerant ascetic, maintains a sort of continuous sacred residence for a further fifteen to twenty-five years. Finally the role culminates in the position of authority assumed by the most senior *abadhuta samnyasin*, who only leaves his permanent sacral abode on special ritual occasions, barefooted.

By renouncing marriage, Mahima Dharma ascetics also renounce being social men. As such they renounce the gender-specific time frames

---

[13] See Dumont 1966, 324-50.

that imply the time of marriage, the time of bringing up children, and the time of managing the household. Here, it might be suggested that leaving the social and gendered world makes a man androgynous. This ascetic androgyny is visible in the appearance of the ascetic. The long hair of the *baba*s recalls that of a woman. *Baba*s have *shakti*, the divine power, and as such they incorporate the goddess. Asceticism in Mahima Dharma seems to be combined with androgyny and thus recalls certain Indian concepts of divinity.[14]

The fact that Mahima Dharma ascetics organize themselves and live in monastic structures in the Joranda monastery and its branches shows how the *baba* doctrine creates a sacred society. The transcending of social time by following an ascetic lifestyle allows ascetics to enter the otherworldly time-frame of the monastic life. Through world renunciation and ascetic exercises, ascetic bodies become a matrix of sanctification and divination and thus symbols of the 'temples of god'. By practising the ascetic life, ascetics enter the 'time of gods' and themselves become the spiritual altars of fire for their ritual performance of the *yagya* ritual.

Temporary lay ascetics

Alongside the permanent ascetic lifestyle of *baba*s who, after a long period of preparation, have decided to renounce social time for the rest of their lives, there are also temporary options of renunciation for laymen. Young men who are critical of their society or are unwilling to marry try to live and exercise like *baba*s for a time. After a period of religious experience as a *tyagi* for up to fifteen years, they must join the religious community of *baba*s or else be excluded from the monastic life. The period as a *tyagi* offers many young men an alternative to ordinary social life. Among the monks they can exercise and improve spiritually, seeing for at least a time or a number of years whether they can resist the temptations of youth and the social world.

Ascetics accept young *tyagi* volunteers who want to live like them. Among the ascetics a *tyagi* is considered a student. He is not yet a real *baba*, only a 'small *baba*' (*chota baba*) who still can return to social life but who is devoting time to examining himself first. Real *baba*s are the more senior *das* who have practised for more than fifteen years at least and have undergone initiation (*dikhya*) into the monastic community, as well as *abadhuta samnayasin*, those tested by the old age and long period

[14] See O'Flaherty 1980.

of their ascetic exercise and endeavour. The older a *baba* becomes, the more he grows in importance and social authority. The relationship between old *babas* and young *tyagis* is thus shaped by the generosity of old age and by the respect of the younger for the older.

A young man trying to find his identity among the Mahima Dharma monks is usually accepted by his family. The shorter the phase of spiritual examination in finding of one's real identity and calling, the less problematic the shift from the religious community of *babas* back to the social life of the laity. More problematic for *babas* is if an older *tyagi* tries to establish his own rules and regulations and thus combine the sacred time of a *baba* with the social time of a householder, with a wife and children. A *baba* who sets out to harm the reputation of Mahima Dharma monks in this way is considered a fraud, and he will be expelled from the *baba* community and punished with isolation and a lack of respect. As long as a separation between the religious community of monks and the social values of laymen is maintained by the volunteers, the temporary choice to become a *baba* for a time is an accepted alternative to ordinary social life.

A temporary change in the conduct of life can be considered here within the broader process of *baba*-ization, one of social options in India today being a *baba* for a time, thus demonstrating the high esteem in which ascetic values are held in Indian society.

Local Practices of Mahima Dharma in the Context of Tribal Religion

Proselytizing ascetics from central Orissa have spread the ascetic religion in Koraput district, which is strongly dominated by tribal ways of life and values. Today in the tribal region many Mahima Dharma adherents, the *alekhs*, can be recognized by their *gerua*-coloured cotton dresses and their abstemious attitude towards life. *Alekhs* do not eat meat or drink alcohol. Besides the local goddesses Basudha and Basmati, they also worship God Alekh. Some of the well-off *alekhs* go on a pilgrimage once a year to Joranda.

Experimental conversion

In examining Mahima Dharma in Koraput, we are first confronted by the phenomenon of 'experimental conversion', that is, new converts testing the power of their new God. The most common reasons given for experimenting with the new *dharma* are physical and psychological afflictions, especially in connection with barrenness. The efficiency of the new *dharma* is examined with respect to its healing properties. If one's life does not improve or if the wish for children is not fulfilled, even after austere asceticism, the disappointed converts will return to their traditional belief. Temporary and experimental conversion can thus be seen as a form of religious pragmatism. This also indicates that religious identity has to be approved by time.

The changing ethics

If conversion is reckoned to have been successful in these respects, a long-term change in the local ethic is visible. For those who decide to stick to the new *dharma*, the new form of conduct transforms the traditional, short-term form of ascetic custom in traditional society. Traditionally, ritual specialists (*gurumai, dissari* [15]) undergo a phase of temporary renunciation before performing ritual activities such as animal sacrifices or divinations. Through fasting or other personally modified and negative rules[16] of diet, traditional *gurumai* and *dissari* qualify for communication with the transcendent sphere. Temporary ascetic preparation finally leads to ecstasy during specific ritual séances. In this context, the altered state of consciousness is accompanied by the consumption of alcohol.[17]

For *alekh*s, the traditional ascetic practice, which is common to all ritual preparations, eventually becomes the new permanent ethic of an abstemious form of life. While non-*alekh*s only temporarily renounce alcohol and meat, *alekh*s abstain permanently.

There are two phases of initiation for adherents of the new abstemious religion:

---

[15] *Gurumai* and *dissari* are the local religious specialists. *Gurumai* are local healing specialists and mediums of the supernatural sphere; *dissari* are local astrologers and local healers. Through ecstatic ritual seances, chants and dialogues, the traditional specialists communicate and mediate with the diyine and with humans, thus healing the former and worshipping the local goddesses and gods. For further details, see Otten, in press, Chapter 3.

[16] What can be called the 'don't rules', for example, 'don't eat meat; don't drink alcohol'.

[17] On this, see Pfeffer 2000, 342-3.

The first phase is the experimental period, which is initiated by the first initiation (*dikhya*) to the religion. It is optional and reversible. This first initiation means that one accepts the new abstemious rules of conduct in one's life and renounces meat and alcohol. The abstemious attitude is symbolized by the permanent wearing of the *gerua*-coloured cotton dress.

The second phase of conversion is the second initiation in order to become a religious specialist or *alekh gurumai*. This second initiation is conceived in terms of a spiritual marriage with God (*alekh biba*), which as a holy alliance is irreversible and compulsory. After this spiritual marriage, the *alekh* specialist, who in most cases is a woman, will be able to perform ecstatic sung séances, which are regarded locally as dialogues with the gods. During the divine communication, the *alekh gurumai* becomes a 'voice of god'. Her[18] ecstatic voice and speech represent a sacred time of the gods. This divine time is conceived as being temporary limited, unstructured, and always dependent on transitory expressions of the altered state of consciousness of the *alekh gurumai*. *Alekh gurumai's* ecstatic song séances are healing rituals for afflicted clients. Those who are suffering from a personal crisis are consoled and mentally strengthened by hearing the 'voices of gods'.

For *alekh*s and their specialists, the restrictive code of behaviour represents an inverted set of age-old ideas and values. Traditionally everyone eats meat; *alekh*s do not. Although traditionally ritual ecstasy demands intoxication, *alekh*s abstain from alcohol. Traditionally rituals require blood sacrifices; *alekh*s refuse to kill animals and sacrifice a coconut instead. Their forms of religious practice are a negation of the carnivorous tradition. The perpetuation of negative rules represents a continuity of the traditional ritual formalism. In the Alekh religion, the traditional temporary limitation of abstinent practice is transformed into a permanent ethic of abstinence. Neither the form nor the function change, only the carnivorous practice. The ritual séances of the *alekh*s remain ecstatic in form and continue to fulfil the same function of healing, but the change to abstinence is made in order to acquire a new meaning. In this manner, the traditional structure of ecstasy is reconstituted through perpetual asceticism. In Alekh religion we discover a transformation from the temporary limitation of traditional forms of renunciation (as in ritual

---

[18] Since empirically there are more female *alekh gurumai* than male, I use the feminine form for purposes of description here. Males are included in the generalization.

fasting) to the permanence of an ethical code, which is systematized by negative rules of behaviour.

Alekhs and their specialists regard themselves as new voices of the Divine alongside the old voices of the traditional ritual and healing specialists. Traditional healers use the same ecstatic techniques for communication with the Divine as the *alekh* specialists, but *alekhs* have a new abstemious attitude towards life. This new religious identity indicates recent social change, perhaps comparable to ascetic developments in Christian societies. Weber,[19] as is well-known, linked particular ascetic tendencies with basic socio-economic changes in Europe. In the same vein, the new tradition of Alekh asceticism, with its abstinent ecstasy, may well lead to fundamental changes with regard to local concepts of time and their transformation from temporary phases into a permanent attitude towards life in south-west Orissa.

Ecstatic Song Séances as Sacred Time

The sacred time of the ecstatic song séance of *alekh gurumai* is strongly connected with social time and the world of the local population. Ecstatic song séances always take place at night, when social activities cease in tribal villages and the voices of the other world can be heard. At night, afflicted patients gather to listen to the 'voices of gods'. The sound of an *alekh gurumai* 's voice can be heard accompanied by her single-stringed instrument, the *dudunga*, which is made out of melon and snake-skin. The *alekh gurumai,* sitting on the ground with her hair loose and the instrument in her hands, keeps her eyes closed. She sings for herself and for the sake of those who are suffering. Those who are sleepless or those who 'carry some pain (*dukho*) in their heart'[20] gather to listen to the voices of the gods. 'The *gurumai* is *baya* (crazy)', people say. It is 'good *baya*', a good or divine temporary 'craziness'.

The spontaneous songs and narrations of the *alekh gurumai,* which are composed during her altered state of consciousness (*baya*), represent *khelo*, or divine play. *Baya* and *khelo* are expressed in a 'religious language'[21] and at the same time in the codes of religious speech, which

---

[19] Weber 1988.

[20] Free translation of an often-used expression.

[21] See Keane 1997, 47-71. The use of religious language is a religious observance that can be defined in terms of religious performance, textual practices or speech situations. Religious language in the form of a speech act differs from common

often are characterized by a polyglot shift between several languages,[22] through glossolalia, invocations, and poetic fragments. Using this language in divine communication makes it a marker of sacred time. Dialogues with the supernatural are characterized by their incomprehensibility. The regular one-stringed drone of the *dudunga* indicates the rhythm of ecstasy. The séances of ecstatic, non-systemic singing last for two to three hours. This period is considered one of divine communication, a sacred time for meditation and mediation. After regaining consciousness, the *alekh gurumai* will not remember a single word expressed during her trance.

The ritual grammar of *baya* and *khelo* is based on the music of the *dudunga.* Repetitive and monotonous in its rhythm, the *dudunga* determines the development of the séance, inducing an altered state of consciousness, accompanying the divine singing, and finally ending *baya* and *khelo*. The time of the trance is sacred, expressed by vocal 'play'. Sacred 'play' is characterized by its finality, its pauses. Thus the specific aspect of any divine appearance is that it ends. Holy time thus has its limits, which are marked by the *dudunga*. *Baya* and *khelo* indicate the close connection between music, song and the sphere of the conceptualized Divine.[23] For *alekh*s, the sacred time is the 'crazy' (*baya*) 'play' (*khelo*) of voices, words, and meanings. The sacred language of the *alekh gurumai* is expressed by unsystematic song compositions, poetic epic fragments, and hymnal sequences. The narration is always impulsive, spontaneous, and situational of the specific mood of the *alekh gurumai*.

The following transcription of a typical *baya*[24] and *khelo,* composed by an *alekh gurumai,* illustrates the local concept of sacred time in ecstatic song séances. The local language here is Desya.[25] This *baya* was induced by the sound of the *dudunga* and lasted two hours at night. Certain

---

speech through its ritual context, namely, the form and the content of communication between this world and another. Uttering, heteroglossia, glossolalia, the use of parallelisms and poetic structures shape the forms of religious speech. Its religious content mostly has a metapragmatic character. Its discursive form (for example, prayer) becomes a matrix for religious experience and the belief in transcendence.

[22] Like, for instance, Desya, Oriya, Kui, or Gutob.

[23] On the close connection between music, social structure and academic terminologies, see Lévi-Strauss 1964.

[24] Recorded in October 2000.

[25] Desya is a mixture of Oriya and the local indigenous languages of the population of Koraput (Desya).

fragments of the *baya* are presented below. Finally, the *alekh gurumai* sacrificed a coconut for the God Mahima Alekh, for Basudha, the earth goddess, and for Basuki, the snake goddess.

Transcription of expressions of an ecstatic religious speech (*baya/khelo*)[26]

O Mother, you have given me life.
Like the ashes form Mother,
The ashes form me.
Tell me, what is truth?
Tell me, how shall I live?
O, Saraswati!
You are protecting me under your feet.

Mother, say how much truth
is in this universe?

You told about thirty-six varieties of love;
you can recognize hundreds, hundreds!

And nothing is true in the universe!

True temple of God!
Who has done this temple of God, O Lord?

That is the truthful message with truth!

My Mother does not know
that oath is God.
My Mother does not know
that this is the path of God.

Listen to Mother's message!

I am the Mother in my ear, I am hearing.
I don't know, I don't know, O Mother, what I am hearing
in my ear.

It is true,
Mother, you said something unknown and true to me.

[Glossolalia, unknown language]

A God is hanging;
Mahima Mother, who is sitting on the stage;
Read Mother's message in Sanskrit.

---

[26] I am indebted to Miss Sunita Dalai for helping me with the transcription.

Who said which message is true?
You tell, O mother!

I myself am the truth in this universe which is yours;
There is no God.

Basuda – the Earth told three times the truth!

Forgive a hundred times;
Forgive, for the name of a healthy creation!

All the creation!
I salute you through my hymns!

Earth hymns … hymns… hymns

Creator's hymn
It is the truth, the truth!

Omnipotent and happy hymn!

Protecting father!
Protecting mother!

You are Basudha – the Earth

How inauspicious for you is your child!

New misery you bring, O Laxmi!

You are peaceful while having no beginning;
but you are the origin!

Truthful God, your children have sorrow!

Thirty-three million Gods, thirty-two million, thirty-six million Gods.
Fifty-two million times you are God!
You are in the mind and the mind is in you;
Keep it!

In the afternoon, you slept under the tree.
I beg blessings and protection from you.
God protects this child.
As much as evil spirits exist, God will destroy them!
It is true, Mother, how much illusion there is in this universe!
Mother, you saw it and also you know it!
Mother, all things exist from father!
Protect my child!

He always sees you and protects you!

God, listen to me

and please give me happiness.

Truthful God, keep your blessing for me.

It is seven times true near the Mahanadi river.

Religious devotion gave me two children.

O great God, one child but two births.

After one year and nine months, again one child.

Your Mother is the female seven-headed serpent Goddess!

Basuki Ma, queen of snakes,
You destroy the magical knot!

Queen of snakes, in your hand is Mother.
She is binding all evil.

O Mother, bind the evil spirit!

O, Mother, you are Basuki,
the queen of female serpents;
You are the queen, O Mother!

These fragments of the ecstatic song séance as religious speech and divine communication illustrate how sacred time becomes manifest in Koraput in the sound of the words of an *alekh gurumai*, in her voice, and in the rhythm of the *dudunga*. The ritual speech can be used to console and heal afflicted patients, as well as for an individual prayer. The ecstatic speech séances are not 'professionalized', since the *alekh gurumai* never takes money for her séances, singing only when 'god comes upon her throat'. Through her ecstatic voice the supernatural manifests itself, while with her ecstatic song séance sacred time starts. An important characteristic of this sacred time is its transitoriness. The transitory expressions appear only during the time of ritual ecstasy. The speech is always fragmented and is only partly understood. Sometimes the ritual speech remains hermetic for the listeners, and sometimes only certain words are deciphered. However, these ecstatic expressions demonstrate the remarkable coexistence of tribal theological concepts with pan-Indian ideas. The fragments presented above reveal the strong attachment of the new religious specialists to the earth goddess, even though the new God Alekh is also being worshipped. Here we discover that the new God, which in the *baba* context is the concept of nothing (*sunya*), in the tribal context is conceived as *Mahima Mother*. The holy Mother is almighty and powerful and incarnates herself in different names and shapes, such as the goddess Basuki, the local snake goddess, or Basudha, the earth. The local earth goddess is the protecting father and mother in one, but she is also connected with goddesses from Hindu mythology, such as Laxmi or Saraswati. When the *alekh gurumai* gives the order to 'read Mother's message in Sanskrit', itself an allusion to the spread of Hindu education in tribal regions, we see how the ecstatic ritual speech reveals the influence of the Sanskrit language. The ritual speech itself continues to have the power of exorcism (*Oh mother, bind the evil spirit*), this being a very common feature in other local ritual traditions in Koraput.

From the ecstatic song séance of the *alekh gurumai*, we see that the narrative creations and poetic fragments, which are always spontaneous and inspirational, combine pan-Indian ideas of goddesses with local belief systems based on a belief in Mother Earth and her divine incarnations. The ritual speeches of the *alekh* tradition in Koraput, which are the expressions and manifestations of a sacred time for *alekh*s, can be seen as a language of cultural creativity that combines traditional local beliefs with the impact of a new ascetic doctrine.

Conclusion

Different concepts of time, as well as the unlike values of transitoriness and permanence, signify the different social and sacred times and worlds of the two communities that adhere to the Mahima Dharma doctrine in Orissa. The world renunciation of the *baba*s transcends social time and thus creates a religious community of monks guided by their own sacred time. Through ascetic practice, ordinary men transform themselves into 'temples of god'. The asceticism of the *baba*s sanctifies the human body through a strict discipline of body and mind. *Baba*s then orchestrate their religious community through the time of internal and external rituals of discipline and the external rituals of fire (*yagya*). The external and internal fire of the *baba*s turns them into symbols of the fire altar itself and thus transforms them into representatives of the God Alekh.

The phenomenon of '*baba*-ization' in rural Orissa shows that individual choices exist for temporary religious experiences. The religious practice of '*being a* baba *for a time*' is a popular short-term option for young men and demonstrates the vitality of ascetic models in shaping young people's identities and futures in India.

In the case of the *alekh*s, a two-fold process of social and religious change can be seen: while on the one hand new *alekh* 'voices of the gods' represent a new community of abstemious moralists, on the other the main ritual of the new converts remains within the same traditional pattern of sacred time as expressed through ecstatic ritual song séances.

The life of abstinence results from the transformation of short-term ritual abstention into a permanent code of ascetic ethics for the day. This change of temporary frames can be seen as an indication that a new religion is coming into being and thus of social change in the tribal context. However, the sacred time of the *alekh*s as expressed in the ecstatic song séances indicates that religious change is always accompanied by the continuity of local concepts.

References

Beltz, J. 2001. 'Healing Practices and Mahima Dharma: A Short Note on Recent Fieldwork in Western Orissa', in *Adivasi* 40/41, 92-102.

— 2006.'Contested Authorities, Disputed Centres and Rejected Norms: Situating Mahima Dharma in its Regional Diversity', in G. Pfeffer (ed.), *Periphery and Centre: Groups, Categories and Values*, Delhi: Manohar.

Dube, I.B. 1999. 'Taming Traditions: Legalities and Histories in Twentieth-Century Orissa', in G. Bhadra, G. Prakash and S. Tharu (eds.), *Subaltern Studies X: Writing on South Asian History and Society,* Delhi: Oxford University Press, 98-125.

— 2001. 'Issues of Faith, Enactments of Contest: The Founding of Mahima Dharma in Nineteenth-Century Orissa', in H. Kulke and B. Schnepel (eds.), *Jagannath Revisited: Studying Society, Religion and the State in Orissa,* Delhi: Manohar, 149-78.

Dumont, L. 1966. 'Appendice B. Le Renoncement dans les Religions de l'Inde', in ibid., *Homo Hierarchicus. Le système des castes et ses implications*, Paris: Gallimard, 324-50.

Eschmann, A. 1986 (1978). 'Mahima Dharma: An Autochthonous Hindu Reform Movement', in A. Eschmann, H. Kulke and G.C. Tripathi (eds.), *The Cult of Jagannath and the Regional Tradition of Orissa*, Delhi: Manohar, 374-410.

Guzy, L. 2001. 'Voices of Gods: Ecstatic Alekhs and Local Configurations of Mahima Dharma', in *Adivasi* 40/41, 61-70.

— 2002. *Baba-s und Alekh-s—Askese und Ekstase einer Religion im Werden. Vergleichende Untersuchungen der asketischen Tradition Mahima Dharma in zwei Distrikten Orissas (Dhenkanal und Koraput)/Östliches Indien*, Berlin: Weissensee Verlag.

— 2006. 'Negative Ecstasy or the Singers of the Divine: Voices from the Periphery of Mahima Dharma', in G. Pfeffer (ed.), *Periphery and Centre: Groups, Categories, Values*, Delhi: Manohar.

Keane, W. 1997. 'Religious Language', in *Annual Review of Anthropology* 26, 47-71.

Lévi-Strauss, C. 1964. *Mythologiques : Le Cru et Le Cuit*, Paris: Librairie Plon.

O'Flaherty, W.D. 1980. *Women, Androgynes and Other Mythical Beasts*, Chicago: Chicago University Press.

— and Duncan J.M. Derrett (eds.) 1978. *The Concept of Duty in South Asia*, SOAS London: Vikas Publishing House.

Otten, T. (in print). *Heilung durch Rituale: Vom Umgang mit Krankheit bei den Rona im Hochland Orissas/Indien*, Berlin: LIT Verlag.

Pfeffer, G. 2000. 'Tribal Ideas', in *Journal of Social Sciences* 4 (4), 331-46.

Senapati, N. 1972. 'Appendix Mahima Dharma', in N. Senapti and P. Tripathy (eds.), *Orissa District Gazetteers: Dhenkanal*, Cuttack: Orissa Government Press, 443-8.

Senapati, N. and P. Tripathy (eds.) 1972. *Orissa District Gazetteer: Dhenkanal*, Cuttack: Orissa Government Press.

Tribal Research Bureau (T.R.B.) 1968-9. 'Impact of Satya Mahima Dharma on Scheduled Castes and Scheduled Tribes in Orissa', in *Adibasi* 10 (1), 44-76.

Weber, M. 1988 (1920). *Gesammelte Aufsätze zur Religionssoziologie I*, Tübingen: J.-C.B. Mohr (Paul Siebeck).

5

Rhythms of Life: Ritual Time and Historical Time

Frédérique Apffel-Marglin

She should have died hereafter;
There would have been a time for such a word,
To-morrow, and to-morrow, and to-morrow,
Creeps in this petty pace from day to day,
To the last syllable of recorded time;
And all our yesterdays have lighted fools
The way to dusty death. Out, out, brief candle!
Life's but a walking shadow, a poor player,
That struts and frets his hour upon the stage...[1]

La continuité temporelle prend l'aspect du tissage perpétuel effectué par deux jeunes filles, le jour et la nuit, l'une défilant ce que l'autre vient de filer...

Ce qui est premier n'est pas un temps qui se déroulerait d'une facon uniformément continue; c'est un rythme dont le rythme solaire apparait comme le prototype...

Tisser cette trame c'est en connaitre les noeuds, les *ritu*... les actes qui propulsent la durée a venir...

...le retour a la matrice...la nuit [qui] détisse ce que le jour a tissé. Mais ce retour exprime avant tout un cycle de renaissance, de rajeunissement et par conséquence, d'immortalité.[2]

---

[1] Shakespeare 1990, Act V, Scene V.

[2] Silburn 1955, 13, 20, 36, 47. Temporal continuity takes the aspect of a perpetual weaving done by two young girls, the day and the night, one unweaving what the other has woven.... .
What is primary is not a time that flows in a uniform continuous manner; it is a rhythm of which the solar rhythm appears as the prototype...
To weave this weft one has to know its knots, the *ritus* ... the actions that propel the coming duration...
...the return to the womb... the night [that] unweaves what the day has woven. But this return expresses primarily a cycle of rebirth, of regeneration and thusly, of immortality.

Introduction

The two quotes I have chosen as epigraphs illustrate two profoundly different notions of time. Shakespeare, a contemporary of Galileo, captures the modern Western notion of time. The repetition of to-morrow, to-morrow, to-morrow, followed by 'Creeps in this petty pace from day to day', powerfully captures the notion of the seamless flow of a homogeneous 'recorded time'. Here the word 'recorded' seems to allude to the measurement of time, this petty pace monotonously advancing minute by equal minute, hour by equal hour, indefinitely, regardless of men's actions. On the scale of this line going on indefinitely, men's lives are but a brief candle. In this sense, time is the stage, the backdrop of men's brief strutting and fretting. 'Recorded', on the other hand, might also signify history, the written record of men's deeds placed on the arrow of time, the uniform line starting with the first written record and going on indefinitely. Time is not made by men; rather, they strut on its stage.

The quotes from Lilian Silburn are taken from the first chapter of her work on the Vedic sacrificial literature. The modern Western notion of time has deep roots going back as far as the period of the Vedic hymns, if we think of the deeds that the oldest parts of the Hebrew bible refer us to. It is there that the notion of linear time, of history, first makes its appearance. When God told Abraham to leave the city of his father, abandon his father's idols, go West to the land of Canaan and there start to worship Him, the event marks the beginning of the story of the Jews, an unfinished narrative waiting for the coming of the *mashiah*, the messiah, to find its end. As Gunther Plaut puts it, in his edition of The Torah: 'This address of the Divine (Gen 12:1-4) to one human being … form[s] the starting point of Israel's history.' [3] The story attaches itself to the line of unidirectional time. Similarly, the rituals that contemporary Oriya villagers enact embody a notion of time that has equally ancient roots in the Vedic literature and is totally different from the modern Western understanding of time.

The topics of this chapter are the enacted time-space of Oriya villagers and the modern notion of homogenous, abstract linear time. In the second part of the paper, I shall endeavour to lay bare the constructed and metaphorical nature of modern, homogeneous, abstract, linear time, the time of history. This seems necessary to me since, although to modern

[3] The Torah 1981, 90.

readers the metaphorical nature of Vedic or contemporary Oriyas' notions of time is obvious, the notion of linear, homogeneous, unidirectional time seems literal and not metaphorical.

I have called the villagers' time 'ritual time' for reasons that will become obvious in the body of the paper. Several of the papers in this volume make us aware of the fact that there are several different kinds of time on the subcontinent. Ritual time, it would seem, belongs in the category of 'common cosmic time' as defined by Angelika Malinar in her essay in this volume. Although I simply use the word 'time' frequently in the paper, it should not be read as meaning 'time in general' but this particular 'ritual time'. I make no attempt here to situate this ritual time in relation to any other notions of time except that of modern time, nor do I maintain that this ritual time is the only notion of time existing on the subcontinent.

In this paper, I shall return once more to the festival of the menses, Raja Parba, to explore this other notion of time, which I call *ritu*al time because this reflects the etymology of Sanskrit *ritu* (cognate with the Latin *ritus*), meaning actions that propel the duration to come. The suffix -*tu* with the root *ri* makes this an action word, the substantive *rita* most often being translated as 'cosmic order', understood as being simultaneously in time and space.[4] It is in Raja Parba that I can best discern the rhythmic nature of time and place, a time that is made by humans in consonance with the alternating rhythms of the more-than-human world. However, what will be said here in the context of Raja Parba applies to many other festivals too.

In Raja Parba also, one sees clearly what Silburn calls 'le retour à la matrice', the return to the womb, the time and place where continuity springs forth, where renewal and regeneration occur. We shall in fact see that ritual is the making of time, a time that is not given and hence has constantly to be made and made well in order to achieve regeneration and continuity. Hence the necessity of periodic re-enactments. There is no ordered continuity without a rhythm, and no rhythm without repeated beats.

It is also in Raja Parba that one sees that the return to the womb, the fount of the possibility of continuity, is the place/time where distinctions, order and forms are all dissolved, just as sunlight dissolves in the night.

---

[4] On the etymology of *ritu*, see Benveniste 1973, 380. The English word 'ritual' comes from the Latin *ritus*, which is cognate with the Sanskrit root *ri*.

Light re-emerges from the womb of night rejuvenated. The womb is both dissolver and regenerator. Time does not flow forward evenly: it is interrupted, or dissolved and then remade. The thread that the young woman has strung on the loom to make the day is untied and rewound by another young woman to make the night. The dissolving alternates with the formed, the ordered, and it is this very alternation that creates continuity and a form of this-worldly immortality through regeneration. The rhythm is marked in two beats, two phases. Without one or the other there is no time, no order, no continuity and no possibility of immortality. They are as necessary to each other as night and day, fallow and cultivation, wet and dry, activity and rest, field and forest, menses and absence of menses.

In the second part of the paper, I shall attempt to de-privilege the modern notion of time and history. When ritual time is apprehended through the lens of historical time, it generates a kind of distortion that seems to have encouraged the view that people have no notion of time, that they are ahistorical. It also fosters the notion that rituals are obsolete and fated to disappear. However, when we can behold ritual as the maker of time, of continuity, ritual acquires the same kind of presence and weight that history has in Western civilization. My aim here is to dispel the view that ritual is expressive of some other, more fundamental reality, or that it represents an aspect of that reality. These tasks will necessitate an ethnographic approach towards historical time, revealing its arbitrariness, its constructedness.

Raja Parba and the Making of Continuity

It seems to me at the outset that, before launching into a brief descriptive account of the festival, we need to dispel certain notions concerning menstruation that are widely shared among educated cosmopolitans. In order to do so, let me quote a passage on menstrual observations published in 1930 by an Oriya writer, Phakira Mishra, which concludes a detailed description of what women should do and not do during the first three days of the menses:

> On the fourth day the woman takes a purifying bath, then with clean clothes and jewels and reciting the *mangala pata*, thinking and speaking nicely she will come to her husband.... Some women bleed for a long

time, seven or nine days. If they have intercourse the sperm will come out with the flow.[5]

This text makes clear that what is at issue is not the intrinsically polluting nature of menstrual blood *per se*, but rather this blood during a particular *period of time* marked by several actions, one of which is bleeding. The woman must do many things during the first three days of her menses, as the main ones being sleeping on a *kusa* mat, eating from leaf or clay plates, eating a restricted diet, not worshipping the domestic fire – that is, not cooking – and not having relations with her husband. But even the bleeding is spoken of as an action rather than something happening to the women. The earth and women bleed themselves: it is not that something happens to them. This stands in sharp contrast to the manner in which American women of all classes and ethnicity speak of their menses. For them, as Emily Martin's ethnography of women's bodies has documented, menses is something experienced by the women passively, something that their 'biology' does to them, not something that they themselves actively do.[6]

I had the opportunity to discuss the phenomenon of menstruation in depth with several women on the occasion of the festival of the menstruation of the Earth, the Goddess and women.[7] This festival, called in Oriya Raja Parba (*raja* meaning menses, and *parba* meaning festival), is celebrated in villages in the coastal districts of Orissa by all castes (including so-called untouchable castes) with the exception of Brahmans. It takes place once a year in mid-June, when the monsoon rains make their first appearance and the earth and the Goddess are said to be menstruating for three days. This festival is the most important and largest festival of the year for the villagers of this region. I participated in it at the shrine of the Goddess Haracandi, c. 30 km. south of Puri on the coast, where villagers from some sixty villages in the region congregate for four days. I also participated in the festival in one of the villages around Haracandi's shrine. Men congregate on the hill of Haracandi, all the men of one village sleeping and eating in the same tent for the four days of the festival. The women celebrate in the villages, where they take over the public spaces,

---

[5] Mishra 1930, 88-9.

[6] Cf. Martin 1987.

[7] I have published several papers on this festival, the most comprehensive being Apffel-Marglin 1995. See also Mishra 1995.

the young girls swinging on gaily decorated swings (*doli*) especially prepared for this occasion.

In a conversation I had with three sisters-in-law in one of the villages celebrating Raja Parba, I asked if women were untouchable during menstruation:

> Sisulata: This blood is something that comes out; if you or we touch it, we become untouchable (*chua*). The blood from a wound is not untouchable, it is not polluted (*mara*).
>
> FAM: Why is the blood of menses polluted?
>
> Dibulata: This blood is not from a wound, not from the lips of a wound. This blood comes by itself. When Satidusi takes care of the child, she leaves the blood in the womb. Otherwise, when the day and time come, the blood comes out. If you touch her during these days, you become polluted.
>
> FAM: Is this blood dirty (*maila*)?
>
> It is not dirty!
>
> Chaya: Dirty blood is something that comes whenever the body is sick. We don't like seeing that sick blood.
>
> FAM: Do you feel bad staying like untouchables for three days?
>
> We feel very bad not being able to wash and scrub.
>
> D: We become dirty not being able to wash and scrub.
>
> FAM: Are you sad in your mind?
>
> S: In our minds (*mana bhitare*) we do not feel sad. Our minds are happy during our menses, but we ourselves feel a little bad because we can't wash and are dirty. But menses are a happy thing. If a girl does not get her periods, it is such a bad thing; she can't have children, she can't marry, nothing will happen, nothing. It is very inauspicious (*amangala*).

On another occasion, I went with the same three sisters-in-law to the hill of Goddess Haracandi, near Brahmagiri, where I have attended the fair there, celebrating Raja Parba on several occasions. I asked them, 'What is Raja?':

> S: Haracandi is at her menses; three days are gone, and tomorrow is Thakurani Gadua (the bath of the Goddess). The women will take a bath and so will Thakurani. Red will be thrown over her so it will appear as if she is bleeding. Pouring this red over her, they will treat her as if she were menstruating.

> D: Tomorrow is the bath of Thakurani, and this will be done tomorrow.
>
> S: Yes, that cloth over which the red is thrown will be put in a bucket of water so that the water will be red. The priest will show it to the pilgrims and say, 'This is the blood of Thakurani.' People will drink this water out of joy and happiness.

The notions of menstrual blood as something biological and as something intrinsically negative both constitute serious obstacles to the task of making evident the fact that it is the conjunction of certain actions done in synchrony with certain points of articulation in the year that is significant here. This will become clearer through a brief summary of the festival.

The earth, the goddess, menstruates once a year in mid-June. This is the articulation between the hot, dry season and the rainy season. The hot, dry season is the period of fallow, when nothing grows in the fields. The rainy season is the season when the newly planted seeds germinate. During the hot and fallow season, there is separation between the earth and the clouds. Women are the earth, and the rain clouds are Indra, King of the gods. The articulation of the seasons, and sometimes the seasons themselves, are called *ritu*, a word which also means menses in Oriya (as in Sanskrit). *Ritu* refers simultaneously to the first four days of a woman's periodic flow, as well as to the actions taken by men and women during that time. The convergence of certain acts with the shift from the dry to the wet season, from fallow to regeneration, is produced by both men and women, in fact by entire communities. And it is these acts which produce continuity and create an orderly time that ensures well-being and regeneration. As we shall see, when the proper order of acts is not observed, the continuity of life is threatened, and destruction ensues.

The festival is observed by women in the villages, where they take over the streets and other public spaces, exchanging food and other gifts, while young girls swing on *rajadoli*s (swings for the festival of the menses). Meanwhile the men depart on the eve of *pahili raja*, the first day of the festival, with their loaded bullock carts. The men from some sixty villages around Brahmagiri converge on the hill of Bali Haraçandi and there set up huge tents (*capa*), usually one per village, or two if the village is very large, as well as cooking hearths. They bring supplies and animals to sacrifice to last them for four days. What characterizes this encampment is that men of all castes, including the 'untouchable' castes, all eat and sleep together. The Brahmin priests of each village join them in order to cook the food, even though they say that, since their own women do not celebrate Raja, it is not their festival. The festival is also attended by Muslims who live in adjacent villages. They clean the sacrificed rams and goats as well as help keep order at the festival and the fair that accompanies it, where a temporary market springs up. In the words of a Mr Fariduddin, who had set up a *pan* shop at the fair:

> We try to see that everything goes well at the *mela*. We join with our Hindu brothers. They also join us at our festivals. We maintain good relations with the Hindus, we exchange with them.... The Hindus say that their Goddess is in her period, but we do not understand this. We don't ask about it, it may offend them. We observe *raja* by stopping our ploughs. Some of our girls and women play on swings and wear new clothes.

And a Muslim farmer added:

> We give rest to the land, the bullocks, and to men. It is the way people do, it is a custom. We also make *pithas* [pastry]. The people stop work. If we cultivate at that time people will surely feel bad.... There is nothing in our book about the earth menstruating.... But this earth is Mother; only because of that do we give rest to her.

Let me start by briefly evoking the women's observances in the village. I arrived in one of the villages in 1990 on the eve of Pahili Raja, where my colleague Purna Chandra Mishra had established ties with a family of four brothers, their wives and children. The next day I got up early and went to the house of the four brothers. Dibulata sent me with her youngest daughter to the village tank. Many girls and women were already bathing there, and more kept arriving. Mothers rubbed their daughters' bodies with *haladi* (turmeric), all of them crowding on to the steps leading down to the water, a joyful, smiling crowd on a clear fresh morning, by a pond fringed with coconut palms. The idyllic setting delighted me, especially after the dusty lanes of Puri.

Dibulata joined us, as did Mahari, Sisulata's 13-year-old daughter. They bathed, splashed, even swam, and giggled every time I took their picture. We walked back to the house and I sat in Dibulata's room, watching her carefully, slowly combing her daughter's hair, lining her eyes with *kajal* (eye liner), spreading talcum powder on her skin, and decorating her feet with *alata* (red lac colouring). She then turned to her eldest daughter and repeated the same gestures, after which she turned to me. Looking disapprovingly at my hairdo, she told me it simply would not do and proceeded to oil my hair and part it in the middle, putting *sindur* in the parting and on my forehead. She also painted the soles of my feet with *alata*. Sisulata then called me over to feed me. Later, the youngest of the four sisters, Hadi, invited me to watch her paint one of the most gorgeous and elaborate *chitta* (drawing or painting) I have ever seen, which filled the wall of her family's room. Children were swinging and shouting on the *rajadoli*s set up at the back of the house. Then we went visiting in the village, carrying gifts of food to other households and watching the girls swinging. The village lanes were full of gaily attired women, girls and young boys, each household having a brightly decorated swing (*doli*) near the house. Some of these girls were wild, swinging so high that they appeared to be on the verge of doing a full circle. Their colourful saris flew in the breeze, along with many of their voices singing *rajadoli* songs. Many of the older women tended to their pots, in which they were steaming the traditional delicacy of Raja, *enduli pitha*, a pastry stuffed with coconut and *ghur*. I was told that some men had stayed in the village, but they were nowhere to bc seen. The streets had been taken over by the women and girls. It was indeed a festival of women, just as I had been told.

Meanwhile the majority of the men, at least one per household, had gathered on the hill of Haracandi, where they sacrificed rams and goats and cooked three meals a day, offering it first to the goddess, then all sharing the meal together, regardless of caste distinctions. They also all slept together in the same tent. Like the women, they played – cards mostly – held song festivals, feasted and rested. No one was allowed to plough or work bullocks or do any work. Their Muslim neighbors also gave rest to the earth, not because she was bleeding, but because she is the Mother and needs a period of rest.

Men and women keep themselves separate during the days of the festival, as they do during the first three days of a woman's monthly periods. They give rest to women and to the earth. This is how one villager, Bhikari Parida, expressed it:

> The Mother, the earth, is bleeding.... We think that women are bleeding too at that time, not really, but symbolically [*sanketika*], and that the Mother bleeds through them. During the menses of the earth, women do no work; they play and sing with their friends. The sole reason is for them to rest, just like during their monthly periods, when they do no work and must not be disturbed, they should not be touched, they are then untouchable. When the Goddess is bleeding, we also stop all work in the fields, and not only we farmers, but all the other men, blacksmiths, carpenters, potters, washermen, barbers, etc. It is incumbent upon us that we should please the Goddess and women at this time. Young women celebrate Raja because they are the centre of creation, and we want to make them happy and please them.

Both women and men halt all productive activities. The women must not grind, cut or paste anything, not winnow, in short not engage in the food-processing activities that are theirs. Husband and wife must not unite, since such activity is also called 'work' (*kama*), being, like all the other works of both men and women, an activity that produces life, a productive activity. It is only the denizens of industrialized, urban societies that have come to associate work almost exclusively with remunerated activity.

What takes place at that time is the collective cessation of productive activity. The land lies fallow, the women are fallow, the men and their bullocks are idle, the artisans lay down their tools, the fishermen their nets. The hill of the Goddess Haracandi is a grove whose trees are never cut, a patch of land that is never cultivated, never worked, never productive. To the alternation in time between productive activity and rest corresponds an alternation in space between the cultivated field and the untouched grove. The making of this landscape, in which untouched grove alternates with cultivated field, corresponds with the making of a collective alternation in time between productive activity and rest. Moreover, the making of these alternating rhythms by the human collectivity is nested within the alternating rhythm between the hot, dry fallow season and the wet, rainy, productive season. It is the making of these rhythms as part of the rhythms of the (common) cosmos that brings about continuity.

The importance of ensuring continuity was also stressed to me when I asked what would happen if the men did not make the women happy during this festival by letting them rest and giving them gifts, in the form of the customary *raja* baskets filled with clothes and other items. The following is a conversation I had on this with a 60-year-old man, Bimbadhara Ṇayak:

> FAM. If women are not happy, what will happen?
>
> BN. We cannot contemplate that....We try to please women and keep them in a good mood during their menses and also during Raja Parba.... We have read Kapatapasa [by Bhima Dhibara, late nineteenth century] and heard about the pain given to Draupadi by the Kauravas, especially Dusa. She was at her menses, and Dusa, the brother of Duryodhana, gave her mental and physical pain, insulted her, irritating her extremely. She became very angry and a spirit moved her, and as a result of her *niswasa* [her curse through exhaling] the whole Kurubangsa was destroyed. This is also told in our Mahabharata.

The following is a similar conversation I had with a young washerman, Ramacandra Nayak:

> FAM: What happened at the dice match?
>
> RN: Draupadi cursed Dusa, and he died. The whole lineage of the Kauravas was destroyed because of this sin.
>
> FAM: What sin?
>
> RN: She was disturbed during her *ritu*; she was taken by the hair and she got angry and the result was very bad. Everything was destroyed, blood was shed.
>
> FAM: What would happen if you did the same thing the Kauravas did and disturbed the earth during Raja?
>
> RN: We would get afflictions (*dosa*). Everything would be spoiled. If you plough, it will not give results. That is why we give sufficient rest to women during their menses. If they rest it will be good for them. They do no work; they are untouchable; we do not disturb them. So the mother goddess should take rest at this time.

During Raja Parba, Haracandi is Draupadi. There are temples to the five Pandavas in five villages close by. Sisulata and Dibulata specifically referred to Draupadi as having been menstruating at the time of Duhsasana's affront, signaled by her untied hair. Sisulata put it as follows: 'Dusa came to the room where Draupadi was and dragged her away when she was menstruating. Then Draupadi said: "When I see your blood, then I will tie my hair". Dusa died, then the *benibandha* (tying up of the hair or braid) was done.' As we know, Draupadi remained in a symbolic state of menstruation for thirteen years, and a great deal of blood was shed, not just Duhsasana's. In his study of the Sanskrit *Mahabharata*, Hiltebeitel has argued that the whole story, including the great war, is propelled by this emblematic violation of Draupadi's menses and her curse, her *niswasa*.[8]

The cessation of continuity in the form of the termination of the *bangsa*, the lineage, of the Kauravas was stressed repeatedly by the villagers in their retelling of the *Mahābhārata* story. We also know that the lineage of the Pandavas barely survived. The blood shed as a result of Draupadi's curse brings about the cessation of continuity. It stands in a parallel opposition to the blood shed at the festival in the sacrifice of male animals, which gives life by feeding the goddess, as well as the human

[8] Cf. Hiltebeitel 1976, 1980a, 1980b, 1981.

collectivity. It is blood shed properly, that is, at the right time and with the right acts, whether the blood of male animals or women's blood during the first three days of their menses, that creates the continuity of life. Men shed the blood of their male animals, while women shed their own blood. In the case of both women and the earth, the shedding of their blood is the act that signifies future life, while with the men is it the act that feeds and nurtures the community so that collective life may continue.[9] It is the violation of this *ritu* that brings about the cessation of life, the cessation of continuity and the negative shedding of men's blood, namely destructive war.

To the several contrasts or oppositions we have mentioned, alternations that constitute the rhythm that creates a continuity of time, we need to add the contrast created at the festival itself between the social divisions enacted during productive time and the social inclusivity enacted during the festival. During the four days of Raja, caste divisions are lifted. Men of all castes sleep and eat together. Women in the village take over public spaces and interact and exchange food with all the other women in the village, regardless of caste. Muslims, untouchables and caste Hindus all intermingle. Such practices during ritual time have been characterized in the literature in various ways, the most popular ones being 'transgressivity' and 'liminality'. These terms do not help make visible what is at the heart of these acts, namely the joint creation of rhythmic alternations in synchrony with the cosmos and thus of continuity.

In the case of 'transgressivity', this term positively confuses and conceals what is at issue here. The term is used to refer to such behavior as the lifting of caste and religious distinctions, which is seen as transgressing the norms of the social order. This usage privileges one of the moments, one of the beats in the rhythm, namely the productive moment. Or rather, it does not grasp the social order as having a dynamic rhythm but rather as a single structural entity. More crucially, it entirely misses the fact that true transgressivity consists in *not* observing the *ritu*, in violating it, as in the case of Duhsasana's violation of Draupadi's *ritu*. Duhsasana simply ignored Draupadi's *ritu* and dragged her into the men's public hall. In the nineteenth-century Oriya version, the *Kapatapasa* of Bhima Dhibara, there is a dialogue between Duhsasana and Draupadi in which Duhsasana tells her that he does not believe she is at her *ritu* and that nothing will happen to him if he touches her and drags her out.

[9] On the enormous importance of the feasts the men prepare and distribute at the festival, see Marglin 1996.

Draupadi responds by listing precisely the terrible calamities that would befall him if he did touch her. The villagers repeatedly told me that if they did not observe this ritual, calamities would result, such as famine, epidemics, floods, earthquakes and war. What they do during Raja Parba is the opposite of transgression; they precisely do *not* transgress.

The term 'liminality' is associated with Victor Turner's work.[10] Turner adopts van Gennep's tripartite schema for rites of passage (in his classic *Rites of Passage* of 1908), as well as his architectural metaphor for social forms.[11] Turner understands liminality as the absence of social structure.[12] This understanding conceives actors as dynamic, but as moving through a fixed structure, which is likened to the architecture of a building. At thresholds, namely liminal places, they are neither here nor there. This structural placelessness is variously expressed, often through egalitarianism or inversions. In other words, this view corresponds to Shakespeare's, where space replaces time as the stage on which men strut and fret in their passages through various thresholds. It is a powerful vision. Nevertheless it is one that not only privileges a single static structure, but that also has embedded within it a view of time as a line. Men go through different stages in their lives, marked by passages. It is still men strutting through a structured stage marked with thresholds, the static, given backdrop of human action. In the Oriya, and perhaps Indian view, neither time nor structure is a given. Rather, these are made in concert with the more-than-human-world, what can also be called 'the common cosmos', by producing a convergence of repeated acts creating rhythmic alternations in the social as well as the natural landscapes, which echo, and participate in, the rhythms of the cosmos.

A more powerful image is that rooted in the Vedic sacrificial vision as interpreted by Lilian Silburn, where the solar rhythms of night and day are paradigmatic of the creation of a well-ordered continuity. The days and the nights, the two young women, weave and unweave the weft on which an ordered continuity is woven. The night unravels the thread that the day has stretched on the loom. During the night the sun dissolves, all forms losing their edges and dissolving in the darkness. But the night, the ocean, are also the womb that nurtures the embryo that is born as the

---

[10] Cf. Turner 1966.

[11] Cf. van Gennep 1960.

[12] Turner 1966, 96 writes the following: '[liminality] reveals ... some recognition of a generalized social bond that has ceased to be and has simultaneously yet to be fragmented into a multiplicity of social ties.'

young sun after dawn. These cosmic deeds, however, are not givens, backdrops, the stage of human activity. The two young women are more than metaphors, and the sun is not just a heavenly body. With the advent of the materialist-mechanical cosmos in the sixteenth and seventeenth centuries in Western Europe, the world ceased to be active. The only subject was Man (women were deliberately excluded[13]), and knowledge became an entirely anthropocentric endeavor. The cosmos, nature and the entire more-than-human world become merely the backdrop to men's actions. In contrast, ritual time is not only created by cosmic agency along with human agency, it is also centrally conceived of as female. *Ritu* is a female activity par excellence, as the periodic bleeding of women, goddesses and the female earth signals the emergence from the womb where time and space dissolve and are reborn.

Historical Time

Although the unidirectional linear view of time of the West is extremely ancient, dating back to the oldest layers of the Hebrew bible, the modern sense of time and history emerged much later in Europe. The earliest clocks are said to have been made around 1300. According to David Landes, 'It is the mechanical clock that made possible, for better or worse, a civilization attentive to the passage of time, hence to productivity and performance'.[14] Time pieces such as sun dials and clepsydras, time pieces powered by water, and others existed from antiquity. What had not existed before was the ability to measure the passage of time in equal, standard units of measurement. In India time units or *prahara*s (see Malinar, this volume) are of different lengths. What was emerging in Europe of the twelfth and thirteenth centuries gave rise to the birth of modern mathematics, and this in turn to the mechanical clock.[15] Landes rhetorically asks of medieval man: 'How much reckoning could he do in a world that knew no uniformity of measurements?' (1983, 77) Measurements before early modern times were not standard. Weights varied locally, based on such measures as a particular local basket, as is the case

---

[13] On the deliberate exclusion of women in the creation of the modern cosmology, there is a wealth of scholarship. But a useful overview can be had in Noble 1992.

[14] Landes 1983, 7.

[15] Landes 1983, however, does not correlate the appearance of the mechanical clock with the previous revolution in mathematics, which happened about a century earlier.

in many parts of rural India today. Distances were reckoned in feet, elbows, thumbs and the like, and time was generally marked by the church bells ringing prayer times such as *matine* and *angélus*. The old church bells ringing the canonical hours for prayer did not mark equal units and hence did not lend themselves to arithmetic, to addition and substraction. Landes continues:

> But the new bells [that kept time in the manufacturing workshops that developed in this period] and the calculations they made possible (how long until? how long since?) were a school for all who listened and began to organize their lives around them. Meanwhile the church clung to old ways and, so doing, yielded the rhythm of life and work to the lay authorities and the bourgeoisie. Equal hours announced the victory of a new cultural and economic order. (ibid., 78)

As both Lewis Mumford and Landes have pointed out, the mechanical clock is a machine, a man-made device which, by its essential nature, dissociates time from human events and from nature.[16] It dissociates time from human events in the sense that human events no longer mark or make time; rather, time becomes an independent variable, a homogenous magnitude underlying all human activity and all natural phenomena.

For the ability to measure equal hours to develop, there had to be a previous step, namely the invention of the notion of 'general magnitude'. Time had been the province of the Church through the early and high medieval periods. Different periods of the day and of the year were imbued with the feel and meaning of the corresponding prayer and liturgy. Time was not uniform, but heterogeneous. Time may have been unidirectional, but it was not homogenous. For time to become a homogenous general magnitude, the stage for men's actions, there had to be a mathematical revolution first.

Not surprisingly, this revolution happened, as with the invention of the mechanical clock, within the milieu of the nascent bourgeoisie. In fact the two events are closely tied together, and it took about a century after the crucial development in mathematics for the first clocks to appear. With the expansion of trade and the growth of cities and manufacturing, there was the growth of what anthropologists call 'all-purpose' money, that is, a standardized money that can be exchanged for any commodity, in contrast to 'special-purpose' money, which can only be exchanged for a restricted range of goods, never labour or land, and often not food either.

[16] Cf. Mumford 1934, 15; Landes 1983, 16.

A very widespread type of special-purpose money is the cowry shell, used in both Africa and India. Other special-purpose moneys, well known in the ethnographic record, are the Trobrianders' banana leaf bundles,[17] the African nomadic cattle-herders' cows and bulls, and the West Africans' cloth .

With the development of commerce and long-distance trade, value as the quantity of money that a thing was worth eventually came to be seen as an intrinsic property of the thing itself. The shift from pre-modernity to early modernity is also a shift from a world where things are primarily for use to a world where things are primarily for exchange. All-purpose money allowed a vast array of different things to be exchanged, including human labour, land and food, besides objects. All of these disparate things became commensurables, this being what all-purpose money enables and what special-purpose money prevents. The early modern mathematicians were merchant-accountants such as Leonardo Fibonacci, whose book *Liber Abaci*, published in 1202, marks the earliest formulation of modern European mathematics. According to the historian of mathematics, Richard Hadden:

> By the thirteenth century, money changers were becoming merchants of exchange. By 1338 there were eight banking houses in Florence and by 1400 there were 120. [...] The firm became an entity in itself whose property could be measured by calculating the legally established gains and losses in goods measured by money. (1994, 95)

The appearance of all-purpose money and the need for complex accounting is what allowed the emergence of the concept of 'general magnitude', which differs from simple magnitude in the following way: magnitude is infinitely divisible, but the unit of calculation is discrete and indivisible. Before the invention of general magnitude the unit of calculation was not seen as a number, since numbers refer to a multiplicity and the unit is by definition not a multiplicity, but single and indivisible. According to Hadden, the birth of modern European mathematics at the turn of the twelfth and thirteenth centuries occurred when one – the unit – becomes a number that itself becomes infinitely divisible. When *one* becomes a number, number and magnitude are reunited, a step which allows the measurability of unlike quantities, of incommensurables. Velocity, for example, is neither time nor distance, but something that can be precisely represented only following a mathematical revolution in

[17] Cf. Weiner 1985.

which a ratio between unlike things, such as time and distance, can be produced.

For the classical Greek philosophers and scientists, and for Aristotle in particular, 'the world of nature remains a realm of quality, genus, and difference. Aristotle compares incommensurables in his work on ethic, but not physics.'[18] Aristotle's and Archimedes' physics are entirely theoretical. There are no measurements and no theory of real numbers, only a theory of proportions. The things related as proportions are always commensurables: force to force, distance to distance, time to time. This prevents the construction of formulas and algorithms for calculating force, time and distance. The development of geometry and mathematics in classical Greece led to Aristotle's views, in which numbers and magnitude are different 'things'.

The invention of general magnitude permitted the quantification of incommensurables. This in turn is what made it possible to replace the view of nature held by the classical Greeks as being made up essentially of difference and quality, and the experience of time in ancient and medieval Europe as being heterogeneous, with a mechanical conception of nature and a conception of time as a homogeneous unidirectional flow. In Hadden's words: 'the formation of the mathematical-mechanical world-picture thus represents a reification of the social relations of commodity exchange.'[19]

The modern view of time as homogeneous, quantifiable and abstract pre-dates (and is necessary to) the emergence of history in its modern form. History acquired its central importance in modernity more or less alongside modern European science. History belongs to a secular domain that was created in western Europe in the mid-seventeenth century. Modern science, like modern history, seeks objectivity and strives to determine the 'facts', what 'really happened', whether in relation to human events in the past or experiments in the laboratory. Truth is no longer based on authority, that is, on that of the Church hierarchy: it is independently arrived at by a community of researchers through the use of a scientific method or, later, a historical method.

The view of history as the recording of the acts of men ordered along a homogenous time line is a modern European phenomenon. However, it has come to be perceived by most as a universal way in which to understand the past, one furthermore that is indispensable for the

[18] Ibid., 80.

[19] Ibid., XV.

building of the nation. When Europeans came to the Indian subcontinent and then conquered it and studied its civilizations, they discovered that Indians were ahistorical. This view was famously articulated by Montesquieu, Hegel, Marx and others, as well as by the scholar-administrators who governed India. Marx's words on this are perhaps the most pithy:

> ...invaders came and left, empires were toppled and installed...and underneath this all life in the village communities...continued as ever, unchanging, unmoving, oblivious to the passing of time.... Vegetating in the teeth of time...the natives witnessed, without so much as the blink of an eye, the ruin of empires, the perpetration of unspeakable cruelties, and the massacre of the population of large towns.[20]

The ahistorical nature of Indian civilization was invoked to explain its backwardness. What I tried to do in the first part of this essay is to illustrate a radically different notion of time – among other notions of time – one that characterizes Indian civilization. However, more needs to be done before we can see this notion of time as simply different, not as primitive or pre-scientific, inevitably destined to evolve toward a proper historical consciousness. The task is not a small one, and the space allocated to it is limited. However, I feel it is necessary to attempt to de-privilege this modern notion of history so that it ceases to make all other notions of time seem metaphorical and obsolete. It would also be refreshing not to have historical time be the universal referent in terms of which all other notions of time should be understood. In other words, my intention is to question the objectivity – and hence privilege – of historical time.

What characterizes the revolutions in mathematics and hence in the reckoning of time in early modern Europe is that they eventually gave birth to a view of space and of time that is entirely abstract, homogeneous and quantifiable, thus removing the understanding of space and time from lived experience. Furthermore, these modern notions of time and space are indispensable to the functioning of the market economy and of the centrally administered nation state, the latter having emerged after the conclusion of the Thirty Years War in 1648, which finally put an end to this international religious conflict in Europe, which pitted two equally dogmatic views of Christianity against each other. As James Scott has

[20] Marx as cited by Lal 2003, 122.

argued in *Seeing Like a State*,[21] making a diverse on-the-ground reality uniform and centralized required the rationalizing and simplifying tools of the new science. Modern history thus provided a new sense of identity, one no longer rooted in diverse local memories, but rather in the recently created memory of the new political entity, the nation state, this new 'imagined community', to use Benedict Anderson's phrase.[22] The new scientific methodology guaranteed the objectivity of this history.

In the twentieth century, the modern scientific cosmology and methodology, as well as the modern notion of time and history, have experienced what may turn out to be mortal blows. With the quantum revolution, Heisenberg's uncertainty principle and Einstein's theory of general relativity, which challenged Newton's notion of absolute time and absolute space, a door has been opened for a reconsideration of what has come to be taken as reality. This reality is made up of two non-overlapping parts, one internal to the human mind or consciousness, the other wholly external to it, purely material. The Einstein-Podolsky-Rosen (EPR) experiment, and the delayed choice experiment in quantum physics in particular, challenge the conceptual framework that modern cosmopolitans bring to everything.[23] They challenge our taken-for-granted assumption that it is the same nature out there, regardless of who looks at it. They challenge our devotedly held belief in objectivity and its clear separation from subjectivity. They challenge our separation between the 'in here' and the 'out there'. They challenge our notion of a homogenous, quantifiable, abstract linear time and space. Time turns out to have warps, simultaneity and other characteristics that make our modern minds reel.

The construction of a clear boundary between the 'in here' and the 'out there' was definitively articulated by Robert Boyle, the father of the scientific experimental method. This construction was an effective response to the irresolvable religious conflicts of his times. Theology and metaphysics were proving incapable of delivering the certainty that European civilization had become addicted to in the course of more than a millenium and a half of the Church's monopoly on the production of knowledge. Boyle's bold step in erecting a boundary between theology and metaphysics on the one hand and the physical and material on the other was the last move in, and an articulate formalization of, a process

[21] Cf. Scott 1999.

[22] Cf. Anderson 1991.

[23] For an introduction for lay readers to these experiments, see Zajonc 1993.

that had started with the accountants and bankers of north Italian cities in the twelfth and thirteenth centuries.[24]

Postmodern deconstruction, along with the quantum revolution, help us see that this abstract quantifiable time and space are inventions made for specific purposes by particular people belonging to a particular culture. They are also thoroughly anthropocentric constructions in which representations in men's minds stand for reality, in other words, in which the map stands for the territory. These can no longer be treated as corresponding to reality, much less as universals. Doing so, according to Owen Barfield, is a form of idolatry.[25]

Conclusion

Due to its weight in history, as it were, I shall conclude by returning to the charge of at the ahistorical nature of village India. I have argued that the ritual of Raja Parba is the making of a certain kind of time, namely the continuity of life – not just any life, but the good life. The enactment of Raja Parba consists of a convergence of actions (*ritu*) on the part of human actors and more-than-human actors, which propel a duration of life until the next Raja Parba. The span of time being determined by the articulation between the fallow, dry season and the fertile, wet season is also the *ritu* of the earth, the sea, the goddess. Humans are not the sole actors in this world. The world is alive and inhabited by many beings – gods, goddesses, demons, and others. Right human action is done in concert and consultation with them. We are not here in a totally anthropocentric universe, where the sole actor is 'Man', the rest of the universe being made up of inert mechanical objects. So, when the wheel of the year has turned to another *ritu* of the earth, the festival needs to be re-enacted in order to propel another span of continuity. This continuity is created by a convergence of acts on the part of both human actors and more-than-human actors.

Neither time nor space are givens, let alone abstract quantifiable entities. A continuity of good life is created by a convergence of actions on the part, first of cosmic actors, such as the earth, the sea, the clouds or the sun, and secondly on the part of human actors. The cosmology is not 'mechano-morphic', to use Barfield's phrase, and what is created is not abstract, homogenous, quantifiable time. It is an experiential time, which

---

[24] On the creation of this boundary, see Shapin and Schaffer 1985.

[25] Cf. Barfield 1988.

is a vision of the good life, free from conflict, from calamities such as famine, epidemics and other disasters, a continuity of generations, of the *bangsa*.

The revolution that produced modern mathematics out of the nascent merchant society in twelfth- and thirteenth-century Europe is, according to Hadden, what made possible the creation of the modern scientific cosmology of a mechanical, quantifiable universe whose motions are calculable due to the existence of general magnitudes, the key ones being abstract, homogeneous time and space. This cosmology won out over rival Renaissance cosmologies that all shared a view of the world as alive, as having agency. It won for cultural and political reasons, not because it was somehow more 'true' in any 'objective' sense. It was more true only in the sense that it was functional to the growing market economy and the new, centrally administered nation state. It won out also because it enabled the recovery of certainty on non-religious, neutral grounds, given that religion could not extricate Europeans from interminable bloody battles. It was and is – as so many have pointed out, starting with Francis Bacon and René Descartes – a knowledge that delivers control over nature and people, that is, a knowledge that is also power. The case of Sir Isaac Newton's real beliefs, which were alchemical, that is, that did not separate spirit from matter, is instructive here. Newton wrote more voluminously about his true passion, alchemy, than about physics, keeping secret the fact that for him gravity was not a blind force but a spiritual one. He knew well that if he divulged his secret beliefs, he would not only be ousted from the Royal Society but would also run the risk of following in the footsteps of Giordano Bruno and other Renaissance magi, who were burned at the stake by the Inquisition.[26] Protestants and Catholics, as well as the new scientific establishment, all joined together in condemning the heterodox Renaissance movements. As the Finnish philosopher von Wright puts it: 'The new science [was] a welcome ally in fighting heresies and exorcising the inferior ghosts leaving the one superghost, the Christian Trinitarian God, sovereign ruler of the universe.'[27] But our own deep immersion in this modernist cosmology should not blind us to the fact that it is no less metaphorical than a cosmology that sees more-than-human beings as expressive of different aspects of an infinitely diverse and varied world.

---

[26] Cf. Stenger 2001.

[27] von Wright 1991, 17.

Finally, I would like to reiterate what I have been trying to say in much of this chapter, namely that the egalitarian moment of these Oriya communities is no less important, no less of an essential aspect of the society, than the hierarchical moment. The one could not exist without the other. Although I have only discussed Raja Parba, very much the same could be said of Ratha Jatra and Naba Kalebara, both of which mobilize Oriya society at the largest level.

Wars, invasions and slaughter are events that result from a transgression of ritual time, which prevent the arrangements of acts that can propel an ordered duration of good life. Speaking of the *Mahābhārata*, Gandhi 'saw very clearly how the program to rewrite history, to turn Krishna into a historical figure and depict the *Bhagavadgītā* as a historical record of Krishna's teaching to Arjuna, has a hard, even cold-blooded, edge to it, a natural link with power politics ('Realpolitik") and an exaggerated masculinity.'[28] Gandhi, unlike other nationalists of his time and since, rejected the historicisation of epic narrative. He sensed that this Eurocentric mode of thinking deeply violated an Indian view of time as an essentially *moral* activity. The enactments of rituals and epic narratives are the *making* of common cosmic time, what I have here called variously experiential and/or ritual time. Humans are only one of the actors involved in this process of making, since they act together with the many other-than-human actors in a non-materialist and mechanical universe.

References

Anderson, Benedict. 1991. *Imagined Communities: Reflections on the Origin and Spread of Nationalism*, London [u.a.]: Verso.

Apffel-Marglin, F. 1995. 'Gender and the Unitary Self: Looking for the Subaltern in Coastal Orissa', in *South Asia Research*, 15 (1), 78-130.

— 1996. 'Rationality, the Body and the World: From Production to Regeneration', in F. Apffel-Marglin and S.A. Marglin (eds.), *Decolonizing Knowledge: From Development to Dialogue*, Oxford: Clarendon Press, 142-81.

Barfield, O. 1988. *Saving the Appearances: a Study in Idolatry*, Middletown, Conn.: Wesleyan University Press.

Benveniste, E. 1973. *Indo-European Language and Society*, Coral Gables, Florida: University of Miami Press.

---

[28] Lal 2003, 126.

Hadden, R.W. 1994. *Shoulders of Merchants: Exchange and Mathematical Conceptions of Nature in Early Modern Europe*, Albany: SUNY Press.

Hiltebeitel, A. 1976. *The Ritual of Battle: Krishna in the Mahabharata*, Ithaca, London: Cornell University Press.

— 1980a. 'Draupadi's Garments', in *Indo-Iranian Journal* 22, 97-112.

— 1980b. 'Shiva, the Goddess, and the Disguises of the Pandavas and Draupadi', in *History of Religions* 20, 147-74.

— 1981. 'Draupadi's Hair', in *Puruṣhārtha* 5, 179-214.

Lal, V. 2003. *The History of History: Politics and Scholarship in Modern India*, Delhi: Oxford University Press.

Landes, D.S. 1983. *Revolution in Time: Clocks and the Making of the Modern World*, Cambridge, Mass., and London: The Belknap Press of Harvard University Press.

Martin, E. 1987. *The Woman in the Body*, Boston: Beacon Press.

Mishra, P. 1930. *Gruhasta Ashrama*, Cuttack.

Mishra, P.C. 1995. 'Gender and the Unitary Self: Looking for the Subaltern in Coastal Orissa', in *South Asia Research* 15 (1), 78-130.

Mumford, L. 1934. *Technics and Civilization*, New York, Harcourt: Brace & World,

Noble, D. 1992. *A World Without Women: The Christian Clerical Culture of Western Science*, New York: Knopf.

Scott, J. 1999. *Seeing Like a State*, New Haven: Yale University Press.

Shakespeare, W. 1990. *The Tragedy of Macbeth*, Ed. Nicholas Brooke. Oxford: Clarendon Press.

Shapin, S. and S. Shaffer. 1985. *Leviathan and the Air Pump: Hobbes, Boyle, and the experimental life*, Princeton: Princeton University Press.

Silburn, L. 1955. *Instant et Cause: Le Discontinu dans la Pensṛe Philosophique de l'Inde*, Paris: Librairie Philosophique J. Vrin.

Stenger, I. 2001. *La Guerre des Sciences aura-t-elle Lieu?*, Paris: Le Seuil.

The Torah: A Modern Commentary, W.G. Plaut (ed.). 1981. New York: Union of Hebrew Congragations.

Turner, V. 1966. *The Ritual Process: Structure and Anti-Structure*, Glenside, PA: Aldine.

van Gennep, A. 1960 [1908]. *The Rites of Passage: a Classic Study of Cultural Celebrations*, Chicago: University of Chicago Press.

von Wright, G.H. 1991. 'Images of Science and Forms of Rationality', in S.J. Doorman (ed.), *Images of Science: Scientific Practice and the Public*, Hong Kong, Singapore, Sidney: Gower.

Weiner, A. 1985. *Women of Value, Men of Renown: New Perspectives in Trobriand Exchange*, Austin: University of Texas Press.

Zajonc, A. 1993. *Catching the Light: The Intertwined History of Light and Mind*, Harmondsworth: Penguin Books.

6

Time for Ritual: The Pañjīs of Puri and Jajpur

Heinrich von Stietencron

The argument in this paper is divided into three sections and involves three different levels of investigation. The first regards the recognition, in ritual calculation, of the simultaneous existence of differently structured forms of time and, consequently, different reckonings of time. This section touches, at least marginally, on some of the technicalities of the lunar-solar calendar (published every year as *pañjī* or *pañjikā*)[1] and its implications for connections between time and identity. The second section examines two ritual calendars of Orissa, one from Jajpur, the other from Puri, asking why there are different ritual calendars in the same area and what this might mean for regional identity. The third section looks at some of these differences in more detail.

Ritual Time

It is a feature common to all religions to mark out certain days in the cycle of the year for the performance of a particular ritual or the organization of a religious festival, the timing of which has normally been handed down for many generations. What distinguishes living Indian tradition from this general pattern of religious calendars all over the world is the simultaneous use of two differently structured forms of time: one for ordinary life, derived from the movement of the earth around the sun, and another for ritual action, derived from the movement of the moon around the earth.

As in most cultures, ordinary life in India is governed nowadays by the solar calendar, with its twelve months and its weeks of seven days of twenty-four hours each. But ritual action also takes lunar time into account, calculating two periods of fifteen lunar days each (called *tithi*), one for the period of the waning moon and culminating in the new moon,

---

[1] The *pañjī* is calculated every year by experts in *horaśāstra* or astrology and forms an indispensable tool for successful ritual practice.

the other for the waxing moon and culminating in the full moon. The names of these two halves, *kṛṣṇapakṣa* and *śuklapakṣa*, that is, dark and bright half, respectively, emphasize a clear dualistic structure inherent in the progression of time, which is, of course, also evident in the opposition of day and night, or in the *uttarāyaṇa* and *dakṣiṇāyana* movements of the sun.[2] Among the two *pakṣas* of the lunar month, the *kṛṣṇapakṣa* is potentially dangerous. It is a time when the deceased ancestors are awake and when ghosts and unpacified spirits of various kinds move about. Demons, like the *asuras* and *rākṣasas*, also tend to be active at this period. This is therefore a time that calls for rites to be conducted to avert danger from evil spirits and also for rituals addressed to Lord Śiva, the vanquisher of demons, and his circle of deities, or to the Goddess, who also fights the demons. The bright half of the month is generally more auspicious, both for ritual action and for various undertakings, unless adverse planetary influences intervene.[3]

Of even greater importance for the interpretation of the lunar period are the twenty-seven *nakṣatras*, or stellar constellations visible near the ecliptic along the orbit of the moon, through which the moon travels.[4] They form a lunar pendant to the constellations of the zodiac. Ideally their number is twenty-eight, but one of them, Abhijit, has no spatial extension and is consequently not counted.

These *nakṣatras* also have a bearing on ritual calculations since some of them are considered auspicious, others less so, and some are clearly dangerous. For marriage rituals, the presence of the moon in the *nakṣatras* Rohiṇī, Mṛgaśīrṣa, Uttara-Phālguni and Svāti is already considered auspicious in early texts; other auspicious rites are recommended to be performed when the moon is in the *nakṣatras* Puṣya, Punarvasu, Tiṣya, Hasta, Śroṇa or Revatī. The ritual calendar must take such astral influences into account.

Of course, such general statements are not yet tuned to the individual sacrificer's needs. Astrological texts dating back to the late classic and early medieval periods affirm that the positive or negative

---

[2] *Uttarāyaṇa* designates the ascending northward movement of the midday sun from the winter solstice to the summer solstice, i.e. its growing height above the horizon, while *daksināyana* indicates the descending southward movement back to the winter solstice.

[3] The planet Śani (Saturn) is considered particularly dangerous.

[4] Also known as asterisms or moon houses. There is some regional variation in their names.

quality of a *nakṣatra* does not really depend on the *nakṣatra* per se. What is important is rather its position in the series of *nakṣatra*s in relation to that particular *nakṣatra* which housed the moon at the time of the individual sacrificer's birth. The *nakṣatra* in which the birth took place is reckoned as *ādya*, the first. The 10th *nakṣatra* after *ādya* is thought to have an influence on professional success, the 16th on social relations or social acceptance, the 18th on material gain, the 23rd on illness and death, and the 25th on mental or spiritual achievements. The position of favourable or unfavourable planets in these *nakṣatras* also reflects a positive or negative influence on the individual,[5] and the moon's passage through the latter marks periods of potential misfortune or illness.

To travel through one *nakṣatra* and undergo in the process its characteristic changes of apparition from one new moon or full moon to the next, the moon requires thirty *tithi*s or lunar days, one *tithi* being defined as the span of time needed by the moon to traverse twelve degrees along the 360-degree circle covered in one lunar month. Thirty lunar days are therefore needed to traverse the full round of 360 degrees. Though the distance which the moon has to cover in a *tithi* is constant, the time needed to do so varies considerably, oscillating between twenty-two and twenty-six hours. Theoretically, an equal distance covered at equal speed would result in equal time for the *tithi*s. But ritual time does not go by theory, it goes by observation. And observation shows that in the course of the lunar month the moon seems gradually to pick up speed and cover a greater distance in the *nakṣatra* circle, only to slow down again and require more time for the fixed distance of twelve degrees per day. This influences the calculation of lunar time, since some lunar days (*tithi*) are longer than others. As a result, each lunar day has to be calculated separately. The reason for this phenomenon is easy to understand. The moon does not revolve around the earth at the same distance. When it comes nearer to the earth it appears to move faster; when it is more remote it appears to reduce speed. The same factor of varying distance of the moon from the earth is responsible for tidal variations on our sea coasts.

The combination of the solar and the lunar time reckonings in the Indian lunar-solar calendar results in a number of complications, of which I shall mention only the most obvious. Since the lunar day is, on average, shorter than the solar day, the beginnings of these two kinds of days do not coincide but move further and further apart. A lunar day can therefore begin at any time of the solar day, whether in the daytime or at night. To

---

[5] For further details, see Kane 1962, vol. 5,1, 523-36 and 559f.

follow lunar time strictly would force people to observe rituals at any time of the day or night and thus make ritual duties extremely difficult to combine with ordinary life.[6] For practical purposes, therefore, all religious performances prescribed for a particular lunar *tithi* can be performed on the solar day into which the beginning of the lunar *tithi* falls.

Since the *tithi* is, on average, slightly shorter than the solar day, two consecutive *tithis* may begin on the same solar day. In this case the first is reckoned as an additional *tithi* of the same name, resulting in a *tithi* of double length. If, on the other hand, during a *tithi*'s presence no sunrise occurs, the *tithi* is dropped altogether.[7] This is why, in the calendar, some *tithis* have a double duration, while others may be missing entirely. Ritual time is thus based on the movement of the moon, but not without relating it to the sun. A lunar day without a sunrise is unfit for ritual.

Given all these complications, why does Indian ritual tradition stick to the lunar calendar? Why are the moon and lunar times so important? For an answer we need to turn to the late Vedic period (eighth to sixth centuries BC), when the early Upanishads indicate a gradual transition from nomadic pastoralism to a more settled way of life,[8] and when the newly developed theory of reincarnation[9] and the search for liberation from the cycle of existences (*saṃsāra*) started to replace earlier priorities. Under its impact, the former expectation that sacrificers and brave warriors would reach Indra's paradise after death began to lose some of its attraction. The joys in paradise would turn out to be impermanent and after a while result in a new incarnation, fraught again with struggles and frustrations or sufferings, and again ending in death.

Among the many consequences of this change two turned out to be of particular importance. First, the escape from *saṃsāra*, the search for final emancipation and the attempt to let the individual *ātman* merge with

---

[6] This applies to frequently recurring ritual observations at home or in the temple; it does not apply to important seasonal festivals, which may take place late at night or, like Śivarātrī, throughout the night. Of course, the individual priest or householder is always free to perform his rituals at the exact *muhūrta* or optimal time prescribed for each ritual. One *muhūrta* has the duration of forty-eight minutes.

[7] This situation arises when a *tithi* commences after sunrise and ends prior to the next sunrise.

[8] This is implied by the formation of *janapadas*, hereditary kingship and cultural contacts based on long-distance trade.

[9] For a study of the beginnings of the theory of reincarnation, see Butzenberger 1996, 1998.

universal Brahman were formulated as the highest aims. Secondly, questions of guilt, punishment, and expiation resulted in the conception of multiform possibilities of life after death, including not only various heavens and hells, but also the realms of animals, plants, and demons.[10]

It was at this stage that the moon came to be considered an important destination for deceased ancestors after their departure from earth.[11] With the necessary ritual assistance of a living son, the soul of a deceased person would proceed via several intermediate stations to the moon, and more precisely to that side of the moon that is turned away from the earth and cannot be seen from it.[12] From there, according to knowledge or merit, the soul might proceed further, again via different stations, to the sun and finally to *Brahmaloka*, or, if negative karmic qualities predominate, to *Yamaloka* and, according to later sources, to various hells. Alternatively, it would return to earth in the form of rain to enter plants, animals, etc., or else wait on the moon for an occasion to reincarnate on earth in a selected family. During their time of residence on the moon, the ancestors were believed to depend largely on food and drink offered to them by their descendents.

At a relatively early period already astronomy and astrology were among the sciences closely connected with ritual, and the moon's orbit, its phases and eclipses influenced ritual practice considerably. Poetically imagined as a heavenly cup and, in the early Upaniṣads, as a receptacle for Soma, the choicest of all the oblations of the gods, in the bright fortnight the moon is gradually filled with Soma by the sacrificial oblations of the faithful and then, during the dark fortnight, is emptied by the celestials who feed on it. Indeed, Soma had become a name for the moon by that time. Moreover, the visual sequence of the moon's birth, growth, fullness, decay, and death, only then to return to renewed life, made it a perfect symbol for rebirth and transmigration. Later Indian literary tradition praises the moon's cool brightness as a symbol of purity and spiritual knowledge.

---

[10] For the early concepts, see Schmithausen 1995; Malinar 2002.

[11] *Kauṣītaki-Upaniṣad.* 1.2-7; cf. *Chāndogya-Upaniṣad* 5.10.1-10; For a different attempt, see *Chāndogya-Upaniṣad* 4.15.

[12] This is implied by the fact that the ritual prescribes food offerings to the ancestors at a new moon, which is midday for them, while a full moon corresponds to their midnight. For the relationship between the moon and the ancestors and the two possible itineraries of the soul after death (to rebirth or to *Brahmaloka*), see Stietencron 1971, 54-6.

Ritual is one of the most unchanging elements of religion. Over the centuries new gods may come to be worshipped, new concepts about man and his liberation may be formulated and propagated, and the entire world view may change; yet ritual continues to preserve its ancient prescriptions and its magic truth. This is true in India also, and to this day the offerings to the ancestors remain an important and regular duty in the life of the Indian householder. In this tradition survives the ancient Vedic knowledge that man is born with three debts which he has to pay off by means of sacrifice and ritual support during his lifetime: one to the gods, another to the ancestors, and the last to his own parents, who will require ritual support at the time of their deaths in order to master the perilous passage into the world of the fathers. Once securely settled there, the ancestors are able to visit their descendants from time to time in order to help them in cases of need or to punish them in cases of neglect. The link between the living and the dead is upheld in ritual giving and ritual memory for up to seven generations. The two ritual calendars (*pañjī*) of Orissa studied here have ample evidence of the continuous ritual care afforded to the ancestors throughout the year, though the *pañjī* of Jajpur, a renowned centre for rites to the dead, has more to say on this subject than the *pañjī* of Puri.[13]

Gods, ancestors, and men are thus bound together by mutual dependence, but they live in different places and experience different dimensions of time. A man's day is structured by the movement of the sun from one sunrise to the next. The day of the ancestors is as long as a month in human time and is structured by the movement of the moon in its relation to the sun. The day of the gods is still longer, lasting one year in human terms and being determined by the movement of the sun along the *rāśis*, that is, the signs of the zodiac. Thus, time has different rhythms in different spheres of existence. For gods, ancestors, and men, the perception of time is constitutive as one of the markers of their respective identities. An awareness of such varieties of experience of time on

[13] The oldest sacred spot in Virajā *kṣetra* is Nābhi Gayā, a place of special importance considered to be the navel of the earth and the entrance to the world of the dead. The place is near the bank of the river Vaitaraṇī, which is believed to separate the world of the living from that of the dead. Purification rites at this place and the donation of a cow help the deceased person cross the river and reach the world of Yama, ruler of justice and king of the realm of the dead. *Yama tarpana* is prescribed at the appropriate time in Virajā *pañjī*, but it is not mentioned in the *pañjī* of Puri.

different levels of existence is fundamental for successful ritual communication with the other spheres of existence.

In ritual calculation, therefore, we are confronted with three levels of time: earthly, lunar, and celestial, corresponding to the three spheres of existence where mutual communication is both possible and necessary for the well-being of their inhabitants. The exchange between these spheres is verbal in terms of praise and supplication; may be material in terms of offerings of food, incense, and various gifts, which are hoped to be answered by the gifts of health, children and prosperity; and is spiritual in the form of blessings, knowledge and emancipation. While time in the realm of the gods is solar, in the abode of the ancestors it is lunar. Thus in order to connect these spheres in ritual, time on earth is lunar-solar. These three forms of time have basic structures in common. In all three cases, the day is divided into two equal parts with twilight periods at the junctures: day and night on earth, bright and dark *pakṣa* on the moon, and *uttarāyaṇa* and *dakṣiṇāyana* in the realm of the sun. The astronomer, who calculates the ritual calendar, must take all three levels into account and coordinate them as best he can, while also seeking to avoid periods of danger caused by inauspicious planetary constellations or lunar mansions. The resulting ritual calendar is published each year and serves as a guide for both public and private ritual action.

Ritual Calendars and Regional Identity

The fact that there are several such calendars in the limited area of Orissa alongside one another, and that they differ both in the calculation of the proper time for starting the rituals and in some of the details prescribed for ritual performance has led me to study two of them more closely: the *pañjī* of Virajākṣetra (Jajpur), the ancient seat of the famous Goddess Virajā in Orissa; and the Khādiratna *pañjī* of Puri, representing the ritual practice of the male state deity of Orissa, Lord Jagannātha. Both *pañjīs* were for the year 2000/2001. The main conclusion of this comparison is that difference in ritual calculation acts as a consciously retained marker of subregional identity.

The two *pañjīs* differ in the calculation of the longitude (or forward movement per day) of the moon, resulting in different determinations of the beginning and end of a lunar day or *tithi*. As a consequence, the same festival will not necessarily start on the same day in Jajpur and in Puri, nor, of course, anywhere where one or the other of these two calendars is followed.

The difference remains mostly within the margin of one or two lunar days, but occasionally reaches three days.[14] It was caused by a discovery made in 1869 by the celebrated astronomer, Samanta Chandrashekhara of Khandpara near Kantilo in Cuttack district, Orissa.[15] With the help of new instruments he constructed, he managed to make important corrections in the measurement of the longitude of the moon. These were put down in his *Siddhāntadarpana*, a famous work on astronomy. In the following decades, the consequences were hotly discussed by learned pandits in Benares and all over India. As a result, Samanta Chandrashekhara's changes were accepted almost throughout the entire Indian subcontinent. The Khādiratna *pāñjī* of Puri relies entirely on his work. Similar corrections had already been made in the West in the latter half of the sixteenth century by the Danish astronomer, Tycho de Brahe, Johannes Kepler's teacher.

The pandits of Virajā-*muktimaṇḍapa* in Jajpur and the greater assembly of the pandits of Virajā-*maṇḍala* discussed the issue intensively at the time, but finally decided not to change their tradition. The Virajā *pāñjī* therefore continued to rely on the Bhāsvatī, composed by Śatānanda Āchārya of Puri in AD 1099. Thus, it appears that the pandits of Jajpur decided to retain an outdated system, probably from the beginning and certainly in later years in the face of better knowledge, in order to accentuate their own autonomous status. Time – in this case ritual time – came to be consciously used as a marker of a separate identity. It is worth reflecting on this change for a moment.

Change from within does not vitiate one's identity. It is change from outside, imposed change, that becomes a threat to one's identity, may be the reason why this innovation in astronomical calculation was rejected in Jajpur in the late nineteenth century. By this time the fame of the Puri temple of Lord Jagannātha outshone by far the fame of the ancient goddess Virajā in Jajpur. Streams of pilgrims from all parts of India were attracted to Puri, and the British controlled both the country and the temple at Puri. Although the decision in favour of the new calculation was

---

[14] For field research I found this difference in time helpful, because if one misses a section of a festival in one place, it is still possible to fill the gap at another place where a different calendar is followed. The prediction of a conjunction of five planets in the sign of Aries during the dark half of the month of *Vaiśākha* (April/May 2000) differed by as much as four *tithis*.

[15] Often he is referred to as Pathāni Sāmanta.

made public by the pandits of Puri, British support for this overdue correction cannot be ruled out.

Centuries earlier, when the Bhāsvatī was introduced in 1099, in both Puri and Jajpur, the situation had been different. At that time the Somavaṃśis were at the height of their power and Jajpur was one of their capital cities, a place that could claim to have been continuously at the centre of power from at least the beginning of the Bhaumakara rule in 847. In the local construction of historical memory, Jajpur was also considered to be identical with Yayātinagara, the first important capital of the Somavaṃśīs in coastal Orissa. Transmitted brahmanic constructions of Jajpur history even foster an image of the unbroken importance of the city as a key centre for rites for the dead and ancestor worship from the early epic period of about 1000 *BC*, when the Pāṇḍava heroes are said to have visited the place.[16] Jajpur can thus claim a history of more than two and a half millennia, during which it always retained its place as a famous ritual and political centre in northern Orissa. This position was only shaken towards the end of the Sūryavaṃśī rule, being lost altogether in the middle of the sixteenth century, when Jajpur suffered more than any other city in Orissa from repeated wars with the Afghans of Bengal.

When the Bhāsvatī was introduced in 1099, the famous Jagannātha temple of Puri did not yet exist. Like Jajpur, Puri was predominantly a *śākta* site, with the goddess Vimalā at its centre and several Śiva temples around, just as Virajā was surrounded and protected by Śiva temples. At that time there was neither a major difference nor competition between the two sacred sites. The introduction of the Bhāsvatī, therefore, was an internal development that bore no threat to regional identity.

In 1869 and in the years that followed, the situation was different. The administration of the Puri temple was a function of the king of Khurda, who accepted progress as a sign of the Lord. By contrast, Jajpur had suffered almost total destruction in the sixteenth century and had not been able to regain equal status with Puri. When it came to accepting or rejecting innovation, the pandits of Jajpur chose the latter course, thus projecting themselves as the guardians of time-honoured tradition and reaffirming the separate and unique identity of Virajākṣetra.

Wherever the Virajā *pañjī* is used today – and this is not restricted to the neighbourhood of Jajpur, but can also be encountered in certain

---

[16] Cf. *Mahābhārata* 3. 114. 3-26. The fame of Virajā tīrtha is also extolled in the *tīrtha* list of *MBh* 3. 83. 6-7. For the *Virajākṣetramahātmya* and traditional praise of Jajpur and its sacred places, see Dhal 1984.

śākta areas of the old districts of Balasore, Mayurbhanj, and Puri, down to Ganjam – we are confronted with the memory of a former centre of political and religious power that predates the British, the Muslims, and even the Gaṅgas.

Regional Differences and Priorities

In this section, I shall examine the two *pañjī*s more closely. Both religious centres politely refer to one another's major rituals. They also refer to a number of other sites where important festivals or rituals are performed, thus indicating the geographical extent of their regional perception, if not of their influence. In spite of the fame of Lord Jagannātha as the state deity of Orissa and the spread of Vaishnavism in the wake of the Caitanya movement, Jajpur still retains its influence in the predominantly *śākta* areas of the hill tracts to the north and west of the central coastal plains. In view of the currency of Virajā *pañjī* from the Brāhmaṇī River in the former Cuttack district right up to Medinipur in West Bengal, Mayurbhanj, and even Singhbhum in Bihar, K.C. Panigrahi was inclined to consider this vast area an ancient Virajā[17] *maṇḍala*.

Also interesting are some differences of content that are relevant for regional identity. Since Jajpur is an important centre of death ritual and ancestor worship claiming equal status with Gayā in Bihar, it is not surprising that the Virajā *pañjī* has several entries on death ritual which the Khādiratna of Puri has not.

There is also a different regional perception due to geographical position: the *Gangāsāgar melā* in Bengal is still within the geographical and ritual horizons of Jajpur, but no longer within those of Puri. On the other hand, whereas the Puri *pañjī* refers to the Pongal festival of south India, the Virajā *pañjī* does not. These are instances of general orientation that also reflect distinct regional identities. Some of the most striking differences can be found in the celebration of the anniversaries of the births and deaths of important people. Here the Puri *pañjī* emphasizes freedom fighters, politicians and social reformers, starting with Śivajī, and ending in 2001 with Biju Patnaik. Gandhi and Netaji Bose, Nehru and subsequent prime ministers, as well as freedom-fighters and the champions of a separate state of Orissa, like Gopabandhu Dās and Madhusūdan Dās, are remembered here. Even the *Utkal Divasa*, the day

[17] Cf. Panigrahi 1973, 13ff., cited by Dhal 1984, 5.

of the creation of the new state Orissa, has its place in the Khādiratna *pañjī* of Puri (on *Caitra śuklāṣṭamī*).

The Virajā *pañjī* on the other hand, mentions only a few of these political figures. It is far more interested in culture. It is scholars, poets, and saints who are remembered here. It betrays the more traditional outlook of this *pañjī* that medieval and pre-modern poets, like Jagannāth Dās, Kabi Abhimanyu Sāmanta Siṅghāra, Kabi Sūrya Baldev Rath, Upendra Bhañja, Kavimañjula Kṛṣṇaprasād and certain others are recorded with the dates of their births and/or the dates of their passing on/passing away (*samādhi*) in this *pañjī*. The Puri *pañjī* has dropped any reference to this important aspect of the past. The same applies to more recent luminaries of Orissan literature, like Fakirmohan Senāpati and Vaiṣṇava Pāṇi. The different perspective of the Virajā *pañjī* is also indicated by the fact that important figures from Bengal, like Rāmmohan Roy and Rabindranāth Tagore, are mentiond in this *pañjī* but not in Puri.

Both *pañjī*s must, of course, mention the major saints whose followers live within their area of distribution. They are too many to be enumerated here. It is therefore more interesting to note who is omitted. Rāmānuja, for example, who is supposed to have come to Puri and to have established the Emār *maṭha* there, cannot be absent from the Khādiratna, but he is missing in the Virajā. On the other hand, the influence of the Caitanya movement appears to be stronger in Jajpur than in Puri. The Virajā *pañjī* mentions not only the birth and *samādhi* of Caitanya and his major followers, it also gives the current date of the Caitanya era. This era is not mentioned in the Khādiratna of Puri, nor are important members of the Caitanya movement like Advaitācārya and Acyutānanda, though both are listed in the Virajā *pañjī*. It is rather astonishing that even Kabir, Dayānanda Sarasvati, and Svāmī Śivānanda, all remembered in Virajā, are neglected in Puri. The same applies to the anniversaries of the birth and death of Bāyābābā,[18] whose influence on the religious life of the Vaiṣṇavas of the Caitanya tradition in Orissa is not reflected in the Puri *pañjī*. The Khādiratna, on the other hand, remembers the anniversary of the death of Balarām Das, who is not mentioned in the Virajā *pañjī*, as well as that of the renowned astrologer, Pandit Vāsudeva Khādiratna, after whom this *pañjī* is named. There are rare cases where the two *pañjī*s differ in respect of the dates of births or deaths by more than one *tithi*. This is the case for the Mahraṭṭa king, Śivajī, whose birthday is given as the 9th

[18] On the life and the network of religious institutions connected with Nāmācārya Bāyābābā, see Malinar 2004.

of *Vaiśākha kṛṣṇa* in Khadiratna and the 1st of *Baiśākha śukla* in Virajā, that is, seven *tithi*s apart.

Finally, there is a demographic element in the differences between the *pañjī*s of Puri and Virajā. The Jajpur district was under Muslim rule for a much longer period than the Puri district, and Muslim settlements of considerable size still exist in the area. This is reflected in the Virajā *pañjī*. While the Khādiratna of Puri mentions only the birthday of Mahāpuruṣa Hazrat Muhammad and the major festivals of Id-ul-Zuhā (in memory of Abraham's sacrifice), Muharrām (mourning for the martyrs) and Id-ul-Fitr (the end of fasting after Ramadan), the Virajā *pañjī* lists several other Muslim festivals, such as ab-i-merāj (Mohammad's ascent to heaven from Jerusalem to look at paradise), the birthday of Hazrat Ali, and Ab-i-Barā't (the night of divine records and forgiving). The Zoroastrian Jamat-ul-Vidā is also mentioned.

There are other aspects worth studying in the ritual calendar, such as the value system, which attributes positive powers to certain seasons, months, and days while seeing others as potentially fraught with danger. Another example is how the lives and sports or exploits of major deities are incorporated into the ritual year by celebrating their birthdays, their dressing for special festivities, their outings, and their going to sleep. The role of women also merits a closer look. Their main task is to use the weapon of fasting to keep their husbands and families safe from the evil influences that threaten in certain months. A detailed comparative study, including the *pañjī*s used in the border regions of Orissa, towards Andhra Pradesh, Chhattīsgarh, Jharkhand, Bihar, and Bengal, would throw more light on the cultural alignments and historical influences that continue to be important almost seventy years after the creation of the language-based province of Orissa in April 1936.

To sum up, therefore, there are, in the Indian cultural tradition, several levels of time: the time of the gods, ancestors, and humans; the time of the sun and moon and also of other planets like Bṛhaspati (Jupiter), which I have left aside in the present context; time stored in cultural memory and time that drops out of it; the time used in day-to-day transactions; and ritual time. These notions of time coexist, but operate on different layers of existence and in different sectors of social consciousness. Identity, whether social, cultural or regional, is not just something created in time, it is also informed by notions of time. Ultimately it acquires relevance and continuity only if it survives the passing of time.

References

Butzenberger, K. 1996-8. 'Doctrine of Transmigration I and II', in *Berliner Indologische Studien* 9-10, 55-119; 11-12, 1-85.

Dhal, U.N. 1984. *The Glory that was Virajā Kṣetra*, Delhi: Nag Publishers.

Kane, P.V. 1962. *History of Dharmaśāstra (Ancient and Medieval Religious and Civil Law in India)*, 5 vols, Poona: Bhandarkar Oriental Research Institute.

Malinar, A. 2002. 'Wiederverkörperung oder Abschied vom Ich: Der Tod und sein Jenseits in der Altindischen Literatur', in J. Assman und G. Trauzettel (eds.), *Tod, Jenseits und Identität: Perspektiven einer Kulturwissenschaftlichen Thanatologie*, Freiburg: Alber, 764-98.

— 2004. 'Mantra Recitation as a Religious Institution: Śrī Kalpataru Sevā Āśrama in Bhubaneshwar', in A. Malinar, J. Beltz and H. Frese (eds.), *Text and Context in the History, Literature and Religion of Orissa*. Delhi: Manohar, 175-202.

Panigrahi, K.C. 1973. *Orisara Saṃskṛti O Itihasare Jājapura*, Jajpur: Virajāvaktramālā Series.

Schmithausen, L. 1995. 'Mensch, Tier und Pflanze und der Tod in den älteren Upaniṣaden', in G. Oberhammer (ed.), *Im Tod gewinnt der Mensch sein Selbst: Das Phänomen des Todes in Asiatischer und Abendländischer Religionstradition,* Wien: De Nobili Reserach Publications, 43-74.

Stietencron, H. von 1971. *Gaṅgā und Yamunā*, Wiesbaden: Harrassowitz.

7

Cosmic Time and its Influence on Rona Girls and Women

Tina Otten

Introduction[1]

Social time is marked by the categories attributed to it by society. It can be structured by cycles and rituals, and disrupted by contingent events. Time can be perceived as good or bad, auspicious or inauspicious, long or short. This question of the quality of time is very probably crucial in all human societies, and it has stimulated some works that have become classics in the field of social anthropology.[2] In India, choosing the right moment in time is essential to start an activity. From the highest governmental offices down to small households in remote villages, the auspicious moments to begin an undertaking are written in calendars and almanacs,[3] and announced by ritual specialists.[4] Moreover, many people identify and explain aspects of their personality with reference to the time of their birth and the auspiciousness of its moment.[5] The positive quality of a particular moment in time may be called *muhurta*,[6] as in many parts of India, or *sub bel* (auspicious time) in the hills of Koraput, Orissa. This auspicious time is important for the performance of rituals, which in turn

[1] This paper is based on eighteen months of fieldwork in two villages of Koraput district, Orissa, conducted between 1999 and 2002. I would like to thank the people who shared their knowledge with me in the villages I lived in or visited frequently, as well as my assistants, Sunita and Susmita.

[2] See, in chronological order of their publication, Evans-Pritchard 1940, Gellner 1958, Geertz 1966, Leach 1966, Ohnuki-Tierney 1990, Gell 1992 and Östor 1993. I agree with Alfred Gell that 'the relevant distinction does not lie between different "concepts of time" but different conceptions of the world and its workings'(Gell 1992, 36).

[3] For Orissa, see Stietencron, this volume, and Mahapatra 1961.

[4] See e.g. Friedman 1982.

[5] See e.g. Pugh 1984.

[6] See Leutgeb 2000 for a detailed discussion of the concept of *muhurtam* in Maharastra.

are important markers of personhood and well-being in general. Gods and demons must be appeased by rituals at the proper time for the performance. Illnesses of great social significance[7] are said to be caused by celestial beings desiring to take the ill person to their realm, away from the world of humans from their identities as persons in their particular society. Personhood is established by a sequence of relationships with both the human and the celestial worlds. It is dependent on activities that bring these relationships into balance. Consequently, rituals and actions carried out at an inauspicious moment have long-term effects on one's personhood by creating disorder and illness through unsatisfied celestial beings.

The inhabitants of the Koraput Hills refer to themselves as 'Desya'.[8] The government census places the Desya in the categories of Scheduled Tribe, Scheduled Caste and Other Backward Classes. While Scheduled Tribes call themselves 'Adivasi',[9] Scheduled Castes and Other Backward Classes refer to themselves as 'Desya' proper, a distinctive category opposed to 'Adivasi'. Thus the word 'Desya' denotes both an inclusive and an exclusive category in relation to the people of the hills.

One of the communities of the Desya are the Rona, who live on the southern fringes of the predominantly tribal[10] Koraput district, concentrated in the areas surrounding the former royal courts of Nandapur and Jeypore. The title 'Rona' refers to the royal Rajput title of 'Rana',

---

[7] See Otten 2006, 93.

[8] From the Sanskrit word *deśa* (land); Sanskrit *deśya* means those of the land, indigenous people.

[9] In India we find the distinction between the first inhabitants of a place and the people who live there now. Sanskrit *Adi-* means 'first', while *vasin* means 'one who dwells'.

[10] Anthropologists debate whether or not the term 'tribe' is politically correct. In the present context the term does not refer to a 'primitive society', but to social systems that are traditionally called 'tribe' in India as an translation of the indigenous term 'Adivasi'. For this historical reason the term has been used as an analytical and structural category, which, in this specific meaning, occurs only in the anthropology of India; see, for instance, Bailey 1960 Dumont 1957, Guha 1999, Pfeffer 1982, Sinha 1980. When I use the word 'tribal' in this paper, it is because of a lack of any other technical term for this form of society and because other possible alternative, like acephalous society, indigenous people, etc., also have their problems. I am writing about people who have a clear sense of social hierarchy and whose historical ideas include past migrations and negotiations with past kings.

applied to the nobles of western India.[11] Most probably the people adopted the name 'Rona' when Rajputisation reached Orissa in the eighteenth century.[12] The Rona consider themselves to be the leading members of the former Paik militia[13] of the king of Nandapur, who has resided for more than 200 years in Jeypore. He is the head of one of the oldest Hindu kingdoms in Orissa.

Nandapur was the capital of a kingdom dating from at least the fourteenth century[14] but as its large temples date back into the twelfth century, it might even be older. The oldest evidence of pan-Indian influence are Jain ruins around Nandapur, which can be dated to the ninth century.[15]

The Rona are divided into a senior section, called *boro* Rona, and a junior section called *sano* Rona or *kuttia* Rona.[16] The only difference between the *boro* Rona and the *sano* Rona is that the senior section enjoys a higher status than the junior section. While the administration has classified the *boro* Rona as an 'Other Backward Class' (OBC) since 1950,[17] the *kuttia* Rona have always been classified as a Scheduled Tribe.

---

[11] Pfeffer 2000a, 162.

[12] See the critical analysis of the concept of Rajputisation in Orissa by Banerjee 1928, which has been discussed in a wider context by Sinha (1962). The myth of Rajputisation appears to have spread eastwards from Rajasthan. The idea has reached Orissa probably not before the eighteenth century (Berkemer 1993, 212f.). On the Rajput problem, see also Schnepel and Berkemer (2003, 15-16).

[13] The Rona stress that they should not be lumped together with other *paik* communities (Choudhury 1964).

[14] Berkemer 1993, 191.

[15] Donaldson 2001, 8.

[16] The word '*kuttia' in* general refers to houses made from mud and straw and has the denotion of 'hut'. It leads to the impression of remoteness (Niggemeyer 1964:11).

[17] The Rona were included in the list of hill tribes under the A.T.I.L.T. Act from 1931 to 1950 (Behuria 1964. Final report on the major settlements operations in Koraput district 1938-1964 (unpublished manuscript, courtesy of Bidiyut Takri). After the division of the Vishakapatnam Agency in 1936 the Rona in Andhra Pradesh retained their status as tribals and are still considered such. The *boro* Rona are known as 'Rena' and 'Rona', the *kuttia* Rona as '*sano* Rona' or '*kuttia* Rona'.

The Rona speak Desya[18] as their mother tongue. They observe an exogamous patrilineal and patrilocal kinship system and use clan categories to differentiate between agnates and affines. They have eight different clans: sun (*kora*), cobra (*hantal*), tiger (*killo*), monkey (*golori*), fish (*macho*), bear (*kimidi*), vulture or hawk (*pangi* or *gidh*) and cow (*goru*).[19] In contrast to other Desya communities, the Rona do not include their clan names in their personal names, but use instead titles like Pujari, Kotelel, Majhi, Patro, Tiltang, Alang or Pardani. They can intermarry with all other clans from their community except their own. The marriage pattern is one of symmetric exchange, and marriage with the *menaboini*, mother's brother's daughter (MBD) or father's sister's daughter (FZD), is of highest status ana is preferred.

I conducted my research among *boro* Rona of Lamtaput Block in Koraput district. The present article deals with their concepts of cosmic time. Since the *kuttia* Rona always refer to themselves as *kuttia* Rona and the *boro* Rona as Rona, I refer throughout the paper to the *boro* Rona as 'Rona'.

In the Rona community of Koraput district, women seem to be more susceptible to the inauspicious effects of an ill-timed ritual. When a woman or her family faces problems, people often give as the reason that one of her life-cycle rituals was carried out at an inauspicious time. From the Rona point of view, one could say that cosmic time and its correct use determine the 'good' and 'bad' moments in a woman's life. A woman who is going through a bad time in her life may say, 'My fortune [at this time] is bad' (*bhagyo korap*), and at good times may say, 'My fortune is good' (*bhagyo bholo*). Moreover, cosmic and cosmological time and life-cycle rituals are important markers of Rona personhood. By personhood I mean the set of roles that describes the relationships of a person to other members of his or her society. The paper contains three main hypotheses:

1. Cosmic time and the achievement of Rona personhood are closely interwoven.

---

[18] Desya is spoken within an area comprising the subdivisions of Koraput City, Jeypore, Nawarangpur and Malkangiri, in Koraput District. It differs to a great extent from the standard Oriya speech of the coastal districts of Orissa in a way that it is 'almost unintelligible to a new-comer' (Bell in Mahapatra 1964, 2)

[19] In one village my interview partners told me that there is one more clan name, 'dog" (*kukur*), and that the people of this clan have the name *kichei*. However, nobody knew where they could be found.

2. Personhood is created through life-cycle rituals, this process being essential for further alliances between the marriage classes of Rona society. If these rituals are performed at inauspicious times, this will have negative consequences for one's future in-laws.
3. Girls are ascribed Rona personhood through life-cycle rituals at an earlier age than boys, but social change, especially the constraints of the education system, allows the creation of Rona personhood for girls to be delayed up to the date of their biological maturity.

Concepts of Cosmic Time

Let us first examine the Rona concept of cosmic time. Certain gods and demons in the Rona pantheon are especially associated with time. Supernatural beings are located not only in space but also in time, the power of a god or goddess at his or her location or shrine being strongest at a particular moment. The influence of many gods and demons is set in time, since they exert their influence on human well-being at specific moments. Sometimes these influences overlap, as in a sacred geography. Thus, each month is ruled by a god or a demon; however, each day of the month is ruled by a certain goddess, and again at each time some moments are suitable for approaching the gods, while other moments are believed to be taken over by demons. As a consequence, some gods and goddesses are creators of human time, while other cause that time to be disturbed. These disturbances are often connected with illness. As I have shown elsewhere,[20] people believe that many illnesses cannot be treated or healed using modern medicines because the illness has been brought by a god or demon who needs to be satisfied in a ritual. Injections and pills are therefore useless.

The god of death, Jomraj (Yama), gives humans their individual spans of life. The goddess, who is most often referred to as Devi Maa, ensures women their fertility at the proper time. Other members of the Rona pantheon also have their preferred times. Shiva likes to incarnate himself in the local spirit mediums on a Monday, Durga on a Tuesday or Friday. Hundi, the village goddess, and the house goddess are worshipped on Mondays and Thursdays. Healing rituals to counter the influences of the celestial troublemakers Sani (Saturn)[21] and Rahu[22] are carried out on

[20] Otten 2006a.

[21] For the role of Sani in southeast India, see e.g. Knipe 1995.

Saturdays and Wednesdays respectively. Moreover, in their appearance as demons, Sani and Rahu are markers of the beginnings and ends of time periods, and can disturb human (life)-times: every day of the week has its special Sani, who brings a certain kind of fever. Rahu is present at twilight every day: his time is before sunrise and after sunset. Twilight is also the time for the souls of the deceased (*duma*) to visit their relatives who are still living as human beings in the villages, and sometimes these *duma* bring illnesses as well. In general, the twilight hours are always kept for rituals through which the community expels demona or *dumas*; they are never used for rituals that should evoke auspiciousness.

I shall now to illustrate how cosmic time influences the ways of life of girls and women, the name-giving ceremony and other life-cycle rituals, as well as serves to create Rona personhood. First we shall see how years, months and days are symbolically structured in Rona society.

Auspicious Times for Rituals

Each month in the Desya calendar stands for certain actions and events: some months are considered good for certain actions, others not. In the yearly cycle, four months are considered to have excellent qualities for rituals and a direct influence on the status of the person. These four months are considered auspicious for marriages (*nor biba*) and many other rituals, which are also called *biba.* In the Rona community, it is not only the union of two persons that is considered a marriage. Every life-cycle ritual, like birth rituals, pre-menstruation rituals, first menstruation ceremonies and death rituals, are considered marriages, not to mention many other rituals that count as *biba* as well. *Biba* or marriage is used to refer to any alliance that establishes a relationship, not only between different kinship groups, but also with specific gods and goddesses over generations. *Biba* must therefore be understood as an alliance with certain other groups in society. Life-cycle rituals establish a girl's status in her society and strengthen the bonds between marriage groups. These groups may be human affines, but they can also be gods. Every death ritual, for

[22] In Hindu astronomy Rahu is the ascending node of the moon (the point where the moon intersects the ecliptic in passing northwards), his counterpart Ketu the descending node. Rahu is also believed to be the cause of solar and lunar eclipses. Among the Rona, Rahu has another connotation: he is a demon, associated with the wind and causes many illnesses. Solar and lunar eclipses are not caused by Rahu, but by the stellar constellation *kand* (Oriya *kandha* sword, Desya arrow).

instance, is believed to be a marriage ritual with a group of gods, especially with the house of Yama, the god of death. The auspicious periods for *biba* rituals are the following four lunar months:

1. *Magh*, the lunar month from new moon in February to new moon in March. This month is the main month for every *biba* ritual. The weather is pleasant, the crops are brought into the houses, there is an abundance of vegetables for the feasts involved, and agricultural work is at a minimum.
2. *Baisak*, the lunar month from new moon in May to new moon in June. In this hot month before the rainy season, many *biba* rituals take place to prevent illness, for example when many marriages are planned (*bato biba*).[23]
3. *Bondapan*, the lunar month from new moon in August to new moon in September, falls in the rainy season and is also less appropriate for grand marriage feasts, but many rituals are carried out to prevent illness.
4. *Dialli*, the lunar month from new moon in November to new moon in December, is especially good for bringing the new bride to the house, but due to the heavy burden of harvest work it is often considered unsuitable for conducting a big marriage feast. The feast will be held in the month of *magh*.

The Rona use the lunar month in relation to solar days.[24] Besides the quality of the lunar month, the auspiciousness of the day has to be considered. Also, like the qualities of the months and days, there are the qualities of the lunar mansions (*nakṣatra*; *nakatra*) to be taken into account. The planetary gods are the rulers of the days in the calendar week, and each planet god governs one calendar day. In addition, each of the 28 wives of the moon god Chandra governs one day of the month. Only the astrologer (*disari*) has the right to announce auspicious and inauspicious times to the village community. For the announcement,

---

[23] A *bato biba* is a ritual carried out when someone has successfully fought off death. The reason is that the person is thought to have been close to the gods and goddesses and the house of dead. Through a *bato biba* ritual, the person who has recovered is established in the world of human society.

[24] The length of a lunar month (the time between two new moons) is 29.53 solar days. During that time, the moon travels through 28 lunar mansions (*nakatra*). The concept of lunar days (*tithi*) is only known to a few of the ritual specialists in the area, and is not used.

almanacs (*pañjī*) printed in Puri[25] and palm-leaf manuscripts (*yogni*) handed down from father to son are used. The character of every day is a mixture of the month it belongs to, of its place in the week's course and of the reigning wife of the moon god. Among the 28 wives of the moon god, some create an auspicious atmosphere for certain actions, while others are quarrelsome and inauspicious. In other words, any quality of time is established through the ruling gods and goddesses and the interference of the demons.

Auspicious times are always followed by inauspicious ones. If a marriage or any activity is going wrong, people believe that the activity was carried out when the auspicious time had passed (*sub bel phitigola*). For instance, the *nakatra* Rohini, which is considered perfect for marriage, is preceded by the *nakatra* Krittika, whose quality is to make the bride quarrel with her mother-in-law, and it is followed by the *nakatra* Mrigasiras, which will make people uncooperative and prone to dispute. However, as already noted, a day is not only governed by a certain *nakatra*, but also influenced by certain gods and demons. Thus Monday and Thursday are lucky days on which the village goddess is worshipped, while Wednesday and Saturday are good for rituals to appease the demons Rahu and Sani and get rid of them.

Days also have times that are regarded as especially auspicious for rituals and other actions. These auspicious moments in a day are, for example, the time before first light, when the first rooster crows, or when one's shadow reaches seven feet long. In the evening, these auspicious moments are when the cows return to the village, and when the colours of the day fade. Other auspicious times are when the lamps are lighted and around midnight. As demonstrated in this section, time has different qualities. A person is influenced, established and pervaded by the quality of time, which is in turn determined by the gods or demons, who are said to be the rulers of time and thus influence the auspiciousness of the moment. This relationship between moment and person starts at the time of one's birth.

---

[25] Almanacs from Puri and Jajpur are available in the local markets. On the difference between the two, see von Stietencron in this volume.

Time of Birth

The dark time of the new moon is a bad time for a person to be born, but so is the second day after full moon, because on that day thc 'arrow of the heavens' (*kand*) starts to eat the moon. Another bad time is at solar or lunar eclipses, which are also believed to be caused by the stellar constellation *kand* (Oriya *kandha* sword, Desya arrow). Pregnant women hope that their infants will not be born in the month of the arrow, *Caitra* (April/May), since this month has the quality of hunting, aggression, and inversion of the social order of Rona society. This month represents something like a reversal of the whole year. Children born in this month are said to be quarrelsome as adults. A son will bully his father or brother, while a girl is said to become destined for widowhood if shc marries. This idea is connected with the fact that, even nowadays, women who are born in *Caitra* cannot marry in the most prestigious manner.[26] We see that individuals are strongly influenced by the quality of time. In the following I shall describe in more detail how good and bad times in life are explained through the influences of cosmic time.

Coming back to the importance of the time of one's birth, let me now describe how the quality or substance of this time influences the timing of the ritual of the name-giving ceremony and shapes personhood among the Rona. In my examples, I shall concentrate on girls and women. For the sake of clarity, the following section is summarised on the accompanying figure.

---

[26] In Desya society, as elsewhere in India, people can marry in different ways. The most prestigious is the 'tying-the-*boi*-pot marriage' (*boi bandiba biba*). This marriage is an arranged marriage, preferably between cross cousins. It is carried out with many guests and implies a huge level of gift exchange and many ritual actions. Other common forms of marriage are the 'simple marriage' (*ubka biba*), an arranged marriage with fewer guests, ritual actions and gift exchange, and lastly 'marriage by elopement' (*udlia biba*), in which the bride and bridegroom elope and demand that they be married. This type of marriage is often performed in order to escape an arranged marriage with another person.

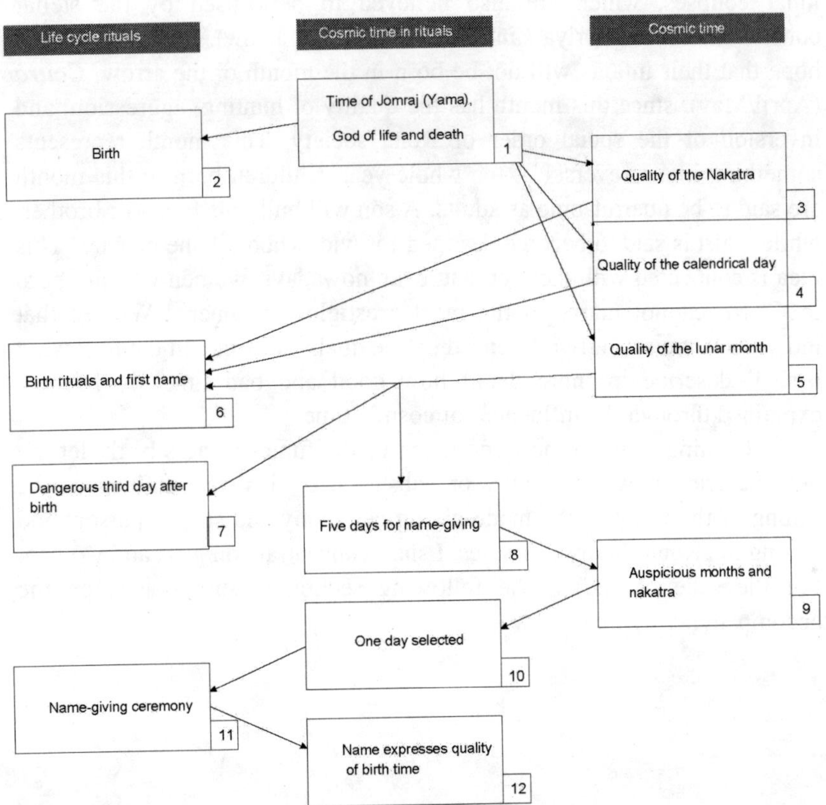
Life cycle rituals
Cosmic time in rituals
Cosmic time
Time of Jomraj (Yama), God of life and death
1
Birth
2
Quality of the Nakatra
3
Quality of the calendrical day
4
Quality of the lunar month
5
Birth rituals and first name
6
Dangerous third day after birth
7
Five days for name-giving
8
Auspicious months and nakatra
9
One day selected
10
Name-giving ceremony
11
Name expresses quality of birth time
12

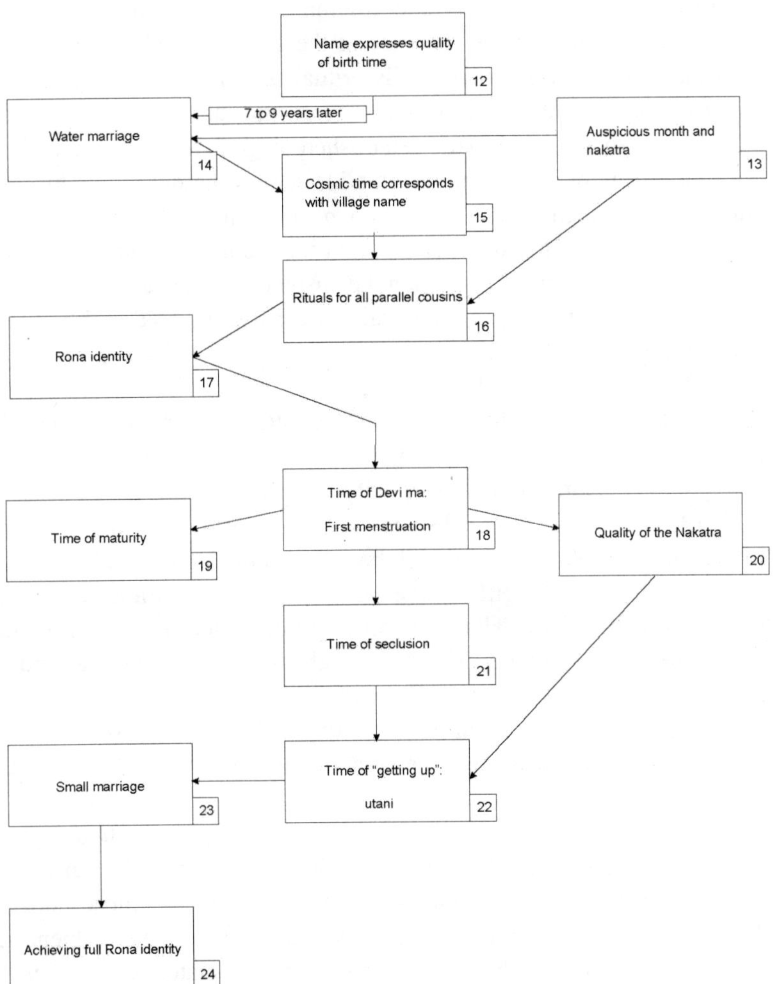
Name expresses quality of birth time
12
7 to 9 years later
Water marriage
14
Auspicious month and nakatra
13
Cosmic time corresponds with village name
15
Rituals for all parallel cousins
16
Rona identity
17
Time of Devi ma:
First menstruation
18
Time of maturity
19
Quality of the Nakatra
20
Time of seclusion
21
Time of "getting up":
utani
22
Small marriage
23
Achieving full Rona identity
24

The chart has three columns, with in the left column the life-cycle rituals undertaken by a Rona girl in order to enable her to achieve exclusive Rona status. The column on the right gives the respective cosmic times, while in the middle column the influence of cosmic time on the girl and her rituals is given. This middle column contains the points where the quality of cosmic time and the state of the girl's personhood cross. Here, with the help of the ritual specialist, ritual action is thought to provide a better quality of life. The proper time, fate and luck, which in Desya are called *bhagyo,* are individually established by gods for each person before the time of his or her birth, and this influences the quality of his or her entire life. Through ritual action *bhagyo* can be influenced in a good way when the ritual is carried out at the right time, but can be shifted on to the wrong side if it is carried out when the auspicious time has passed (*sub bel phiti gola*). Each section of the ritual process is numbered both in the text and the figure.

The god of death, Jomraj, is the ruler of the time of birth (**1**). He decides at what time he will push the little human being out of its mother's womb with his big thumb. As the creator of the life of a human being, he is responsible for the quality and length of life of the new-born child (**2**). The quality and substance of the moment of birth is influenced by the *nakatra* (**3**), the calendrical day (**4**), and the lunar month (**5**).

The name that a girl receives at the time of her birth is derived from the day of her birth (**6**). Her first name will be a modification of the name of that day. For example, Monday is called *Sombar* in Desya, and girls born on that day will be named 'Somari'.[27]

The position and quality of the day of birth in the week will have life-long consequences for the individual concerned. One of these consequences is that this calendrical day is considered auspicious for her. However, the most inauspicious day of the week comes just two days after this most auspicious day (**7**). Thus if the individual's day of birth was on a Monday, each Wednesday will be a day of danger. For those born on a Tuesday, the day of danger is Thursday, etc. All rituals are influenced by one's date of birth and the auspicious *nakatra* associated with it. This also becomes clear in the different birth rituals, like the first bath, and the

---

[27] The other names for girls are: For Tuesday Mangali; for Wednesday Budri; for Thursday Gouri or Gurubari; for Friday Sukri; For Saturday Sobei; and for Sunday Roilu.

offering or 'selling' of the child when it is handed over from the midwife to the mother in a ritual way.[28] Then the ritual of 'touching the cooking pot' will be performed in order to terminate the period of birth impurity. In this ritual, the child is brought as a guest into the house of his or her parents.

The next important ritual for establishing Rona personhood is the name-giving ceremony (**8**). The day of birth influences the date in the following way. The name-giving ceremony should take place in the second year. In this year, only five days are acceptable: one year, one month, and one day after birth (1/1/1), one year, five months, five days (1/5/5), and also at 1/7/7, 1/9/9 and 1/11/11. However, in the Rona world view it would be the greatest error to conduct the ceremony on the date 1/3/3, because of the danger of the third day (see above). Among the acceptable five days, there might be days governed by inauspicious *nakatras* (**9**), and these have thus to be ruled out. Additionally, some months or parts of them are considered unsuitable for rituals.

Taking all these obstacles into account, in most cases there is no choice of days at all. The sole suitable day (**10**) will be the day of the name-giving ceremony, and the girl receives a name that expresses the quality of that particular day (**11**). While the first name denotes the weekday on which the child was born, which in turn influences the date that is chosen for the name-giving ceremony, the second name is important for future rituals.

During this day of name-giving, a girl (and a boy, for that matter) is believed to alter her substance. From now on, she will partake in the quality of the day from which she has taken her name. This name is important for her future life-cycle rituals (**12**), through which the child achieves increasingly greater degrees of personhood. The name that is given is suggested in almanacs and is appropriate to the *nakatra* of the day. The next life-cycle ritual for boys is marriage. Girls undergo two additional life-cycle rituals before marriage, one before maturity, one

[28] The midwife puts the newborn child in a winnowing fan and offers the child to all women present. By doing this she asked every woman in a standardised formula: 'Look, what I have brought from the market (the child); you want it?' Every woman, except the mother, will answer: 'No it is too bitter, I will not take it.' A ritual selling of the child takes place, when the child is weak or siblings of the child have died before. The child will be sold to a status lower community and will be bought back on the same day. See also Skoda in this volume.

afterwards. The first ritual represents a 'water marriage' (*pani biba*, **13**).[29] The second ritual is performed after maturity and includes a *homa* sacrifice and a 'marriage' to a substitute groom, that is, to three branches of different fruit trees that are symbols of fertility.[30] This is called 'small marriage' (*chota biba*) or 'getting-up marriage' (*utani biba*, **22**).

The 'Water Marriage' (13-17)

Every seven to nine years, a village should perform a 'water marriage' for the pre-pubescent girls of the village. This cycle is fixed by the importance placed on girls undergoing this ritual before their first menstruation. Finding an auspicious day for the ritual is again a question of finding a suitable month and an auspicious *nakatra*. A 'water marriage' is performed in the months that are deemed suitable for marriages (**14**). Most of them will be performed in the month of *Magh*. There are seven suitable *nakatra*[31] for the ritual, of which Anuradha is considered the best. As an additional condition, the selected *nakatra* and village name should 'mix well' (**15**). After a suitable date has been found, a girl is selected for the water marriage. She then becomes the representative of her age group and of all the girls who are her parallel cousins in the village. Many of the following rituals will be carried out with her on behalf of the whole group (**16**). Two criteria are important in making the selection: (1) the name of the girl should match with the name of the village; and (2) her parents must have enough money (approximately 2000 to 5000 rupees) to pay for the 'marriage'. Among the eligible girls, one or two will be found whose names 'mix very well' with the village name and the *nakatra*.

The auspicious time for the ritual must be strictly observed. Early in the morning, the sacred water for the water marriage will be fetched from a pond. Pond water is considered 'pure' at this time because no daily activity has taken place there as yet. At the time when one's shadow has reached seven feet long, soil and bark from holy places within and around the village will be collected by women. Soil and bark are necessary to create a sacred space in front of the main house of the local lineage, which contains the shrine of the deity of that local lineage. Next, a canopy and a

---

[29] For more details of this ritual, see Otten 2006, 191ff. To my knowledge, there exists only one other description of a pre-puberty ritual in Middle India (Dube 1953).

[30] These are mango, jackfruit and banana.

[31] Rohini, Punarvasu, Utoro pha, Hosta, Swati, Anuradha and Dhanista.

pole consisting of three unripe branches of fruit trees will be erected in front of the house. Since this main pole represents the former bridegroom, it is erected by a male affine, in most cases someone in the category of elder sister's husband (eZH). However, if nobody suitable is found, a person in the category of mother's brother (MB) can perform this ceremony on behalf of his son.

The generation of the 'grandfathers' (FF and MF) is also involved in the ceremony. Many maternal grandfathers refer to the girls as their brides. In Rona society the alternating generations are considered identical, regardless of a person's age. Therefore ideally only two generations exist, the generation of the 'children' and that of the 'parents'. When a child grows up, marries and has children itself, its parents are equated with its children as their 'younger siblings or spouses'. The idea of alternating generation sets allows an equation to be made between the end and beginning of life and personhood: a person near to death will go to the house of Jomraj, the god of death, soon, however, being sent back to the Rona community to become a child again.

The 'water marriage' ritual continues with a *tika* ceremony. Every woman present gives *tika* (blessings and money) to each girl. Afterwards, at the time when the cows return to the village, the little girls are carried on the backs of their mother's brothers to the important households of the village. From time to time the crowd of cattle and the crowd of girls become mixed while roaming around the village.[32] Now the girls have achieved the status of an exclusive Rona personhood (**17**). The ritual water marriage should end before the time of Rahu starts, that is, before sunset.

Thanks to social change, however, especially the education system, some parents refuse to conduct a water marriage for their girls, meaning that the latter do not attain exclusive Rona personhood. Without this personhood, they are allowed to share food in boarding schools with students of other castes. Parents who intend to send their daughter to a boarding school will therefore not perform the water marriage for her.

The Small Marriage (18-24)

Three to ten years after the water marriage, the goddess determines the time of fertile years to the girls (**18**). She governs the biological time when

---

[32] The symbolism behind this image is that brides and calves are equated in marriage rituals (Otten 2006, 283).

they become mature (**19**) and therefore also the *nakatra* for conducting the maturity ritual (**20**).

When a girl discovers that she is having her first menstruation, she returns straight home, whether she is in the fields working or in a far-off boarding school. Once back home she sits in seclusion and experiences a period of ritual impurity (**21**).[33] An auspicious time must be chosen by the ritual specialist to break her seclusion, 'to make her to get up' (*utani*, **22**). This auspicious time is chosen according to the *nakatra* that governs the day when the 'getting up' should be performed (**20**). The maturity ritual must be performed seven, nine or eleven days after the girl achieves her maturity (**23**). A *utani biba*, also called 'small marriage' (*chota biba*), is held, involving feasting and the exchange of gifts, as in a marriage between two Rona (*nor biba*). During the days of seclusion the daughter's father goes to the villages of his relatives, namely his sisters who have married out to other villages and the relatives of his wife, and invites them. He will later marry his daughter into one of these villages. His sister's son or wife's brother's son, who are cross-cousins (*mena bhai*) to his daughter, will be her preferred marriage partners.

The observance of auspicious moments in the small marriage is similar to that in the water marriage. The women fetch sacred water, soil and bark according to the auspicious time. Then the sequence of rituals continues. All invited relatives and the older people of the village assemble at the temporary sacred space next to the house. From here they go to a brook suitable for the *homa* sacrifice, which is performed on a small makeshift altar and accompanied by the offering of five different coloured fowls and a billy goat. After the ritual at the brook, the people proceed to the house.

The rituals are performed according to the same structure as described for the water marriage. The relatives should start giving blessings and the gifts accompanying their good wishes at an auspicious time, which is often when the cattle return to the village. The ritual comes to an end before the time of Rahu, that is, before sunset. After the ceremony, the substitute groom is 'drowned' in a pond by the bride and her (unmarried) friends, but the marriage festivities continue into the night. The girl has completed one more step towards Rona personhood, one which boys do not undergo (**24**). She now wears now the sacred thread (*brata*) and is not allowed to take food outside of her own community.

---

[33] The role of ritual impurity and the control of female sexuality in coastal Orissa has been analysed by Tokita Tanabe 1999.

The correct performance of the small marriage is important because the girl's future in-laws may blame any illness she suffers later in her life, or even death in their house, on a previous ritual having been carried out at the wrong time.

Conclusion

Life-cycle rituals among the Rona create and represent personhood through ascribed social roles. These rituals are also carried out by other 'OBCs' (Other Backward Classes), like the Kamar (potter), Gauda (herdsman) and Mali (gardener). All these communities share the same culture, but even though they have the same life-cycle rituals, these rituals serve as markers for their exclusive group identity.

The different parts of the Rona world represent different kinds of existence and different ways of perceiving time in them. There are the great spheres of the cosmos, including the worlds of the gods and the dead, where change can be foreseen and time moves in predictable ways. The time of the cosmos of the planetary gods and stars, including the sun, moon and *nakatras*, repeats itself in certain rhythms, which are only disturbed by the intervention of the demons. But the main field of demonic interference is the world of the humans, where order and sudden change coexist. The central parts of the Rona world, like the villages and the fields, the passing of generations and the affinal ties between clans are closely linked with the cosmic order. Fate (*bhagyo*), that is, the specific life quality of the individual human being, personal relationships, affinal ties between local lineages and influences from 'outside', including the results of social change, are more uncertain and always threatened with failure. In this world of instability, cosmic time, which is determined by and calculated according to the solar and lunar calendars, is the marker of good and bad in the fate of the individual member of society. The good comes from good relations with the gods; the bad, like the interference of demons or unsatisfied gods, disturbs that order, and it is the task of the ritual specialists to determine at what moments in time the bad influences can be avoided or contained.

Whether now or or later, a crucial point in the life of a women is the period following her marriage. In fact, the water marriage and the *chota biba* that cosmic time is in favour of the woman at her time of marriage. A marriage is seen as bringing the goddess Lakshmi to the house. If the groom's household faces great problems after the marriage, like the death of the groom or his father, the woman is seen as having no good luck at all, which also effects her in-laws. Such a women is referred to as 'non-Laksmi' (*alaksani*), that is misfortune.

The life-cycle rituals of Rona girls are representations of such efforts to bring forth *bhagyo* by linking personhood and the good influences of the cosmic world. They allow the positive influences to predominate over the times of a person's life, from brief periods such as days to the entire lifetime.

Almost all actions in daily life and all rituals need auspicious times for their performance. In the Rona world-view, a life-cycle ritual carried out at an improper time is always a source of problems. Illness and sufferings are often explained with reference to a life-cycle ritual that was carried out after the auspicious time had passed. This misfortune can be seen in the context of personhood. The ill are often perceived as not being fully integrated into Rona society, but as suspended halfway between the worlds of the gods and the demons, a state in which they are particularly exposed to good and bad influences respectively.

Water marriage and small marriage both determine the achievement by a girl of full status as a Rona. Rona are proud of the fact that, just as Brahmans carry out life-cycle rituals for their sons, they do so for their daughters. Girls seem to be more susceptible to the laws of cosmic time: an inauspicious day of birth, the inappropriate timing of a ritual by the ritual specialist, a life-cycle ritual carried out in an improper way, or maturity achieved at an inauspicious calendrical date are said to cause misfortune in the future in-laws' house. Connected with the attaining of exclusive personhood is the responsibility to observe the rules of the society and to obey the laws of cosmological time.

References

Bailey, F.G. 1960. *Tribe, caste, and nation: a Study of Political Activity and Political Change in Highland Orissa*, Manchester: Manchester University Press.

Banerjee, R.D. 1928. 'Rajput Origins in Orissa', in *Modern Review* 43 (March), 285-99.

Behuria, N.C. 1964. *Final report on the major settlements operations in Koraput district 1938-1964*, unpublished manuscript, courtesy of Bidiyut Takri.

Berkemer, G. 1993. *Little Kingdoms in Kalinga: Ideologie, Legitimation und Politik Regionaler Eliten*, Stuttgart: Steiner.

Choudhury, B. 1964-5. 'Notes on the Ranas of Koraput', in *Adivasi*, 2, 51–6.

Donaldson, T.E. 2001. 'Jaina Art in Orissa', in *Ravenshaw Historical Journal* 2, 7-10.

Dube, S.C. 1953. 'Token Pre-Puberty Marriages in Middle India', in *Man* 53, 98-119.

Dumont, L. 1957. *Hierarchy and Marriage Alliance in South Indian Kinship*, London: Royal Anthropological Institute.

Evans-Pritchard, E.E. 1940. 'Time and Space', in idem. *The Nuer*, Oxford: Clarendon Press.

Friedman, B. 1982. 'Astrologers and Astrology in Bengal', in *Journal of Indian Folkloristics* 5, 12-21.

Geertz, C. 1966. *Person, Time, and Conduct in Bali: An Essay in Cultural Analysis*, New Haven: Yale University Press.

Gell, A. 1992. *The Anthropology of Time: Cultural Constructions of Temporal Maps and Images*, Oxford: Providence, Berg.

Gellner, E. 1958: 'Time and Theory in Social Anthropology', in *Mind* 67, 182-202.

Guha, S. 1999. *Environment and Ethnicity in India: 1200-1991,* Cambridge: Cambridge University Press.

Knipe, D. 1995. 'Softening the Cruelty of God: Folklore, Ritual and the Planet Sani (Saturn) in Southeast India', in D.D. Shulman (ed.), *Syllables of Sky: Studies in South Indian Civilization in Honour of Velcheru Narayana Rao*, Delhi, Bombay, Calcutta: Oxford University Press, 206-48.

Leach, E. 1966 [1961]. 'Two Essays Concerning the Symbolic Representation of Time', in Edmund R. Leach, *Rethinking Anthropology*, London: Athlone Press, 125-43.

Leutgeb, A. 2000. *Muhurta: Das indische Wissen um den Günstigen Augenblick*, Pune: Sanjay Godbole Oriental Research Foundation.

Mahapatra, K.N. 1961. 'Reckoning of Cha-turma-si-, Lunar and Solar Months and Different Eras in Orissa', in *Orissa Historical Research Journal 11*, 135-46.

Mahapatra, S. 1964. *Desia: A Tribal Oriya Dialect of Orissa*, Bhubaneshwar: Creation Printing Industries.

Niggemeyer, H. 1964. *Kuttia Kond: Dschungel Bauern in Orissa*, Munich: Renner.

Ohnuki-Tierney (ed.) 1990. *Culture Through Time: Anthropological Approaches*, Stanford: Stanford University Press.

Östor, A. 1993. *Vessels of Time: An Essay on Temporal Change and Social Transformation*, Delhi, London: Oxford University Press.

Otten, T. 2006. *Heilung durch Rituale: Vom Umgang mit Krankheit bei den Rona im Hochland Orissas, Indien*, Münster: LIT Verlag.

— 2006a. 'Given From God and Come In Its Own Will: The Hierarchy of Illness Causes among the Rona of Orissa', in G. Pfeffer (ed.), *Periphery and Centre,* Delhi: Manohar.

Pfeffer, G. 1982. *Status and Affinity in Middle India,* Wiesbaden: Steiner.

— 2000. 'Tribal ideas', in *Journal of Social Sciences* 4 (4), 331-46.

Pugh, J.F. 1984. 'Concepts of Person and Situation in North Indian Counseling: The Case of Astrology', in Daniel, Errol Valentine and Judy F. Pugh (eds.), *South Asian Systems of Healing*, Leiden: Brill. 85-105.

Ramadas, G. 1931. 'Vedullavalasa copper-plate grant of Vira Sri Viswambaradeva Maharaja', in *Journal of the Andhra Historical Research Society* 6, 8-15.

Schnepel, B. and G. Berkemer. 2003. 'History of the model', in G. Berkemer and M. Frenz (eds.), *Sharing Sovereignty: The Little Kingdom in South Asia*, Berlin: Klaus Schwarz, 11-20.

Sinha, R.R.P. 1980. *Tribal and non-Tribal Intelligence*, Delhi: Classical Publications.

Tokita-Tanabe, Y. 1999. 'Women and Tradition in India: Construction of Subjectivity and Control of Female Sexuality in the Ritual of First Menstruation', in M. Tananka and M. Tachikawa (eds.), *Living with Śakti: Gender, Sexuality and Religion in South Asia*, Senri Ethnological Studies 50, Osaka: National Museum of Ethnology, 193-220.

8

Children Sold and Thrown Away: Temporary Identifications in a Converging Tribal and Caste Society

Uwe Skoda

The title of this paper might lead one to think initially of child bonded labour and the tragic fate of children in the carpet-knotting industry[1] or elsewhere, or of children sold to be sacrificed as *meriah*.[2] However, in none of the cases of the symbolic selling or throwing away of children described here is any harm done to them. Quite the contrary: by selling them or throwing them away, their parents are hoping to improve the health of their children and to help them to survive.

The north-western part of Orissa, especially in the Sambalpur district, is an area with a mixed tribal and caste society. Historically in the second half of the nineteenth and first half of the twentieth centuries, peasant castes such as the Aghria, among whom I conducted field research (Skoda 2005), migrated into a predominantly tribal region, where they started to clear a large part of the forests, became revenue collectors for various little kings, managed to establish themselves as 'village kings', and were certainly effective in integrating the tribal population into emerging state structures.

The aim of this paper is to introduce and describe the so far apparently little-known practice of selling and throwing away children in the wider perspective of a converging tribal and caste society, in which inter-group[3] relations and hierarchical ranking are constituted by temporarily identifying children with other, lower communities.[4]

---

[1] Gupta and Voll 1999, 113.

[2] Padel 1995, 8-9.

[3] When speaking of groups I am not referring to substantial entities or fixed organizational units but rather to situational or contextual collective representations.

[4] As far as I know, the practice of throwing away children has been mentioned for only three tribal cases in the literature: by Grigson 1991 [1938] for the Gond, Roy 1999 [1928] for the Oraon of the neighbouring regions of Bastar and Chhotanagpur respectively, and Choudhury 1977 for the Munda.

Endangered children are deliberately made impure and a low status is intentionally ascribed to them, since this provides them with protection from life-threatening forces.
Identification – and children's identity by identification – can be understood here as a quality of becoming or of being 'the same as'.[5] However, identity and identifications are negotiated in categories of 'selling' and 'buying' or 'throwing away' and 'purifying'. Both are related to notions of time or to life phases as relatively more or less dangerous or socially more or less restricted, as well as to the notion of a person being 'ripe' or 'unripe'. The ethnographic cases of selling children and throwing them away presented here clearly show that identities and identifications may be multiple, changing or variant as well as hybrid, and that they are explicitly related to the social construction of both time and space. I argue that the children must be transferred, which necessarily involves movement in space from 'one's own' (household) to a space that the selling community usually considers polluted, restricted, or even forbidden (e.g. an 'untouchable' household). In order to deceive or misguide the God of Death or evil forces, such spaces or 'danger zones' are temporarily sought to protect endangered children. However, the transaction is limited to a certain period of time, namely prior to marriage. Before marriage, and before reaching a ripe and less endangered state within the life-cycle, the transaction must be reversed, and the now grown-up children are purified, formally reintegrated into, and re-identified with, their original community.

The Selling of Children

Before analysing this phenomenon, let me describe a few concrete cases of selling (*bikri* in Sambalpuri/*bikiba* in Oriya) that I came across, in which children were sold to communities of lower status.

The Selling of an Aghria Child to a Pathan Family

An Aghria man, now forty years of age, was sold at the age of one year to a Pathan widow living in his mother's natal village. The Aghria family already had three daughters. An elder brother, the firstborn son, had survived for only a few days after birth. The boy himself was rather weak in his early childhood and suffered from back pain. Under these

[5] See http://en.wikipedia.org/wiki/Identity (accessed 21/09/2004).

circumstances, the family became very worried about his condition. His maternal uncle (*mamu*) arranged for the boy to be sold to the Pathan family, to whom a rather low status is ascribed. The Aghria family hoped that the boy would then survive.

As the father of the sold remembered it, the selling itself was quite simple. The Pathan lady was invited to the boy's house. She put a copper coin, with a picture of Hanuman, around the young boy's neck. The father interpreted the image of Hanuman on the coin as a symbol of strength being transferred to the boy. A Brahmin was not required. The rather loose relationship between the selling and the buying families continued after the deal had been made. The boy remained in his original family, but occasionally visited the Pathan lady. The now grown-up informant argues that his parents might also have been afraid of the wrath (*abhisap*) of a saint who might have been treated badly, for which reason his elder brother might have died. He also remembers to have eaten in the home of the Pathan lady during these visits, though his father denies that. The boy received the nickname 'Pathan'.

Before his marriage the boy was bought back by his family, and the copper coin returned to the Pathan lady. The boy had to be purified in a ritual performed by a Brahmin, and a feast (*bhoji*) had to be given to the *jati* (the members of his caste in the village), formally re-admitting him into his caste (the Aghria).

The Selling of an Aghria Child to a Kisan Family

A young Aghria woman of about twenty-two was sold at the age of seven to a local Kisan *gunia* or traditional healing expert in her village, who had already been summoned frequently due to her continuous back pain. Her father's mother then suggested selling her to this Kisan family. At the time of her being sold, the *gunia* spoke a few *mantra*s and water was exchanged between the two families involved. After being sold, the girl was seen as a daughter of the *gunia* and later, after his death, as the daughter of his son.

She was bought back by her family immediately before her marriage four years ago. The Kisan family came with their own *jati* (caste members) and a Kisan priest to offer a coconut in a minor ritual. The Kisan then gave some coins (Rs. 5) to the Aghria, which was described as the delayed selling price on their part, since at the time of the sale no money had actually been handed over. They also offered a *sari* and a brass pot for the girl. Again, water was exchanged. Subsequently, her father (Aghria) paid Rs. 51 and offered clothes for the whole Kisan family in order to repurchase his daughter. The grown-up girl then sat in her father's lap as a sign of his parentage and his legal rights over her (she had also sat in the lap of her 'Kisan-father' when she was sold). Her father argued that the child should actually sit on a *purug* (a kind of cask for storing rice made of straw ropes, which may be filled with five bags of 75 kg each or 375 kg in total) filled with *dhan* (paddy), and should have a basket in her hand to collect gifts for herself. However, in her case the *purug* was replaced by a smaller basket, and she kept a metal plate in her hands, in which she collected more than Rs. 100 for herself.

As the Kisan family explained to me, they also demanded some items that had been used by the child, for example used clothes and dishes as a symbol of their parentage, things they still keep in their home. The Kisan also claimed that the girl's illness was not transferred to their family when the girl was bought, but was cured while she was living with them.

The selling of an Aghria Child to a Chamar Family

In this case an Aghria girl, now an old lady of about sixty-five, was sold at a very early age, between six months and one year. Her elder sister had died at the age of three, before she was born. She too was considered very weak and was often ill. Her parents were afraid that she would die as well. Subsequently she was sold to a Chamar family in the village of her *mamu*. There was a particular belief, she explained to me, why she was sold to Chamars. As leatherworkers, the Chamars used to put the leather on a line after tanning and then moisten it with water. The salty water dropping from the leather was collected in pots placed under the line. Anyone who took a bath in such a pot would be cured of all illnesses. The old Aghria lady was not sure whether she had taken such a bath or not, but said it was quite likely that she had.

After being sold she received a leather necklace from the Chamar family, which she wore until she was bought back. It was given to her when she was sold, and was seen as a mark of identification with the Chamars. She called the Chamars 'mother' and 'father', although she continued to live with her Aghria family. Later on she would visit the Chamar family occasionally and eat some light snacks (*murhi*) there, though not boiled rice, which is regarded as a potentially more polluting substance.[6] The old lady also said that she was treated by her family to some extent as not belonging to her original caste. For example, she was given less food at feasts (*bhoji*), though in contrast to ordinary, 'full' Chamars, she was allowed to enter the kitchen and use the same dishes at that time.

Many years later, immediately before her marriage as a child, she was bought back by her birth family. A *purug* filled with preboiled rice (*usna chaul*, not paddy) was prepared, and she was made to sit on top of it. Her 'Chamar-family' offered a *sari*, which she wore while sitting there. In exchange the Chamars demanded a new *sari*, a metal pot, a substantial amount of money (Rs. 5 as silver coins, 10 grams each at that time) and the filled *purug*.

The Selling of a Kisan Child to a Harijan Family

Last year a very weak Kisan child was sold to a Harijan (Ganda) family in the same village. The child's parents explained that it had been so weak that it had almost died. The child was sold for Re. 1 to the Harijan family, but immediately afterwards the Kisan family gave them two chickens, one black and one white, which they offered in their own home to *dharmadevta*, the Sun God, as a witness of the transfer.

According to the Kisan family, having been sold the child is considered a Harijan, if only temporarily. However, the child can take part in caste feasts and is distinguishable as a Harijan by the white thread (*suta*) which, after being soaked in some herbal medicine, was given to the child as a necklace by the Harijans at the time the child was bought. The white thread is a symbol of the Harijans as the traditional weaver community. The child was also given the nickname Ganda, the old caste name of the Harijans.

To have a 'Harijan child' in their family, the Kisan believe, excludes or at least reduces the negative effects of the evil eye (*najar*), evil spirits (*bhut*) and witches (*tandhei*). The Harijan purchaser, however, argues that it is the change of caste, particularly from higher to lower, that is helping the child to survive. He also adds that the Harijan's rather simple food (less oil, less spices, a lower quality of rice, etc.) helps the sold children – or from his perspective bought children – to become physically stronger and thus to have a better chance of survival. Usually

[6] For a discussion of different substances and their potentially defiling character, see Marriott 1968.

he takes the children – he has already bought around fifty, he said – to his house for one or two days after buying them and feeds them there. Unlike the Kisan, he did not see the evil eye as a cause of the children's illnesses.

The child has not yet been bought back, but the Harijan argues that the money he had given for it must be returned with interest. In addition the child will be made to sit on a *purug* filled with paddy, in his view containing roughly 40 kg. Then he will take off the white thread around the child's neck and extend the thread with some half-prepared threads (*mudha suta*), so that he can wind it around the child's body seven times. This is seen as freeing the child from the Harijan family, who will receive the paddy in the *purug* plus four coconuts, seven chickens, and money from the Kisan family, the chickens being used by the Harijans to feast their *jāti*. The whole procedure will take place in the presence of two members of each *jati* as witnesses. The Kisan must also provide a feast to their *jati* to reintegrate the child into it.

Empirical Situation

Including the four cases just described, I came across almost forty such cases in which children were temporarily identified with other communities (see Table 1).

Before analysing the pattern of exchange, a few remarks would be in order on social organization. According to the administrative classification, apart from a small number of Scheduled Caste households belonging to the Harijan or Chamar communities, the majority of the population belongs to the category of Scheduled Tribes (for example, Kandh, Gand, Munda, Kisan). Because of this very high figure, the whole of Kuchinda *tahsil* in the Sambalpur district has been declared part of a Scheduled Area. Thus, according to the government's classification, the Kuchinda region is numerically a tribal area.[7] However, as far as cultivatable land is concerned, a different picture emerges. Most of the land, particularly the high quality land, is owned by peasant communities such as the Aghria (or Chasa), who can be described as the 'dominant caste' of many villages in the sense of Pocock.[8] (For the hierarchy in terms of purity, see Table 2.)

---

[7] For a critical analysis of the terms tribe and caste, see Skoda 2005.

[8] By the term 'dominant caste', I do not associate that which is locally in the numerical majority, but, following Pocock 1972, 26, that which controls political

Another possibility is to sell children to certain semi-nomadic groups wandering through the area. I met two such groups during my stay, the Gugunadia and the Mahuntia. While the former are named after the bull Nandi symbolizing the God Śiva, the latter received their name because they ride on elephants (the person who rides being a mahant) representing the Goddess Lakṣmī. Both claim to be able to solve problems like barrenness and offer medicine for all kinds of problems. They state that they also purchase children from castes such as the Aghria, Gaud, Harijan, and Chamar. In the case of the Mahuntia, the children touch the elephant to receive the blessing of the Goddess. However, their own claims to high status, for example, their conviction that they are Gaud, are doubted by local people.

The Symbolic Acts of Selling and Buying Back: Motives for Selling

Despite variations in the four cases presented earlier, some general points can be made. First, common to them all is the fact that the child sold is considered weak or ill, suffering from various diseases and pains. In addition, older siblings have often died earlier. In any case the parents feel that the life of their child is in danger and hope to improve its chances of survival by selling it. However, the strategies pursued for its survival vary in details, with some believing in the healing capacity of the water used by the Chamars in the tanning process (case C), others in the white thread dipped in herbal medicine given by a Harijan (case D). In all cases the children are sold to families with healthy children.

Second, except in one Chamar case, to which I shall return later, all the children were transferred into another community. Apart from the Chamar, selling a child within ones own community is impossible. People claimed that it was the change of caste or tribe that was helping the child to survive. Some people speculated that selling children helped avoid or reduce the negative effects of the evil eye, evil spirits or witches (case D). However, in all cases the transaction and identification remained symbolic

---

and economical power, especially over landholding, and which usually occupies the ritual status below the Brahmins (priests) and which maintains reciprocal relations with a series of specialized service castes, both religious and secular. The members of a caste like the Patidar are certainly not not the dominant caste in all the villages of a region, and where they are, not all Patidar are necessarily landowners. In this regard, the notion of a 'dominant taste' is purely relative.

Selling group	Buying group	Number of cases (38)
Tihari (Brahmin)	Ghansia	1
Gaud	Munda	1
Gaud	Harijan (Dom)	1
Aghria	Kisan	1
Aghria	Munda	1
Aghria	Harijan	3
Aghria	Ghansia	4
Aghria	Chamar	2
Aghria	Pathan	1
Aghria	Gand	1
Aghria	Dhoba	1
Kandh	Mali	1
Kandh	Kisan	2
Kandh	Ludha	1
Kandh	Harijan	2
Kandh	Chamar	1
Gand	Harijan	2
Gand	Chamar	1
Kisan	Harijan	1
Kisan	Chamar	1
Munda	Gaud	1
Munda	Chamar	1
Khadia	Ghansia	1
Luhura	Gand	1
Harijan	Oram	1
Harijan	Luhura	1
Harijan	Chamar	1
Chamar	Luhura	1
Chamar	Chamar	1

Table 1: The selling of children: empirical examples*

* Since I conducted my research primarily among the Aghria, the figures for them are naturally higher. However, I verified my data among the other communities in the area and included their cases.

		Communities selling children														
	Caste	Tihari	Gaud	Aghria	Kandh	Gand	Chasa	Mali	Kisan	Munda	Luhura	Khadia	Oram	Harijan	Ghansia	Chamar
Communities purchasing children	Tihari															
	Gaud									1						
	Aghria															
	Kandh															
	Gand			1							1					
	Chasa															
	Mali				1											
	Kisan			1	2											
	Munda		1	1												
	Luhura													1*		1
	Khadia															
	Oram													1		
	Harijan		1	3	2	2			1							
	Ghansia	1		4								1				
	Chamar			2	1	1			1	1				1		1

Table 2: Simplified model of the local hierarchy and the transfer of children

* This Luhura lives together with a Gand and has been expelled from his community.

only, with all the children continuing to live with their original family after taking food in the house of those who had bought them.

Third, in many cases the children spent some time in the house of the family that had purchased them and, perhaps even more significantly, almost all the children who were sold ate in the home of their new 'family', even if it was only a symbolical act of offering rice in which the child did not eat a full meal. If we take into account the idea in Marriott's[9] transactional theory, according to which the person in South Asia is seen as a 'dividual' rather than an 'individual', his or her inherent quality being changed by the food ingested, then eating in another community, eating their food – not to mention food as such – transforms the person and obviously has repercussions on his or her own identity. In particular, the 'bodily substance-codes of [...] low castes are necessarily expected to become the most unselectively heterogeneous, their powers diluted and restricted, their temperaments gross and animal-like. As removers also of what the higher castes conceive as "pollution", the lowest among them are masters of negative transformations...'.[10] Since 'dividuals' are always 'composites of the substance-codes they take in',[11] identification with another group, the intended transformation and lowering of the child's status, is achieved to a large extent by sharing the same food, by eating *their* food, which in any other context would not even be touched. This corresponds to the argument put forward occasionally by informants that the less refined quality of the food eaten in these lower-status families helps the child become physically stronger. This argument relates to a cliché sometimes found in upper castes, according to which lower castes are physically stronger, and therefore hard manual labour or agricultural work is more suitable for them.

Fourth, the act of selling is indeed an 'economic' transaction in the sense that it involves a transfer of money. This means at least one coin is handed over to the family who is selling the child, even though the coin may only have a purely nominal value or is handed over at a later stage. Similarly, money is paid when the child is bought back, but usually this time a rather substantial amount compared to the initial selling. At the same time, the selling, and especially the repurchasing, is often

---

[9] Marriott 1976.

[10] Ibid., 128.

[11] Ibid., 111. Marriott (ibid., 109) further argued that 'what goes on *between* actors are the same connected processes of mixing and separation that go on *within* actors', and he stressed the divisibility of the person.

accompanied by a gift exchange (*sari*, paddy, etc.), for example, in many cases the now grown-up child sits on a *purug* of rice while being transferred back to his original group.

Fifth, although the act of selling is not necessarily accompanied by a ritual performance, it is noteworthy that in many cases the child's mother's brother plays a vital role in arranging the selling. Often the children are sold into his village. Although the selling does not require the presence of a priest, buying the child back does, and sometimes also the presence of *jati* members, usually from a different clan, as witnesses of the performance, in order to reintegrate the child back into his or her original group. For full re-identification a feast for the members of one's own caste is obligatory, indeed unavoidable if one wants to marry. Usually the reintegration is effected immediately before one's marriage.[12]

Sixth, in many cases the child is given the attributes of his new group when it is sold in order to be visibly identified with them and temporarily marked as 'other'. For example, a necklace made of leather is offered by the 'new Chamar parents', and the Harijans give a white thread as a necklace and symbol of the Harijans as traditional weavers.[13]

As far as I am aware, these attributes or amulets were given mainly by untouchable castes. Obviously these groups are essentialized, in particular by their occupation, and these differences are marked publicly, which, in the long run, has repercussions on the hierarchical order. Fewer attributes were given by groups classified as Scheduled Tribes, like the Kisan or Munda, when they purchased high-status children. Only a Gand, locally known as a healer or *Gunia*, purchased an Aghria child and offered a *daunria* or small amulet (a little copper box filled with herbs and roots

---

[12] Only in the case of the Khadia, I was told, is it necessary to have been bought back already to start the marriage negotiations.

[13] Choudhury (1977, 73) mentions that in similar circumstances a strip of goatskin is given to Munda children by the Lohar (blacksmiths) or Ghasi (untouchables). He notes: 'When the children of a couple die shortly after birth or if they have only girls and boys die after birth a strip of goat-skin … is tied around the neck of the next child on the sixth day of his/her birth. This is done by a Lohar or Ghasi man after making an offering of a white chicken to the Sing-bonga [supreme deity of the Munda, U.S.]. It is believed that it will protect the child from evil spirits and help him to grow into a normal healthy being. […] it is discarded at the time of marriage of the child. Marriage cannot take place without first ceremonial removing the skin. This ceremony is known as *chamargu*.' This may hint at a Chamar function in such rituals or the Lohar/Ghansi being equated with Chamar in them.

to be worn around the upper arm). However, in other cases the Chamar also gave some pieces of bullock's horn or some roots as a medicine to be worn around the neck. With regard to other situations in India,[14] one could also argue that groups of low or very ambivalent status often seem to be relatively closely linked to the divine sphere and are thus able to use their nearness to it for ritual healing.

Seventh, in addition to their material attributes, the children are usually given the name of the caste into which they are sold as nicknames, for example, they are known as 'Pathan', 'Ganda' (the old name for Harijans), or as 'Chamaren', that is, 'Chamar woman'.[15] Thus identification with the new group is not only expressed visibly by using amulets, but also linguistically. Generally a variety of names are used in different contexts: a name fixed in one's horoscope and used in rituals; a name used in official papers such as identity cards; first names used by close family members, etc. The nickname one receives after being sold is just one name among many others, though it is particularly used by others, friends or relatives. While it may be considered a serious insult in certain contexts to call someone who has not been sold a Chamar, these nicknames may be used to call or tease the person sold. And long after sold children have been bought back, these names continue to stick to them, are remembered, and might become a permanent part of a multiple identity, even though they were only intended as a temporary form of identification.

Hierarchy and Purity

Another common and important factor has yet to be discussed, namely, that children are mainly sold to, and thus identified with, low-status families or communities. Parents deliberately try to sell their children into a lower-status environment. Thus one obvious characteristic of the selling is the direction of the transfer. However, for a better understanding of what is involved here, the local hierarchy must be described in greater detail.

From my own observations regarding the acceptance of food, etc., as well as my discussions with informants, a model of a hierarchy in terms of

[14] I am referring here to the example of the Sidi documented by Basu 1994.

[15] The use of such nicknames is also known from the Desya context of Koraput, for example among the Gadaba, where names like Ghanzi or Dombru are common (G. Pfeffer/P. Berger/T. Otten, personal communication).

purity has emerged, which should not, however, be confused with considerations of rank within the context of kingship, in which the Aghria dominate as landowners. The local hierarchy can be presented quite simply, as in Table 2.[16]

In this table, communities are classified according to the relative purity of the selling group. Apart from the Brahmins, to whom the highest status is usually ascribed, the upper category includes communities from the Gaud up to the Gand, who are considered *bal lok* (good people) or *bada lok* (big people), in the sense that only they are served by the high-status Brahmins as well as barbers and washermen. This implies that such services are not offered exclusively to the Aghria as the dominant peasant caste (and so-called Other Backward Classes), but also to communities like the Gand or Kandh, who are traditionally considered tribal or so-called Scheduled Tribes, though here they display a high degree of Hinduization. Within this category, the highest position in terms of purity is unambiguously ascribed to the Gaud as former water carriers (Paenti) and herdsmen (Nariha). Another group in this category, the Kandh, take pride in the fact that they are the original settlers of the village, a claim apparently not disputed by other communities. The second clearly marked category consists of the so-called Untouchables (called *achhua* in contrast to all 'touchables' or *chhuati*). However, this category is not homogeneous but rather sharply stratified internally, with the Harijans considering the Chamars 'untouchable' for themselves. Between these two categories lies a third consisting of communities which are undoubtedly 'touchable', but nevertheless too low to be served by Brahmins, barbers, etc. Within this category, described as *choṭ lok* or small people, the Kisan, for example, certainly rank quite high, while the Oram and Khadia, both Christian communities, are said to rank lower.

Since apart from the Chamars children are never sold within one's own group, the corresponding fields in Table 2 are black. The selling communities are noted at the top of the table, the communities into which the children were sold being listed on the left. Thus, one can determine the direction of selling which, as already stated, is mainly to lower status groups, which generally appear below the diagonal line of black fields in

---

[16] Unlike in Table 1, I have left out the Pathan (or Muslims), who are very small in number in the region, but are usually considered as having an ambivalent status, with a tendency towards a rather low status. I also do not list the Ludha and Dhoba because I could not gather sufficient information regarding their status. They are not present in the villages I visited personally.

contrast to the very few cases of selling to groups that are higher in status, which appear above this diagonal line. Exceptions are the cases of selling within a status category, for example, by Aghria to Gand, but the different status categories just mentioned are separated by bold black lines. It is therefore clear that most higher-status communities or *bal lok* sell their children to lower-status communities, preferably to so called 'untouchables', among whom one finds the highest concentration of cases.

The material here is also significant in terms of the interactional or transactional theory put forward by Marriott,[17] as well as to earlier attributional theories of status, which had placed the emphasis on standards of behaviour, occupation, diet, marriage or remarriage, and the performance of rituals in order to determine status. Marriott stated a theory 'which holds that castes are ranked according to the structure of interaction among them'.[18] Two kinds of interaction were highlighted in particular: the giving and receiving of food of various categories, such as raw foodstuffs, food cooked in clarified butter, food cooked in water, etc.; and the giving and receiving of ritual services. Interactional ranking as a local concept placed the givers of food in a higher position than the takers, the order being inverted as far as service was concerned.[19] The theory holds good in the present case if one substitutes the giving of children to lower communities for their acceptance of food. However, the children are not just given but sold, and the accepting of money as an apparently neutral medium does not affect the ranking of the higher-status taker.

Turning again to the ethnographic examples in Table 2, it becomes clear that most children were sold by higher-status groups to lower-status ones. For instance, Aghria children were identified with 'untouchable' castes or lower-status tribal castes. In some cases, one can even discern a ladder-like effect to selling downwards, for example, Aghria or Kandh selling to Kisan and Kisan to Harijan, or Aghria selling to Munda and Munda to Chamar. The table also makes it clear that most children are sold to the lowest strata; indeed, the lower the status of a category, the more children are transferred to it. However, although people often talked freely about which children they had sold, they were less prepared to elaborate on those they had purchased from higher-status communities, thus avoiding an implicit acknowledgement of inferiority to those communities in terms of purity.

---

[17] Marriott 1959, 1968, 1976.

[18] Marriott 1959, 96. See also Marriott 1968, 145-6.

[19] Ibid., 142.

To sell children to groups of lower status also means deliberately making them impure (*asudha*); this is a central motif of this practice. Often this is related to the hope that having a rather impure member of a low-status caste or tribe in their own family will ward off the envy of other persons or evil forces in general. Usually the parents of a young child try to protect the child against the evil eye by performing several rituals, giving it protective amulets (*tawiz*) to wear or adding a black *ṭīka* on the child's forehead to make it deliberately ugly. The adoption of a low-status identity by selling the child seems to be another step in this direction. A Kandh, who was himself sold in his childhood to a Harijan, even argued that Yama, the God of Death, did not like to take low-status children, especially 'untouchable' children.

If relatively higher-status communities are able to identify their children with lower, impure communities by having them fed with relatively impure food or bringing them into contact with the defiling attributes of these lower communities, what about the lowest community, the Chamars? How can they sell their children, and to whom? As Table 2 shows, the Chamars provided the only case of a child being transferred within its own community, one being sold to his own mother's father. To put it slightly differently, the child was actually transferred to his mother's brother's house. It is possible to sell children within one's own community provided the buyer belongs to another clan and a senior generation: that is, the child must be sold to someone belonging at least to the father's generation. Thus the lowest group replicates functions from which it is excluded within its own community, as Moffatt[20] observed among other 'untouchable' communities.[21]

Exceptions

Selling in the opposite direction, to a community that is higher in status, is usually excluded. For example, one Kisan argued that he would not buy a child from an 'untouchable' caste. However, there are a few exceptional cases which do not conform to the hierarchical order, for example, an

---

[20] Moffatt 1979.

[21] In addition, the Chamars argued that they can sell children to other, so-called 'untouchable' communities, namely, the Pano (similar to the Harijans) and the Ghansia, although they are regarded higher in status. However, there was no such empirical case in the families among whom I enquired, and this might have been a way of their claiming a higher status.

Aghria child being sold to a Gand, that is, a sale within the same status category. Apart from searching for a family where children are not suffering from any disease, some parents prefer a local healer or *gunia* as a buyer and expect him to have a positive influence on the child or to have some knowledge of herbal medicine, etc. *Gunia* are often called in to get rid of the evil eye or of the disturbing influences of evil spirits (*bhūt*) whom they claim to be able to dominate. In one case a Gand *gunia* also agreed to purchase a Luhura child in the same village.

In another case, a Luhura decided to buy a Harijan child and explained that, from his perspective, the buying was a kind of aid in order to save the child. However, this Luhura lived together with a Gand and had already been expelled from his community. In the same Luhura family, but in a part not excluded from the community, a Chamar child was purchased. Their fellow caste members do not seem to have taken any action against the family, which, however, is the only Luhura family in the village. Other Luhura disagreed and argued that a *jati* feast would be obligatory if a Luhura did buy a Chamar child. Choudhury's observation[22] according to which Lohar blacksmiths or Ghasi tie a piece of goatskin around children's necks, underlines the rather low status of the Lohar, who are most likely identical to the Luhura.

The same notion of lending a helping hand was also suggested in the case of an Oram family who bought a Harijan child. Here the Oram emphasized that a kind of humanitarian aid was involved, the caste not being important. However, they also said that the child was given the nickname *bhiku*, derived from *bhikia* 'to beg'. Thus in this case the 'selling' was considered rather a kind of begging.

Often people argue that it is difficult to refuse a transfer if someone wishes to sell a sick child into a certain family. As a Kandh once explained to me, usually the Kandh sell their children to Kisan or Munda – as he had in the case of his son – though if, for example, a Kisan had offered to purchase his child, he would probably have sold it to him. No such case has happened yet. However, these are all theoretical considerations: in many cases people are not sure whether they could buy a child and what their *jati* would do in such a case.

---

[22] Choudhury 1977, 73.

The Buyer's Perspective

If accepting children also implies a lower hierarchical rank, what, then, are the motives for buying? On the one hand, it seems obvious that lower-status communities, which are often quite poor, gain materially from the transfer. The price for buying back is much higher than the price for purchasing in the first place. Apparently, by providing a temporary low-status identity for the child, the buying family acquires material wealth in the long run, that is, at the time of the repurchase by the birth family. Thus, the transactions or exchanges are financially beneficial to them. On the other hand, there is also the motif, already mentioned, of the lower-status family lending a helping hand to a family in need, and it would be difficult to refuse to help in such a situation. It is important to note here that the buyers are clearly not afraid of any negative influence affecting their own families, even if it is believed the child has attracted the evil eye, etc. Obviously no evil effects are being transferred with the child, at least not as long as one has paid a price for it.[23]

However, there is also the risk of the child dying before being bought back, and the *jati* of the lower-status group might demand an expensive feast as part of any funeral. An old Harijan who had purchased several children, some of whom had died, said that he had had to celebrate a funeral (*kam ghar*) in such cases. A *jati* had to be called on the third day to act as barber and washer-man. In such cases the Harijan must avoid oil for three days and must give a feast to his *jati* on the seventh day, the food for which – rice, vegetables, but no chicken – is usually provided by the child's natural parents. There is no consent if the child has to be bought back in the case of death, which seems to express a certain ambiguity in respect of the child's status in the sense that, although the child has been symbolically transferred, if it dies it usually does so in the house of the natural parents with whom it is still connected. While the Harijan, and also an Aghria whose child died before being bought back, argued that this is not necessary, some Chamars disagreed. In one case among the Chamars, after death a child had been bought back symbolically in the form of a puppet on a leaf plate. Its birth parents then paid some money to

[23] There might be a similarity here to the *meriah*, where the buying of a child frees the buyer from any negative influence or sin. As a priest argued before the sacrifice, 'we bought you with a price, and did not seize you, now we sacrifice you according to our custom, and no sin rests on us' (Russell cited in Padel 1995, 111).

the Chamar. Because it was bought back, there was no need for a feast among the Chamars. In any case it is likely that the natural parents must offer a feast to their caste members, as some Aghria did. However, the risks for the buying family seem to be rather limited compared to the financial benefits, since the selling family shares the costs of a feast, the buyers must offer to do so, or else they still repurchase the child, even after its death.

Throwing Away of Children and Other Symbolic Acts

Apart from selling, there are other symbolic forms of dealing with weak or endangered children. Compared to the practice of identifying them with lower-status groups, these ways offer an intra-group alternative which, although not as common as the selling of children, also involves the child being made impure deliberately.

Thrown Away

One such practice is to throw (*phingiba*) a child into the dust (*kechara*) or dustbin (*kechara daba* or *kechara gada*). As in the case of sold children, here the child – as in case of an Aghria girl I came across – is usually rather weak and has been suffering from various illnesses before the parents decide to act. By throwing away the child symbolically or by practically putting it into the dust, the parents are hoping that it will survive. The child is then known as *kechara*, with which it is thus linguistically identified.

Another very similar way of dealing with this situation is to throw a child into cow dung (*khat*). There are two places, usually in the garden, where cow dung and other biological waste is collected and where the child might be put, one known as *khat dhuda* (*khat* = cow dung; *dhuda* = rubbish hole, though rather in the sense of a heap of compost), the other place as *khat kur* (also 'heap of compost'). While in the first place biogas is occasionally produced nowadays using cow dung and other biological waste, in the latter location natural and sometimes even industrial waste, such as plastic bags, is collected. Although cow dung itself is considered pure, both places are regarded as impure and therefore as possible places in which to dump the child.[24] However, either is possible. Afterwards the child is usually given the nickname *kathu* if it is a male child or *kathi* if it

[24] The *khat kur* is regarded as more impure than the *khat dhudā*.

is female. In one case a child was placed on the *khat dhuda* first, but then sold to a Harijan family, thus showing that these forms are not mutually exclusive and might be combined if desired.

Slightly different is a third practice, in which a child is placed into the leftovers of a meal. Thus the child is sat on a plate containing some food remains or garbage (*aentha*) for a short while. As Marriott et al. observed,[25] garbage is regarded as being polluted 'by saliva flowing from the mouth of the eater', meaning that it should be handled by inferiors only. Accordingly, as an elder Aghria lady whose late husband was a case in point told me, this is done to make the child impure (*asudha*).[26] This man was also called by his nickname of *aentha* (leftover food). The impure child remains in this condition until his or her marriage. A ritual purification and a feast for the *jātis* is obligatory immediately before the wedding, as is also the case when the child is thrown away (in either form).

A conjunction of the first two methods described had apparently already been observed by Grigson[27] among the Bison-horn Maria Gond (Gand). He noted:

> I once witnessed an unusual naming ceremony. A son had been born after three elder brothers had died. It was considered that their deaths had been due to the hostility of some demon or of the familiar spirit of some magician, and on the medium's advice the baby had been suspended in a rough cradle over the rubbish-heap by the fence of the *bari* garden, and all the men present threw cow-dung and filth all round the cradle, shouting out '*Kacharu*' or 'Filth!', which name was given to the child in the hope that thereby the malignant power would be deceived into thinking that the parents set no value on the child.[28]

---

[25] Marriott 1968, 142.

[26] However, in none of these three practices is the child itself considered inauspicious (*asubha*).

[27] Grigson 1991 [1938], 270.

[28] Similarly, Roy (1999, 120) stated for the Oraon (Oram): 'The new-born babe of a woman who has lost one child after another, soon after birth, is [...] deposited on the manure-heap by one woman and taken up by another. This is believed to protect the child from the evil attentions of malignant spirits, for it [is] said, that evil spirits do not care for a babe thus thrown into a manure-pit as a useless refuse. Such a boy is named either as *Fekua* (cast-away) or as *Gundura* (belonging to cattle-dung) or as *Mali* (pertaining to manure), probably to deceive evil spirits.' Both authors mention the child being thrown into impure places and emphasize the deceiving of evil spirits as a main motif, but neither, known as

Given Away

Apart from selling children and throwing them away, there is – at least in some communities like the Aghria – another practice, of simply transferring them or giving them away within one's own community. This is known as *deba*, 'to give', and although not everyone considers it as effective as selling, it is practised occasionally. In one case among the Aghria, a mother, who had already lost two daughters, gave her son to her husband's elder brother's wife who had had three sons and three daughters, all of them strong and healthy. The mother believed that her son would stay alive and healthy if she gave him to her sister-in-law.[29] Most importantly here, the son was given to another family, because both families had already separated their property as well as the household. In another case an astrologer, after noting an inauspicious constellation of stars, recommended that a mother give away her son, who was in a weak condition at the time. Spontaneously the child's mother's brother's wife, who was present and who had no children of her own at that time, stated that she would take the child. Till today the mother's brother's wife is addressed as 'mother' by the child. A third case concerned a girl child who had suffered since her birth from nosebleeds and was generally weak; furthermore, her mother could not produce enough milk to feed her. It was decided in the family to give the daughter to her father's younger brother's wife, who had already had two healthy children. Again the family had already been divided. The girl was returned after six months, once her condition had stabilized. Since giving a child away within one's own community does not involve any impurity, no purification is needed before he or she is married.

---

keen observers of local cultures, observed any cases of the selling of children. However, Roy's example also shows that transferring the child is important, since it was placed on the dung heap by a different woman from the one who retrieved it.

[29] Her husband's elder brother's wife.

Selling Yourself to God: The Kṛṣṇa Guru Parties

Finally, another way of transferring children to others is to sell them to Kṛṣṇa, or rather to a so-called Kṛṣṇa Guru Party.[30] Such a party is held around a throne or *gaddi* of Kṛṣṇa, which anyone can set up in his house after being initiated by a Guru and can quite often be recognized by a picture of Krishna outside the house. Often the group brings together the members of different tribes and castes. The difference from the practices already described is the aspect of self-selling. The story of one particular Munda is exemplary here. While looking for work in another region, the Munda met a guru who read his palm and told him that he might die in an accident or be afflicted by other serious problems. A little later, he barely survived an accident and subsequently became a follower of the Kṛṣṇa Guru Party. In order to become a member, he sold himself in a kind of *dikhya* or initiation. Before undergoing the *dikhya*, he had to choose a guru (*guru kariba*). In this brief ritual, the devotee or *bhakt* provided a brass plate on which the guru placed his foot. The foot was then washed by the *bhakt*, who drank some drops of the water that had been used for the washing. Later the *bhakt* offered a cloth (*dhoti*) and money to the guru in order to sell himself (*mui biki hele*, I sold myself). This act, however, is also seen as *saran padiba* or as giving oneself to Lord Krishna, the *saran guru*, who is now directly responsible and holds the *bhakt*'s life explicitly in his hands.

The elder brother's daughter (*jiari*) of the same Munda was also given to Kṛṣṇa because an open wound on her leg refused to heal. Several doctors were consulted and different sorts of medicine applied, but only after she joined the Kṛṣṇa Guru Party did she recover. People disagree over whether children can sell themselves or only adults. Parents can offer their children to Krishna in this manner, but they must perform the necessary daily rituals themselves, because it is believed that children are not able to observe the ritual routine properly. However, this act of selling to a God seems to be irreversible. No impurity is involved. In any case the parents hope that under the influence of Kṛṣṇa the child will be cured and positively influenced, and not be taken away by Yama, the God of death.

---

[30] Apparently the English term 'party' has been incorporated into the local vernacular, in which it denotes a group of people meeting more or less regularly to worship Lord Krishna.

The Identification of Children: Transactions and Impurity

Contemporary society in the Sambalpur district, involving a convergence of tribe and caste, is held together not only by the common worship of Hinduized tribal deities[31] and by the continuing power structures of the former little kingdoms,[32] represented most notably by the still powerful landlords as described in the literature, but also by a rather subtle network of relationships established by, for instance, selling children. Apart from common rituals, from work as labourers in the fields of the landlords or from newly established schools, inter-group relations are created by the transfer of children. However temporary and legally incomplete these transfers and relations may be, they form an important sphere of interaction and mutual influence.

With respect to the whole picture of selling, throwing away, and giving away, there are two overlapping goals that people are striving to achieve through these transactions. First, the child is transferred into a family or house that has not been affected by any misfortunes, illnesses, or mishaps, particularly with regard to its children. Secondly, the child is made impure in the hope of diverting the evil eye, the attention of Yama, but also to grow stronger physically in a lower-caste environment. The practice of selling, which people regard as the most effective way of saving the children, obviously combines both aspects: the child is saved by being transferred into another, but impure setting. By being handed over to and identified with a lower-status family and becoming impure at the same time, the child is being given the best chance to survive.

	Child is transferred[33]	Child becomes impure
Giving away	X	
Throwing away		X
Selling	X	X

Table 3

[31] Eschmann 1994 [1975], 211ff; Sontheimer 1994, 117ff; Pasayat 1998, 103ff.

[32] Kulke 2001 [1993], 114ff; Schnepel 2001, 271ff.

[33] Here being transferred is mainly related to movement outside one's own family and home. However, placing a child on a compost heap, for example, also includes a certain spatial movement and element of transfer.

The deliberate polluting or defiling of children shows, as Marriott had already observed, that 'pollution is not dreaded as an absolute evil, instead it may be manipulated or even enjoyed'.[34] A state of self-induced impurity may be a *protected* state as well. Obviously here pollution is being sought deliberately, even though for a restricted purpose and a limited time frame. Furthermore, not only pollution prior to marriage, but also value is attached to the act of transfer itself.

It should be noted that the child's transfer to and identification with a lower and impure caste has no negative effect on the high-status giver, neither when selling the child nor when buying it back. The same is true in reverse: the low-status recipient of the child cannot improve his status by selling it back. The transaction does not affect the ranking of either the giver or the taker, presumably because it is a market-like transfer in the sense that selling or *bikri* is exactly what happens at a local market (*hat*). Although a market transaction is in itself conceived as permanent, it can always be reversed by another act of selling. Money can be accepted from anyone, and contrary to what Marriott suggests,[35] money does not actually seem to involve 'the slightest degree of subordination'. Rather, it seems to block the transfer of any substance-code. However, in line with Marriott's transactional theory showing 'rankings established by food transfers'[36] and the frequent avoidance of pollution in regard to food, here the child is not only sold first, it then eats in the taker's house in order to defile it deliberately.

The temporary identification of children establishes inter-group relations that reflect a local hierarchy, but at the same time also creates and reinforces the hierarchical structure of this mixed tribal and caste society. Through the Chamar giving amulets such as leather necklaces, the selling expresses a process of 'identifying differences'[37] as it essentializes differences between categories in public and thus hierarchically ordering them. Children are sold from groups of higher status – including higher

---

[34] Marriott 1968, 143.

[35] Ibid., 144.

[36] Ibid., 169-70. Marriott also emphasized the aspect of dominance rather than purity in ranking communities. Thus he suggested: 'Gaining dominance over others through feeding them or securing dependence on others through being fed by them appear to be comprehensive goals of actors in the system of transaction. Purity and pollution, among other values, are used as expressions of achievement towards these goals' (ibid., 169).

[37] Jeffrey 2000, 286.

tribal groups like the Gand or Kandh – to lower-status groups such as the Munda or Harijan, and usually not the other way round. Thus, the selling also shows that tribal groups are not always, and exclusively, integrated into lower strata of the hierarchy, as is sometimes assumed, but into higher levels too.

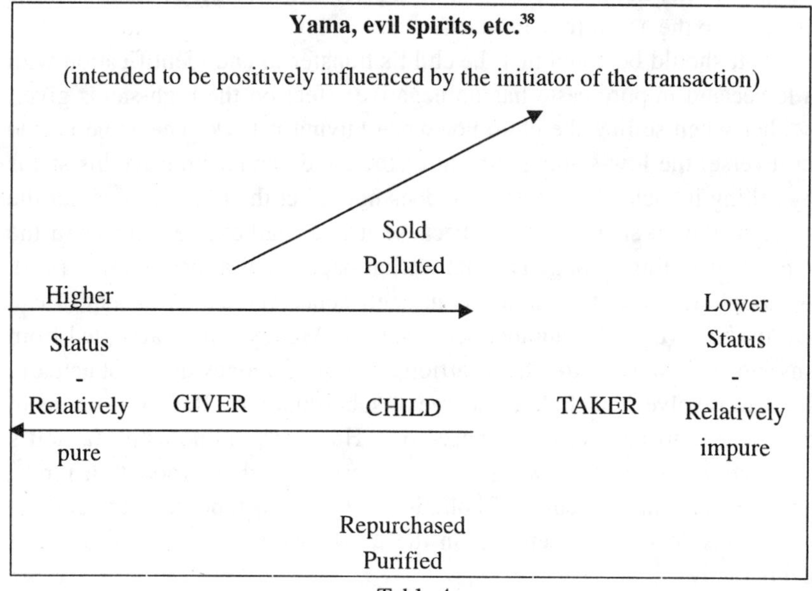

Table 4

Furthermore, the transactions described here are undertaken more or less explicitly with a third party in mind (see Table 4). Children are made impure or are transferred in order to deceive, distract the attention of, or even fool Yama, the God of Death, malignant spirits or anyone having an evil eye, etc. Obviously there is nothing wrong in trying to cheat evil spirits or Yama. This can also be seen with regard to the Brahmins, who are occasionally cheated too. In times of illness and need a family might offer Brahmins certain gifts known as *dan*, in which the hair or nail of a sick person, etc., might be hidden. In this way, the hope is that the disease or negative influence will be transferred to the Brahmin, who is also

[38] In the case of the Munda (Choudhury 1977, 73), it is not an evil spirit or Yama that has to be fooled, but rather Sing-bonga, the supreme deity, who is asked for protection. See also footnote 14.

aware of the potential 'poison in the gift'.[39] However, in the case of children there is a fixed time frame for the transaction and the deception. Every child, once grown up, must be bought back and purified before marriage. As regards the gods, one could also argue, as is widely believed, that at the time of marriage Lakṣmī, the Goddess of wealth and happiness, comes into one's house, in particular in the form of the bride, and is expected to help counter the evil forces that may be threatening the members of the family.[40] Thus, marriage is vital for the social construction of life phases and the notion of time in general (see Table 5).

Phases of life	
premarital (childhood)	postmarital (adulthood)
unripe (*apurnna*) person limited social personhood	ripe (*purnna*) person full social personhood
time of relatively increased danger	relatively safer, less endangered time
time of relatively limited social restrictions socially devalued time time of possible transfer / identification	socially more restricted time socially highly valued time re-identification obligatory to enter the phase

Table 5

The transfer of children is clearly embedded in the life-cycle; that is, prior to marriage a person is not considered to be a full – or mature – social person. An unmarried man or woman cannot become an ancestor, has not yet reached his or her maximum purity, and is excluded from certain rituals, which can be conducted only by husband and wife together. The identification of children – formally leaving one's own community, the marked difference and the loss of a relatively higher status – is thus an attempt to guarantee continuity within the life-cycle in order to share a collective identity as a full member of one's own group, in particular of one's own caste, at a later stage. Therefore, the intended loss of status and

[39] Raheja 1988.

[40] This idea originated in a discussion with Prof. D.K. Behera, and I am grateful to him for his inspiration.

the crossing of caste boundaries possibly occur only in, and are limited to, a relatively devalued, less restricted period of the life-cycle. To solve a life-threatening crisis at a later, much more regimented stage of life using the same means is impossible.

Children must be bought back and purified after being sold or thrown away in order to be reintegrated into their own group and in order to marry. On the one hand this might signify the persistent influence of the caste system in the region, in which the value of purity plays a crucial role.[41] On the other hand, it might be also a continuity of local, tribal concepts of ritual purity.[42] However, the selling, and even the temporary breach in commensality, does not endanger the separation of groups according to their relative purity, which is rather reinforced. While some boundaries, like group boundaries, may be crossed for a certain period, other perhaps more essential boundaries like marriage are maintained, meaning that the changed identity remains incomplete and mainly restricted to childhood. For women marriage initiates a new process of identification, in that the bride is integrated and henceforth identified with her husband's family and clan.

Children are sold to communities that are considered to be physically strong due to their diet. But they are also strong against transcendental dangers such as the evil eye. In being sold, the social status of children is lowered by placing them in an impure, yet transcendentally more protected or immune state. An exchange of transcendental protection, occasionally visualized by certain attributes, for material protection, resembles to some extent the relationship between a sister and a brother in rituals like *Rakhi Bandhan* or *Bhai Jiuntia*.[43] However, here a temporary low status is exchanged for material wealth. What seems to be absurd from a Western, 'economic' point of view is actually conceived as a way of dealing with evil forces and at the same time as a means of creating and reinforcing a local hierarchy and of integrating tribes into it. The temporary identity of children shows that status, like identity, is not permanently fixed, but rather continuously negotiated, and may even be voluntarily lowered for a certain period in order to acquire personal advantages within a collectively constructed framework.

---

[41] Dumont 1980 [1966].

[42] Pfeffer 2000, 342.

[43] During these two rituals, after fasting, sisters offer a thread to their brothers, which is tied around their right wrists. This is said to protect the brother, who in exchange offers gifts to his sister.

References

Basu, H. 1994. *Habshi-Sklaven, Sidi-Fakire: Muslimische Heiligenverehrung im westlichen Indien*, Berlin: Das Arabische Buch.

Choudhury, N.C. 1977. *Munda Social Structure*, Calcutta: KLM Private.

Dumont, L. 1980 [1966]. *Homo Hierarchicus: The Caste System and Its Implications*, Chicago: The University of Chicago Press.

Eschmann, A. 1994 [1975]. 'Sign and Icon: Symbolism in the Indian Folk Religion', in G.C. Tripathi and H. Kulke (eds.), *Religion and Society in Eastern India*, Delhi: Manohar, 211-33.

Grigson, W. 1991 [1938]. *The Maria Gonds of Bastar*, Delhi: Vanya Prakashan.

Gupta, M. and K. Voll (eds.). 1999. 'Child Labour in India: An Exemplary Case Study', in K. Voll (ed.), *Against Child Labour: Indian and International Dimensions and Strategies*, Delhi: Mosaic, 85-144.

Jeffrey P. 2000. 'Identifying Differences: Gender Politics and Religious Community in Rural Uttar Pradesh', in J. Leslie and M. McGee (eds.), *Invented Identities: The Interplay of Gender, Religion and Politics in India*, Oxford: Oxford University Press, 286-309.

Kulke, H. 2001. *Kings and Cults: State Formation and Legitimation in India and Southeast Asia*, Delhi: Manohar.

Marriott, M. 1959. 'Interactional and Attributional Theories of Caste Ranking', in *Man in India* 39, 92-107.

— 1968. 'Caste Ranking and Food Transactions: A Matrix Analysis', in M. Singer and B.S. Cohn (eds.), *Structure and Change in Indian Society*, Chicago: Aldine.

— 1976. 'Hindu Transactions: Diversity without Dualism', in B. Kapferer (ed.), *Transaction and Meaning*, Philadelphia: Institute for the Study of Human Issues, 109-42.

Moffatt, M. 1979. *An Untouchable Community in South India: Structure and Consensus*, Princeton: Princeton University Press.

Padel, F. 1995. *The Sacrifice of Human Being: British Rule and the Konds of Orissa*, Delhi: Oxford University Press.

Pasayat, C. 1998. *Tribe, Caste and Folk Culture*, Jaipur: Rawat.

Pfeffer, G. 2000. 'Tribal Ideas', in *Journal of Social Sciences* 4 (4), 331-46.

Pocock, D.F. 1957. 'Inclusion and Exclusion: A Process in the Caste System of Gujerat', in *Southwestern Journal of Anthropology* 13, 19-31.

Pocock, D.F. 1972. *Kanbi and Patidar*, Oxford: Clarendon Press.

Raheja, G.G. 1988. *The Poison in the Gift*, Chicago: The University of Chicago Press.

Roy, S.C. 1999 [1928]. *Oraon Religion and Customs*, Delhi: Gyan Publishing House.

Schnepel, B. 2001. 'Kings and Rebel Kings: Rituals of Incorporation and Dissent in South Asia', in B. Schnepel and H. Kulke (eds.), *Jagannath Revisited: Studying Society, Religion and the State in Orissa*, Delhi: Manohar, 271-95.

Skoda, U. 2005. *The Aghria: A Peasant Caste on a Tribal Frontier*, Delhi: Manohar.

Sontheimer, G.-D. 1994. 'The Vana and the Ksetra: The Tribal Background of Some Famous Cults', in G.C. Tripathi and H. Kulke (eds.), *Religion and Society in Eastern India*, Delhi: Manohar, 117-64.

9

Memory, Performance and the Regeneration of Society Among the Koya

Ulrich Demmer

Introduction

In many societies, performances like rituals and ceremonies constitute the privileged contexts for the generation and reconstruction of identities. This is particular so in times of crisis and suffering, where performances, as anthropologists since van Gennep[1] and Hertz[2] have argued, are conducted in order to regenerate social structures and to remind people of their key cultural values. Pioneering work in the field of social and cultural remembrance has shown that rituals are, in fact, primary modes of organizing what Assmann[3] has called 'cultural memory'. Among the various forms of ritual (like healing séances, initiation rituals and so on), it is especially death rituals that provide an arena for cultural memory and for the regeneration of identities.[4] This is because in many cultures death not only disrupts actual social relationships but is seen as a violation of proper moral and social norms and behaviour. In fact, in most societies death is seen as a volatile act which is traced back to the misbehaviour of either the deceased or of other living people in the community. The task of death rituals, then, is twofold. First, performers have to rebuild the damaged social ties between the dead person and the living, while secondly, they must also renew the moral orientation of the living through acts and performances of social memory. In this chapter, I explore how the Koya death ritual can be interpreted in this sense as a context for social memory and for the reconstruction of society.

---

[1] van Gennep 1909.

[2] Hertz 1960.

[3] Assmann 1992.

[4] Cf. Bloch and Parry 1982.

Ritual, Memory and the Construction of Identity

As Turner[5] and many other scholars have demonstrated, rituals often mediate social concepts, moral values and meaning systems, thus contributing vitally to the reconstruction of social and cultural identity when this is faced with crisis and conflict. This usually implies the performance of symbolic action as a means of representing meaning and cultural and social principles. Moreover, more recent research has shown that the reconstruction of identity in ritual also implies the use of social and cultural memory. In other words, rituals have a mnemonic dimension.[6] In the following, I would like to foreground two aspects of ritual memory, namely, the modalities of its construction and the objects of remembrance.

A closer examination of ritual processes shows the various ways in which memory and remembrance are constructed and generated. In some extreme cases meaningful action is reduced to a minimum, and ritual memory takes the form of what has been called 'flashbulb memory'.[7] According to Whitehouse, this is widespread in Melanesian initiation ceremonies, where cognitive and affective processes seem to *write* memories into the bodies and psyche of the novices. In most other rituals, however, memory is brought about by semiotic and/or verbal activities in which actors employ elaborate symbolic and meaningful action. Among the Ndembu in Africa,[8] for example, ritual actors experience symbols like the *mudyi* tree or an anthill, which evoke the remembrance of social principles like matrilineality or moral values like the respect for ancestors. Moreover, those modes of symbolic representation often entail poetic constructions, creative processes, and what Fernandez[9] has called the 'performance of images', which serve to predicate and remember collective as well as personal identities.

Other rituals, in contrast, are dominated by linguistic and verbal modes of social and cultural memory. Thus, performance studies,[10]

---

[5] Turner 1969.

[6] Cf. Assmann 1992 for cultures like early Egypt; Taylor 1989 for modern Western culture; Connerton 1989.

[7] Whitehouse 1996, 703.

[8] Turner 1969.

[9] Fernandez 1986, 20.

[10] Ibid. 1986.

research indebted to the 'ethnography of speaking',[11] and poetic approaches to ritual[12] all demonstrate how participants around the world use figurative language and poetic imagery that recall the core elements and meanings of their cultures and identities. Others have also pointed out the relevance of narratives or storytelling[13] in organizing the mnemonic process. Moreover, all these devices are often embedded in dialogue and discourse, especially in shamanic rituals.[14] Verbal means and artful language are used in these cases actively to reconstruct memories and to remind actors, as Roseman puts it, 'who they are and how the world works'.[15]

Ultimately, a good many performances combine both methods and constitute arenas in which symbolic action and verbal discourse are intertwined in the construction of memories and identities. In Jenu Kurumba death rituals,[16] for example, the community is remembered as a protective household, and its construction involves a series of meaningful ritual actions, as well as the dialogic, verbal reworking of past social relationships.

What is the object of ritual memory, and which aspects of identity are reconstructed? Memory in ritual is used for a range of issues that relate to the construction of identities. As Connerton[17] shows, public ceremonies often serve to memorize collectively the cultural and social norms of a culture. This also holds true for tribal societies, where, in rites of initiation, for example, basic cultural meanings and social values are transmitted. The practice of remembrance in a Chinese village conducted by Jing[18] demonstrates that states and nations also depend vitally on the public celebration of memories as a process that entails subtle strategies of legitimation and even of the manipulating of memories. Diaspora communities,[19] which perform rituals to keep their cultural roots and histories present in their consciousness, also have a particular incentive to construct their identity in time.

---

[11] Cf. Sherzer 1983; Kuipers 1990.

[12] Cf. Laderman and Roseman 1996.

[13] See Briggs 1988; Sherzer 1982.

[14] Demmer 2001.

[15] Roseman 1996, 259.

[16] See Demmer 1999, for a detailed description.

[17] Connerton 1989.

[18] Jing 1996.

[19] Cf. Basu 2000.

In other cases, the focus of ritual is not the memory of a cultural history and heritage, but the remembrance of personal affairs and social relationships. A well-studied instance is the practice of confession in the Catholic Church, where people reconstruct their personal and moral histories in dialogue with the priest.[20] In contrast, anthropologists have usually foregrounded the fact that the social relationships and structural principles of a community are made the focus of ritual memory. Turner,[21] for example, has shown how, in Ndembu performances, the principle of matrilineality, which is structurally in danger of being forgotten,' is represented symbolically in the form of a specific tree and thus made to be remembered in a virilocal society. Ritual memory, then, serves to regenerate the central moral values of this society through time. Performance studies also show that the values and structures of kinship play an important role in identity. The anthropology of India provides vivid examples. Thus Dumont[22] and Pfeffer[23] have investigated how, in death rituals, the relations between the segments and/or categories of a society are expressed by means of the exchange of gifts, services or symbolic representations. The social order is framed in these contexts as an exchange relationship between institutions and/or their representatives. The basis of this order is the system of kinship of the tribes and/or castes. In these performances, actions such as gifts or services have a symbolic, referential function because they represent the principles of the social order, for example, reciprocity between kinship segments. Thus the Gadaba[24] perform their specific self-understanding as a kinship-based community during the performative process of the death ritual, while the Jenu Kurumba of south India[25] also publicly enact the presentation of kinship-based values and morality in their death rituals.

In the following I shall analyse this latter aspect, namely, how the Koya perform, re-create and thus remember their kinship-based values through ritual action when death has put them into doubt and crisis. First, however, I shall briefly describe the basic ethnographic background.

---

[20] Cf. Hahn 1995.

[21] Turner 1969.

[22] Dumont 1986 [1957].

[23] Pfeffer 1991.

[24] Ibid.

[25] Cf. Demmer 1999.

Ethnography

The Koya, who are also known as Bison Horn Maria,[26] are settled in the southernmost part of Orissa in what is today the Malkangiri district. Large sections of this tribe also live in the eastern parts of the neighbouring region Bastar. The Koya I am referring to in the present chapter live in the southernmost part of Malkangiri district, in settlements close to Mottu village. As traditional slash-and-burn cultivators, they practise cultivation of, for example, rice and millet, but they also herd cattle and buffalo or work in the fields of neighbouring farmers.

Linguistically the language the Koya speak belongs to the Dravidian family of languages, which in Orissa involves tribal cultures like the Khond or Oraon and the many sections of the Gond.[27] However, the Koya communicate easily in other local languages, in particular Telugu. In fact, as Tyler[28] has shown, the Koya language itself is linguistically closer to Telugu than to any other language in the region, though undoubtedly a distinct language in its own right.

The Koya are organized in terms of what can be called a 'group model' of society. In contrast to the Jenu Kurumba of south India,[29] for example, the Koya represent their social organization as a clear-cut network of kinship-based groups. According to this model, their social organization consists of five exogamous phratries (*saga*), namely, *ko:vasi* (tortoise), *ma:ni* (goat), *so:di* (buffalo), *madkami* (tortoise) and *podiya:mi* (bird).[30] Each phratry in its turn consists of a number of partilineal clans (*katta*), with each phratry and clan having its own totem. Both units, phratries and clans, are exogamous, to the effect that all the phratries intermarry, marriage within the clan or phratry being prohibited.

While actual kinship on the personal level is certainly the dominant factor in the structuration of both domestic and local units, locality is no longer thoroughly structured by clan affiliation. Even in the times of the early ethnographer Grigson,[31] this was no longer the case.

---

[26] Cf. Grigson 1938; Elwin 1943.

[27] Tyler 1969, 1965.

[28] Tyler 1969.

[29] Demmer 2001a.

[30] Grigson (1938, 306ff.), who mentions the *kuhra:mi* (or *kadiari*) phratry instead of *podiya:mi*. My own inquiries found no evidence of the former.

[31] Grigson 1938.

The linkages between the segments are determined by the kinship system, which is of the Dravidian type, differentiating all kin people into two categories, namely those with whom one can have marriage ties and those with whom one cannot. The former category, what we call affinal relatives, is termed *akomama*.[32] The latter category, those with whom marriage is forbidden, are the *dadabhai*.[33]

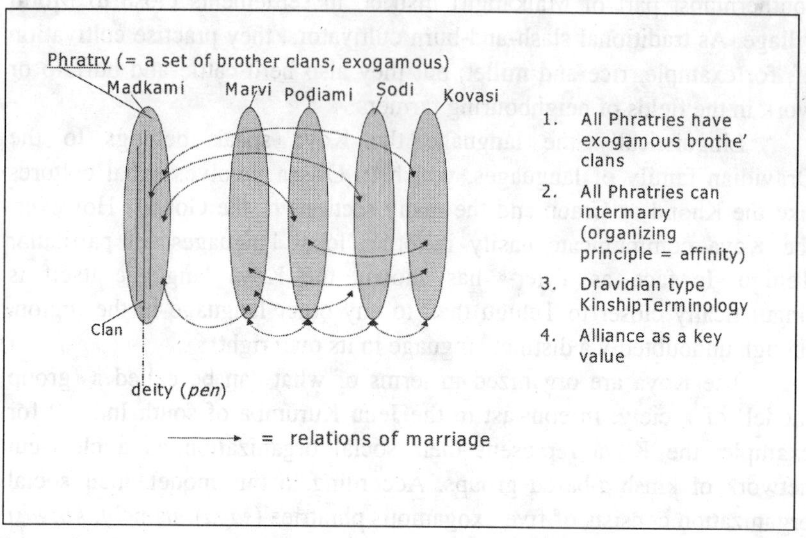

Fig. 1: Model of the Koya society. The clan names translate as follows: Madkami (tortoise), Mani (goat), Podiami (a bird), Sodi (buffalo), Kovasi (tortoise).

This classificatory system is employed on the clan level as well, so that ego has a number of *dadabhai* (fraternal) clans with whom he or she cannot intermarry and a number of *akomama* (affinal) clans with whom marriage is conducted. This conforms to an overall Middle Indian pattern where, as Pfeffer[34] has pointed out, relations through marriage are repeated in time and over generations in the same pattern. This pattern, namely, affinity, organizes the society as a whole and can be seen as a key social principle of these cultures.

---

[32] Cf. also Grigson 1938, 244-5.

[33] Ibid. 1938, 244-5. See Table 1 in the appendix to this chapter for a list of kinship terms.

[34] Pfeffer 1982.

This is also the case among the Koya, where the category of *akomama* (affinal) relatives plays a central role. Moreover, not only are the phratries seen as affinal categories because they are defined as *akomama* clans but, as the analysis in the present chapter shows, actual kinship relations, as well as social and ritual life are also based on affinity as a key value. However, these kinship-based social structures are not fixed per se but have to be renewed and maintained. It is in rituals like the death ritual where the meaning and significance of this principal value are reinforced and kept alive.

The same holds true for relationships between human beings, the departed (*hanal*) and the deities (*pen*), all of whom are seen as members of society. The latter has, in fact, an extended character. As among many other cultures in the world, here too the society is not confined to human beings but includes the dead and deities as well. Among the latter this means in particular the clan deities (*pen*) and the earth, which is worshipped as the village mother in every settlement. All of these deities, that is, the clan deities as well as the village mother, influence the well-being of the community and are worshipped in the course of the many rituals (*padum*) that are associated with the fertility of the soil, prosperity and agriculture. Moreover, people also communicate and talk with them in times of difficulty and suffering, for example, when they are ill. This 'divine discourse' is only practised in séances, where Koya shamans embody the deities and act as their mediums.

Like the deities, the dead too are regarded as important and active members of the society. In fact, they are really a part of everyday life. In every Koya hut a part of the storage room (*wijalon*) is set aside, where the 'pot of the departed' (*hanal kunda*) and the hearth of the departed are set up. Usually the dead are thought to live in the underworld, but in times of ceremonies and rituals they are thought to reside in the pot, in front of which they are offered food, drink and the smell of incense sticks. Moreover, in most of the *padum* that are associated with the prosperity of the land, the Koya also seek to maintain good relationships with the dead in order to secure fertility and well-being. The burning of bushes on the land can only be carried out with the help of the dead because a burning log from the hearth of the departed must be used to start the bush fire. But even in everyday life, the dead are recognized as active beings with whom good relationships must be secured, for example, when people pour a little of their drinks on to the floor 'for the *hanal*'. The first ritual, however, through which good relationships with the dead and ultimately a good society itself are established, is the death ritual itself.

The Death Ritual and the Performance of Identity

As mentioned in the introduction, in many societies death means not only sorrow, grief and loss, but also a severe break in time, a crisis of moral relations and of the social structure. It leads to a state of, as Turner[35] has called it, 'betwixt and between', often putting into question the central axioms and values of a society. Most often, and among the Koya too, death is understood as an event that puts in doubt the good relationships between the living and the person who has died. But the departed continue to live and act, though in a different state of being. Accordingly, to secure good future relationships with the dead, these must be re-established and they must be reintegrated into society, otherwise the well-being of the society and its very identity as a social body of security, solidarity and exchange is placed in danger. Thus the death ritual is performed in order to cope with this crisis of society.

A death ritual among the Koya proceeds in three different phases: the 'funeral ceremony', the 'stone-setting ceremony' (*kallu padum*), and what is called the 'ceremony of (bringing back) the dead person's soul' (*hanal jiva padum*). They all have two significant features. First, they involve the performance of manifold obligations, which in turn derive from the prominent role of kinship relations, most importantly the links that emerge from the system of affinity (and seniority). Secondly, they all involve certain dimensions of social memory and are carried out to cope with time and the unavoidable social crisis that it brings about, namely, the partition of social relations and the danger of forgetting their moral implications. Social memory is employed to remind the people, and in particular the deceased, of the ongoing relationships that, in fact, do not and should not die. Taken together, both aspects, social memory and the performance of affinity, serve, as it were, to bring about the 'regeneration of society'.

The Funeral Ceremony

Among the Koya, the deceased are cremated. When a man dies, one of his close affinal *akomama* (e.g. the son-in-law or brother-in-law) is sent for. On his arrival he climbs on top of the roof of the deceased's hut and beats a drum to announce the death of the person and call the other relatives of the deceased to come to the cremation ceremony. He also makes a small

---

[35] Turner 1969.

hole in the roof (or removes some of the tiles), so that the message of death can spread out of the hut in all directions.

At the same time, messengers are sent off to bid other relatives to join the ritual. When all have assembled, the body is taken out of the house and a first act of social memory is performed. The body is washed by close female relatives with different types of warm water and wrapped in white cloth. The wife and/or sisters of the deceased tie small bundles of leaves around the waist of the corpse and rub black soot on to the chest. Others, usually the granddaughters, tie a string or a piece of cloth round a finger of the dead person's hand.

All this is done, as people say, for the memory of the dead. The soul of the departed (*hanal jiva*) should remember where it came from and should keep its hut and family (*kutumb*) in good memory in order to help them in the future.

The ritual then continues with a number of performances that show the value of kinship relations. Thus, the body is carried by certain male relatives to the cremation ground.[36] The deceased's wife or sisters take cooked rice and *haldi* with them and offer them in front of the pyre, while a son and the brother-in-law throw rice in all directions. The body is then laid on the pyre and the fire is kindled. Again this is performed not only by the son but also by affines, thus underlining the value of that relationship. All the relatives then return to the deceased's hut for food. The deceased, however, is given its food and drink outside the settlement. The soul of the departed is troublesome and angry, people say, and for the time being it should not return to its hut.

The Stone-Setting Ceremony (*kallu padum*)

The second ritual phase is the so-called 'stone-setting ceremony' (*kallu padum*). Among the Koya, memorials are erected for everybody, men, women, and children. The site of memory is usually located opposite the funeral ground, a little outside the settlement. At the memorial site, all the local clans (including those of different phratries) erect memorial stones (*uraskal*). Sometimes, however, wooden pillars or simply a forked piece of wood can be used as a substitute for the stone or pillar.

---

[36] See Fig. 2.

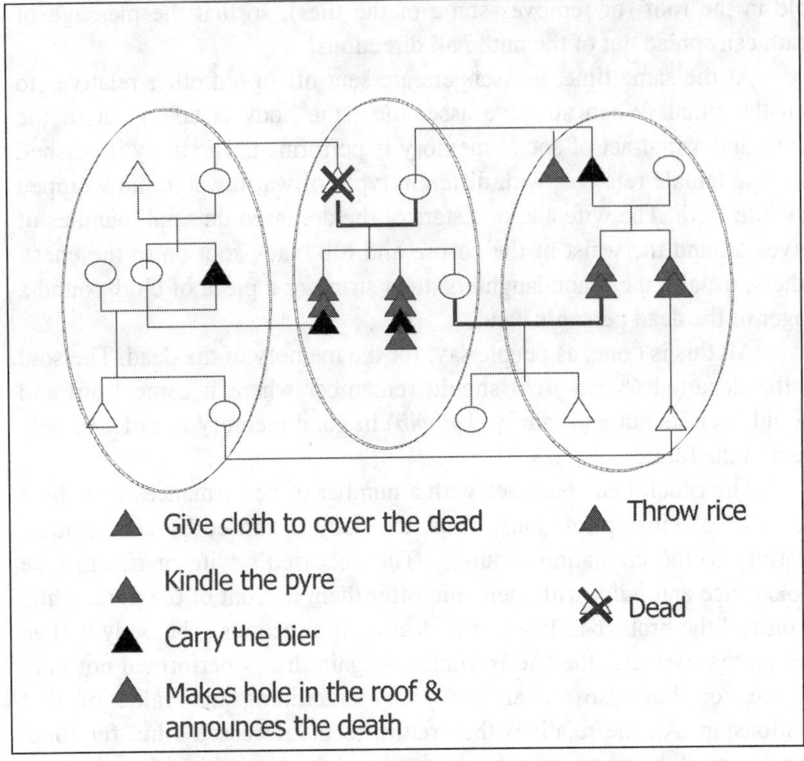

Fig. 2: Performances of relatives in the funeral. The figure shows the contributions of the actors according to their kinship relations to the dead.

As in the first phase, social memory and the performance of kinship ties are central to this ritual. In the first sequence the stone or pillar is brought to the site, and sometimes, people say, one of the important affines (*akomama)*, such as a sister's son (ZS) or daughter's husband (DH), actually sits on the stone or post. Affines also dig the hole for the pillar, while a son makes an offering of a chicken to the dead person's soul (*jiva*). It is again the affines who slaughter the buffalo or pig for the dead person and who erect the stone or wooden post. Then an affine, in our case the DH, performs another offering in front of the post, while the sons or brothers of the dead take the tail of the killed animal and hang it right on top of the post.

These performances of kinship ties are also accompanied by acts of social memory. This often implies the singing of what can be called memorial songs, that is, the good deeds of the departed are recounted in sung narratives. Moreover, the deceased's son reminds the departed of his or her home and former good relationships, asking the dead not to harm his or her people. To do this, he takes a piece of straw from the dead person's hut, throws it at the bottom of the stone(s), and addresses the dead as follows: 'You have built that hut; think of your wife and family and don't take anybody.'

Then all the participants throw rice and go to a nearby pool, waterhole or river to bathe and then walk to the dead person's hut, where they eat and drink. The drum is always beaten on the way by the son-in-law or other affines. The sons, brothers, etc., of the deceased present gifts to the drummers (being affines), most often a piece of cloth. From now on the soul or spirit of the dead (*hanal jiva*) is said to reside near to the memorial stone.

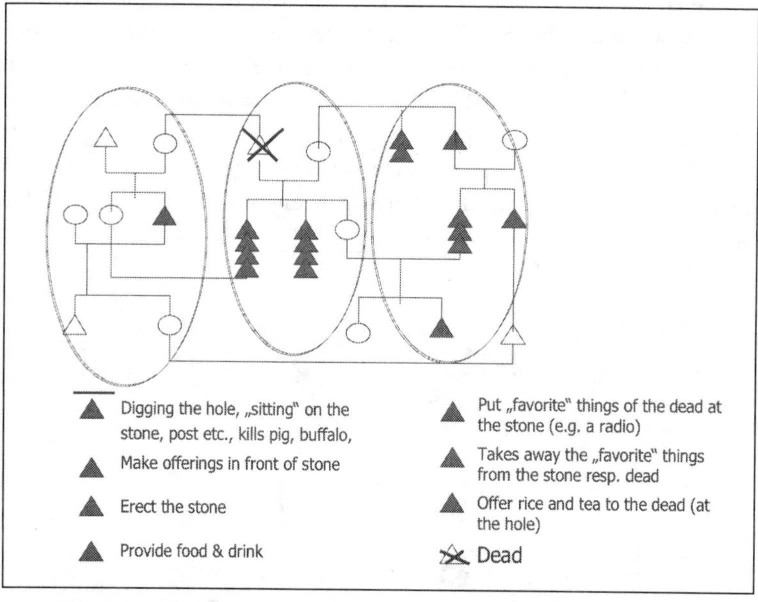

Fig. 3 Performances of relatives in the 'stone setting ceremony'. The figure shows the contributions of the actors according to their kinship relations to the dead.

Bringing Back the Dead Person's Soul (*hanal jiva*)

The final phase consists of 'bringing back the dead person's soul.' As in the earlier phases, both categories of relative, *akomama* and *dadabhai*, are needed to achieve this. After these have assembled at the dead person's hut, they walk ceremoniously to a nearby river or water pool, taking with them a small earthenware pot and a ring. At the water they perform a *puja* and fill the pot with water, and then the close relatives step into the water. They cry, lament, and invite the dead person's soul to join them. Simultaneously they try to catch some living creature from out of the water, a fish, frog, crab or something even smaller, like a worm. When someone catches something, this is understood as the arrival of the dead. Then they put the captured animal along with the ring into the small water-filled pot, and from now on the dead is said to be inside the water in the pot.

Then one of the affines (*akomama*) rubs some oil on the pot, and finally a girl (a daughter or daughter-in-law of the deceased) carries the pot to the clan god's shrine (*penu, hanal-kot*), where an *akomama* relative (ZS, WB, DH) sacrifices two chicken, one for the affines and one for the dead person's family (S,D,W, F,B,Z), before the pot, with its water, ring and living creature, is poured on the ground. Finally, the ring is tied to a tree close to the clan god's shrine and an *akomama* relative sprinkles water to, as one informant put it, 'clean' the place. Finally they celebrate a small feast at the clan god's shrine. In this way, it is said, the deceased reaches his or her home after having been out in the forest, hills, and rocks.

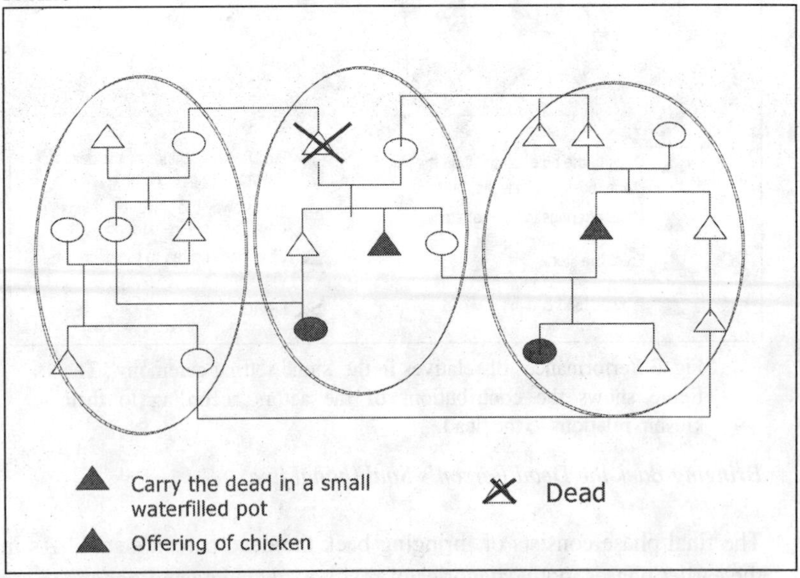

Carry the dead in a small waterfilled pot

Offering of chicken

Dead

Fig. 4 Performances of relatives in the last phase of the death ritual. The figure shows the contributions of the actors according to their kinship relations to the dead.

Conclusion

In conclusion, we can identify the following as the outcomes of these performances. Apart from dividing people, death gives rise to the anger of the deceased and thus puts social relationships into crisis. Yet, the participants overcome this state of 'betwixt and between' and remind themselves, including the dead, of their 'good' relationships and of how a society should work or what it should look like. Memory plays a central role in this process.

However, while in some cultures 'flashbulb memory'[37] evokes only a dim and transient image of the past, memory in the Koya death ritual is constructed highly elaborately and is performed through symbolic actions and verbal activities. Moreover, it is explicitly the social memory that is at issue here, since both personal social relationships and collective social principles are made the focus of ritual remembrance.

With respect to the former, the Koya remind the dead of his home and his responsibilities to his close family. Social memory thus helps re-establish peaceful and collaborative relations with the dead. At the same time, social memory is also employed on the second, collective level. As the above analysis makes clear, the ritual actors perform a series of symbolic actions affirming their relationships as a kinship-based society. At the heart of this are the performances of the *akomama*, who actively present affinal ties as a bond of solidarity and support.

In the first sequence, it is an *akomama* (e.g. the son-in-law or brother-in-law) who announces the death by beating a drum and calling people together for the funeral. Affines also play a central part in the funeral itself in placing the body on the pyre and kindling the fire. In the second sequence, affines dig the hole for the memorial stone, slaughter the animals, and make a number of offerings. In the final performances, too, affines enact important roles by rubbing *haldi* and oil on to the pot and making offerings to the deceased at the clan god's shrine. These findings also correspond to the spectrum of tribal societies in Middle India as a whole, where, as Pfeffer,[38] for example, has shown, affinity is one of the key values, which is equally reinforced in ritual. Among the Koya, this is accompanied by verbal memories of the dead and their relationships with their living relatives. In sum, then, central social relationships, in particular affinal ties, are renewed in the death ritual. Social memory and

---

[37] See above note 7.

[38] Pfeffer 1982

the performance of kinship relations contribute to the overall outcome of the ritual, that is, to the regeneration of society.

Appendix

Parallel Relatives	Cross Relatives (Affines)
da:da:l (father's father) [FF], emma (father's mother) [FM]	ta:ta:l (mother's father) [MF], ka:ko (mother's mother) [MM]
tappe (father, father's brother; F, FB), evva (father's brother's wife, mother, mother's sister; FBW, M, MZ)	ma :ma :l (mother's brother, father's sister's husband, wife's father, husband's mother) [MB, FZH, WF, HF] po:ye (father's sister, mother's brother's wife, wife's mother, husband's mother) [FZ, MBW, WM, HM]
enna (elder brother, father's elder brother's sister) [B, FBeS], ekka (elder sister, father's brother's elder daughter) [eZ, FBeD]. tammundu (younger brother, father's brother's younger son) [yB, FByS], e:la:di (younger sister, father's brother's younger sister) [yZ, FByD]	ba:ta:l (father's sister's elder son, mother's brother's elder son, elder sister's husband) [FZeS, MBeS, eZH], enge (father's sister's elder daughter, mother's brother's elder daughter, elder brohter's wife) [FZeD, MBeD, eBW] erundu (father's siter's younger son, mother's brother's younger son, younger sister's husband; FZyS, MByS, yZH), e:nda (mother's brother's younger daughter, father's sister's younger daughter, younger brother's wife) [MByD, FZyD, yBW]
marri (son, brother's son) [S, BS], maya:di (daughter, brother's daughter) [D, BD]	a:ne (sister's husband, daughter's husband) [ZS, DH], kodiya (sister's daughter, son's wife) [ZD, SW]

Table 1: The kinship terms of the Koya. These are all classificatory terms that can refer not only to the genealogical relatives but to a category of relatives. The anthropological transciptions are given in square brackets. Cf. Pfeffer 1991.

References

Assmann, J. 1992. *Das Kulturelle Gedächtnis: Schrift, Erinnerung und politische Identität in frühen Hochkulturen*, München: Beck.

Basu, H. 2000. 'Theatre of Memory: Ritual Kinship Performances of the African Diaspora in Pakistan', in A. Rao and M. Böck (eds.), *Culture, Creation, Procreation in South Asia*, Oxford: Berghahn, 123-45.

Briggs, Ch. 1988. 'Introduction', in C. Briggs (ed.), *Narrative Resources for the Creation and Mediation of Conflict, Anthropological Linguistics* 30 (3-4), 271-7.

Bloch, M. and J. Parry (eds.) 1982. *Death and the Regeneration of Life*, Cambridge: Cambridge University Press.

Connerton, P. 1989. *How Societies Remember*, Cambridge: Cambridge University Press.

Demmer, U. 1999. 'How to make the Spirit of the Dead Happy: The Rhetoric of Words and Deeds in a Jēnu Kuṟumba Death Ritual', in E. Schömbucher and C.P. Zoller (eds.), *Ways of Dying: Death and its Meaning in South Asia*, Delhi: Manohar, 68-87.

— 2001. 'Always an Argument: Persuasive Tools in Jēnu Kuṟumba Death Rituals', in *Anthropos 96*, 475-90.

— 2001a. 'The Social Structure of the Jēnu Kuṟumba', in G. Pfeffer and D. Behera (eds.), *Contemporary Society, Tribal Studies,* Vol. 4, New Delhi: Concept Publishers Co., 230-65.

Dumont, L. 1986 [1957]. *A South Indian Subcaste: Social Organization and Religion of the Pramalai Kallar*, Delhi: Oxford University Press.

Elwin, V. 1943. *Maria Murder and Suicide*, Bombay: Oxford University Press.

Fernandez, J. 1986. *Persuasions and Performances: The Play of Tropes in Culture*, Bloomington: Indiana University Press.

van Gennep, A. 1909. *Le Rites de Passage*, Paris: Editions A. and J. Picard.

Grigson, W.V. 1938. *The Maria Gonds of Bastar*, London: Oxford University Press.

Hahn, A. 1995. 'Identität und Biographie', in M. Wohlrab-Sahr (ed.), *Biographie und Religion: zwischen Ritual und Selbstsuche*, Frankfurt/M., New York: Campus, 125-55.

Hertz, R. 1960. *Death and The Right Hand*, Aberdeen: Cohen & West (first published in French in 1907).

Jing, J. 1996. *The Temple of Memories: History, Power, and Morality in a Chinese Village*, Stanford: Stanford University Press.

Kuipers, J. 1990. *Power in Performance: The Creation of Textual Authority in Weyewa Ritual Speech*, Philadelphia: University of Philadelphia Press.

Laderman, C. and M. Roseman (eds.) 1996. *The Performance of Healing*, New York, London: Routledge.

Pfeffer, G. 1982. *Status and Affinity in Middle India*, Wiesbaden: Steiner.

— 1991. 'Der intra-agnatische 'Seelentausch' der Gadaba beim großem Lineageritual', in M. Laubscher (ed.), *Beiträge zur Ethnologie von Zentral- und Südindien*, München: Anacon, 85-106.

Roseman, M. 1996. 'Pure Products Go Crazy: Rainforest Healing in a Nation-State', in C. Laderman and M. Roseman (eds.), *The Performance of Healing*, New York, London: Routledge, 233–71.

Sherzer, J. 1982. 'The Interplay of Structure and Function in Kuna Narrative, Or: How to Grab a Snake in the Darien', in D. Tannen (ed.), *Analyzing Discourse: Text and Talk, Georgetown University Roundtable Talk on Language and Linguistics 1981*, Washington DC: Georgetown University Press, 124-46.

— 1983. *Kuna Ways of Speaking*, Austin: University of Texas Press.

Taylor, C. 1989. *Sources of the Self: The Making of the Modern Identity*, Cambridge, Mass: Harvard University Press.

Turner, V. 1969. *The Ritual Process: Structure and Anti-Structure, Ithaca*, New York: Cornell University Press.

Tyler, S.A. 1965. 'Koya Language Morphology and Patterns of Kinship Behavior', in *American Anthropologist 67*, 1428-40.

— 1969. Koya: An Outline Grammar, Berkeley, Los Angeles: University of California Press.

Whitehouse, H. 1996. 'Rites of Terror: Emotion, Metaphor and Memory in Melanesian Initiation Cults', in *Journal of the Royal Anthropological Institute* (n.s.) *2 (4)*, 703-15.

10

Maṇikeśvarī and Ḍokrī: Changing Representations of Two Tribal Goddesses and the Dynastic Histories of Orissa

Cornelia Mallebrein

Introduction

The goddesses Maṇikeśvarī[1] (lady of the jewels) and Ḍokrī[2] (old lady) are worshipped in large parts of Orissa, especially in its western and southern regions, namely in the districts of Kalahandi, Gajapati, Raygada and Ganjam, as well as in Bastar (Chhattisgarh), which borders Orissa.[3] It is striking that although both goddesses are extensively worshipped in Orissa, astonishingly little is known about them within academic discourses, only Maṇikeśvarī receiving a modicum of scholarly attention.[4] This is surprising, as Maṇikeśvarī is considered the family goddess (*iṣṭadevī*) of well-known royal families such as the Kimedi family (Parlakimedi, Badakimedi and Sanakimedi) and the royal family of Kalahandi, along with quite a number of *zamindari* families that are linked with them. Furthermore, she is worshipped by the royal family of Jagdalpur in Bastar (Chhattisgarh) as the older sister of their family goddess Danteśvarī.

---

[1] The word Maṇikeśvarī (Māṇika-iśvarī) has been translated in different ways as 'Lady of Ruby' (Mishra 1992, 37), 'Goddess of the Gem Stone' (Singh Deo 1991, 1) and 'Golden Goddess' (Fischer, Pathy 1996, 33). One Kondh informant explained *maṇik* as 'red soil' in the Kui language, a type of soil characteristic of Kondh areas. Thus Māṇika Devī is a goddess of the soil and hence of fertility, being closely connected with the Kondh concept of the earth goddess Dhārnī and with Jakeri penu, e.g. in the Kui language.

[2] The name Ḍokrī is translated as 'old woman'.

[3] The present paper forms one part of a wider study on Hinduized tribal deities at royal courts of Orissa, which is supported by the German Research Council (DFG) within the Orissa Research Programme. I would like to thank the DFG for making this research possible. I am grateful to Mr Dillip Sethi (M.A.) for his assistance during my fieldwork in Orissa.

[4] Cf. Singh Deo 1991; Mishra 1992; Schnepel 2002.

It is one aim of this paper to present and discuss a range of varied opinions and statements about Maṇikeśvarī and Ḍokrī and their places of origin, as well as of the different legends referring to their relationship with the various royal families of Orissa who worship them as their tutelary deities.

The present study is based on data collected through fieldwork at the places concerned and oral traditions, as well as on information, legends and myths taken from published sources. The various aspects of the goddesses are presented descriptively.

Both goddesses originate in a tribal milieu, mainly in the environment of the Kondh tribes.[5] Their gradual transformation from tribal goddesses of the earth and fertility to Maṇikeśvarī/Kālī and Dakṣiṇakālī, which took place under Brahminical influence mostly in the nineteenth century, is a striking example of how tribal deities are assimilated into the fold of the Hinduism. In this paper, I shall concentrate on the worship of Maṇikeśvarī and Ḍokrī in Kalahandi district and the adjacent regions of Bastar and South Orissa. In Kalahandi district the main focus will be on their worship in the tribal villages of Jugsaipatna and Merkul, as well as in the former *zamindaris* of Thuamul-Rampur, Jaypatna/Talgud and Madanpur-Rampur, and in Bhawanipatna, the capital of the former Kalahandi State.

In the first part I shall examine the iconography of Maṇikeśvarī and Ḍokrī, its development and gradual change, which is closely linked with the growing importance of these two goddesses as the tutelary deities of royal families, who financed the construction of the major temples to Ḍokrī and Maṇikeśvarī. It will be shown how the fame that Ḍokrī/Dakṣiṇeśvarī and Maṇikeśvarī acquired over large parts of Orissa resulted from a theological shift from tribally based goddesses to the powerful goddess Kālī, which took place in the nineteenth century under Brahminical influence. However, both goddesses have retained their identity as tribal deities, as is evident from their general depiction as just a trunk for a body, with no hands, legs or head, and as closely related to Buḍhā Rāja and Jenā, their male companions, who also have tribal roots.

---

[5] Numerically, the Kondh are the largest group among the 62 tribes of Orissa, with a population of around one million, most of whom live in the Baudh-Kondhmal, Kalahandi, Rayagada, and Bolangir regions (Singh 1994, 590-8; Boal 1982, 1999; Niggemeyer 1964; R. Nayak et al. 1990, 1999 and P.K. Nayak 1989).

Their autochthonous forms of worship and iconography are still maintained at the tribal and village levels.

The second part discusses the various legends and historical records concerning Maṇikeśvarī and Ḍokrī, which differ from region to region. Each royal family preserves its own story of its encounter with the goddesses. Besides a few inscriptions discovered in Bastar (Chhattisgarh district) which mention a goddess Māṇikya[6] most of the available information is based on oral records, which are rarely historically accurate and often refer historical events back to a legendary past. However, analysis of the various ideas about the goddesses further reveals that narratives which are located in a distant past do actually reflect historical events, mostly of a political nature, which are embedded in mythical narratives that attempt to legitimize certain political claims linked to these goddesses.

While I shall therefore discuss various ideas about these goddesses from different sources, thanks to their heterogeneous character no final conclusion about their historical development can be offered, and even their places of origin are unclear. Maṇikeśvarī and Ḍokrī present themselves in manifold forms, not any one definite form. This also has consequences for scholarly discussion concerning the possibility of a relationship between the Nāgavaṁśī goddess Maṇikeśvarī in Bastar and the tutelary goddess Maṇikeśvarī of the Nāgavaṁśī royal family of Kalahandi. As will be seen later, this discussion remains unsolved due to a lack of reliable historical facts.

The Transformation and Change of Tribal Deities

In the present day, the process of change by modernizing rituals and cults and incorporating tribal deities into the fold of codified Hinduism has reached a so far unknown dynamic level in Orissa. This change has also had a great impact on the temples and shrines of Maṇikeśvarī and Ḍokrī. Therefore I shall start with a general consideration of certain aspects of Hinduization.[7] In western Orissa and in the adjoining southern districts,

---

[6] Cf. Hira Lal 1907-8; 1932.

[7] In this paper, the term 'Hinduization' is used in the sense of A. Eschmann 1978a, 82: 'Hinduization may be defined as a continuum operating in both ways between the two poles of tribal religion and codified or "High" Hinduism ... the process of Hinduization acts in both ways ... tribal elements are incorporated into Hinduism, but also implies that features from Hinduism are integrated into tribal

where the worship of Maṇikeśvarī and Ḍokrī is attested, various tribal religious ideas merge with Hindu, that is, Brahminical as well as tantric concepts. This fusion has characterized the culture of this region from ancient times.[8] The religious pluralism of this region manifests itself in various festivals, some of which are often celebrated only locally[9] in specific music traditions,[10] and various dance forms, which have their roots in the tribal context. The rich architectural heritage manifests itself in a great variety of temples and shrines[11] that are devoted to local but also to pan-Indian deities.

Traditional autochthonous forms of worship are still maintained in these once thickly forested regions, which are still inhabited today by various tribal communities. The deities are represented by a simple stone under a tree or within an open mud shrine (*gudi*), their home often being an anthill outside or within these *gudi*s.[12] Male as well as female deities are often represented by a simple sword.[13] All these various forms of worship exist side by side with colourful modern temples in either the Cuttack or Andhra styles.[14] The countless gods and goddesses of the vast Hindu pantheon assemble, all of them peacefully united, within these

---

cults.' Eschmann published several articles on this topic (e.g. 1978a, b and 1994). On the process of Hinduization, see, among others, Urhahn 1985, 38-65; Kulke 1978a, 1992, 1993b; Schnepel 1993, 2002; Pasayat 1997, 1998; Mallebrein 1999.

[8] For further information, see Basa and Mohanty (eds.) 2000.

[9] Cf. Patnaik 1982 on the Sulia and Sikerpat festivals in Bolangir, cf. Mallebrein 2004a, 143-53.

[10] Cf. Guzy (forthcoming).

[11] Cf. Donaldson 1985-7, Dehejia 1979.

[12] The anthill represents the mother earth, her body. But it is also considered a mountain. The anthill/mountain is compared to the womb of mother earth and represents fertility and stability, as well as the entrance to the underworld, cf. König 1984, 85-8.

[13] The sword contains the energy (*śakti*) of the deity and represents her power. In many village shrines, like in the Buḍhārāja shrine at Banbir in Nuapada district (N 19°45'5", E 83°11'40"), the deities Buḍhārāja, Durgā and Pāṭkhaṇḍā are represented by several swords offered by devotees. Deities also speak to their devotees through the sword.

[14] In the year 2003/4 the small mud shrine of the goddess Pendrānimātā at Umarkot (N 19°39'55" E 82°11'58"), Nawrangpur district, was modernized into a huge colourful temple complex. The temple trust commissioned architects and craftsmen from Andhra Pradesh to carry out the work.

modern temples.[15] In the process of modernizing local shrines and temples, the temple compound is extended by new shrines to other deities.[16] As a result of this process, the original simple cult image is also given a new shape, with a splendid aureole of shining, golden brass now surrounding it. The stone image is wrapped in costly dresses and ornaments, and decorated with silver eyes. To mark its divine power and energy a protruding silver tongue is attached to it.[17] Often a new sculpture showing the deity as a Hindu goddess is placed beside the original image. Representations of Durgāmahiṣāsuramardinī, or Durgā riding a tiger, are popular. In the course of this process, a Brahmin priest may take over the whole worship or parts of it from the former tribal priest. One result of this is that animal sacrifice is shifted from the inner part of the temple compound to the periphery.[18] A further step involves replacing animal sacrifice with vegetarian offerings, since the goddess is now considered as having been pacified. This change in the cult and the ritual also has consequences for ritual specialists like the medium (Sirhā, Kalisi, Dehuri, etc.) who represents a deity while being in a state of trance. As 'living gods on earth' they are the mouthpiece of the divine and thus a channel of communication between man and god. In this role they are considered to be the direct recipients of the blood sacrifices, but the abolition of these at temples has made their role redundant.[19] By incorporating the local deity into a new, Brahminical form of temple cult and worship, a Sanskrit name is added to her former autochthonous designation, giving her now two

[15] As a result of the increasing number of temple constructions, a new imagery of gods has been developed, documentation and analysis of which forms one part of the research project on Orissa being carried out at the University of Tübingen under the guidance of Prof. H. von Stietencron.

[16] At the side of the former tribal goddess Barāḷā Ṭhākuraṇī at Balasgumpha near Phulbani (N 20°25'48" E 84°19'0") a shrine for Śiva was constructed, and recently a new temple for goddess Lakṣmī, financed by the business people of Phulbani. For more information on Barāḷā Ṭhākuraṇī, cf. Eschmann 1978a, 95.

[17] The protruding tongue is a characteristic feature of many goddesses with a tribal background. Although they are part a temple cult, they still retain certain distinctive marks. On Samaleśvarī/Samaleī, see Pasayat 1998, 140-3.

[18] Since the construction of the new temple of Markamā in Bissamcuttack 2003 (N 19°30'9" E 83°30'36"), the trustees have adopted plans to shift the animal sacrifice from the inner temple compound to the periphery.

[19] Cf. Mallebrein 2005.

names. The change from a 'sign' to an 'icon',[20] as from an elementary symbol or an-iconic sign, such as tree, stone, post etc., to the Hindu idol of a god, was formerly a long process associated with the growth of a particular religious centre. This shift from 'sign' to 'icon' shows how a changing iconography can reflect a historical process. The symbolic power of the new icon reveals at the same time the strong continuity of theological concepts: the indigenous forms change, but the local idea of the power of the goddess remains, being transferred from a living and moving being/medium to a fixed sacred place, which becomes a temple. Detached from the body of a non-Brahmin medium, the time of the ritual becomes more systematic and enclosed in temple structures. The sacred time of a human medium is therefore transformed into a controlling and controlled institution organized by Brahmin priests or able administrators of tribal descent.

As a result of modernization and thus Hinduization some goddesses acquired a supra-regional reputation and fame, most prominent among them in Orissa being the goddess Tārinī of Ghatgaon, a small village in Keonjhar district.[21]

Until the independence of India, a deity's rise to fame was strongly linked with a royal family and its patronage of her.[22] According to Kulke, the royal patronage of autochthonous deities was an essential precondition for the consolidation and legitimation of political power in the Hinduized tribal zone of Orissa.[23]

---

[20] Eschmann (1994, 210-3) discusses the development from 'sign' to 'icon'. 'The signs are not considered to be icons, i.e. representations of a form of the deities, but nevertheless they represent the presence of the deities' (215).

[21] On the Goddess Tārinī and her development, cf. Mallebrein 2004b, cf. further the Tarini webside: www.maatarini.com. For other goddesses, like Tārā-Tārinī from Purusottampur and Maṅgalā from Kakatpur, cf. Das, 1999.

[22] Even after the India's independence in 1947, the royal families financially supported the temples they had founded. Their patronage ceased in 1971 with the abolition of their privileges and compensations, the 'privy purses', under Indira Gandhi. Without this financial support it is nowadays very difficult for the temple trusts to raise the money for their maintenance. As a result many temples are falling into ruin.

[23] Cf. Kulke 1978a, 33.

Maṇikeśvarī and Ḍokrī: Various Iconographic Forms

In this section, I would like to examine in more detail the iconographical development of Ḍokrī and Maṇikeśvarī in the regions of the former Feudatory State of Kalahandi. As the tutelary goddesses of various royal families, such as the Nāgavaṁśī of Kalahandi,[24] the Zamindari-Rājas of Karlapat, Kashipur,[25] Mahulpatna (Jayapur), and the royal family of Thuamul-Rampur and Madanpur-Rampur, these goddesses were acknowledged and worshipped in the former region of Karond,[26] an area formerly comprising the present-day Koraput, Nuapada, Rayagada and Bolangir districts.

The Tribal Village of Merkul

The traditional Kondh village of Merkul[27] provides an idea of the tribal roots of Ḍokrī worship and the original form of her depiction.[28] Merkul lies at the foot of a great mountain, and even a four wheel jeep has great difficulty in reaching it. In this village lives the Pāṭmāji, a senior Kondh headman who traditionally plays a central role in the coronation ritual of the Kalahandi kings. In Merkul the deities called Dhārnī/Ḍokrī[29] and Buḍhā Rāja are worshipped in a manner that is characteristic of the earth goddess worship of the Dongria Kondhs, who live on top of the mountain. A temporary 'house' on earth is built for the earth goddess Dhārnī on the occasion of the great buffalo sacrifice (*meriah*), which is held every three to six years. In a Dongria village, the Dhārnī stones that represent the

---

[24] According to the family history of the Nāga House of Kalahandi, a prince from Chota Nagpur called Raghunāth Sai founded the Nāga line in 1005. He gave a *zamindari*, as such Thuamul, Karlapat, Narla and Dadpur, to each of his sons. In course of time other *zamindari*s were attached, like Madanpur, Mahulpatna and Kashipur; cf. Senapati, Kuanr 1980, 51, 52, 41.

[25] Kashipur now belongs to Rayagada district.

[26] Cf. Mishra 1992, 38. The land of 'Kurund' or 'Kurund-Maṇḍal' was named after the availability there of gem stones.

[27] Merkul is a small village about thirty kilometres from Bhawanipatna (N 19°45'9" E 83°10'02").

[28] I would like to thank the members of the royal families of Kalahandi, Mahārāja Udit Pratāp Deo, Śrī Bīrkeśari Deo and his son Laṅkeśvari Deo for their valuable information, assistance and support during my fieldwork in their region.

[29] One informant told that Dhārnī is the Kondh name, Ḍokrī the Pāik name.

goddess Dhārnī/Ḍokrī stand at the centre of the 'house'. Around this the Dongria Kondh erect an elaborate construction made of wood, bamboo and clay, with painted inner and outer walls. The wooden planks inside the ceremonial hut are carved with representations of human breasts. In the distance Koteiwali, who is thought to be her male companion, is represented by a stone.[30] During the buffalo sacrifice, he too is given his own 'house'.[31] Since this wooden construction is discarded after the sacrifice, only parts of the wooden house still exist in Merkul. Koteiwali is called Buḍhā Rāja in Merkul, and the stones (Jakeri/Dhārnī) are called Ḍokrī. The worship is performed by the Jani, the traditional priest of the earth goddess. On this level, Ḍokrī is part of the Kondh pantheon and closely connected with Buḍhā Rāja, her male partner.

Jugsaipatna, the Former Capital

Whereas at Merkul goddess Ḍokrī is the focus of worship, at Jugsaipatna it is Maṇikeśvarī. This place[32] is considered to be the original centre (*mūlpiṭha*) of the goddess Maṇikeśvarī and the first capital of the royal family of Kalahandi. Recently the former tribal form of worship has undergone a great change, the previous open mud shrine having been dismantled and replaced by a modern cement temple, in which two small stones besmeared with *sindūr* represent the goddess. Her male companion, Buḍhā Rāja, is represented in the temple by a separate stone. Since in form and size the stones resemble the Jakeri/Dhārnī stones of Merkul, we can assume that both may originate with the same concept of the earth goddess, Dhārnī. This change from tribal shrine to cement temple was financed by the Divine Life Society, the most prominent member of which in Orissa is the Gajapati of Puri.[33] Along with the new modern cement architecture, the local non-Brahmin priest has been replaced by a Brahmin, who is now in charge of the deities, being the key-holder for the

[30] According to Roland Hardenberg (personal communication) Koteiwali is considered to be Dhārnī's husband. He is linked or even represents the sun god, and has the role of a king and judge. He is like an old wise man.

[31] On this topic, and for the depiction of the earth goddess house, cf. Mallebrein 2001, 143-4.

[32] N 19°45'5", E 83°11'40".

[33] Svami Chidanandji Maharaj is the founder of the Divine Life Society. In Orissa the main centre is 'The Divine Life Society, Chidananda Hermitage Shanti Ashram', near Puri.

new temple door. For the local tribal devotees, however, it is painful to see their goddess now locked up. By handing over her worship to a Brahmin priest, the Divine Life Society is hoping to increase her following among caste Hindus. Close to the Maṇikeśvarī temple, the Society has erected a temple for Subhadrā and installed a Brahmin as priest. People say that originally the plan was to build a temple for the God Jagannātha, but then his sister Subhadrā[34] intervened demanding a temple for herself. She is now considered a sister of Maṇikeśvarī.

Maṇikeśvarī and Ḍokrī in Mixed Tribal-Hindu Villages

Whereas in Merkul and Jugsaipatna the deities Ḍokrī, Maṇikeśvarī and Buḍhā Rāja are the focus of worship and are represented by an unhewn stone, their iconography changes in villages with a mixed tribal and Hindu population, where the shrines (*gudi*) are made out of mud with a permanent roof. A priest performs regular worship. These shrines are made in order to provide shelter to a multitude of deities represented by anthills of various sizes and heights. To give an example, in the Ḍokrī shrine of the village of Purunaguma near Bhavanipatna, several anthills mark the goddesses Ḍokrī, Maṇikeśvarī, Samaleī, Bainī and Pardesan, as well as male deities like Ratankumār, Paban Kumār and Khandual. Buḍhā Rāja occupies a separate place within the hut and is represented by a stone. A Kṣatriya priest performs his worship. The close connection of these deities with the earth is visibly expressed, and they need the blood of sacrificial animals for nourishment in order to replenish their lives and fertility.

Gunpur, a Small Taluk Village

The Ḍokrī shrine at Gunpur near Thuamul is a striking example of the present tendency to modernize traditional shrines (*gudi*). The worship of the goddess Ḍokrī is patronised by the still powerful local Ghontia, who was formerly in charge of tax-collecting. On this level a sword replaces the former depiction of Ḍokrī as a stone or anthill. A throne made out of cement has been constructed inside the old shrine. The sword as a symbol of Ḍokrī's divine power (*śakti*) is placed at the centre. To enhance her importance, a large new cement temple is under construction just behind

---

[34] For more information on Subhadrā, cf. Eschmann, Kulke, Tripathi 1978, 177-8.

the old shrine.[35] After this is finished, there are plans to install a carved stone image of Ḍokrī there, depicting her as Durgā.

The Goddesses and their Male Companion
Buḍhā Rāja – Mahākāla Bhairava

One remarkable feature in the worship of Maṇikeśvarī and Ḍokrī is their close relation to Buḍhā Rāja,[36] who is considered a male partner, friend, protector, or even a brother. Buḍhā Rāja is always worshipped at some distance from the goddesses, but all informants agreed that the goddesses Maṇikeśvarī and Ḍokrī should be worshipped together with Buḍhā Rāja. Like Maṇikeśvarī he is well-known all over western Orissa, and like her he has manifold forms, his name incorporating various tribal and Hindu gods. In this way he is linked to Śiva in his form as Bhairava, Beru or Baḍa Deo (great god). The Kondh call him Buḍhā Penu (god), and other tribal communities, like the Bhuiya, Oraon and Maler, worship him as a deity of light and the sun. For the Gond he is one of the most powerful deities in Orissa, a ruler and an independent deity. In Athgaon, a former *zamindar* in Bolangir district, Buḍhā Rāja is depicted in his temple as powerful god with four arms holding a sword and shield. The Bhunjia worship him as their main deity (*iṣṭadevatā*). In Nuapada district, bordering Bastar, there are many shrines devoted to Buḍhā Rāja. The village of Babir, close to Khariar, is considered a centre of Buḍhā Rāja worship. The god is regarded as the ruler of 22 villages. He is represented by a mud figure depicting a rider on horseback, a form he is also worshipped as in Bastar, where he is called Rāja Rao. At Babir, Buḍhā Rāja has a big family, Ḍokrī Budhī being his wife and Bahar Bhīma his son.

Jenā and Human Sacrifice

Apart from Buḍhā Rāja, another god, Jenā, is also closely associated with the worship of Ḍokrī and Maṇikeśvarī; he forms an essential element in their rituals, especially within the Dasahrā festival. The Jenā *khālo* is a secret spot were human sacrifices were performed in former times. During Dasahrā, in the night from *mahāṣṭamī* to *navāmī*, countless animal

---

[35] The construction of the new temple was started in 2002.

[36] Some informants call Buḍhā Rāja a wise old man (buḍhā). For further information on this, see Rahman 1936.

sacrifices are offered at this spot. Jenā is also called Bali-Rāja and considered Yama's assistant. He demands blood. Jenā is remembered in the temples and shrines. In one corner of the Maṇikeśvarī temple at Thuamul Rampur, for example, there is a place called Jenā where old broken iron chains are kept, having been used formerly to bind the human victims of sacrifice. This close relationship of Maṇikeśvarī and Ḍokrī with Buḍhā Rāja and Jenā respectively is a characteristic trait of their cult and worship.

Maṇikeśvarī and Ḍokrī, the Tutelary Deities of Royal Families

In the present section, I shall consider the striking depictions of Maṇikeśvarī and Ḍokrī as only a trunk for a body, with no hands, legs or permanently fixed head, this being a characteristic feature of their iconography as tutelary deities in the former *zamindaris* of Jayapatna/Mohulpatna, Thuamul-Rampur, Madanpur-Rampur and Bhawanipatna.

Goddess Ḍokrī at Talgud and the Royal Family of Jayapatna

The royal *zamindari* family of Mohulpatna lives in Jayapatna, a small town approximately ten kilometres from the village of Talgud, which has a Ḍokrī temple. This temple was constructed in the early twentieth century, at the same time as the new palace in Jayapatna. The goddess Ḍokrī is represented by a simple conical cement trunk approximately one metre in height, with a flattened top. Above this trunk is a small hole in the wall, where, according to the priests, small stones, considered her *yantra,* are kept. It was a Kondh who discovered the goddess in the form of small bleeding stones while digging for sweet roots. Every day the Pāika priest dresses the body of the goddess. It is only during the Dasahrā festival that a richly decorated head made out of clay is placed on this trunk. The goddess then assumes the visible form of Dakṣiṇeśvarī, with wide open eyes and a protruding tongue, which give her a fierce appearance. Buḍhā Rāja is not worshipped within the temple compound. His place is a large stone boulder in a hamlet called Adivasipada, though for the Dasahrā festival he is invited to the temple, together with the six sisters of Ḍokrī, each one represented by a stick wrapped in a sari. The place of Jenā-*khālo* is far away in the deep mountains, where, in former times, a fort of the Gaṅga dynasty was situated.

Ḍokrī and Maṇikeśvarī at Rampur and Thuamul-Rampur

At the newly constructed cement temple in the village of Rampur,[37] the deities Ḍokrī, Maṇikeśvarī and Buḍhā Rāja are represented by three small, red, conical cement trunks. This modern temple has recently replaced the former mud shrine. Rampur was formerly the residential place of the Rampur Pāṭ-Rāja family before they shifted their capital to Thuamul-Rampur in the nineteenth century to construct a large new palace and temples for their tutelary deities. The new temple to Ḍokrī/Dakṣiṇakālī and Maṇikeśvarī at Thuamul-Rampur is situated close to the palace. Since Ḍokrī is the old local goddess, Maṇikeśvarī having come later, Ḍokrī is considered senior and as such every Dasahrā she is given a head made out of clay. At one corner of the temple parts of an iron chain mark the place of Jenā.

The Goddess Maṇikeśvarī and her Worship in Bhawanipatna

The Maṇikeśvarī temple at Bhawanipatna is the main centre of the worship of this goddess in Kalahandi, where she is considered extremely powerful and is hardly visible inside the sanctum. No photograph exists of her, but we may assume from descriptions that her image corresponds to the general iconographic form of a conical trunk. The impressive temple is located within the palace compound. In the middle of the nineteenth century, the royal family moved their capital from Junagarh to Bhawanipatna. The present temple was completed by Brājamohan Deo (1917-39).[38] In Bhawanipatna, a permanent head made out of metal is placed on the conical trunk. This head is also substituted by a clay head during Dasahrā. A separate shrine for Buḍhā Rāja was constructed to the right of the temple. The place of worship for Jenā lies about 3 km from the temple.

---

[37] N 19°34'25" E 83°2'27" .

[38] Cf. J.P. Singh Deo 1991, 4-10; Mishra 1991, 17-26; P.K. Deo 1991.

Ḍokrī and Maṇikeśvarī at Madanpur-Rampur

The depictions of Ḍokrī/Dakṣiṇeśvarī and Maṇikeśvarī in Madanpur-Rampur differ from those elsewhere. Here the goddesses are represented not by a conical trunk but by an umbrella, which gives the impression of a slightly conical pillar. Madanpur, formerly the capital of the royal family of Madanpur-Rampur,[39] is close to the present-day Bolangir district. In the middle of the nineteenth century the royal family moved their capital to Rampur, where they constructed a new palace and a temple for Ḍokrī/Dakṣiṇeśvarī and Maṇikeśvarī within the palace compound. Their former tutelary goddesses, Pāṭmaheśvarī and Pāṭkhaṇḍā,[40] remained at Madanpur. At Rampur the original local goddess was Ḍokrī, Maṇikeśvarī later being added by the Brahmins who came from Ganjam to perform the worship in the various newly constructed temples. They also introduced a tantric form of Ḍokrī and Maṇikeśvarī worship. Among the goddesses Maṇikeśvarī occupies the first place in hierarchy, followed by Ḍokrī/Dakṣiṇeśvarī, Chattarbāutī, Laṅkeśvarī and Jamlatī.[41] Within the Maṇikeśvarī temple, a huge umbrella and a sword placed on a cement throne mark the presence of Ḍokrī/Dakṣiṇeśvarī, the goddesss Maṇikeśvarī being represented by a big sword placed to the right of Ḍokrī. The umbrella, called Chattarbāutī, is made out of a black and gold sari, wrapped around a long bamboo stick in such a way that it gives the

[39] Madanpur Rampur claims to have been an independent kingdom since it came to be in existence in *AD* 1061. In contrast to the Kalahandi royal family, the rulers of Madanpur-Rampur refused to cooperate with the British, and freedom fighters took refuge in their territory. As a retaliatory measure, the British brought the kingdom of the rulers of Madanpur-Rampur under the control of the Kalahandi kings (Panda 1997, 176). Their struggle for independence is also reflected in their family history, which stands in contrast to that of Kalahandi. According to their genealogical tradition, the Nāgavaṁśī Rājput prince, Ragunāth Sai came not alone, but with his four other brothers from Chota Nagpur to this region (*AD* 1061). Each prince married the daughter of a Gaṅga ruler, who gave the territory to his son-in-law to rule. They were the sons of Mahārāja of Navratangarh-Satrangarh in southern Bihar (now Chota Nagpur). The four brothers (one died) married Gaṅga Rājkumāris at Bastar, Dadpur (later shifted to Karlapat), Madanpurgarh and Junagarh. Madanpurgarh was the capital of Karonda-maṇḍala (Mihirendra Singh Deo, personal communication 2003).

[40] For more information on the Pāṭkhaṇḍā *jātrā*, see Mallebrein 2004 (c).

[41] Laṅkeśvarī and Jalmatī are not represented by a symbol or icon, but they are included in the worship.

impression of a long slightly conical pillar. According to the royal family a small brass plate depicting Durgā is set into the upper part of the bamboo stick. This umbrella is regarded as the movable image (*calanti pratimā*) of Dakṣiṇeśvarī.[42] During the Dasahrā festival the umbrella (*calanti pratimā*) is brought outside the temple to the site at which animals are sacrificed. Also here we have the tradition of preparing a temporary head made out of clay, but here the head is not placed on the trunk of the goddess but on the throne within the sanctum, being considered a representation of Jaya Durgā. Immediately after the *pūjā* in the night of *mahāṣṭamī*, this head is immersed in water. Buḍhā Rāja is called Mahākaleśvar, and white goats are offered to him.[43] The secret place of Jenā-*khālo* lies outside the village, and close to it a villager has constructed a small shrine for Jenā Buḍhā. His worship is carried by Brahmins in Rampur, but by Pāika priests in Madanpur, where the main goddess Pāṭmaheśvarī is considered a form of Durgā, though Maṇikeśvarī and Dakṣiṇeśvarī at Rampur are worshipped as forms of the goddess Kālī.

Maṇikeśvarī and Ḍokrī/Dakṣiṇeśvarī in the Nineteenth Century and the Revival of Tantric Worship

In the nineteenth century, the worship of Ḍokrī and Maṇikeśvarī underwent a great change, and they achieved region-wide fame. This goes along with yet another form of representation of the goddesses as the tutelary deity of royal families. This increasing importance of both goddesses for the royal families can be linked to changing patterns of ritual and doctrine that emerged in the nineteenth century. This theological shift from a more tribal form of worships towards a revived form of tantrism started when the Kalahandi royal family moved their capital from Junagarh to Bhawanipatna in the mid-nineteenth century. In this respect they were simply following a tendency which started mainly under the British Supremacy in the nineteenth century, when the local rulers left their former small capitals to establish new, splendid,

---

[42] At several places the movable image (*calantī pratimā*) of a goddess is a long wooden pole wrapped in saris, the most prominent being the wooden pole images of Birajāimātā and Kāṭhi Ṭhakurānī from Banpur (Khurda district) and Khilāmuṇḍā in Rampur and Mandasa (AP).

[43] According to the family tradition, Buḍhā Rāja came from Chota Nagpur along with the five Nāga princes, the founder of various Nāgvaṃśi families in this region.

representative seats of government, with impressive palaces and temples for the major Hindu gods.[44] In Bhawanipatna the change in ritual and worship started during the time of the Nāga ruler Udit Pratāp Deo (1853-81) of Kalahandi, whose main aim was to develop this new centre of power. He invited a great number of Brahmins, mainly from Sambalpur[45] and Ganjam, to take care of the gods in the newly established temples, giving generous land grants for their maintenance.[46] These Brahmins reshaped the ritual by introducing their traditional ways of tantric worship, and thus their presence became indispensable for the control of the powerful divine energy. It was under this Brahminical influence that the cult of Maṇikeśvarī developed, which finally led to her fame and worship being spread across Orissa. Attracted by her new divine power, the other *zamindari* Rājas of the nearby regions called Brahmins into their territory to start the tantric worship of their tutelary goddesses Ḍokrī and Maṇikeśvarī. Within the tantric form of worship they are addressed as Māṇikeśvarī-Kālī and Dakṣiṇa-Kālī, thus being linked with the Daśamahāvidyās, the ten great cosmic powers. Following the Vaiṣṇavite idea of the ten *avatāras,* the idea of the Daśamahāvidyās brings together distinct strands under a unifying great deity, Mahādevī.[47] The ten goddesses are divided into three categories. Kālī belongs to the first group, along with Chinnamastā and Dhūmāvatī, whose worship is tantric. For the royal families the powerful tutelary goddess is also of great importance on the political level. The *tāntrika* conceive the world as *śakti*, the power that creates, sustains and destroys the entire universe, but it is also the power that flows through the social and political world. 'Tantric ritual seeks to harness and exploit this power, both as a means to spiritual liberation and as a means to this-worldly benefits, such as wealth, fame and supernatural abilities.'[48] For the Brahmins, introducing tantric rituals

---

[44] Cf. on this topic, Kulke 1993a.

[45] The Brahmins from Sambalpur belong to two groups, the Jhadua (Aranyaka) Brahmins, and the immigrants, i.e. Oriya (Utkalika) Brahmins, who are considered higher than the Jhadua and are said to be of tribal origin. See Pasayat 1998, 88; Russell, Hira Lal 1975 (Vol. 2), 398-9.

[46] Udit Pratāp Deo was married to Aśā Kumārī Devī, the only issue of Mahārāja Nārāyaṇa Siṅgh, the last ruler of Sambalpur. Therefore he had strong ties to Sambalpur, and the Brahmins were part of the 'dowry'. Another strong group of Brahmins came from Ganjam.

[47] On Mahādevī, see Kinsley 1986, 132-50 and Rajeshwari 1989.

[48] Urban 2003, 275.

is a means 'by which Brahmin society perpetuates the perception of itself as privileged in the midst of radical social changes that do not always privilege Brahmans'.[49] Animal sacrifice still plays a crucial part in the worship of the goddesses Maṇikeśvarī-Kālī and Ḍokrī/Dakṣiṇeśvarī Kālī, as it is considered extremely powerful. Śrī Kṛsṇānanda Āgamavāgīśa, the composer of the *Bṛhat-Tantrasāra* (Great Essence of the Tantras), one of the most frequently used texts in Hindu ritual and iconography, writes that by unleashing the terrible power of the Goddess through sacrificial violence, the *tāntrika* can slay his enemies, enchant women and ultimately even bring the entire region under his control.[50] Performing these rituals is regarded as very dangerous, as are the deities linked to it. Therefore, Maṇikeśvarī appears in mystic darkness to her devotees in her temple in Bhawanipatna. In the worship of Maṇikeśvarī-Kālī and Ḍokrī/Dakṣiṇeśvarī the *yantra* that is hidden in their image plays an important role as representing their *śakti*. Through yogic visualization (*dhyāna*) and *mantra* recitation (*japa*), the goddess appears through the *yantra,* and the worshipper can identify himself with the goddess.[51] The concept of the *yantra* is the underlying concept of all the *iṣṭadevī*s of royal families discussed so far. This elaborate form of esoteric tantric ritual can only be performed by highly skilled priests.[52] According to Preston, 'the ultimate goal of goddess worship is to reach emancipation through total identification with the deity ... a dangerous path requiring careful attention to intricate ritual details ... which are believed to yield enormous spiritual power'.[53] The power gained through the tantric ritual was one reason why the other *zamindari* families established this form of worship in the temples of their tutelary goddesses. Their conic shape testifies to their origins as tribal goddesses.

---

[49] Brooks 1992, 188.

[50] Cf. Urban 2003, 282-3, who also provides a list comparing Vedic sacrifice with tantric sacrifice.

[51] Cf. Hudson 1999.

[52] Cf. Brooks 1990, 70 'Tantrism ... does not intend to be revolutionary in the sense of establishing a new structure of social egalitarianism ... It opens its doors only to a few who ... seek to distinguish and empower themselves.'

[53] Preston 1980, 50-1.

Various Legends about Maṇikeśvarī

After the discussion of the remarkable iconographic change in the depiction of Maṇikeśvarī and Ḍokrī, I now turn to the various legends concerning the relationship between Maṇikeśvarī and different royal families. It is striking to see that the goddess Ḍokrī does not play any role in these quite heterogeneous stories. As already mentioned, the presented information is based on oral records, which are rarely historical accurate, and thus there are different views about the origin of Maṇikeśvarī, each informant having a different opinion as to what is the truth. We shall start the discussion with the oral tradition of the Kondhs at Merkul, then shift to the royal family of Kalahandi, and finally discuss the only historically dated references found in Bastar. The section ends with myths of the first encounter of Maṇikeśvarī with the Kimedi royal families and the final extension of their worship in southern Orissa.

Maṇikeśvarī, a Goddess from Salapgarh

The Kondh Pāṭmāji of Merkul explain the former relationship between the Kalahandi royal family, the Kondh and Maṇikeśvarī as follows. The Kondh selected a member of the present Kalahandi royal family as the ruler of various Kondh clans and their territory. During this time the first fort of the kings was at Salapgarh, a village high up in the mountains. For the Kondh Salapgarh is also the original place of Maṇikeśvarī worship, a local goddess closely linked to the earth and fertility, hence her name was Māṇika, a word which originates from '*māṇika*', the Kui word for red soil. To invest their newly selected king with divine power, the Kondh presented all their gods to him with a demand that he build shrines for them at every corner of his new territory. Later these Kondh kings shifted the fort from Salapgarh to the plains, to a place called Jugsaipatna, where they erected a new fort and constructed a shrine to Maṇikeśvarī.

This legend reflects the ties between the Kondh and the Kalahandi Rāja that have a historical basis. While for the Kondh the time of Salapgarh goes back to legendary past, but by moving to Jugsaipatna the king enters history since archaeological findings of the fort do exist, but they have not as yet been dated. As the Kondh consider the Rāja of Kalahandi to be a member of their community, it was customary till recently for the him to take a Kondh girl as his first wife (*pāṭrānī*). It was also a custom in the royal family that the coronation of a new king should take place on the lap of the Kondh Pāṭmāji of Merkul.[54] C. Elliot, the Deputy Commissioner of Raipur, was the first to report about this 'curious' ritual.[55] This custom was still followed by P.K. Deo, the father of the present Mahārāja Udit Pratāp Deo in Jugsaipatna, who mentions in his biography that before his official investiture ceremony was celebrated on 16th March 1940, a *rājyābhiṣeka* was performed for him on an auspicious day at the ancestral stone in Jugsaipatna. While sitting on the lap of the Pāṭmāji, the turban was tied by the *zamindar* of Lanjigarh,[56] who also gave a *tilaka* with *sindūr* taken from the Maṇikeśvarī stones inside the temple.

The legend of Salapgarh clearly shows that the Kondh regard themselves as the real owners of the territory: the new king rules with their permission and on their behalf. For Mahārāja Udit Pratāp Deo, this coronation ritual is a sign 'that they have accepted us as members of the tribe, as sons of the soil'. This ritual was mainly of political importance: the new Rāja needed the support of the Kondh tribes, who constituted more than eighty percent of the population till the nineteenth century. According to F. Deo, 'the Rāja took a Kandh women, and on this basis the Rāja could later claim to be the Rāja Mahāpuru, with its suggestion of divinity, as the head of the Kandhs, especially by the 19th cent'.[57] In the nineteenth century, Kalahandi had to cope with several Kondh uprisings, the major one occurring in 1882, when the Kondh revolted against the Kulta cultivators who had been brought to Kalahandi from Sambalpur to improve the local agriculture. Today it is hard to believe that the small jungle village of Jugsaipatna was once the first capital of the Kalahandi royal family.

Maṇikeśvarī, a Goddess from Gadapur, Kondhmal Area

Although the Kalahandi royal family acknowledges the right of the Kondh to be present at their coronation ritual, they claim that the goddess Maṇikeśvarī came from Salapgarh, having been brought from Gadapur to

[54] The tradition of sitting on the lap of a tribal chief is also known from the royal families of Gangpur/Sundergarh, Pallahara, Keonjhar, Bonai, and Patna/Borasambar. See Deo 1990, 75-76.

[55] Cf. Cobden Ramsay 1950, 202 (citing Lieutenant Elliot).

[56] Cf. Deo 2000, 51.

[57] Deo 1990, 187. 'The Rāja did not collect regular revenue from the Kandhs even up to the coming of the colonial rulers.'

their region in the thirteenth century. According to the family history (*rājavaṃśāvali*) of the Nāgavaṁśī dynasty of Kalahandi, the sixth ruler, Rāja Harichand Deo (*AD* 1201-34), encountered political difficulties and died young. His pregnant wife fled to her father's house in Gadapur, today in Kondhmal district, where she gave birth to a boy. The people of Kalahandi asked her to bring her son back so that he might assume rule over their area, a request with which she complied.[58] From Gadapur she brought her family goddess Maṇikeśvarī, a goddess belonging to the Gaṅgā dynasty who took over rule in this region after the defeat of the Kalachuri kings in *AD* 1211. Her son was crowned the new ruler in Jugsaipatna, where he constructed a temple for Maṇikeśvarī, as well as one in Bundeseer, which later became the final capital of the Kalahandi dynasty.

Whereas the former story explains the place of origin of Maṇikeśvarī, the following gives the reason why she became the main family goddess of the Kalahandi Nāgavaṁśī dynasty. The miracle happened in 1849, during the rule of Fateh Nārāyaṇa Deo (1831-53), when a cholera epidemic broke out in Junagarh, at that time still the capital. His first son, Udit Pratāp Deo (1853-81), was affected by it. Out of despair he took his son to the Maṇikeśvarī shrine at Bundeseer, placing him in front of Maṇikeśvarī and clsoing the door. After some time he could hear a weeping sound, and he found his son completely cured. His son narrated a vision of the mother Maṇikeśvarī. Since then the Nāga dynasty of Kalahandi recognised Maṇikeśvarī as their main tutelary deity. From Junagarh they first moved their fort to Medinipur, and later to Bhawanipatna, where they constructed an impressive temple to the goddess.

The statement that Maṇikeśvarī came to Kalahandi in the early thirteenth century after the death of the sixth ruler, Rāja Harichand Deo, presupposes that the history of the Kalahandi royal family started with Raghunāth Sai, a Rajput prince from the Nāgavaṁśī line of Chota Nagpur,[59] who usurped the throne of Jagannāth Deo, the last Gaṅgā ruler. The latter had no male heir, and only one daughter called Surekhā. He married her to Raghunāth Sai, who started the Nāgavaṁśī line of

[58] Cf. Senapati and Kuanr 1980, 53.

[59] Dalton remarks on the mythical origin of the 'Chutia Nagpur Rajas'. 'The boy selected was a brother of the Satranjigarh chief'; cf. Dalton 1978, 165-7.

Kalahandi in *AD* 1005.[60] He also moved the capital to Junagarh[61] and installed the goddess Laṅkeśvarī there, [62] still today the main goddess. However, historians are rather doubtful that Nāgavaṁśī rule in Kalahandi goes back to the eleventh century, since they consider it unlikely that a Chota Nagpur Rājput dynasty existed so early. Hence, if there was a family relationship with the Chota Nagpur Nāgavaṁśī line, it was not before the thirteenth century.[63]

Especially in the eighteenth and nineteenth centuries, there was a trend within royal families all over India, not only in Orissa, to establish their own family histories with the help of court genealogists. In most cases they traced their family origins back to one of the famous Rajput clans.[64] The family history of Kalahandi was also compiled in this period. In 1896 Mahārāja Raghukeśari Deo (1894-98) had it written down in order to be able to hand it over to the Political Agent of the Chhattisgarh feudatories, as the Rājas were asked to provide proof of their sovereignty.[65]

The story of the miraculous healing of the young boy at Bundeseer provides a reason for changing the capital from Junagarh to Bhawanipatna, as places where such wonders happen are regarded as being endowed with great divine power (in this case represented by Maṇikeśvarī), thus being ideal for prestigious new projects.

---

[60] Cf. Senapati, Kuanr 1980, 50-2 (including genealogical chart), for another version, see Deo 1990, 183ff.

[61] Junagarh was formerly called Junabali, after the human sacrifices which were offered to the goddess Laṅkeśvarī.

[62] On Laṅkeśvarī of Junagarh, cf. Das 1999, 200; J.P. Singh Deo 2001, 47-8. On Laṅkeśvarī of Sonepur, also called Pascima Lanka, cf. Das 1999, 152-5. At Junagarh there is no temple to Maṇikeśvarī, but one to Kanaka Durgā. She remained there even after the family had moved the capital to Bhawanipatna in 1850.

[63] Cf. Deo 1990, 183ff.

[64] Cf. on this topic Schnepel 2002, 147, fn. 30: 'the widespread production of *vaṃśāvalis* and genealogies proclaiming Rajput descent is probably to be dated to the period between 1770 and 1820, when early colonial interests provided a stimulus to such productions'; also 155-7; Sinha 1962, Banerji 1928.

[65] The Kalahandi royal family had good relations with the British. In 1918 Rāja Brajamohan Deo was awarded the Order of the British Empire, and on 16.10.1926 he was honoured with the title of Mahārāja, which was made hereditary on 20.10.1932; cf. Rao 1993, 8.

Maṇikeśvarī and Bastar

Some scholars have suggested that Maṇikeśvarī has her origin in Bastar and that the Kalahandi Nāgavaṁśī are the descendants of the Chakrakoṭa Nāgavaṁśī of Bastar.[66] Their argument is based on the fact that both the dynasties worship Maṇikeśvarī, and that both families belong to the *kaśyapa gotra*, their emblem being a cobra (*phaṇi patāka*). As this suggestion is quite central to scholarly discussions concerning Maṇikeśvarī, it is necessary to take into account the worship of Maṇikeśvarī in Bastar.[67] Prior to her appearance in the Kalahandi area, a goddess called Māṇikyadēvi is mentioned in inscriptions found in Bastar (Chhattisgarh). The inscription from Bhairamgarh, a village in the vicinity of the Indravati River, speaks about a king who was a worshipper of Māṇikyadēvi.[68] The king may be identified with the ruler Jagadēkabhūṣaṇa Mahārāja, who is also mentioned in inscriptions dated *AD* 1218 and 1224. He is the ruler of the Chhindaka Nāgavaṁśī Dynasty of Chakrakoṭa-maṇḍala, which is mentioned in several inscriptions. Barsur, on the right bank of the river Indravati, was the capital.[69] This Chakrakoṭa-maṇḍala comprised portions of the Bastar, Koraput, Nawranpur, Nuapada and present-day Kalahandi districts. The Nāgavaṁśī kings describe themselves as lords of the mythical capital Bhagavatī of the Nāgas in the subterranean world, the best of all cities.[70] There are various opinions concerning the origins of the dynasty.[71] It is not clear when the Chhindaka Nāgas came to power as rulers of the Chakrakoṭa-maṇḍala.[72] The earliest known record is a fragmentary inscription from Errakot, dated 1023.[73] After the Cōḷa invasion in that year, small principalities were

---

[66] For a discussion of the origin of the Nāgas, cf. Grant 1984 (reprint from 1870); Rajguru 1979; Mahapatra 1982; Sahu, Mishra and Sahu 1980, 192-203.

[67] For a list of all Bastar inscriptions of the Nāgas of Chakrakoṭa, see Sharma 1998, Vol. 1, 331-3; Hira Lal 1907-8.

[68] *Śrī-Māṇikyadēvi-divya-śrīpāda-padm-ārādhaka*; cf. Hira Lal 1907-8, 164; for a map of Bhairamgarh, 160

[69] On Basur and its remains, see Postel, Cooper 1999, 13 ff.

[70] For more information on the Cakrakoṭa-maṇḍala and the Chindaka Nāga kings, see Sahu 1997, 193-7.

[71] The origin of the Nāgavaṁśī Dynasty is discussed by Singh Deo 1987, 233-42; Shukla 1988, 71-3.

[72] Shukla 1988, 63-6 discusses each ruler in detail.

[73] Cf. Hira Lal 1932, 166.

united in the name of Cakrakoṭa-maṇḍala under a Chhindaka Nāga king. Nāgavaṁśī rule continued at least till the middle of the fourteenth century. The Sati Stone Inscription from Temara records the immolation of Māṇikya [dēvī] after the death of her husband in 1324.[74] This shows that Māṇikadēvī was also used as personal name.

The Chhindaka Nāgas extended their power up to eastern Kośala in the early twelfth century and established their rule at Suvarṇapura (Sonpur). The Telugu-Choḍa general Jasarāja I (*c.* 1040) took part in a successful campaign against the Somàvaṃśi kings led by Nāgavaṃśī Someśvara I in Kośala and, as a reward for his services, was made the ruler of eastern Kośala or of parts of it, to administer on behalf of the Nāgavaṃśi kings.[75] According to Panigrahi,[76] who follows other dates of the Telugu Chōḍas in Sonepur, the last ruler, Someśvara III (*c.* 1095-1119), known as Bhujavala, was driven out of Sonepur by Jājalladeva I (*c.* 1090-1120), the Kalachuri king of Ratnapura, who remained there till it was annexed by the Gaṅga kingdom at the beginning of the thirteenth century. According to Sahu, about this time Anaṅgabhīmadeva III conquered the eastern part of Kośala, and the Gaṅga governor was placed in charge of Kamala-maṇḍala (modern Kalahandi), as is known from the Narla temple inscription of Śaka year 1153, i.e. 1231.[77]

The Chhindaka Nāga ruled in Bastar till 1324, when the last ruler, Hariśchandradeva, was killed. The Nāga Dynasty was supplanted by the

---

[74] Cf. Hira Lal and Rai Bahadur 1909-10, Inscription no. 8 – Temara Sati-Stone Inscription of Saka-Samvat 1246, where this inscription is linked with the Nāgavaṃśī dynasty.

[75] Sircar and Venkataramayya 1949-50, analyse the conquest of the Nāgavaṃśī kings up to eastern Kośala and the establishment of the Telugu Choḍa, their subordinates in the early twnefth century, at Suvarṇapura under Someśvaradeva II (1105-30), who called himself Lord of Kośala. The Telugu Choḍas claim descent from the Coḷa royal family in their inscriptions, and they came into contact with the Chhindaka Nāgas around 1040. The tutelary deity of the Telugu Choḍa ruling family was Vaidyanātha (Śiva). Someśvaradeva styled himself Lord of the entire Kośala. In his inscription from the year 23 he mentions that he stood before Laṅkāvarttaka on the bank of the river Chitrotpalā (i.e. Mahānadi). The modern Laṅkeśvarī, a hillock in the bend of the Mahānadi at Sonepur, seems to have been referred to as Lāṅkāvarttaka in the inscription. Someśvaradevavarman III (*c.* 1155-80) is the last ruler whose name in mentioned as ruler of the Telugu Choḍa Line in Suvarṇapura,

[76] Panigrahi 1981, 117-20.

[77] Sahu 1997, 196-7.

Kākatīya of Warangal, who ruled Bastar from 1323 until 1947, when the last king of the dynasty, Pravīr Chandra Bhanj Deo, acceded to the Indian Union. The founder of the dynasty was Annamadeva,[78] who brought his tutelary goddess Danteśvarī from Warangal to Bastar. Dantewara became the main centre of her worship.[79] Most probably, Dantewara already was a centre of Māṇikeśvarī worship at that time, and under the new Kākatīya dynasty, Danteśvarī became the central goddess, the *rāṣṭradevatā,* Maṇikeśvarī being considered her elder sister.[80] Māṇikeśvarī, usually called Māulī, is still venerated all over Bastar today. Her main temple is in Jagdalpur, close to the palace. During Dasahrā, at first important rituals are performed in the Māulī temple. Three splendid brass figurines representing Danteśvarī, Maṇikeśvarī and Rāja Rao, a form of Śiva, are displayed in a small side shrine within the Danteśvarī palace temple.[81]

The theory of a connection between the Maṇikeśvarī of the Nāgavaṁśī family of Kalahandi and the Nāgavaṁśī dynasty of Chakrakoṭa-maṇḍala in Bastar receives support from a legend which refers to an incident placed in the fourteenth century. This story is mentioned by Shukla,[82] according to whom Maṇikeśvarī, the tutelary goddess of the Nāgavaṁśī dynasty from Chakrakoṭa-maṇḍala in Bastar, was brought to Kalahandi by a marriage alliance between the Nāgavaṁśī of Kalahandi and the Nāgavaṁśī of Chakrakoṭa-maṇḍala. The last Gaṅgā ruler of Kalahandi, Jagannāthdeva had no sons, only two daughters, Puṣpā and Surekhā. The elder daughter, Puṣpā, was married to Rāmachandradeva of Athagarh, the younger daughter to Raghunāthadeva, a Chakrakoṭa Nāga prince and a relative of the last Nāgavaṁśī ruler Harischandradeva, who died in 1324. As Rāmachandradeva of Athagarh was not willing to leave his state, Raghunāthadeva accepted the offer from Kalahandi, going there, and founding the Nāgavaṁśī dynasty at the beginning of the fourteenth century. As Māṇika Devī was his tutelary

---

[78] Cf. Sundar 1997, 48. Shukla 1988, 148 speaks of Annamadeva as the founder of Cālukya rule. He discusses the various rulers in detail at pp. 148ff.

[79] Cf. Sundar 1997, 61.

[80] There are different opinions about the relationship between Danteśvarī und Maṇikeśvarī. For some historians the Kākatīya merely adopted her and renamed her Danteśvarī, whereas for others Maṇikeśvarī and Danteśvarī both came from Warangal; cf. Sundar 1997, n. 59.

[81] On the Daśaharā festival in Jagdalpur, see Mallebrein 1996; Sundar 1997, 61-76. On Bastar bronzes, see Mallebrein 1993, 1998.

[82] Shukla 1988.

goddess, he introduced her worship in Kalahandi. The Nāgavaṁśī of Chakrakoṭa dispersed, and, in search of a new empire, they went to the Kalahandi region. The legend told by Shukla offers an explanation of the relationship between the Bastar Nāgavaṁśī family and the Kalahandi family, but unfortunately Shukla does not reveal his source for it.

Māṇika Devī, a Deified Girl from Bastar

A legend current among the priests of the Maṇikeśvarī temple in Thuamul Rampur actually reflects a historical incident which took place in the nineteenth century, although the story takes place in the tenth century. The story links Maṇikeśvarī with the Chakrakoṭa dynasty of Bastar as a daughter of Nṛpatibhūṣaṇa, a Nāgavaṁśī king said to have ruled in Thuamul in the tenth century.[83] According to this tradition the name of the king's daughter was Māṇika. She was married to the king of Kashipur. Due to personal problems she decided to leave her husband and to return to her father's home at Thuamul, but her father-in-law prevented her. Out of despair she told him that she would divide herself in two, her head to remain at Kashipur, while her body would return to her parents' place in Thuamul. As a result of this division, her head is worshipped in Kashipur and her body in Thuamul.

The legend of the self-sacrifice and the later deification of the girl reflect an incident that took place in the nineteenth century. In 1866, the former *zamindari* of Thuamul was divided between the Pāṭ Rāja and the Tāṭ Rāja, who were at odds with each other. Thuamul remained with the Pāṭ Rāja, while the Tāṭ Rāja was confirmed in the administration of Kashipur as a separate *zamindari*.[84] Endowed with their own *zamindari* they now demanded part of Maṇikeśvarī's *śakti*, as the goddess endows the ruler with power and grants protection. In the legend, the girl therefore divides herself into different parts.

But what about the claim of Jugsaipatna to be the *śaktipīṭha* of Māṇikeṣvarī? The answer is provided by the priest: the feet of Maṇikeśvarī went to Jugsaipatna. By means of this legend, the claim to the *śakti* of Maṇikeśvarī made by the royal family of Bhawanipatna, the Zamindar Rāja of Thuamul-Rampur and Kashipur, was legitimized.

---

[83] This king is mentioned in the Errakot Telugu Inscription, dated 1023, and may have been Nṛpatibhūṣaṇa; cf. Hira Lal 1932, 166.

[84] Cf. Aitchison 1973 , Vol. II, 334-5.

Maṇikeśvarī and the Kimedi Families

In this final section I shall deal with the shift of Maṇikeśvarī worship from Kalahandi to the southern parts of Orissa, and the adoption of Māṇikeṣvarī as the tutelary goddess of the Kimedi families.

Of special interest in this connection is the legend recorded by one Captain Frye while Special Assistant Agent in the Kondh region in the nineteenth century, referring to an incident which took place in the legendary past. Also in this account, the origin of the goddess Maṇikeśvarī is traced back to the deification of a girl. A prince called Bhīma Deo went in search of a kingdom of his own. After he had established himself in a small tract in Kimedi, he 'carried his arms into Kalahundy country, and subdued it. The capital … was attacked and the inhabitants forsook it. In it there was a Brahmani, a widow, who had an only daughter, whom she tenderly loved. But the girl had died, and the mother had formed an image from her jewels and golden ornaments. When the village was deserted, the widow fled and abandoned the image. … In her the prince found his "Ishta Devi", and to her sacrificed his victim; and when resigning Kalahundy … he took the image with him and enshrined it in his new capital'.[85]

According to Schnepel the acquisition of the image is depicted as having been crucial to, even constitutive of, the foundation of a kingdom, in this case the kingdom of Parlakimedi.[86] Thus the legend of Prince Bhīma Deo was constitutive of the foundation of the Parlakimedi kingdom. It also shows that the iconographical change from a tribal to a tutelary deity had already been completed at that time.

The legend mentioned above is only one among many which link Maṇikeśvarī to the royal Kimedi families, who were once united. The family split in 1607, when the Parlakimedi Rāja gave the main territory of Parlakimedi to his elder son, and the younger founded Bada- (big) kimedi. In 1776 one brother left Badakimedi and founded Sanakimedi, the smallest of the three Kimedi kingdoms. The Parlakimedi family has its own story about its relationship with Maṇikeśvarī. This is part of the Kāñcī-Kāverī legend,[87] which refers to the successful expedition of

---

[85] Cf. Carmichael 1869, 88-9, cited by Schnepel 2002, 259.

[86] Ibid. 259, 260.

[87] The Kañcī-Kāverī-story mentions that Maṇikeśvarī, disguised as a milk maid (Māṇikya), gave a ring to King Puruṣottama which had previously been given to her by Jagannāth as a sign of his support in the fight with the Coḷa king; cf. Dash

Gajapati Puruṣottama (1468-97) against the king of Kanchipuram. The legend tells that the family goddess Maṇikeśvarī appeared to Puruṣottama in a dream and told him to make peace with his brother Kala Hammīra-Narasiṃhadeva, who had founded the Parlakimedi kingdom in Gudari (*Gunpur taluka*). With their combined forces they won the battle against the Coḷa ruler.[88] In Parlakemundi Maṇikeśvarī has two places of worship.[89] Within the huge palace she is worshipped in a side corner of the kitchen, having the shape of a small red stone wrapped in a sari. In the town temple she is depicted by a bronze figure of Durgā, with two other bronzes of Durgāmahiṣāsuramardinī beside her.

In another legend of the Badakimedi royal family, the goddess Maṇikeśvarī is linked to Suvarṇabhānu, who is, apart from Puruṣottama und Kala Hammīra, one of the eighteen sons of Kapilendra, the founder of the Sūryavaṃśa dynasty in Orissa. The story tells that the daughter Māṇiyabatī of the sage Kapila worshipped the goddess Maṇikeśvarī. But the king of Vijayanagar kidnapped Kapila's daughter. In revenge Kapilendra defeated the Vijayanagar king, and the girl Māṇiyabatī was married to Suvarṇabhānu, then being made king of Badakimedi. The sage Kapila gave to his daughter a figure of Maṇikeśvarī as a wedding present.[90]

Due to the worship of Maṇikeśvarī as the tutelary goddess of the Parlakimedi, Badakimedi and Sanakimedi royal families, she also enjoys great popularity at the village level, and her portraits are popular motif in

---

1978, 212-19; Kulke 1978b, 206-8; Mukherjee 1953, 48-63; Panda 1999, 224-5. On the Parlakemundi version, see Rajguru 1972, Vol. 2, 72-5; Berkemer 1993, 205; Schnepel 2002, 159-60.

[88] Berkemer (1993, 206) assumes that the Kāñcī-Kāverī legend rose in importance for the Rājas of Parlakimedi after the Sūryavaṃśa Gajapatis lost power, i.e. after 1510, and most probably after the downfall of this dynasty in 1568.

[89] On Parlakemundi Maṇikeśvarī, see Das 1999, 200-1.

[90] Cf. Dash 1978, 216-7; Schnepel 2002, 159. The royal family of Badakimedi has left its palace in Digapahandi and now lives in Berhampur. The family worships a small bronze figure of Maṇikeśvarī as Durgāmahiṣāsuramardinī at its family shrine. The royal family of Sanakimedi also worships Maṇikeśvarī at its palace shrine at Podamari as Durgāmahiṣāsuramardinī. I would like to thank Dr U.N. Deb, Rājasaheb of Sanakimedi and Māṇikeśvari Prasād Deo, Rājasaheb of Badakimedi for their valuable help and suggestions.

Osakothi ritual paintings.[91] In the countless village shrines she is often represented by a simple red coloured stone, as in the tribal context.[92]

Concluding Remarks

The analysis of indigenous iconographies and their change in the local religious history of Orissa, as of the migration of rulers and their tutelary deities, indicates multiple changes of locality and of the social contexts which have resulted in the shifting iconographic representations of the deities. This historical development can also be seen in the changing forms of architecture and the ideas reflected in orally transmitted legends. As the account of the goddesses Māṇikeśvarī and Ḍokrī shows, the history of the Hinduization of tribal deities covers a considerable area, though each manifestation of the deity must be studied locally. Although identity is transmitted across time, it remains bound to its place of origin and to the shifting localities of the ruling patrons.

One of the problems involved in tracing the history of these goddesses is the differently constructed memories of the ruling families as determined by their migration to new areas or settlements (*gaḍa*). Determining this also depends on the memories of the tribal devotees of these goddesses, who link the latter to their original encounter with one of their ancestors in a mythical past. Time is bridged by memory, as is space. And even though the present location of the deity might be a place of great divine power, the original seat (*mūlpīṭha*) retains its dominant role. In rituals of central importance, such as the coronation ritual of a king, the original place of the goddess is always present, even if only in symbolic form.

I have shown that identity is maintained even over long distances in space and time. And if deities are replaced at the top of hierarchy by a new favourite deity of the ruling house, they still retain their share of worship and a prominent place in the ritual.

It is remarkable that even in remote and often deserted places the memory of divine energy is kept alive over centuries, usually being revived and renewed in ritual at least once a year. Thus although the shifts in historical and social contexts may change their presence in

[91] Cf. Fischer, Pathy 1996, 33.

[92] Cf. the Maṇikeśvarī village shrine in Gadasamantrapur, Ganjam district.

iconographic depictions and rituals, neither space nor time can limit divine power.

References

Aitchison, C.U. 1973 [1930]. *A Collection of Treaties, Engagements and Sanads*, Vol. II, Nedeln/Lichten-stein: Klaus Reprint.

Banerji, R.D. 1928. 'Rajput Origins of Western Orissa', in *Modern Review* 43, 285-329.

Basa, K.K. and P. Mohanty (eds.). 2000. *Archaeology of Orissa*, Delhi: Pratibha Prakashan.

Berkemer, G. 1993. *Little Kingdoms in Kalinga: Ideologie, Legitimation und Politik Regionaler Eliten*, Stuttgart: Franz Steiner Verlag.

Boal, B. 1982. *The Konds: Human Sacrifice and Religious Change*, Warminster: Aris & Phillips.

— 1999. *Man, the Gods and the Search for Cosmic Wellbeing*, Bhubaneswar: National Institute of Social Work and Social Sciences (NISWASS).

Brooks, D. 1990. *The Secret of the Three Cities: An Introduction to Hindu Śākta Tantra*, Chicago: The University of Chicago Press.

— 1992. *Auspicious Wisdom: The Texts and Traditions of Śrīvidyā Śākta Tantrism in South India*, Albany: SUNY.

Cobden-Ramsay, L.E.B. 1950. *Feudatory States of Orissa*, Bengal Gazetteers, Howrah: Glasgow Printing Co. Ltd.

Dalton, E.T. 1978. *Tribal History of Eastern India*, Delhi: Cosmos 1978. [1st pub. 1872 under the title *Descriptive Ethnology of Bengal*, Illustrated by Lithograph Portraits copied from Photographs, Calcutta: Office of the Superintendent of Government.]

Das, H.C. 1999. *Sākta Pithas: A Study*, Bhubaneswar: Bharati Prakashan.

Dash, G.N. 1978. 'The Evolution of Priestly Power: The Sūryavaṃśa Period', in A. Eschmann, H. Kulke and G.C. Tripathi (eds.), *The Cult of Jagannath and the Regional Tradition of Orissa*, Delhi: Manohar, 209-21.

Dehejia, V. 1979. *Early Stone Temples of Orissa*, Delhi: Vikas.

Deo, F. 1990. *History of Interaction between Tribal Peoples and their Socio-Cultural Environment in Chhattisgarh Region*, (Jawaharlal Nehru University, New Delhi, unpublished PhD. thesis).

Deo, P.K. 1991. 'Manikya and Ma Manikeswari', in J.K. Behera (ed.), *Maa Manikswari (The Tutelary Deity of Kalahandi)*, Bhawanipatna: Mahabir Sanskrutik Anusthan, 11-16.

— 2000. *Memoirs of a Bygone Era*, Delhi: Minerva Press.

Donaldson, T.E. 1985-7. *Hindu Temple Art of Orissa* (3 vols.), Leiden: Brill.

Eschmann, A., H. Kulke and G.C. Tripathi (eds.). 1978. *The Cult of Jagannath and the Regional Tradition of Orissa*, Delhi: Manohar.

— 1978. 'The Formation of the Jagannātha Triad', in A. Eschmann, H. Kulke and G.C. Tripathi (eds.), *The Cult of Jagannath and the Regional Tradition of Orissa,* Delhi: Manohar, 167-96.

Eschmann, A. 1978a. 'Hinduization of Tribal Deities in Orissa: The Śakta and Śaiva Typology', in A. Eschmann, H. Kulke and G.C. Tripathi (eds.), *The Cult of Jagannath and the Regional Tradition of Orissa,* Delhi: Manohar, 79-97.

— 1978b. 'Prototypes of the Navakalevara Ritual and their Relation to the Jagannātha Cult', in A. Eschmann, H. Kulke and G.C. Tripathi (eds.), *The Cult of Jagannath and the Regional Tradition of Orissa,* Delhi: Manohar, 265-83.

— 1994. Sign and Icon: Symbolism in the Indian Folk Religion', in G.C. Tripathi and H. Kulke (eds.), *Religion and Society in Eastern India*, Delhi: Manohar, 211-33.

Fischer, E., D. Pathy. 1996. *Murals for Goddesses and Gods: The Tradition of Osakothi Ritual Painting in Orissa, India*, New Delhi/Zurich: Indira Gandhi National Centre for the Arts and Museum Rietberg.

Grant, Charles (ed.). 1984. *Central Provinces of India*, Delhi: Usha Publications [rpt. 1870].

Guzy, Lidia. (forthcoming). 'Dulduli: the music which "touches your heart" and the re-enactment of culture', in G. Berkemer and H. Kulke (eds.), *Centres out There? Facets of Subregional Identities*, Delhi: Manohar.

Hira Lal, Rai Bahadur. 1907-8. 'Inscriptions of Bastar State', in *Epigraphia Indica*, IX, Calcutta: Government Press.

— 1909-10. 'Temara Sati-Stone Inscription of Saka-Samvat 1246', in *Epigraphia Indica*, X, 39-40.

— 1932. *Inscriptions in the Central Provinces and Berar,* Nagpur: Government Printing.

Hudson, D. 1999. 'The Ritual Worship of Devi', in V. Dehejia (ed.), *Devi: The Great Goddess. Female Divinity in South Asian Art,* Washington: A. Sackler Gallery, 73-98.

Kinsley, D. 1986. *Hindu Goddesses: Visions of the Divine Feminine in the Hindu Religious Tradition*, Delhi: M. Banarsidass.

König, D. 1984. *Das Tor zur Unterwelt: Mythologie und Kult des Termitenhügels in der schriftlichen und mündlichen Tradition Indiens*, Wiesbaden: Franz Steiner Verlag.

Kulke, H. 1978a. 'Early State Formation and Royal Legitimation in Tribal Areas of Eastern India', in R. Moser and M.K. Gautam (eds.), *Aspects of Tribal Life in South Asia I: Strategy and Survival*, Studia Ethnologica Bernensia 1, Bern: The University of Berne Institute of Ethnology, 29-37.

— 1978b. 'Jagannātha as the State Deity under the Gajapatis of Orissa', in A. Eschmann, H. Kulke and G.C. Tripathi (eds.), *The Cult of Jagannath and the Regional Tradition of Orissa,* Delhi: Manohar, 199-208.

Kulke, H. 1992. 'Tribal Deities at Princely Courts: The Feudatory Rajas of Central Orissa and their Tutelary Deities', in S. Mahapatra (ed.), *The Realm of the Sacred: Verbal Symbolism and Ritual Structures*, Calcutta: Oxford University Press, 56-78.

— 1993a. 'Legitimation and Townplanning in the Feudatory States of Central Orissa', in idem, *Kings and Cults*, Delhi: Manohar, 93-113.

— 1993b. 'Kṣatriyaization and Social Change: A Study in the Orissa Setting', in idem, *Kings and Cults*, Delhi: Manohar, 82-92.

Mahapatra, K.N. 1982. 'Kalahandi under the Gangas and the Nāga Kings', in H.K. Mahtab (chief ed.): *The Orissa Historical Research Journal*. Special Volume. Dedicated to the Memory of Late K.N. Mahapatra. Bhubaneswar (Orissa State Museum), 23 (1-4), 1-13.

Mallebrein, C.1993. *Die Anderen Götter: Volks- und Stammesbronzen aus Indien,* Köln: Rautenstrauch-Joest-Museum/Heidelberg: Edition Braus.

— 1996. 'Danteśvarī, the Family Goddess (*kulsvāminī*) of the Rājas of Bastar, and the Daśaharā-Festival of Jagdalpur', in A. Michaels, C. Vogelsanger and A. Wilke (eds.), *Wild Goddesses in India and Nepal*, Bern: Peter Lang, 483-511.

— 1998. *Darshan: Blickkontakte mit indischen Göttern. Die ländliche und tribale Tradition*. Berlin: State Museum of Ethnography.

— 1999. 'Tribal and Local Deities: Assimilations and Transformations', in V. Dehejia (ed.), *Devi: The Great Goddess. Female Divinity in South Asian Art*, Washington: A. Sackler Gallery, 137-56.

— 2001 'Tribal Art: Continuity and Change', in P. Pal (ed.), *Orissa Revisited*, Mumbai: Marg, 142-61.

— 2004a. 'Ruler, Protector and Healer: The Clan Gods Sulia, Patkhanda and Sikerpat of the Kondh Tribe', in C. Mallebrein and L. Guzy (eds.), *Facets of Orissan Studies* (Special Issue), *Journal of Social Sciences* 8 (2), 143-53.

— 2004b. 'Creating a *kshetra*: Goddess Tarini of Ghatgaon and her Development from a Forest Goddess to a Pan-Orissan Deity', in C. Mallebrein and L. Guzy (eds.), *Facets of Orissan Studies* (Special Issue), *Journal of Social Sciences* 8 (2), 155-65.

— 2004c. 'Entering the Realm of Durgā: Pāṭkhaṇḍā, a Hinduized Tribal Deity', in A. Malinar, J. Beltz and H. Frese (eds.), *Text and Context in the History, Literature and Religion of Orissa*, Delhi: Manohar, 273-305.

— 2006. 'When the Buffalo becomes a Pumpkin: The Animal Sacrifice Contested', in G. Pfeffer (ed.), *Centre and Periphery: Groups, Categories, Values*, Delhi: Manohar.

Mishra, B. 1991. 'Manikeswari Temple of Bhawanipatna', in J.K. Behera (ed.), *Maa Manikswari (The Tutelary deity of Kalahandi)*, Bhawanipatna: Mahabir Sanskrutik Anusthan, 17-26.

Mishra, B. 1992. 'The Cult of Manikeswari', in *Journal of Orissan History* 12, 37-42.

Mukherjee, P. 1953. *The History of the Gajapati Kings of Orissa and their Successors*, Calcutta: S. Mukherjee General Trading Company.

Nayak, R. (et al.) 1990. *The Kondhs: A Handbook for Development*, New Delhi: Indian Social Institute.

Nayak, R.; N. Soreng. 1999. *The Kuvi Kondhs: A Handbook for Development*, Bhubaneswar: NISWASS.

Nayak, P.K. 1989. *Blood, Women and Territory: An Analysis of Clan Feuds of Dongria Konds*, Delhi: Reliance Publishing House.

Niggemeyer, H. 1964. *Kuttia Kond: Dschungel-Bauern in Orissa*, Haar bei München: Klaus Renner Verlag.

Panda, B.P. 1997. 'Resistance Movement in British Orissa', in J.K. Samal (ed.), *Comprehensive History and Culture of Orissa*, Vol. 2, Delhi: Kaveri Books, 163-89.

Panda, Sh. K. 1999. *Political and Cultural History of Orissa*, Delhi: New Age Publishers.

Panigrahi, K. Ch. 1981. *History of Orissa,* Cuttack: Kitab Mahal.

Pasayat, Ch. 1997. 'Tribal-Non-Tribal Interaction in Orissa: A Study of Samalei/Samaleswari Devi in Sambalpur', in G. Pfeffer and D.K. Behera (eds.), *Contemporary Society: Tribal Studies,* Vol. 2, Delhi: Concept Publishing Company, 304-16.

— 1998. *Tribe, Caste and Folk Culture*, Jaipur, Delhi: Rawat Publications.

Patnaik, Dh. 1982. *Festivals of Orissa* (With a foreword by Raicharan Das), Bhubaneswar: Orissa Sahitya Akademi.

Postel, M. and Z. Cooper 1999. *Bastar Folk Art*, Mumbai: Franco-Indian Research.

Preston, J. 1980. *Cult of the Goddess: Social and Religious Change in a Hindu Temple*, Delhi: Vikas Publishing House.

Rahmann, R. 1936. 'Gottheiten der Primitivstämme im nordöstlichen Vorderindien', in *Anthropos* 31, 37-96.

Rajeshwari, D.R. 1989. *Sakti Iconography,* Delhi: Intellectual Publishing House.

Rajguru, S.N. 1972. *History of the Gaṅgas*, 2 vols., Bhubaneswar: State Museum.

— 1979 'The Naga Dynastiy of Chakrakota', in *The Orissa Historical Research Journal*, 24-26, 25-44.

Rao, B.R. 1993. *History of the Ex-State of Kalahandi: 1905-1948* (thesis Berhampur University).

Russell, R.V. and Hira Lal Rai Bahadur. 1975. *The Tribes and Castes of the Central Provinces of India* (4 vols.), Delhi: Rajdhani Book Centre.

Sahu, J.K. 1997. *Historical Geography of Orissa,* Delhi: Decent Books.

Sahu, N.K., P.K. Mishra and J.K. Sahu. 1980, *History of Orissa*, Cuttack: Nalanda.

Schnepel, B. 1993. 'Die Schutzgöttinnen: Tribale Gottheiten in Südorissa (Indien) und ihre Patronage durch hinduistische Kleinkönige', in *Anthropos* 88, 337-50.

— 2002. *The Jungle Kings: Ethnohistorical Aspects of Politics and Ritual in Orissa*, Delhi: Manohar.

Senapati, N. and D.Ch. Kuanr. 1980. *Orissa District Gazetteers (Kalahandi)*, Vol. 6, Gazetteer Unit Department of Revenue Government of Orissa.

Sharma, R.K. 1998. *Encyclopaedia of Art, Archaeology and Literature in Central India*, Delhi: Aryan Books International.

Shukla, H.L. 1988. *Tribal History: A New Interpretation*, Delhi: B.R. Publishing Corporation.

Singh Deo J.P. 1987. *Cultural Profile of South Kōśala*, Delhi: Gyan Publishing House.

— 1991. 'Goddess Manikyadevi', in J.K. Behera (ed.), *Maa Manikswari (The Tutelary deity of Kalahandi)*, Bhawanipatna: Mahabir Sanskrutik Anusthan, 1-3.

— 1991. 'Manikeswari Temple and the Icon of the Deity', in J.K. Behera (ed.), *Maa Manikswari (The Tutelary Deity of Kalahandi)*, Bhawanipatna: Mahabir Sanskrutik Anusthan, 4-10.

— 2001. *Tantric Art of Orissa,* Delhi: Kalpaz Publications.

Singh, K.S. 1994. *The Scheduled Tribes.* People of India. National Series, Volume III. Anthropological Survey of India, Delhi: Oxford University Press.

Sinha, S. 1962. 'State Formation and Rajput Myth in Tribal Central India', in *Man in India* 42 (1), 35-80.

Sircar, D.C. and M. Venkataramayya. 1949-50. 'Mahada Plates of Somesvaradevarman: Year 23', in *Epigraphia Indica* 28, 283-92.

Sundar, N. 1997. *Subalterns and Sovereigns: An Anthropological History of Bastar, 1854-1996*, Delhi: Oxford University Press.

Urban, H.B. 2003. 'The Power of the Impure: Transgression, Violence and Secrecy in Bengali Śākta Tantra and Modern Western Magic', in *Numen* 50 (3), 269-308.

Urhahn, M. 1985. *Grenzen und Übergänge von Kasten- und Stammesgesellschaft in Indien.* Heidelberg: Südasien Institut.

11

Casting a Glorious Past: Loss and Retrieval of the *Ol Chiki* Script

Barbara Lotz

The focus in this paper is on different concepts of time as imagined both within and outside the Santal community, concentrating on the promised return of the 'golden past' as a key motif of self-orientation. First, nineteenth-century Western interests in documenting the past of the Santal in search of a history of the 'original' high civilization of India will be discussed. This will serve to provide a background in contextualizing the attempt of the Santal schoolteacher Raghunath Murmu (1905-85), from Mayurbhanj, Orissa, to preserve the narrative heritage and mythic history of his people. Murmu created a body of texts ranging from mythological tales and dramas to school textbooks in Santali, and written in a script designed by himself. The reinvention of the allegedly formerly existing Santali script, *Ol Chiki*,[1] was the centrepiece of Murmu's vision to revitalize the cultural and spiritual consciousness of the Santal by ascribing to them a written tradition that they had once possessed in bygone days of imagined glory, when the Santal were independent and free. The cultural movement that was initiated through Murmu's efforts from the 1940s onwards will then be compared with previous and contemporary socio-political and religious movements of the Santal, which had also mobilized the masses by means of claims of a returning golden age of 'Santal Rule' (*Santal Raj*). The paper will analyse interpretations of time and history with regard to (1) colonial and missionary interests in historizing time and extracting scientific facts from orally transmitted concepts of time; (2) attempts by leaders of the community to employ the emotional value of a commonly shared concept of time in revolutionary or reform movements; and (3) Raghunath Murmu's intricate handling of a concept of mythic time to increase the status of Santal culture in the past, present and future.

---

[1] For an example, see figure page 249.

Documenting a Tribal Past

Santal legends and mythological tales assumed a written form for the first time in the middle of the nineteenth century, when British civil servants and Western missionaries began to document the Santali language. If we examine the early ethnographic material on the Santal that was published by British officers such as Dalton, Man, Hunter and Risley, the insertion of the Santal myth of origin figures prominently in all their texts, since any traces of the 'history' of the community were clearly of the greatest interest to these foreign observers. The narratives were taken down from various Santal informants and were mostly translated by missionaries familiar with the language. These versions, in spite of variations due to the different geographical, religious and social backgrounds of the informants,[2] reflect the existence of a quite consistent and clearly outlined oral text in the cultural memory of the Santal, as transmitted in the form of a recitation performed twice in the life of every Santal individual.[3] The myth ranges from the very beginnings of the world to the creation of the first human beings, then moves on to their genealogy and separation into clans or septs, i.e. into the twelve different families of the tribe, and on to the mixed fate that the community experienced during long years of migration.

These oral traditions certainly did not meet the expectations of a proper source for historical research by Western standards, as they did not conform to the notion of a chronological or factual account. With its range of narration encompassing a whole cosmogony, namely the influence of the supernatural as well as mundane developments, the myth was more likely to reflect a construction of time that was intricately linked to the spiritual concepts of the community as well as to its wanderings on earth.

---

[2] The selection of the informants, who often came from Christianized circles or were by profession used to dealing with outsiders, had to lead to selective information as they may have been influenced by Christian or Hindu world views or by the intentions of the researchers or missionaries themselves.

[3] The traditional legend of the creation of the world is recited in connection with the life-cycle rituals of every Santal, first at the Chaco Chatiar ceremony (*chaco* lit. means 'toddling', i.e. the ceremony may be performed when the child starts to move), when the child is symbolically given full social rights as a member of the Santal community, and finally at the Bhandan, the funeral ceremony, when the deceased is handed over to the next world and to the care of the already departed ancestors. Cf. Bodding 2001, 2. The recitation of the myth is thus essential for the integration of the individual into the lineage.

As a literary genre, the myths could not compete with the refinement and dimensions of the classical Sanskrit epics that had fascinated indologists earlier (and they too had expected to identify a historical core to these works), nor did the narrative expansion of the lineage into the past provide any royal chronicles or biographies, or valid references to friendly or hostile dynasties on the outside. Compared to the stock of Sanskrit texts that had already failed to counter Western accusations of the 'ahistorical' character of Hindu culture, these orally transmitted myths seemed to be situated at an even lower stage of historical self-consciousness.[4] Yet, as the only available record of the tribe's past, they had a fascination of their own, since they served these Western scholars as a basis for various conjectures concerning not only the origin of this specific community, but also the still hazy early migratory history of the sub-continent. The few 'hard facts' in the mythical narratives of the Santal, especially the host of geographical names mentioned along their migration route, therefore seemed the most promising basis for scientific verification to Western historians and ethnographers, whether by examining historical sites or comparing Santal tales of migration with the similar, recorded legends of neighbouring tribal communities. Once the beginnings of Indian civilization had been associated with the spread of the Aryan race, the interest in the pre-Aryan period was aroused among Western scholars, especially as the Munda languages obviously did not belong to the Indo-Aryan family. Extracting possibly embedded geographical information out of the narratives, one missionary to the Santal, Skrefsrud, assumed that they had entered India via the Punjab (on the basis of the 'seven-river land Campa'), while Dalton argued that they must have come from Assam, and Risley, rejecting both theories, sought to locate their migration route much closer in both time and geographical space.[5]

---

[4] That the oral traditions were expected to be of either epical or historical dimensions is visible in several disappointed statements. Dalton thus complained that the Santal lacked 'a song commemorative of ancient glory'; Man remarked with resignation: 'Once upon a time gives all the chronological data I could ever extract from them'. Risley stated that these legends could be acknowledged 'neither as a record of actual wanderings nor as an example of the workings of the myth making faculty .... of a people whose only means of recording facts consists of tying knots in strings and who have no bards to hand down a national epic by oral tradition'. Cf. Dalton 1872, 210; Man 1989, 42; Risley 1891, 225.

[5] Risley, while dealing with Skrefsrud's and Dalton's respective theories on the Santal migration, criticised them for their trust in the narration. To support his own migration theories, however, Risley willingly resorted to the same tales: 'If

The people who eventually facilitated the study of the Santal legends started their work much earlier, since the beginnings of the documentation of Santali culture and language can be traced to the arrival of the American Free Will Baptist Mission in 1835. On the initiative of Amos Sutton, who had come to Orissa in 1824, Revd and Mrs Eli Noyes and Revd and Mrs Jeremiah Phillips were sent to India, starting their mission in the western portion of Midnapore district and in Balasore district, Orissa.[6] It was Revd Noyes who in December 1838 'discovered' a people in the jungles between Orissa and Bengal who were 'neither Oriyas nor Coles' and 'kept themselves aloof from the Hindus'.[7] From 1845, when a mission began in that remote area, Revd Phillips started to learn the language from a Santal teacher, in the study of which he became a pioneer,[8] producing translations of school materials and of numerous scriptures into Santali using the Bengali script). Phillips established the first Santal school in 1845 and, as early as 1852, published the first 'Introduction to the Santali Language' in the Bengali script.[9] Phillips' expertise is widely acknowledged, for example by E.G. Man, who thanks him in his foreword for his assistance 'in the Sonthalia language and songs'; similarly, W.W. Hunter, in his *Annals of Rural Bengal* (1868), relied largely on information supplied to him by Phillips.

The widespread recognition of the Santal as a distinct people, different from the 'Coles' and Mundas,[10] can be directly related to the

---

the legends are regarded as an account of recent migration, their general purport will be found to be fairly in accord with actual facts'. Ibid., 225.

[6] The Balasore station was founded in 1835. Cf. Swaro 1990, 2.

[7] Culshaw 1949, 2; Swaro 1990, 143. We find an incidental remark regarding the 'industrious Sonthars' in a report of 1817 by Jt. Magistrate Sutherland of Monghyr. Cf. Man 1989, 10.

[8] The Annual Report of the Free Will Baptist Mission for the year 1846 states: 'During the past year Brother Phillips has acquired some knowledge of the language of these people (the Santals).... He has published a tract of 8 pages, which is the first work ever published in the Santal dialect' (Culshaw 1949, 3-5).

[9] Swaro 1990, 147-9.

[10] Also the Gossner missionaries (Berlin), to whom Skrefsrud belonged initially before he founded his own Santal mission in 1867 near Benagaria, mention the Santal by name ('The Santal-tribes of our Coles') first in Schatz's report of 31 July 1855, after the news of the *Hul* (Santali for 'rebellion') had reached them. Cf. *Biene* Dec. 1855, 90. From then on, in the words of Gossner missionary Batsch, 'we started to especially focus our mission on these people' (Batsch from Hazaribagh, 20 Oct. 1856, in *Biene*, Feb. 1857, 14).

impact of the Santal *Hul*, the violent Santal insurrection of 1855/56. This originated in an isolated area of the Raj Mahal Hills, but soon threatened to spread to other Santal-populated areas, creating a great stir among the British administration and the resident missionaries who, perhaps for the first time, realized the extensive area of settlement of these people.[11] Among the Santal, too, the *Hul* became one of the most important turning points in more recent collective memory, where legends and tales sprang up dealing with its origin, reasons for failure, and impact on the community.[12] The Santal rebels, Sido and Kanhu, emerged as agents inspired by divine orders to restore independence and bring about the long-awaited *Santal Raj* (Santal Rule). Their eventual failure was later assigned to their personal moral misbehaviour, which had probably infuriated the gods. Nevertheless, in Santal memory they are hailed as the first real national martyrs, who actually preceded the rebels of the 1857 mutiny.

Parallel periods were forcefully interconnected[13] at this point: while for the Santal the uprising meant a phase necessary to bring about the return of the golden age in the course of revolving cycles of glory and decay, for the colonial rulers it marked the official entry of the Santal as a distinctive ethnic community. This official registration paved the way for further investigations into the Santal's past and present and a gradual integration of their time into the chronological framework of the West. Although earlier uprisings had been formally noted, it was only the 1855 *Hul* that eventually attracted the attention of the rulers to the grievances of the tribals. The revolt triggered in its wake a wave of sympathy for the Santal and a feeling of remorse over the atrocious exploitation of the British Raj and their local administrators. For the British rulers and Western missionaries, siding with the tribals also gave vent to the expression of their simmering contempt for the 'cunning' practices of the

---

[11] As the Gossner missionaries Schatz and Batsch mention in their reports of July and August 1855 respectively, they had to fear for their stations in Hazaribagh and Ranchi in case the rebellion would reach these areas. Although condemning the violence of the tribals, Schatz explicitly states that the government alone was responsible for the uprising, as it had continued to support the 'most horrible suppression' by landlords and officials (*Biene*, Dec. 1855, 90).

[12] P.B. Andersen, in a paper presented at 17 ECMSAS, Heidelberg 2002, concentrates on Santal statements and narratives about the *Hul* and the Kherwar movement he had collected from archives and Bodding's folkloristic collections. Andersen 2002, unpublished paper.

[13] Cf. Malinar in this volume.

dominant Hindu society.[14] A patronizing concern was adopted towards a people whose caste-free and self-governed social system came ideally close to the concept of the noble savage on the one hand, and who, on the other, with their neglected and abandoned position in society seemed to personify the downtrodden and meek of the earth, making them ideal recipients for the teaching and preaching of the West.[15] To compensate them for the previous official neglect, the new district of Santal *pargana*s was created around the Damin-i-Koh, with a decentralised, village-based administration, while on the educational and social levels, the government explicitly encouraged the missions to concentrate their work on the Santal.[16]

As a result, documentation and literature on the Santal increased to such an extent that, by 1872, Dalton obviously had good reason to declare the Santal 'the most honoured of the aboriginal races in Bengal in the attention that enquirers have [of late] directed towards them'.[17] The first book exclusively on the Santal, published in 1867 by Assistant Commissioner E.G. Man, reflects this spirit of sympathetic affinity, especially when he presents his later highly acclaimed five-point analysis of the 'primary causes of the rebellion', recounting the injustices inflicted on the Santal by moneylenders, the police, government officials and the law courts from 1832 onwards. In unrestrained admiration of the administrative measures taken by his superior, Sir Ashley Eden, Man judges the developments following the uprising as 'the first step towards raising the Santals from a state of misery ... to comparative prosperity and

---

[14] Missionary Skrefsrud, in his preachings on the abolition of spirit worship, compared the greediness of the spirits (*bonga*s) with that of the exploiting Bengalis, making clever use of the word 'similarity' (Saeter 1938, 159).

[15] The *Christian Observer*, Calcutta, of August 1862 strongly recommended further missionary work among the tribals: 'The Hindoos look down upon these people ... [but] these are the victims that please God, with a broken and shattered heart, ... whosoever shall abase oneself shall be exalted, this is the first step towards acceptance of Christianity. That is why the despised aborigines are much easier converted than the clever and proud Hindoos.' Cf. *Biene*, Jan. 1863, 6.

[16] After the *Hul*, several missions started to work among the Santal. By 1857, the Church Mission had started work around Bhagalpur, the Gossner mission was active around Hazaribagh from 1856 onwards, the Baptists expanded their earlier work in Birbhum and Orissa, and the Methodists worked among the Santal in Bankura (Saeter 1938, 145; H. Batsch from Hazaribagh, Dec. 1864, in *Biene*, July 1865).

[17] Dalton 1872, 208.

contentment', thereby determining a turning point in their existence, dividing it into a (gloomy) past and a (promising) future, the change for the better having been brought about by his own countrymen.[18] Apart from moulding contemporary history, he displays in his book a prominent interest in the ancient history of the Santal, an interest which is, however, twofold, since he does not just seek to explore their past for its own sake, but rather with the aim of throwing light on the roots of his own culture.

In his endeavour, Man first presents substantial extracts from the Santal legends of origin, and then, with great effort, relates their mythological elements to similarities in Greek, Sumerian or Egyptian mythology. His interest in tracing the 'golden past' of the Santal is inspired by his passion for the ancient glories of Egyptian and Sumerian culture. In his quest to find parallels, the Santal, in his view, achieve the status of being the source of all Indian civilization, and he acclaims them as the 'most ancient, perhaps the most primitive race in India', and wonders about a time 'when the Sonthals and the Greek, the Persian and the German, the Feejee and the Maori ... all the races of men were gathered at one place'.[19] His romantic interest in the unity of the derivation of mankind conspicuously excludes the Hindu population, when he considers the 'Sonthal traditions ... pure and unadulterated ... the Sonthal as a distinct race, has every appearance of being older than the Hindoo'.[20] Similarly he disputes the idea of 'Sanscrit being the older sister of most civilised languages' and rather suggests Santali to be the 'ancient and uncorrupted dialect' of the subcontinent. Interestingly, his assessment seems to echo the Santal's own world view when he supports their concept of a (once glorious) people who were perennially driven out of their habitat by the invading and dominant *Dekos*.[21]

What is generally considered the most detailed and authentic version of the legends of origin was published about twenty years later, having been

---

[18] In contrast to this evaluation, Bodding states that although most Santal consider the *Hul* to be the beginning of a new era, in their estimation it is rather one of deterioration (Bodding 2001, 10).

[19] Man 1989, 60-2.

[20] Ibid., 66-9.

[21] Bodding in his Santal Dictionary translates *Diku* or *Deko* as 'A Hindu or Bengali of the better class, not low caste Hindus e.g. Domes, Bauris, Hadis. Mohammedans are not called *deko*.'

noted down in Santali[22] by Missionary Revd L.O. Skrefsrud (1840-1910), as told to him by the Santal Guru Kolean.[23] In the texts translated by Bodding, we have a relatively 'uncommented' compilation of myths, social customs and rituals, as indeed the text was initially designed by Skrefsrud 'as a guide for the Santals, especially in the customary matters', and it did not primarily address the foreign reader.[24] Compared to the earlier accounts of officers-cum-anthropologists, this text therefore offers a less altered view of Santal concepts of their past, present, and future.

The legends of origin and consequent migration as preserved in the oral narratives of the Santal and documented in these texts reveal several patterns of remembrance. Time is accounted for in a linear sequence as it follows the origin and genealogy of the tribe, though not in terms of chronologically correct data and events. Simultaneously, we find the idea of a revolving pattern, as a once existing golden era is expected to return in the future after a present period of decay. Most remarkable in the narrative of their migration are the oscillating sequences of prosperity and destruction in their destiny, sometimes assuming biblical dimensions of collective sin and heavenly reprisal through the expulsion of the whole clan. Time periods are rarely marked by ruling dynasties or kingdoms,

---

[22] Skrefsrud noted down the Santali text in Roman letters. The use of Bengali characters, initially meant to make printed matter accessible to literate Santals, ended in around 1868, when Revd Puxley published *A Vocabulary of the Santali Language* in the Roman script. In 1873, Skrefsrud, an excellent linguist and phonetician, edited *A Grammar of the Santhal Language*, which has been the foundation of all works on this language. He also used Bengali characters initially, but in this grammar adopted the Roman alphabet with a number of diacritical marks. His system of transliteration is still in use with a few exceptions.

[23] Kolean's dictation was finished on 15 February 1871, and the text published in Santali (in Roman script) in 1887. It was re-edited by P.O. Bodding (in 1916 and 1929), and finally translated into English in the 1930s by him; however, the translation only appeared after Bodding's death in 1936, with a foreword by Sten Konow.

[24] Skrefsrud was, of course, first and foremost a missionary, who, despite all the deep affection, respect and scholarship he devoted to 'his' Santal and their culture, was determined to lead them away from spirit worship and superstition. Bodding therefore rightly doubted Skrefsrud's statement that the book contained absolutely nothing of his own, and attributes at least the arrangement and the 'easy and fine' language to Skrefsrud's influence (Bodding 2001, 1).

neither their own nor those of their neighbours,[25] although their legends and tales are replete with 'royal' individuals, perhaps in emulation of Hindu terms to denote the chiefs of a clan. Instead, periods are marked and remembered by their respective locations of settlement: the memory of the past seems to be preserved in predominantly spatial dimensions.[26] Therefore, the memory of the route appears to be the core of a sense of continuity in a nomadic and migratory community; furthermore, the route is also able to preserve the memory of the localities where the segregation or integration of other members took place, thus ordering the hierarchy of genealogical links.[27] Although there are variations or omissions in the sequences of sites mentioned in the memories of the different gurus, the respective qualities attached to each of these locations varies amazingly little. Memory has imprinted the names of locations with the ineffaceable stamp of the sojourn, advantageous, hostile or disastrous, that the Santal experienced there.

However, once the oscillating movement of ups and downs seemed to have reached a climax, as between periods of unsteady wanderings, they reached a promised land and experienced a golden age of self-rule

---

[25] In the version presented by Man, they were once persecuted by one 'Mirjadurrik', believed by many to be a 'Mussalman king' (Man 1989, 38). In another version of the legend, a Santal king destroyed himself and his family at Chae on hearing of the approach of a Muslim army under a general of Muhammad Bin Taughlaq (Ghosh 2000, 153).

[26] Thapar refers to the spatial form of description and 'the total orderliness' as a marker of cosmological time in distinction to historical time, as 'the orderliness emphasises its unreality'. However, memories of the Santal migration route seems to alternate between the cosmological spheres and quite realistic geographical conditions (cf. Thapar 2000, 142). For example, in a song given in Kolean's version, the route is remembered in an abbreviated version: 'In Hihiri Pipiri we were born, in Khoj Kaman we were called for, in Harata we grew up, in Sasan Beda we became septs', and so on. Cf. Bodding 2001, 9.

[27] The route up to Chae Campa coincides with the greater portion of the Munda traditions, indicating that both, Santal and Munda, were once members of a single tribe that they refer to as the Kherwar (or Kharwar). Cae Campa is mentioned in Munda and Santal traditions as the point of separation for the Kherwars, the Munda remaining in what is now Ranchi District, the Santal moving on, crossing the Damodar to Hazaribagh, then further on to Manbhum and Santal Parganas. The dispersal of the other Kherwar branches allegedly also started from Campa (Bodding 2001, 12; Roy 1995, 65; Ghosh 2000, 151f.). According to Skrefsrud, a later settlement of the Santal, Saont in the present-day Midnapore district, gave them their name.

and independence. All Santal traditions agree that, after a number of unsuitable places, they stayed in Cae (or Chattro) Campa for a very long time and built many forts for all their sub-families;[28] it was also here that they placed their gods, the Highest Spirits, in the sacred grove called the *jaher*.[29] The end of this golden age is explained with reference to a weakening from within through infighting among the families and illicit relationships, which led to their final defeat by the *Dekos*: not obeying the ancestor's rules and mixing with people from outside is considered the reason for their exodus from Campa.[30] In the narrator's perspective, the appeal of the golden past is enhanced by a contrasting perception of the present as a period of degeneration and a miserable time of transition.[31] This perception characterises the generally gloomy end of the Santal's

---

[28] According to E.G. Man's version, in Cae Campa the descendants of Pilchu Haram, the first man, and Pilchu Furhi, the first woman, 'split up into tribes or families, ... the Hansdah, ... the Murmu, Soren, Tudu, Mardi, Kisku, Besra, Kedoar, Baski, Marmoren, Bisra and Hemron, twelve tribes in all (Man 1989, 41). In Kolean's version, however, the families were formed earlier than Cae Campa, around four stations in Sasan Beda . In his version, each family had its 'special work', i.e. the Kiskus were kings, the Murmus priests, the Sorens peons and fighters, the Hembroms the nobility, the Marandis the wealthy class, the Baskes the merchants and so on (cf. Bodding 2001, 9-10).

[29] A cluster of trees (where possible of the original forest) consisting of *sal* trees and at least one *mahua* tree, to be seen in the vicinity of every Santal village as a place of worship. The grove is also known as *Sarna*, the word that came to be used by the Santal to differentiate their religion from Hinduism.

[30] The key story in the expulsion from Campa by Mando Sin (also Madhwa or Madho) is told in many versions; here is Kolean's: One Sin (descendants of Kherwars who had joined in marriage with Dekos) had an illicit relationship with the daughter of a Kisku king. When the girl bore a child she was forced to abandon it. The boy was found by Marandi girls who named him Mando Sin, and he grew up to be a powerful Divan in the royal Kisku family. Mando finally demanded a Kisku girl for marriage. As no one was willing to give his daughter to Mando because his sept was unclear, he threatened to apply *sindur* as a sign of marriage forcibly to all the daughters of the tribe. Terrified, the whole population fled (Bodding 2001, 12).

[31] In Bodding's assessment, 'The traditions generally end with lamenting the present deplorable state of the people; they are living under the feet of the Dekos; they are unable to stay anywhere; are very poor and so on. As a consequence they have forgotten their old customs; they have no Guru-training; and besides this they have no records (written), their records are all 'in the mouth'; therefore so much has been lost, mixed up and brought into disorder' (Bodding 2001, 22).

tales of origin, thus rapidly establishing a rapport with a possibly latent feeling of discontent with their present status among the audience, while simultaneously appealing to a reorientation towards the former power, independence, and unity of the community. The narrative itself acquires importance by implying that the former stages of glory could be attained again if proper consequences were to be drawn from the narratives. Furthermore, the melancholic yearning for the past, which is invariably intertwined with a self-characterization as the eternal victim of the *Deko* outsider, serves to increase the prestige of the community in competition with its neighbours, as it implies that, in spite of the present degradation, the bygone civilization was greater than everything presently existing.

Invent a Script and Write Back

By the 1930s, the Santali language and literature had attracted great interest, resulting in a substantial and steadily growing number of profound articles based on linguistic and grammatical research, the publication of excellent grammars and dictionaries, and extensive collections of transcribed and translated oral literature. In fact, there were so many different researchers, administrators and missionaries working on Santali and other Munda languages that the question of a standardized script arose. In view of the 'deplorable long war'[32] over how to write the Munda languages, especially Santali, in 1925 Bodding pleaded with the Asiatic Society of Bengal to decide on a single, scientifically rigorous system of writing, for which, as Grierson too had stated, the Roman alphabet with diacritic marks devised by Skrefsrud would be the most suitable, not only for publications by foreign scholars, but also as a

[32] Bodding refers to the 'violation of an agreement of 27 years ago' between the three principal missions working among the Santals to adopt the system of writing introduced by Skrefsrud, i.e. the Roman script with systematised diacritics. Bodding complains, that since the discontinuation of Bengali characters for Santali, a haphazard use of the Roman script lacking correct diacritics had led to several grave mistakes in scientific publications. Cf. Bodding 1925, 13. Grierson, who was assisted in his survey by Bodding in the section on the Munda languages, also favourably refers to the proposed standardization of spelling in the context of Bodding's translation of the Old Testament. Grierson 1906, 37.

standardized medium for teaching the Santal to write in their own language.[33]

Against this backdrop of 'being written' for more than eight decades, a change of agency becomes apparent when, from the 1930s onwards, a Santal schoolteacher, Raghunath Murmu, became the initiator of a cultural movement that originated in his village in Orissa but later spread to all Santal areas. The inspiration to engage himself in the promotion of his mother tongue seems to have arisen from Murmu's first experiences at school. Born in the village of Dandbose near Rairangpur, Mayurbhanj, into a family of agriculturists and carpenters,[34] he was sent to primary school but is said to have protested early against being taught in Oriya, not Santali. He went on to study in Bahalda Middle School and matriculated at the high school in the state capital, Baripada. After serving an apprenticeship in the Baripada Power House, he engaged himself in Cottage Industry by weaving carpets, where he developed some innovative methods and was sent by the then Diwan for further industrial training to Calcutta, Serampore and Goshaba. Upon his return, he was appointed instructor of Purna Chandra Industrial Institute in Baripada, but had to quit the job because of the death of his father. He was then posted near his home as headmaster of Badamtaliya Model School, teaching Oriya and English. Since his apprenticeship at Baripada, he had been experimenting with a script for the Munda languages, but it was only during his comparatively steady job at Badamtaliya that he finally designed the *Ol* alphabet, manufactured the hand press and wrote his first successful drama, *Bidu-Chandan* (1942). The superintendent of education of the state was impressed by these endeavours and had the hand press sent to the Mayurbhanj State exhibition of 1939, whereupon he was even

[33] Bodding defended this system as 'something which is in accordance with their [the Santal's] mental character. We have very little trouble in teaching them to write correctly when they use our system. A better proof of its soundness is not required' (Bodding 1930, 5). Like Skrefsrud, who used medical mirrors to control the proper pronunciation of the Santali sounds, Bodding too was concerned with utter correctness. To arrive at a correct distinction of the vowels, he even 'succeeded in getting X-ray photographs of the Santal tongue when pronouncing nine different vowels', for which purpose he took 'half a dozen Santals' with him to Calcutta (ibid., 5).

[34] His father and brothers were known for well-designed cart wheels and agricultural tools, a background that proved useful when Murmu later manufactured his own printing blocks and a hand press for printing *Ol Chiki* (Badha Bishra 2001).

summoned by the Maharaja of Mayurbhanj, Pratap Chandra Bhanj Deo, to explain the alphabet.[35] He was promoted to Rairangpur High School, but in 1946 he resigned from the service to devote his life entirely to language and literature.

Murmu's biographical background is presented here in some detail in order to highlight his ability to cross traditional boundaries. Compelled to learn two and more languages from childhood, he grew up to negotiate between different cultural spheres. Although trained as an academic, he further developed his skills in traditional crafts. He travelled not only all over Mayurbhanj and Orissa, but also the neighbouring states of Bihar and West Bengal, not as a migrant labourer, but in the comparatively respected position of a tribal among non-tribals. It was then that he learned of the low respect his community had in the world and took the decision to work towards improving its image. Lastly, he managed to acquire a reputation in the outside world as a learned 'tribal' intellectual and writer. His home district of Rairangpur can itself be described as border area in a double sense: first, regarding its location on the northern confines of Orissa, which is linguistically, culturally and economically closely linked to Bihar and the tribal belt of Chota Nagpur, especially to the industrial town of Jamshedpur; and secondly, regarding the district's position within the Santal area of settlement at its southernmost pocket, quite distant from the heartland around Santal Parganas. This cultural and geographical distance from significant centres, combined with his unusual experience of the outside world, including a firm idea of the large settlement area of his tribe, may have reinforced his desire to create a common script as a cultural bond that would reconnect the Santal to former times of unity and establish a new centre extending across several linguistic and political zones.

Unlike previous combinations of Western writer and tribal informant (often with the additional mediation of a missionary as translator), for the first time, one and the same person was now writing texts of his own cultural heritage, being in the true sense 'authorized' as a community insider. Whereas before outsiders extracted internal Santal knowledge and made it intelligible to the outside world, now a member of the community was rewriting ancient Santal knowledge for his own contemporary people. Murmu would have been qualified to contribute to the existing stock of texts on Santal culture and literature in English or Oriya, but he chose to reject these languages and their scripts, as he

[35] Hemrom 1972, 2.

thought them unsuitable to represent the Munda languages properly. In his wish to increase the cultural prestige of his community, he seized one of the most powerful instruments with which to establish a dominant culture: a language, a script and a written tradition of its own.

A change of perspective can be assumed especially through the use of the *Ol Chiki* script for his texts: whereas earlier it was the translation of oral texts that had started a process of communication with the world, now a process of the community itself re-appropriating the texts was envisaged, to such an extent that the contents were not only rewritten, but virtually encoded with a script that was only intelligible to the initiated (though actually excluding most of his fellow tribesmen). A process of the concealment and re-privatization of cultural knowledge was initiated, without intending to challenge or halt the ongoing translation activities of researchers and missionaries.[36] By reconstituting the oral literature in the form of written texts, he reversed the process of the historization of the legends and initiated a kind of re-mythologization of time and space.

In this reinterpretation of myth and tradition, the adoption of a separate script played a significant role. The *Ol* script (see illustration) was perceived and represented as a divine tool intended to serve much more dignified purposes than mere communication. Basic communicative needs were already being met by the respective state languages of Oriya, Bengali and Hindi and their scripts, plus European languages in Roman script. The *Ol* script was meant to instil a feeling of pride in the former achievements of the community and to remind it of a once close relationship with divine beings who had been in possession of that script. The 'rediscovery' of the script sought to provide a link between the present community and its own past existence, characterized by spiritual guidance, discipline and learning; the re-appropriation of the script therefore appeared as a major component in achieving the superior status of earlier times. The 'disappearance' of the script in turn was interpreted as a loss of discipline and solidarity that the community had experienced in the course of time or, according to Murmu, to 'an emptiness of spirit

[36] In fact, during his lifetime some of his own works were translated into English by S. Mahapatra, such as extracts from *Hital* and song collections. Realizing the complexity of the issue, Murmu never openly referred to the 'Christian' character of the Roman script, nor did he turn against the missionaries' works. One reason might be that this pocket of Mayurbhanj saw little missionary activity. Moreover, Christian converts had played a significant role in the shaping of a tribal identity during the Jharkhand movement.

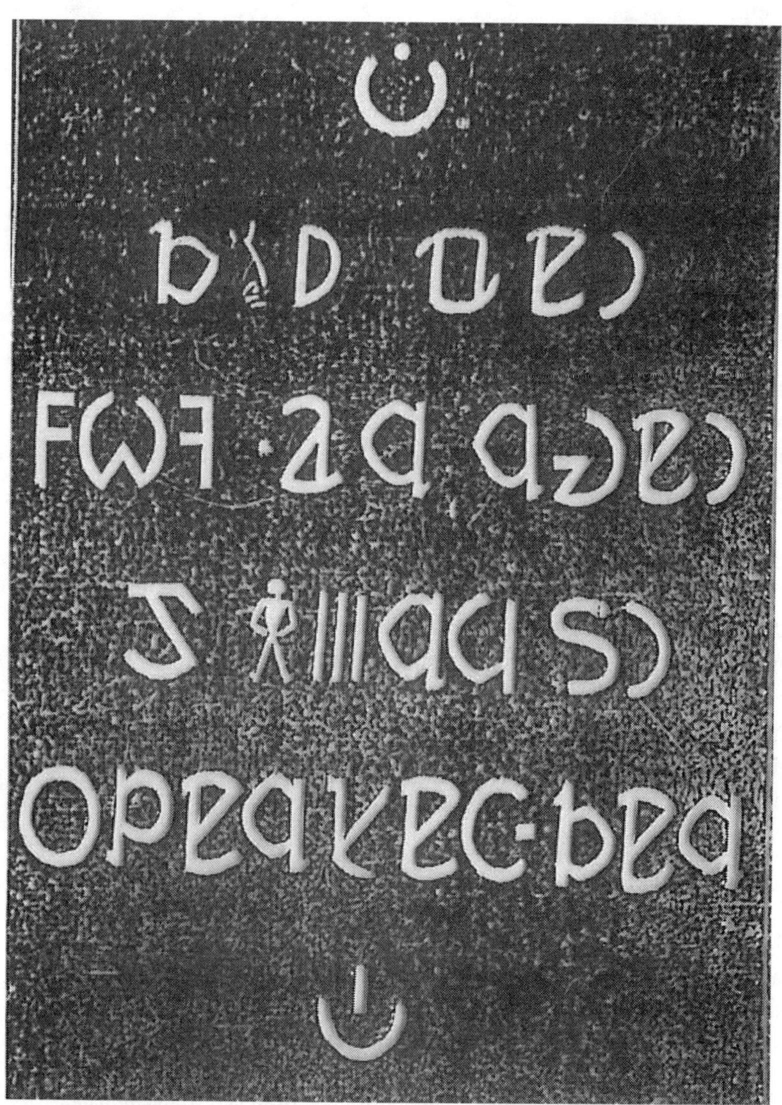

Ill.: Ol Chiki Script

and of softness in approach to life' that the community was facing in the present.[37]

The 'loss' of the script thus became a symbol of all that had been lost or corrupted in the course of time, and its 'rediscovery' assumed the dimensions of a spiritual renovation. The connection between the newly created script and the self-projection of the community's former existence in a timeless, sacred past becomes even more evident in the context of a certain wave of 'rediscovering' tribal scripts. These had been 'revealed' to their inventors around 1936, especially in Orissa and adjoining Chota Nagpur, where in almost all cases the script was conceived or received within a context of worship and spirituality.[38]

On a broader scale, the nationalistic fervour to defend one's mother tongue and cultural roots was certainly inspired by the rise of the Gandhian movement, which reached the area in the 1920s. Moreover, in the case of the tribal languages concerned, the attempts to establish scripts and grammars must be seen as a commitment to the tradition of the revolutionary Birsa movement, which had instilled a new cultural, spiritual and economic self-consciousness in the tribals of Chota Nagpur around 1900.[39] However, perhaps the most immediate incentive for the tribal language activists can be attributed to the success of the Oriya language movement, which had resulted in the formation of the first independent province on a linguistic basis that very year. The strategy of consolidating a language by equipping it with a body of literature, journals, and textbooks for primary education could be certainly studied in the example of the Oriya campaigners, who had been especially active in

[37] Mahapatra 1986, 68.

[38] Scripts for Santali, Saura, Ho, Kui etc. were devised from 1935 onwards. Guru Mongei Gomango (1916-81) invented the Saura script in 1936, when it 'materialised' in front of him as an incarnation of the god Daru Devata in the form of the alphabet. The 24 letters were designed to symbolize 24 important gods in their religion. The stone on which the script 'became visible' soon turned into a place of worship, and Gomang founded a religious sect based on the script (Mahapatra 1997, 77). In 1937, Samuel Ranka designed four alphabets for Kurukh (Oraon), none of which lasted (Pinnow 1972, 825). Lako Bodra designed *Varang Kshiti* for Ho and created an unpublished trilingual dictionary (Ho-Hindi-English) of which Zide writes, 'this is an esoteric work which is not mainly concerned with everyday Ho ...' (Zide 1991, 2535).

[39] Ho activist Lako Bodra, for example, was deeply influenced by the famous Munda leader Birsa Munda (1875-1900) and considered himself a medium keeping up Birsa's teachings and his political-patriotic tradition (Pinnow 1972, 826).

remote tribal areas such as Singhbhum.[40] The spread of a distinct wave of linguistic consciousness was obviously enhanced by their agitation, as much as by the frequent inquiries of border and language commissions, even if the aspirations of the tribal language activists originated in different contexts and motives.

The reason why, of all the tribal scripts invented, and in spite of its contested status, only the Santali *Ol Chiki* could establish itself over the years to a certain degree in teaching, publications, and distribution is partly due to the sound self-esteem of the Santal community, with its powerful urban pressure groups. Besides, Santali, in comparison with other tribal languages, cannot be defined as either marginal or endangered, in view of the large number of its speakers. But it was mainly Murmu's pragmatic and progressive outlook that helped the script to survive what was basically a short-lived fashion, since he was not indulging in any purely traditionalist or esoteric endeavour: from his own educational background, he was well aware that the language and script could only prosper if it was integrated into modern networks of teaching, communication and knowledge. Textbooks and reading material had to be prepared and printed, and, most importantly, an institutional network for training, printing and propagation had to be set up, all of which tasks he attended to more or less single-handedly and with great devotion.[41]

Although Murmu saw the script as a major achievement in his vision of spiritual and cultural reform, he was reluctant to project himself as a tool of divine inspiration. Soon after the script's invention, a mystification of its origin had become established in local belief, linking it to supernatural contexts. According to one of these myths, the first five characters were said to have been created from the five elements, thus emulating similar concepts of the 'holiness' of the Devanagari script and proclaiming the *Ol* script to be something primordial. Other

[40] Although the Oriya initiative in Singhbhum concentrated on the Oriya population there in order to consolidate its status, Oriya leaders, such as Godavarish Mishra in 1916, toured in this disputed border area, as the tribal Ho-population played a significant role in regard to which regional language they would call their own when asked by border or census commissions.

[41] The ASECA (Adibasi Socio-Educational Cultural Association) that he founded in 1954 has spread as a wide network over all states with a Santal population. That in Rairangpur, Orissa, is still the headquarters for teacher-training, text book production and administration. However, the acceptance of the script by both learners and the State Education Department is an issue that cannot be dealt with in this chapter.

interpretations endowed the script with a sacred and divine status by assigning its revelation to the Santal gods Bidu and Chandan, who had granted it to Raghunath Murmu after he had prayed to them.[42] However, Murmu preferred to point to the linguistic achievement of his creation of a scientific writing system that was initially devised for all the Munda languages, which would end the practice of noting down one language in four different scripts and which would create a feeling of a common linguistic identity among its users across political boundaries.[43] He was convinced that he had only reinvented and developed something that must have existed in former times, as he thought the elaborate usage of tattoo marks, way signs and other symbolic pictographs among the Santal were the survivals of a once comprehensively developed skill. In his view, the existence of the word '*Ol*' for 'writing' in Santali[44] served as a further basis for his assumption and justified his efforts.

Concerning the quality of secretiveness that the orally transmitted texts once possessed before they caught the attention of Western translators, Murmu's position may have been ambivalent. While on the one hand the translations had given proof to the world of the rich literary and mythological heritage of the Santal, on the other the gradual alienation of these texts from their originally restricted background may have caused concern for the desecrating or even polluting effects of their exposure to an atmosphere outside their proper context of worship and ritual. With the help of a separate script, however, texts that had been decoded by outsiders could again be encoded, thus protecting intimate spiritual knowledge from the outside world. The concern for the sacredness of the contents becomes evident, for example, in the introduction that Murmu wrote to his mythological drama *Bidu Chandan* (1942), where he stresses: 'it is a divine play. It should not be staged just

---

[42] For myths surrounding the making of the *Ol* script, cf. Mohapatra 2001, 75.

[43] The alphabet does not imitate other scripts in the area, but limits itself to thirty characters, some of which are derived from the physical environment or common postures of everyday life. All the vowels are indicated by separate letters ordered linearly on the Roman model, although the ordering of the letters follows the *varga* model of Devanagari. Six vowels are identified, and in the alphabet, each vowel 'leads' four consonants respectively, forming monosyllabic words for ease of remembering (Hemram 1972, 4; S. Mahapatra 1986, 117; Kh. Mahapatra 2001, 65; Mohapatra 2001, 74). According to Zide, the script 'provides some interesting and elegant representations', especially for the final checked sounds (Zide 1969, 426).

[44] The script was accordingly named *Ol Chiki*, or 'script for writing'.

any day. The best time to perform it is between the new moon day of Magh Bonga and Maha Bonga.'[45] His commitment obviously did not end in creating texts to add to the folkloric heritage of the Santal, but he intended to standardize their contents and re-create the sacred atmosphere they incorporated, thus re-ritualizing their performance within a traditional framework.

Among Murmu's major literary works, the play *Bidu Chandan* will be presented briefly here because in it we find the *Ol* script (which at the time of writing the play had just been created!) embedded in a mythical lore, suggesting that it had existed since time immemorial, when it had been used by semi-divine heroes. In his double function as the inventor of the script and the author of the drama, therefore, Murmu cleverly uses the literary form to convey obliquely the message that the script is not a recent invention but a revival of formerly available knowledge. The drama takes up strands of Santal legends that are traditionally rendered in *Binti* songs[46] and allows the divine dancers, Bidu and Chandan, come to earth to sing and dance, and to spread their message of peace and brotherhood among the people. The traditional story was reshaped to match the form of the drama, combining well-known features with newly invented details. Yet the attempt is not intended primarily to achieve the modernization of legendary material, but, as in many of Murmu's texts, is concerned rather with the integration of modern contents and messages into allegedly traditional folklore.[47]

In *Bidu Chandan*, the possession and use of a secret script forms a central strand in the development of the plot, since the script is exclusively used for secret communication between the heroine Chandan and the hero Bidu. The story relates how the outsider Bidu is caught up in feuding between the two Santal kingdoms of Chaigadh and Mangad, and due to misunderstandings, he ends up hiding from both sides. Chandan,

---

45 Murmu 1987, introduction.

46 *Binti* songs give an account of the creation and of migration from the mythical kingdoms of Chaigal, Champagal and Bahagal, and are recited at marriages (Mahapatra 1986, 8).

47 In Murmu's mythological play *Kherwar Bir*, which describes an epic battle between evil and good forces which are threatening to destroy the community, he projects moral values through the protagonists, who to his mind represent essential features of the Santal character. *Hital* is a voluminous collection of songs in praise of the creator, based on the origin myths of the Santal. Several disputed practices, such as eating meat and drinking alcohol, are dealt with in this text.

the daughter of the Chaigad chief, makes use of an encoded script to leave messages on rocks and walls for him.[48] At one of their clandestine meetings, Bidu equates her with a goddess for her cleverness and creative skill in using the script, but she in turn is amazed at his divine gift in being able to decipher the writing. Bidu replies that the miracle is entirely hers, since he has only read out what she has created. Both agree in the end that it is only through their bond of love and trust that they have become receptive enough to 'read each other's feelings'.[49] The scene ends with their secret marriage in the forest and their blessing by the gods. Later, written messages are exchanged when Bidu has to flee from Chandan's father, who is out to kill him. Chandan leaves a message on a rock for him, but when she comes there later in search of an answer, she only finds Bidu's bloodstained cloth. While everybody falls for the trick and thinks Bidu has died, Chandan suddenly discovers that the blood stains conceal the 'written' message that he is alive and has received her warnings in time to escape. In a later scene, however, Chandan finds a message from Bidu that he has been caught and carried off by his enemies. In the end, Bidu and Chandan disappear from the scene of turmoil and return to their heavenly spheres, taking their knowledge with them, and leaving the fighting humans to themselves. Only then are they recognized as divine beings, whereupon both the earthly parties resolve to follow the path of love and sacrifice in the future.

In the play, the script projects several functions and qualities. Although the signs are created by the goddess Chandan, even the god Bidu needs to be empowered by the 'bond of love' to decipher them and successfully communicate through them. The script functions as an exclusive and secret survival kit, protecting the knowing few from those who are 'blinded' by hatred, making them unable to read the signs or even to recognize them as something that might hold a message. It is presented as a divine offering that can be used by humans provided they abide by the rules of good and devout living. In spite of the opportunity missed in the past, nothing is lost, since time can repeat itself: the play suggests that there is hope for the future if the guidelines laid down by the gods are

[48] In the printed text, these 'messages' are set off against the *Ol Chiki* flow of text as white characters on black boards, and their somewhat crude or 'carved-like' script show a combination of pictorial signs and *Ol* letters, making these 'messages' appear as an 'early' stage of the script. See also the attached sample page.

[49] Murmu 1987, 71.

followed in the present. In-fighting and the loss of solidarity among the members of the tribe appear as the greatest impediments in recognizing the divine gift of the script, which has the unique quality of permitting the tribe to stand out and excel over all others. Mystical power is needed to decipher the script; the script in its turn is a means whereby to recognize the mystical power; and finally the script becomes the mystical power itself in its manifestation as the imperishable sacred alphabet.[50] The divine gift is timeless and thus primordial, as is man's ability to make use of it.

Reforms and Visions

Despite its overtly 'scientific' attitude, Murmu's vision for the reorganization of the Santal still had a distinct spiritual character. In his concern to revive a golden past by disciplining the members of the community in the present, he seems to have come close to other contemporary or earlier reformist movements among the Santal that had developed in the wake of the *Hul*. The idea of *Santal Raj* had already guided the heroes of the rebellion, Sidho and Kanhu, who claimed to be acting under a mandate from the gods. After the *Hul*, drought and famine led to the tribe's dispersal, and reasons for the failure of the rebellion were sought. In order to appease the gods, who were obviously disturbed, and to revive the ancient days of Santal independence, a group of Santal leaders in the Santal Parganas proclaimed the need for a reform of religious and social customs under the name of the Kherwar movement.[51] Parallel to the wave of Christianization among the Santal,[52] a distinct tendency towards Hinduization set in, when the first Kherwar leader, Baba Bhagirath Manjhi, announced around 1871 that he would restore the

---

[50] This concept, similar to the syllable *Om* as the unperishable Highest Being (*Akshar Brahma*), can be found among other newly invented tribal scripts such as Saura, where the script was believed to be an incarnation of the gods.

[51] The term the Santal use for themselves is 'Hor', meaning 'man'. 'Kherwar' is allegedly an old name of the tribe. Kolean narrates that 'up to Campa, we and the Mundas, the Birhor, the Kurmbis and others were called by the name of Kharwar.' This is supported by similar statements from Bagh Rai as recorded by Dalton. The Kherwars or Kharwars reigned earlier in the Damodar-Sone Valley, Chota Nagpur, and in the process of Hinduization became *jagirdar*s under the Chero kings. Cf. K.S. Singh, quoted in Chaudhuri 1993, 24.

[52] Skrefsrud and Bodding were quite critical of 'some present-day Santal who have wanted to effect a kind of reformation and have styled themselves Kherwars' (cf. Bodding 2001, 12).

golden age of the Santal if they gave up belief in spirits and returned to the worship of a single god, preferably the Hindu deity Ram Candra, whom he identified with the Santal god Cando, the Light Spirit.[53] In 1880, his successor Dubia Gossain introduced the worship of 'holy men', otherwise alien to Santal belief, and encouraged the Santal to demand an independent tribal administration during census operations in 1881. The Sapha Hor or Sapai movement was launched with an even stronger stress on purity, largely invoking Hindu concepts of pollution by demanding that the Santal renounce their 'objectionable' practices of eating meat and drinking alcohol, and reform their social customs.[54]

Although between 1908 and the 1920s the Kherwar movement was dormant or even in decline, the eventual rise of the Satyam Shibam Sect in Barind (Malda district) can be linked to these widespread Sanskritizing campaigns, especially of the Sapha Hor sect, whose aim was the revision of tribal customs. The Satyam Shibam leader, Jitu Santal (or Jitu Sardar), reinforced the process of gradual emulation when, around 1924, he became associated with the *Swaraj* movement, whose leaders' aim (especially those of the Arya Samaji) was to reclaim aboriginals, Christian and Muslim converts and Untouchables into the Hindu fold through ritual purification or *shuddhi*. Jitu Santal not only linked the return of Santal Raj to the abolition of certain 'degrading' practices, he also demanded proper conversion to Hinduism, thus radicalizing the already paradoxical attempts of his predecessors to become better Santal by embracing Hindu beliefs.[55] In his outspoken hatred for the non-Hindu, he announced the

---

[53] The Christian missionaries followed the same strategy, and, according to Skrefsrud, declared the Light Spirit Chando to be identical with God the Almighty, who should be addressed as 'Thakur' by the Santal. The Gossner missionary D. Notrott, the first translator of the bible into Mundari, similarly decided on 'Ishwar; Parameshwar' for Mundari (Saeter 1938, 156; cf. D. Notrott in Biene, September 1917, 132).

[54] For details of the sects and their practices, see Bodding 1921, 227f.; Chaudhuri 1993, 96f.

[55] However, Jitu's 'explicit rejection of Santal identity and unambiguous quest for Sanskritization' (Sarkar 1985, 154) was in practice diluted, as the marriage and social customs of the Satyam Shiba sect remained largely unaffected by the reforms. Jitu invariably preached in Santali, made no effort to learn Bengali, and in many other ways demonstrated his great loyalty to traditional tribal norms.

advent of a new order of Santal Raj from the Adina mosque, starting out with an apocalyptic final battle that would begin right there.[56]

The Jitu Santal movement was prominent between 1924 and 1932 on another periphery of the area of Santal settlement as seen from Orissa, like the Kherwar movement, which had been centred in the Santal Parganas. It is unlikely that the educated and widely travelled Raghunath Murmu was entirely ignorant of the main objectives of these movements. Moreover, as a result of the community's contact with its Hindu, Christian and Muslim neighbours, the issues of meat-eating, drinking *handia* (rice-beer), the free mixing of men and women, keeping pigs and chickens, and beliefs in ghosts and superstitions, were not raised merely by the Kherwar leaders, but also resurfaced periodically within the community. Murmu was a reformer himself, envisaging a healthy and vigorous community that had shunned its bad habits and was no longer ridiculed by its neighbours. He shared with the Kherwar leaders the invocation of the allegedly ancient traditions of the Santal and the dream of a return of the golden age by following the correct prescriptions.

However, he declined to make speeches or otherwise appear at mass gatherings like a self-styled religious or fanatical political leader. Nor was he convinced that the Santal could be disciplined in accordance with Hindu principles. His vision circled around the institution of a new religious and cultural image, which sought to trace and consolidate typical features of Santal culture, all of which came to be subsumed under the name of *Sarna*.[57] Thus he declared practices that had been considered degrading to be sanctioned by tradition, as long as they retained their association with the proper spiritual context and were performed with self-restraint and pride. Although he was deeply concerned about the abuse of alcohol in the community, he thought it wrong to condemn the use of rice-beer, wanting instead to restore drinking to its traditional context of

---

[56] In 1932, he was shot dead by the police at the Adina mosque, which he and his men had occupied to transform into a temple. From the mosque he declared the end of the British Raj and proclaimed his own government of Santal Raj (Sarkar 1985, 138).

[57] As a result of this new 'tribal' consciousness, which echoed the demands of the Jharkhand movement, a large number of Santal entered 'Sarna', not 'Hinduism', when asked their religion during the 1951 census. To discern themselves as followers of *Sarna*, Santal were urged to return openly to old practices such as eating beef, drinking rice-beer, observing traditional festivals and not participating in the festivals of non-tribals (Mahapatra 1986, 52).

community feasts and worship. Similarly, singing, dancing, hunting and meat-eating were to be respected as parts of ancient rituals that marked Santal identity, rather than remaining a constant cause of a sense of inferiority. Instead of emulating the Hindu mainstream by 'cleaning out' dirty habits (especially in the *Sapha* movement), Murmu sought to reconstruct the vital aspects of Santal tradition and insisted on keeping its principles out of the Hindu fold, although the model for the projection of the Santal's cultural self-image remained largely a Hindu one.

To convey his message of respect towards tradition, Murmu relied on the texts he created. It is significant that his dramas and collections of songs and stories were intended to constitute a corpus of literature in Santali, preserving knowledge in written form and making it in principle available to everybody. But the genres he chose still allowed mediation by interpreters in a wider sense, as well as permitting the dispersal of texts by actors, narrators or singers, even to largely illiterate 'readerships', as is especially evident in the case of Murmu's very successfully staged plays. A brief example of his narrative technique of integrating religious and cultural issues into his literary works has already been provided here concerning the message of cultural superiority connected with the script embedded in the play *Bidu Chandan*. Similarly, in his revised narrative of the tale of creation, *Hital*, which may have been meant as a book of common reference in spiritual matters, exemplary incidents are inserted in which erring humans are guided by the judgements of Maran Buru, the Highest Spirit. Thus, when a bird suddenly flies into the fire before the starving Pilchu children, Maran Buru 'officially' grants them the consumption of its meat: 'In this world there are all kind of foods/ ... in appropriate time/ keeping *dharma* as witness/ if animals are shot by arrows/ and roasted and eaten/ there is no guilt, no crime.' Similarly, consumption of *handia* is given a catechetic explanation by Maran Buru: 'It is a medicine, it is also a poison/ it enlivens and freshens./ It is wrong to use it out of time/ but is it necessary to drink it/ at the time of *dharam karam*.'[58] Hindu principles such as *dharma* and food purity are borrowed from Hinduism, but adapted fully in accordance with Santal traditions. As the voice of Maran Buru appears as the source of the comments dry lecturing on social concerns is avoided, and the messages are transformed into authorised spiritual guidance, thus updating and refreshening old tales by giving them a new impetus.

---

[58] Chapter IV, 15-17; Chapter IX, 10-11. Translation Mahapatra 1986, 138.

One further difference from earlier Santal movements is that there was no explicit political agenda associated with Murmu's dreams of a return of the former high status of the Santal, nor did he project himself as the revolutionary leader of an exploited population, being himself a rather unassuming, withdrawn and intellectual individual.[59] His strategy was to strengthen the self-esteem of his fellow tribesmen from within by enhancing their cultural prestige and sense of solidarity, since he regarded the supremacy of the Santal culture as being rooted in its songs, dances and arts, language, customs and beliefs. Accordingly he came to be venerated as a spiritual and cultural leader in the true sense, since he managed to reshape the outlines of the Santal's identity as a group as perhaps no leader before him, filling it with new values and ideals from inside, while establishing boundaries against the faith and practices of the outsider.[60]

In spite of the 'soft tools' that Murmu used in contrast to other militant or more dogmatic Santal tendencies, his proved to be a less utopian and more sustainable vision in enforcing a sense of self-respect within the community. The *Ol* script faced and still faces controversy concerning its somewhat elitist aims of imposing it on Santali speakers in the areas of education and communication, yet on the level of ideals and ideology, today the script constitutes one of the foundation stones of cultural prestige, being propagated by several cultural and educational bodies in all Santal-populated states. The Jharkhand movement too, with its large support among the Santal, was keen in its early pamphlets to

---

[59] Reform movements such as those described above were hardly initiated in Mayurbhanj. The Santal uprising of 1917 in Mayurbhanj had as its immediate cause the campaign in the area to recruit 2000 local tribals to serve in Egypt during the First World War (Mahapatra 1986, 16). Murmu was also never actively associated with the Jharkhand movement, but the cultural-religious organization (*Sarna Dharam Semlet*) he founded gave an important cultural impetus to inculcating a sense of tribal heritage among the young people of the movement.

[60] Statues and images of Guru Gomkey, as he is also called, are revered like those of a saint in his village, in Rairangpur and even in Bhubaneswar, where his statue adorns the court of the Academy of Tribal Dialects and Culture (ATDC). Murmu used to work in a small hut, in a grove near a lake outside the village, where he is buried. As a ritual in his honour, visitors light a Charminar cigarette (his favourite brand) and leave it for him to smoke between the stones.

invoke the existence of a highly developed tribal language with a script as one of the main reasons for the formation of an independent tribal state.[61]

In the self-imagination of the Santal, the vision of a golden age is supported by an assiduously pursued desire to prove themselves the original dwellers of the subcontinent, and quite a number of voluminous publications, not only by Santal scholars, are concerned to demonstrate the antiquity and refined nature of their culture. In particular, linguistic approaches examining the relationship of Santali to Sumerian and Sanskrit roots give ample room for conjectures about Santali being 'the mother of all languages', or about links between early Santal culture and practically all the civilisations of antiquity, from Greek to Harappan. Contrived and questionable though these findings might be in certain cases, they are an integral part of nurturing a sense of resilience and pride within the community, and, in combination with its literary achievements, often serve as a basis for the somewhat superior status that the Santal claim over other, neighbouring tribal communities. Their insistence on the value of the *Ol* script and the pressure of some Santal spokesmen to impose it on other tribal languages of Chota Nagpur have already earned them the ironic description of the 'Brahmins of Chota Nagpur', given to them by the renowned Bengali author Mahashweta Devi.[62]

The return of the golden age may have been visualised differently by Raghunath Murmu, but he too would have been amazed at the cultural self-consciousness displayed on recently installed websites, where the identity of the Santal appears to be almost exclusively based on the documentation of the literary and cultural achievements of the community.[63] In this context of world-wide exposure, the existence of an independent script is not only a signifier for high cultural prestige, it also has specific political implications in view of the Santal's persistent demand for Santali to be recognised as an official language of India on the basis of the superiority of its linguistic and literary status, a demand that

---

[61] In the newly formed Jharkhand state, disputes over the official language of the state are still going on, the tribal languages being offered at most 'associated' status next to Hindi and English, let alone the introduction of a different script, which would be a highly contested issue among the many different and competing tribal groups in Jharkhand.

[62] Quoted in Zide 1991, 2535.

[63] http://wesanthals.tripod.com/santals/id24.html. This site offers a good introduction to the *Ol Chiki* alphabet, with details of orthography, pronunciation and word formation, textual examples, on-line journals etc. Other sites include www.allindiaaseca.org and www.aiswacs.org.

has finally been on course for fulfilment since 2004.[64] To underscore this claim, not only is the development of the script described and a fairly exhaustive bibliography in or on Santali provided, the script is also projected as an up-to-date means of communication, with a font in *Ol Chiki* being offered for downloading, besides links to programmes that can transcribe the Bengali, Oriya and Devanagari scripts into *Ol Chiki* and vice versa. The internet, with its potential to offer access gradually to both the elite and the masses, might constitute a new forum to preserve and convey cultural heritage, like, in its own way, the enormous range of audio cassettes with traditional and modern Santali songs or drama (and video) film texts, which are readily available in countryside markets and enjoy tremendous popularity.[65] Popular media like these, which have the additional advantage of reaching illiterate listeners and viewers, might eventually provide practical but nevertheless vital links between the imagined glories of a mythical past and the arduous task of securing a promising future for the cultural and linguistic identity of the community.

As we have seen in the invariably spiritual contexts that surrounded the invention of tribal scripts such as *Ol Chiki*, the quest for an independent script for tribal languages like Santali did not originate mainly in the need to create a medium for communication and education. The tribal scripts were not needed as an instrument, but served as a symbol of continuity, as they were presented as the remnants of an allegedly disrupted tradition of writing. In being intended to fix orally transmitted information, they constituted historicity. Possession of a script was seen not only as raising the 'primitive' status of the tribal communities, but as raising them to the status of a civilization in and of themselves. The gift of the script provided reassurance of the intact spirituality of the community, as this was considered a gift of the(ir) gods. The mystical power of the script was therefore employed in order to preserve the sacred contents of the past, as well as to transform the past itself into a golden age in retrospect. And lastly, rewriting the tribe's own traditions and creating its own script proved to be a catalyst in the process of cultural self-assertion, in response to decades of being historicized and written about by western agents and interests.

---

[64] The bill seeking to include Santali in the Eighth Schedule of the Indian Constitution has finally been passed by both the Lok Sabha (22.12.03) and the Rajya Sabha (23.12.03).

[65] Often these audio cassettes carry lines or titles on their covers in *Ol Chiki*.

References

Badha Bishra, 2001. Interview by Barbara Lotz at Rairangpur, 31.3.2001.

Bodding, P.O. 1921. 'The Kharwar Movement among the Santals', in *Man in India* 1, 223-32.

— 1925. 'A Plea for a Standardized System of Writing the Munda or Kolarian Languages', in *Journal and Proceedings of the Asiatic Society of Bengal*, New Series, Vol. XXI, Calcutta: Asiatic Society of Bengal, 9-20.

— 1930. *Materials for a Santal Grammar. I. Mostly Phonetic,* 2nd edn., Dumka: The Santal Mission of the Northern Churches.

— 2001 [1942]. *Traditions and Institutions of the Santals*, being a translation of Horkoren mare Hapramko reak' Katha, Delhi: Gyan Publishing House.

Chaudhuri, A.B. 1993. *State Formation among Tribals: A Quest for Santal Identity*, Delhi: Gyan Publishing House.

Culshaw, W.J. 1949. *Tribal Heritage: A Study of the Santals,* London: Lutterworth Press.

Dalton, E.T. 1872. *Descriptive Ethnology of Bengal,* Calcutta: Office of the Superintendent of Government Printing. (rpt. 1960)

Datta, K. 1940. *The Santal Insurrection of 1855-57,* Calcutta: Firma KLM Private Limited. (Repr. 2001)

Die Biene auf dem Missionsfelde: Monatsblatt der Goßnerschen Missionsgesellschaft. Issues Dec. 1855, Feb. 1857, Jan. 1863, July 1865, Sept. 1917. Berlin-Friedenau: Buchdruckerei Gutenberg [Referred to in this paper as 'Biene'].

Ghosh, G.K. and S. Ghosh. 2000. *Legends of Origin of the Castes and Tribes of Eastern India,* Calcutta: Firma KLM Private Limited.

Grierson G.A. 1906. *Linguistic Survey of India,* Vol. IV. Ed. S. Konow, Calcutta: Superintendent Government Printing.

Hemram, S.M. et al.. 1972. *Adibasi Ol Script,* Calcutta: Adibasi Socio-Educational Cultural Association (ASECA).

Kisku, D.B. 2000. *The Santals and their Ancestors,* Dumka: Career Press.

Mahapatra, Kh. (ed.) 1997. *Tribal Language and Culture of Orissa,* Bhubaneswar: Academy of Tribal Dialects and Culture (ATDC).

Mahapatra, S. 1986. *Modernization and Ritual: Identity and Change in Santal Society,* Calcutta: Oxford University Press.

Man, E.G. 1989 [1867]. *Sonthalia and the Santhals,* Delhi: Mittal Publications.

Mohapatra, S.S. 2001. 'Formation of Ol Chiki Script and Process of its Transmission', in N. Mathur (ed.), *Santhal Worldview*, Delhi: IGNCA and Concept Publishing, 74-88.

Murmu, R. 1987. Written 1942. *Bidu Chandan: A Santali Drama. In Ol Script,* Rairangpur: Adibasi Socio-Educational and Cultural Association, Orissa.

Orans, M. 1965. *The Santal: A Tribe in Search of a Great Tradition,* Detroit: Wayne State University Press.

Pinnow, H.J. 1972. 'Schrift und Sprache in den Werken Lako Bodras im Gebiet der Ho von Singbhum (Bihar)', in *Anthropos* 67, 822-857.

Risley, H.H. 1891. *Tribes and Castes of Bengal: Ethnographic Glossary,* Vols. I & II, Calcutta: The Bengal Secretariat Press.

Roy, S.C. 1995 [1912]. *The Mundas and their Country,* Ranchi: Catholic Press.

Saeter, I. 1938. *Lars Olsen Skrefsrud: Der Gründer der Santalmission,* Stuttgart und Basel: Evangelische Missionsverlag GmbH.

Sarkar, T. 1985. 'Jitu Santal's Movement in Malda, 1924-1932: A Study in Tribal Protest', in R. Guha (ed.), *Subaltern Studies IV*, Delhi: Oxford University Press, 136-64.

Swaro, D. 1990. *The Christian Missionaries in Orissa,* Calcutta: Punthi Pustak.

Thapar, R. 2000. 'Society and Historical Consciousness: The Itithasa-purana Tradition', in R. Thapar, *Cultural Pasts: Essays in Early Indian History,* Delhi: Oxford University Press, 123-73.

Zide, N. 1969. 'Munda and Non-Munda Austroasiatic Languages', in T.A. Sebeok (ed.), *Current Trends in Linguistcs*, Vol. 5, The Hague/Paris: Mouton, 411-30.

— 1991. 'Lexicography of Other Languages of the Indian Subcontinent: The Munda Languages', in F.J. Hausmann et al. (eds.) *Wörterbücher: Ein internationales Handbuch zur Lexikographie.* Dritter Teilband, Berlin, New York: Walter de Gruyter, 2535.

12

Changing One's Own Identity: The Role of Language in the Transformation of a Subregional Tradition

G.N. Dash

The present paper* presents a rare case from Orissa of a cultural and linguistic identity, which had only recently been established after a long and successful struggle, undergoing change. It will focus particularly on the competing socio-cultural forces that have brought about these changes in a subregional identity.

In 1894 the first steps were taken towards the abolition of Oriya in the government offices and courts of the Sambalpur region,[1] which had been a part of the Central Provinces since 1862, and to replace it with Hindi.[2] As soon as the news spread, the people of the region started vehement protests against the proposed change. The *Sambalpur Hiteisini,* the Oriya news and literary periodical of the region, began to publish protest notes in its columns. Public meetings were held and memoranda submitted to the government under the leadership of Dharanidhar Mishra, a local lawyer of considerable fame and the first person from the region to pass the matriculation examination.[3] Even the celebrated poet Gangadhar Meher, who belonged to the region, published poems in *Sambalpur Hiteisini,* criticizing the proposed change, making emotional appeals to the people and the ruling chiefs of the princely states of the region to take

---

* I am grateful to J.K. Nayak, Department of English, Utkal University, for improving the language of the paper.

[1] I would prefer to call it a subregion, but in this paper the term region is used. For the historical background of the region, see Cobden-Ramsay 1982; O'Malley 1909, 22-43; Dash 1969; Sahu 1985, 1-71.

[2] See Mohanty 1982, 31-3.

[3] Ibid. 1982, 31-3; Padhi and Supakar 1996, 5-6. The celebrated poet Gangadhar Meher mentioned Dharanidhar Mishra's name in one of the poems published in the *Sambalpur Hiteisini* on 3 October 1894. See fn. 4.

appropriate remedial measures without delay, and pleading with the government to do justice to the people.[4]

The unhappiness of the people of the region and the rightness of their cause persuaded even government officials like the Deputy Commissioner, who wrote to the Chief Commissioner opposing the proposed change.[5] But despite the protests of the people, the government went ahead and finally gave notice in the gazette of the Central Provinces for 19 January 1895 that Oriya would be replaced by Hindi in the courts and government offices with effect from 1 January 1896.[6]

In the following year, although the language agitation continued in latent form, it never completely faded away.[7] It appears that the census operations of 1901 provided another opportunity for the people to revive their agitation with renewed vigour. The new Chief Commissioner of the Central Provinces, Andrew H.L. Fraser, and the new Viceroy, Lord Curzon, seem to have aroused new hopes in the people that they might obtain justice. Baikunthanath Pujari, the person in charge of the census operations in the Sambalpur district who came from Baragada, near Sambalpur,[8] worked hard to collect and report accurate census data on language and education in the district.[9] The census operations,[10] which had

---

[4] In *Sambalpur Hiteishini*, 3 October 1894 and 6 March 1895, two poems by Gangadhar Meher entitled *Bharati Rodana* and *Utkala Bharatinka Nivedana* were published which purported to record the lamentation and appeal of *Utkala Bharati* (i.e. Oriya language and literature), which was in fear of being suppressed by *Hindi Bharati* (i.e. Hindi language and literature). See *Gangadhara Granthabali* 1977, 476-7, 478-9. In the context of the colonial administration of the nineteenth century, all these activities may be regarded as agitational activities; see fn. 16.

[5] *Sambalpur Hiteisini* 6, 21 (1894). See Mohanty, 1989, 283-4; Mohanty 1982, 31-3.

[6] Mohanty, ibid.

[7] Mohanty 1989, 289-94, Nanda 1993, 36-7, for information on the role played by the *Sambalpur Hiteisini* in publishing protest notes and reports on problems people were facing through the use of Hindi, etc.

[8] Padhi and Supakar 1996, 19-35. It is said that both Baikunthanath and his father (Dasarathi Pujari) were known to Andrew H.L. Fraser, the then Chief Commissioner of the Central Provinces, who was posted to Baragada at the beginning of his service career.

[9] See Padhi and Supakar 1996, 19-35. For the importance and role of the census data, see Cronin 1981, 29-35.

[10] Ibid. 1981, 33; Padhi and Supakar 1996, 26-9.

to be conducted in Oriya, and the census data[11] again made it clear that a great injustice had been done to the people of the Sambalpur region. In January 1901, therefore, a memorandum was submitted to the chief commissioner by certain prominent people of Sambalpur making a strong plea either for the reconsideration of the language issue and a reversion to the earlier position or 'if, for administrative reasons, the district can not be allowed to possess an official language distinct from that in use in any other district of the [Central] Province', to transfer the district and its Gurhjat Mahals to the Orissa Division of Bengal.[12] In March and July of the same year deputations on behalf of the residents of the Sambalpur region met the Chief Commissioner to press their demand.[13] In September 1901 a deputation even went to Simla with the intention of meeting Lord Curzon, the Viceroy,[14] but it was unable to contact either him personally or the Chief Commissioner, who was also at Simla. However, they did meet Andrew Fraser, the chief secretary of the Central Provinces, who also happened to be at Simla. It appears that this meeting bore some definite results in that it speeded up Fraser's plan to visit Sambalpur in order to assess the situation personally. He visited the district and submitted his report on 5 October, in which he strongly emphasized that the people of the district desired Oriya, not Hindi, to be the language of the administration and courts.[15]

Finally, as a result of this sustained agitation,[16] Oriya was restored in the courts and government offices of the Sambalpur district in early 1903. This agitation also made the colonial government aware of the need to amalgamate the Oriya-speaking tracts under one administration. This ultimately resulted in the transfer of the Sambalpur region from the

---

[11] Out of the total population of 796,413, the number of Oriya speakers was 595,601. See Padhi and Supakar 1996, 27.

[12] See Cronin 1981, 29.

[13] Ibid., 31, 33.

[14] This delegation consisted of the following five individuals from Sambalpur: Sripati Mishra, Balabhadra Supakar, Mahanta Bihari Das, Brajamohan Pattanayak, and Madan Mohan Misra. They arrived in Simla on 16 September 1901. See Padhi and Supkar 1996, especially p. 43.

[15] Ibid., 16-7.

[16] The Oriya term *andolana* (which means agitation/movement) was used in the pages of the *Sambalpur Hiteisini* of 6, 35 (January 1895) and 8, 45 (April 1897). See B. Mohanty 1989, 285, 290-1. The Chief Commissioner, Andrew H.L. Fraser also used the term 'agitation'. See Cronin 1981, 33.

Central Provinces to the Orissa Division on 16 October 1905,[17] apart from some areas like the princely state of Khariar which were only finally merged with the newly created province of Orissa in 1936.

The agitation was successful because the people of the region considered themselves to be Oriyas, speakers of the Oriya language, despite the linguistic differences between the varieties of standard Oriya[18] spoken in coastal Orissa, and the speech of the Sambalpur region, who considered their speech to be a variety or dialect of Oriya. There were, of course, other historical and cultural reasons besides the linguistic one for defining their identity in this way. But the primacy of language is beyond doubt.

Historically, too, the people of the Sambalpur region used to look upon themselves as Oriyas.[19] Its medieval poets, such as Pratap Ray, author of *Sasi Sena*,[20] Ratna Das, author of *Saraswata Gita*,[21] Bhima Dhibara, author of *Kapata Pasa*,[22] Chaitanya Das, author of *Bishnugarbha Purana* and *Nirguna Mahatmya*,[23] Gopinath Sarangi, author of the bilingual (Sanskrit and Oriya) work *Cikitsa Manjari*,[24] and Gopala Telenga, author of *Adhyatmya Ramayana*[25] used the same variety of Oriya in their literary works as the medieval poets in the coastal districts of Orissa. The Baragada copper plate inscription of 1845, issued during the time of King Narayana Singh of Sambalpur, may also be mentioned in this connection.[26]

The concentration of the *Bhagavata Tungis* in the Mahanadi valley of the Sambalpur region, as shown by Heinrich von Stietencron in an unpublished map,[27] is also very significant. These *Tungis* were places where palm-leaf manuscripts of the Oriya *Bhagavata*, translated from Sanskrit by the sixteenth-century saint-poet, Jagannatha Das of the coastal

---

[17] See Cronin 1981, 32-8. Bonai and Gangpur princely states were also transferred from the Chotnagpur Division to Orissa at this time.

[18] The term 'standard Oriya' is used rather loosely in this paper.

[19] See Dash 1996.

[20] Dash 1969, 403.

[21] Mahapatra 1969, 164-5.

[22] *Orissa District Gazetteer. Sambalpur*. 1971: 446-7; Dash 1969: 398.

[23] Mahapatra 1969, 116-9, Dash 1969, 390-4.

[24] See Dash 1969, 263-5.

[25] Mahapatra 1969, 231-3.

[26] See Dash 1969, 337, 399.

[27] See also O'Malley 1909, 91, where it is mentioned that 'Most villages, too, contain a *bhagabatgadi*....'

district of Puri, and other medieval religious texts in standard Oriya, especially the Puranas, were kept. These used to be recited in the evenings and on special religious occasions and were listened to by the ordinary people, most of whom were illiterate. The concentration of Jagannātha temples in the Sambalpur region is another important indicator of the Oriya identity of the people of that region, as Lord Jagannath ultimately became a symbol of Oriya identity.[28]

During the colonial period, the people of Sambalpur continued to look upon themselves as Oriyas and as speakers of the Oriya language, in spite of the fact that they were separated from Orissa proper. After 1889 the weekly periodical, the *Sambalpur Hiteisini* was published in standard Oriya from Deogarh, the capital of the princely state of Bamra in the Sambalpur region. It was popular among the educated people and became the mouthpiece of proponents of Oriya during the entire period of agitation under its chief patron and publisher, Basudeva Sudhala Dev, the ruling chief of Bamra. During this period, the literary activities of the people of the Sambalpur region were carried out exclusively in the standard Oriya, outstanding examples being the contributions of the tribal saint-poet, Bhima Bhoi (1855-95), and of Gangadhar Meher (1862-1924). In Gangadhar's perception the Sambalpur region was a part of greater Orissa or Utkal, a view he particularly expressed in his recently published poetical work *Utkala Lakshmi*.[29] It may also be pointed out in this connection that Gangadhar Meher and his young friend and patron, Braja Mohan Panda, both of whom belonged to that region, used standard Oriya in their private correspondence with each other.[30] This is quite significant, as it is evidence of their sincere quest for an Oriya identity. This trend continued unabated almost throughout the twentieth century. Many literary figures from the Sambalpur region wrote in standard Oriya, immensely enriching Oriya literature through their contributions and achieving considerable fame. This is still the main, if not the only, trend.

It may be remembered here that this was the time when the 'imagined community' of Oriya-speakers was finally taking concrete shape. The Oriya language agitation against the imposition of Bengali in the coastal districts of the Oriya-speaking tracts in the sixties of the nineteenth century[31] provided the opportunity for its construction. It is

---

[28] See Dash 1978.

[29] *Utkala Lakshmi* was published for the first time in 1894.

[30] *Gangadhar Patrabali* 1955.

[31] See Dash 1993.

quite likely that the success of this agitation inspired the people of the Sambalpur region to start their own language agitation against the forcible imposition of Hindi. Although throughout the entire period the people of the coastal region wholeheartedly supported this agitation in the Sambalpur region, it was primarily an indigenous and spontaneous movement. The restoration of Oriya and the subsequent transfer of the Sambalpur region to Orissa in 1905 were therefore applauded by the people of the Sambalpur region.[32]

More recently, however, for a little more than a quarter of a century, a section of intellectuals and educated people from the Sambalpur region have started a new agitation, claiming that their speech is not merely a regional variety or dialect of Oriya, but a completely separate and independent language. Some call it Koshli, whereas others prefer to use the name Sambalpuri. In order to establish this form as a separate language the differences between the standard and other varieties of Oriya on the one hand and Koshli/Sambalpuri on the other are overemphasized and their mutual intelligibility and structural-cum-lexical similarity underplayed or denied. Even the close genealogical link between Oriya and Koshli/Sambalpuri is rejected. As Oriya is supposed to have been derived from Magadhi or Magadhan Prakrit and is therefore closely related to Bengali and Assamese, efforts are made to show that Koshli/Sambalpuri is derived from Ardha-Magadhi and is therefore closely related to Western variants of Hindi like Awadhi, Bagheli, and Chattisgarhi.[33]

---

[32] (a) Andrew Fraser, who visited the district after the restoration of Oriya, records: 'Sometimes [*sic*] after this, I had again to visit the Sambalpur district, and it was most touching to see how people turned out, at every village through which I passed with my camp and at every railway station where my train halted, to return thanks for the restoration of their language.' Quoted in Padhi and Supakar 1996, 34-5.

(b) Similarly, as the partition of Bengal coincided with the transfer of Sambalpur to Orissa, some people in coastal Orissa, such as Pt. Nilakanth Das, declined to celebrate the occasion (16 October 1905) in sympathy with the Bengalis, who observed the day as a day of mourning. They even tried, in vain (which is significant), to persuade the people of the Sambalpur region not to celebrate the occasion. See Bharatachandra Nayak's autobiography as quoted in Padhi and Supakar 1996, 65-6.

[33] For more information about this claim, see Udgata 1997. This claim has been contested, on the basis of structural, lexical and genealogical considerations and mutual intelligibility, as well as in other ways, by linguists such as Bijaya Prasad

The champions of Koshli/Sambalpuri publish articles in Oriya-language periodicals and journals, and books in Oriya and English. They organize meetings and seminars in support of their claim, which they are also trying to establish in different universities and state-level seminars. In order to obtain recognition of Koshli/Sambalpuri as a separate and independent language in the scholarly world, several Ph.D. and D.Litt. theses in support of this claim have been submitted to Sambalpur University in recent years,[34] where one can also follow a diploma course in the Koshli language, itself a recognition of its separate and independent status. Proponents of this movement are making great efforts to publish periodicals, books, and literary works in Koshli/Sambalpuri in order to create a literary heritage.[35] Even a few feature films and TV films have been produced in Koshli/Sambalpuri. Demands have also been made to conduct primary and secondary education in Koshli/Sambalpuri, to withdraw textbooks written in standard Oriya from primary and secondary schools in western Orissa and to replace them with textbooks written in Koshli/Sambalpuri. In short, certain educated people in the Sambalpur region (in fact a subregion) are now earnestly trying to create a regional tradition out of a subregional tradition and seeking a different, subregional identity for themselves, based primarily on their speech.

In order to understand why certain people in the Sambalpur region are now trying to change their identity, which achieved recognition more or less exactly a century ago after a sustained agitation, and why they are again making language the symbol of their new identity, we must examine the socio-political context of this development. It is not enough to point out that in the nineteenth century the people of the Sambalpur region were under colonial rule. The situation was much more complex and demands a detailed explanation. It may not be entirely wrong to state that at that time the Oriya-speaking tracts were divided into three 'smaller colonies' within a larger British colony. The Oriya-speakers in these 'smaller colonies', the

---

Mohapatra, Panchanan Mohanty and G.N. Dash, all of whom, incidentally, hail from the coastal Orissa. See Mohapatra 1995, 266-300, Mohanty 1992, 1993 and Dash 1996.

[34] For more information on this, see Udgata 1997.

[35] For more information, see Udgata 1997; Patel 2002. Only after Orissa became a separate province in British India in 1936 did occasional publications of creative writing in Sambalpuri appear, making a slow start. The number of such publications has increased considerably in the recent past.

Bengal and Madras Presidencies and the Central Provinces,[36] felt dominated, looked down upon, cheated and unjustly treated by the Bengali-, Telugu- and Hindi-speakers who outnumbered them in each of these administrative units and were the middle-ranking officials of the colonial government. The Oriya-speakers felt that they were on the receiving end simply because they were outnumbered, divided into different administrative units, and spoke a language different from those that these middle-ranking officials spoke. Whenever a government position fell vacant, these officials saw to it that one of their fellow speakers, preferably one of their relatives or friends, got the job. As the Oriyas were considered 'Other' by their neighbours, the Bengali-, Telugu- and Hindi-speakers, they felt the need to construct an imagined community of Oriya-speakers and to view those Bengali-, Telugu- and Hindi-speakers as the political 'Others'. In such a situation, the people of the Sambalpur region needed moral as well as material support from other Oriya-speakers, especially those living in the coastal districts of Orissa, and they received such support in abundance.[37] Further, as was mentioned earlier, the success of the Oriyas of the coastal districts in their own language agitation provided inspiration to the people of Sambalpur to start a language agitation of their own. The coastal Oriyas, in their turn, needed the Oriya-speakers of the smaller colonies too, as numerical strength was necessary in their fight against injustice, ill treatment, and colonial exploitation. What was therefore really required was unity among all Oriya-speakers, irrespective of differences in their socio-cultural behaviour and speech, which after all only amounted to dialectal differences. Under these circumstances, similarities rather than differences between the people of the Sambalpur region and of coastal Orissa were emphasized. The struggle for survival in the face of what they thought to be an onslaught by Hindi-speakers prompted this behaviour and is how the imagined community of Oriya-speakers gradually emerged.

But the picture started changing after the merger of the Sambalpur region with Orissa. In most cases, the people of coastal Orissa not only gradually replaced the Hindi-speakers in government offices but also grabbed the newly created positions as middle-level officials. This process gathered momentum after 1936, when Orissa became a separate province of British India, and even posts at the higher levels of the administration were appropriated by coastal Oriyas at the cost of local elites.

---

[36] This was precisely the case in 1862.

[37] See Mohanty 1982, 31-7.

After independence this trend went even further when the people of coastal Orissa emerged as the dominant force in the state administration. They occupied most of the posts in government offices, not only at the district and subdivisional levels, but in particular at the highest level at the headquarters of the administration, located first in Cuttack and subsequently in Bhubaneswar. This was mainly because they had earlier been more strongly exposed to western education, whereas western Orissa was educationally backward[38] and the headquarters of the administration in Orissa had always been concentrated in coastal Orissa.

The people of western Orissa resented this trend. Increasingly they felt that they were being neglected, differently treated and discriminated against by government officials who had come from coastal Orissa.[39] In short, the dominance of the Hindi-speakers was replaced by the hegemony of coastal Oriyas. At least this is what the people of western Orissa, especially the elites among them, felt. Apart from the well-known impersonal and lengthy bureaucratic procedures with which the people were not at all familiar, the generally negative attitude, inefficiency, nepotism, and habit of demanding and accepting bribes on the part of petty government officials might also have been responsible for such a negative public perception, which was made worse by the fact that these government officials invariably tried to help and favour their own relatives and friends, who were, as was to be expected, from coastal Orissa. This well-known feature of subcontinental social behaviour was already noted during the colonial period with respect to Bengali-, Telugu- and Hindi-speakers. These administrative evils greatly strengthened the awareness of 'Us' *versus* 'Them' in the minds of the people of western Orissa.

It is sometimes argued that this feeling of alienation crystallised particularly during the Second World War, when the provincial secretariat, till then located in Cuttack, was temporarily shifted to Sambalpur. The people of Sambalpur now had the opportunity to observe at very close quarters the government officials from the coastal region who mostly manned the secretariat, and to get to know how they managed the provincial administration and, perhaps, also how they demanded and accepted bribes. They realized that the coastal Oriyas were just as exploitative as their Hindi-speaking counterparts. Furthermore, to those

[38] Thus, for instance, BA classes started at Cuttack in 1876, at Sambalpur only in 1946.

[39] See Ghose 1991, 65-6.

who had been less exposed to western education, these government officials appeared to be not at all straightforward, but crafty, deceitful, and basically dishonest, on the whole quite different from their own social norms. This proved to be a lasting impression. The feeling that they were being neglected and discriminated against by these government officials originated at around this time. Since then, the coastal people, irrespective of the districts to which an individual belonged, have earned the derogatory epithet *sale kataki* (brother-in-law from Cuttack).[40]

Both before and after independence, the ruling chiefs of the princely states of western and north-western Orissa, such as Bolangir-Patna, Kalahandi, and Seraikella, made an attempt under the leadership of R.N. Singh Deo, Maharaja of Bolangir-Patna, to create a Union of Eastern States, comprising the princely states of the Orissa, Chota Nagpur, and Chattisgarh regions and, if possible, also the Sambalpur district of Orissa. Their primary goal was to prevent the merger of their princely states with Orissa and to create instead a separate state within the Indian Union, where their influence would remain unchallenged for many more years to come. In order to legitimize and strengthen their claim, they invoked the memory of the Koshala kingdom of *puranic* and historic fame.[41] They claimed that these princely states and the district of Sambalpur (i.e. the erstwhile princely state of Sambalpur) had once belonged to this Koshala kingdom and not to Orissa, having always differed, and still differing greatly, from coastal Orissa linguistically, socially and culturally. In their view, 'the tract of Sambalpur and States bordering it and Singbhum, though speaking Oriya language, differ to a great degree from the

[40] Perhaps the epithet *kataki* originated much earlier, along with the coming of traders from coastal Orissa. The traders were and are often looked down upon as cheats. Their status may be compared with Doms among the Kutia Kondhas or *Diku* among the Santal. Chintamani Misra (1983, 120-1) records that hostility towards the coastal Oriyas, all of whom were called *Kataki*, was due to the corrupt practices of the petty officials, from the former Cuttack and Puri districts, who were engaged in settlement work in Bolangir even before 1920. This epithet perhaps marks the line of demarcation between 'Us' and 'Them'.

[41] Note presented to the Resident, Eastern States, on 30.07.1946 by the Ruler of Seraikella. See Mahatab 1972, 92, 95. See also Ghose 1991, 60-1, 66; Sengupta, Jayanta 2002: 227, 229-30. It may be mentioned here that the Sambalpur and adjacent areas, including Bolangir-Patna, once belonged to Dakshina Koshala or the Koshala kingdom of the early medieval period over which the Panduvamsis and Samavamsis once ruled. See Panigrahi 1981, 7-8, 96, 105-6; Sarma 1983, 2-8, 17-8, 20-3, etc.

language used in and around Cuttack. Habit and custom of the people inhabiting these tracts also differ fundamentally from the coastal districts of Orissa'.[42] This statement may be contrasted with the claim made earlier in the *Sambalpur Hiteisini* during the language agitation. As we have seen, at that time it had been claimed that historically the Sambalpur region had never had any political, archaeological, or social relationship with central India or Chattisgarh.[43] The proponents of the Union of Eastern States also claimed that, if the princely states were to merge with Orissa, the people of these states would be subjected to economic, political, and administrative exploitation 'by the politically more conscious people' of coastal Orissa,[44] and the unexplored forests and mineral resources of the region would only enrich coastal Orissa at the expense of the people of the Sambalpur region. All these claims and apprehensions were widely publicized in order to mobilize public support for them.

Although the Koshala movement failed to achieve its primary objective of preventing the merger of these princely states with Orissa, it gave birth to a political party called the Koshala-Utkala Praja Parishad, the Ganatantra Parishad of later days,[45] which claimed to champion the cause of the people of western Orissa. As never before in the recent past, this early Koshala movement made the people of the region aware of their separateness from the people of coastal Orissa, who were considered the 'outsiders', the political 'Others'. This became even more acute in the former princely states after their merger with Orissa. The seeds of a separate cultural identity[46] were sown, which, although remaining dormant for a few years in the euphoria of the merger, in more recent times blossomed into a separate language movement.

Although the electoral process after independence created the impression that the people held the reins of power through their various elected representatives, it became increasingly clear that the real power

---

[42] Note presented to the Resident, Eastern States, on 30.07.1946 by the Ruler of Seraikella. See Mahatab 1972, 97-8. See also Ghose 1991, 60-1; Sengupta 2002, 227-9.

[43] *Sambalpur Hiteisini* 6, 35 (January 1895). See Mohanty 1989, 286-8.

[44] Mahatab 1972, 87. See also Sengupta 2002, 209.

[45] Ghose 1991, 65-7. R.N. Singh Deo, leader of this Koshala movement and also of the Koshala-Utkala Praja Parishad and Ganatantra Parishad, eventually became the Chief Minister of Orissa in 1967.

[46] See also Sengupta 2002, 229-31.

remained centralized in the state capital, not at the levels of subdivisional or even district headquarters. The sense of distance from the centre of power increased the feeling of alienation and estrangement, which was aggravated further by the very poor state of communications between the state capital and Sambalpur and other places in western Orissa. This situation must be contrasted with that of the pre-independence period, when the real power was vested in the ruling chiefs of princely states in the region. Here, the distance of the local population from the centre of power was shorter, and a rapid implementation of decisions could be expected. Some rulers of these states were even benevolent rulers.[47]

In the political sphere, it soon became apparent that the politicians of the coastal districts were in a stronger and more influential position because of their numerical strength in the Orissa Legislative Assembly, as these districts were more densely populated. In this situation, it was quite natural for the people of western Orissa to think that they were neglected and that their interests were repeatedly being sacrificed for the sake of the people of the coastal districts. There was some truth in this belief.[48] But it was also true that, in the new democratic set-up, politicians from western Orissa began to indulge unscrupulously in vote-bank politics, taking advantage of the situation, and exploiting the dissatisfaction and resentment of the people to further their own interests. Thus, for instance, when the famous Hirakud dam was built near Sambalpur, they claimed that it was being built only for the welfare of the people of coastal Orissa, to protect them from floods and to produce electricity for them. It was alleged that hundreds of villages would be submerged under water and their people rendered homeless and landless for the sake of the people of the coastal districts. Moreover, the rumour was spread that the dam-based irrigation projects, which were actually intended to irrigate areas of western Orissa, were meaningless and fraudulent, as the water would lose its energy and fertility through the generation of electric power by the dam. Irrigating the land with this water would, it was claimed, be harmful and make the land barren. Many people believed such assertions, which

[47] Misra 1983, 123-6.

[48] As, for example, in some former princely states, where medical facilities that used to be free ceased to be so after the merger. In Bolangir there was a good Siemens X-ray machine, one of the only three in India, and that was left uncared for. See Ghose 1991, 65-6.

stimulated the agitation against the construction of the Hirakud dam.[49] In fact, some prominent leaders of this agitation had very personal reasons to oppose the building of the dam.[50] Some fertile land and the double-storey house belong to a prominent leader of the agitation would be submerged.[51] On the other hand, it should also be mentioned that some families whose lands were submerged in the water reservoir of the dam did not receive compensation till very recently, almost half a century after the dam was built – a poor comment indeed on the state administration.[52]

The traditional local elites, especially those who were attached to the courts of the princely states, were certainly the worst sufferers in the post-independence political dispensation. Once influential and powerful, they now felt neglected and ignored and became the disgruntled elements who tried to sow the seeds of dissatisfaction in the minds of the people of the region.

The government took several steps to contain this kind of dissatisfaction. It established the very first engineering college in the state near Sambalpur in 1956 and the second at Rourkela in 1961, the second medical college in the state (the first being at Cuttack) again near Sambalpur in 1959, and Sambalpur University in 1968. But despite these laudable efforts, the problems remained the same and even became aggravated. Kalahandi in particular became a symbol of backwardness, poverty, and unsolved problems. Therefore the feeling continued to grow in intensity and made the people of western Orissa even more aware of their marginal position.

Educated people in western Orissa also felt that the press and the print media, which were based in coastal Orissa, were not giving adequate

---

[49] The Hirakud dam agitation started in the pre-independence period. See Routray 2001, 224-5; Ghose 1991, 61.

[50] Ibid. R.N. Singh Deo, the leader of the Koshal movement, was believed to have been behind this agitation. See Mahatab 1972, 143-4, 146, 149, 226-9, etc.

[51] He was Sraddhakar Supakar. Leadership in the Hirakud dam agitation brought him to political prominence. He joined Ganatantra Parishad, founded by R.N. Singh Deo, and eventually became the leader of the opposition in the Orissa Legislative Assembly as the leader of that party. In his autobiography he mentions his loss. See Supakar 1993, 4.

[52] As, for example, a news item in the *Sunday Times* (Orissa Special) of *The Times of India* dated 9 June 2002 which states, 'The state has taken steps to pay compensation to the Hirakud land oustees after 44 years of its completion .... Around 370 families belonging to the land oustee category are yet to be traced', etc.

coverage to western Orissa and its problems. This was certainly true to some extent but was also due to the poor communication system of those days. But in their perception it appeared that the voice of western Orissa was being deliberately muted. Furthermore, intellectuals, especially writers, journalists, and academics, felt that they were being ignored by their colleagues in coastal Orissa, despite their literary and academic merits and achievements. In this way the perceived hegemony of the coastal people became a source of resentment for the intellectuals of western Orissa and their 'Us' *versus* 'Them' awareness.

This awareness led in its turn to the 'rediscovery' of the socio-religious and cultural traits that were increasingly regarded as special or exclusive to western Orissa as opposed to coastal Orissa. In other words, the people of Sambalpur became conscious and felt proud of the markers of their own subregional tradition and identity. The beauty and greatness of the folk songs, music, dances, and textiles of Sambalpur were rediscovered; the popular festival of Nuakhai was celebrated with great enthusiasm and conscious efforts were made to popularize it throughout western Orissa; the greatness of the goddess Samalai, the most prominent deity of western Orissa other than Marjara Ḳesari or Nrusimhanath, was praised. Furthermore, the glorious past of the Sambalpur region was rediscovered and 'imagined',[53] including as part of it the bravery and patriotism of Surendra Sai, the nineteenth-century claimant to the throne of the kingdom of Sambalpur and Orissa's hero in the so-called freedom struggle against the British. It was also claimed that Lord Jagannātha of Puri was in fact a deity of western Orissa who had been appropriated by the coastal people. In all these exercises, the differences between western and coastal Orissa were strongly emphasized. The first full-scale history of Sambalpur was written in 1962 with the aim of establishing the subregional identity of the Sambalpur region.[54]

In short, the people of western Orissa lost faith in the fairness of government officials and their political masters. They held the coastal people responsible for all kinds of inefficiency and for corrupt and discriminatory practices in the state administration and resented what appeared to them as the hegemony of the coastal Oriyas. While they were thus becoming gradually alienated from the people of coastal Orissa, they tried to discover their own greatness, as well as their differences from the coastal Oriyas. This development was often also rooted in the quite

---

[53] See Dash 1969.

[54] Ibid.

personal sentiments of the intellectuals of western Orissa, who suffered from the experience that even educated people at times made fun of their speech when they came to coastal Orissa for administrative work and for the sake of higher education. They resented the fact that the speech of the coastal people was considered the standard language, whereas their own speech was merely regarded as a dialect and thus attributed an inferior or subordinate status.

It is unfortunate that linguists, and now also sociolinguists, all over the world are still maintaining the distinction between what they call 'standard language' and 'dialect' and that they use this terminology without hesitation. However scientific this distinction and terminology may be, it often causes psycho-sociological problems for the speakers of a dialect. It should not be forgotten that what is called the standard language is in fact itself based on a dialect, which is also, for extra-linguistic reasons, of the same language. Therefore, it would be more appropriate to call it 'the standard dialect' or 'the standardized dialect', not 'the standard language'. Then the speakers of dialects other than the standard will not feel embarrassed.

In the context of Orissa, it is even more unfortunate that the term 'dialect' has been translated into Oriya as *upabhasa*. The prefix *upa-*, borrowed from Sanskrit, imparts a meaning of inferiority or subordination to the noun or other word to which it is added, as in *upa devata, upa graha, upa dvipa, upa purana*, etc. At times even a derogatory sense is given to the word to which it is added, for example, *upapati* (a paramour) or *upapatni*. Therefore, whenever the term *upabhasa* is used for their speech, some intellectuals from western Orissa react sharply, especially when the speech of coastal Orissa is called a *bhasa* or 'standard language'.[55] This sentimental reaction must be situated in the already existing public perception of alienation that is rooted in the administrative and political arena in order to understand its implications properly. Such reactions are quite common in Orissa and, indeed, in India and beyond. As Hobsbawm observes, 'the force of the sentiments which leads groups of 'us' to give themselves an 'ethnic'/linguistic identity against the foreign threatening 'them' cannot be denied'.[56] To cite an instance from Orissa, Sridhar Das of Puri district narrates in his autobiography that, when he was in the princely state of Boud in western Orissa in the 1930s, he published two articles on the speech of Boud. After their publication some

[55] See Udgata 1997, 160-5.

[56] Hobsbawm 1995, 170.

educated people of Boud raised a hue and cry, accusing him of making fun of their speech. The reactions from Boud were so strong that he was obliged to discontinue writing on its speech.[57]

Apart from these more sentimental reasons, there appears to have been a more practical speech-related reason for people in western Orissa to change their identity. School students in western Orissa found their textbooks difficult to understand, if not unintelligible, as they were allegedly written in a variety of Oriya spoken in the Cuttack and Puri regions. This was already pointed out about half a century ago by Aswini Kumar Pujari in his plea for the standardization of Oriya and the incorporation of a number of lexical items from the Sambalpuri variety of Oriya as a remedial measure.[58] So far, however, no such measures have been implemented.[59]

On the whole, when the people of western Orissa became estranged from the people of coastal Orissa, they were no longer prepared to accept an inferior, much less a derogatory status for their speech as an *upabhasa*. They were proud of their own speech and regarded it as the boundary marker between 'Us' and 'Them'. To quote Hobsbawm again, 'Why, indeed, should language be such a criterion of group membership, except perhaps where language differentiation coincided with some other reason to mark oneself off from other community'.[60]

The articles written by Aswini Kumar Pujari, referred to earlier, were perhaps the first steps taken in claiming an independent status for the Sambalpuri variety of Oriya, despite his ambivalent position.[61] In 1977

---

[57] Das 1996, 87. I have been able to trace only one of these two articles. See Das 1931.

[58] Pujari, 1951a, 1951b, and 1952.

[59] In 1996, G.N. Dash suggested that in school textbooks, for the subject of Oriya language and literature, prose and verse or poetry pieces from different regional varieties of Oriya, including Sambalpuri, should be included. See Dash 1996. But so far nothing has happened on that front.

[60] Hobsbawm 1995, 56.

[61] Pujari's position with regard to the Sambalpur or western Orissa variety of Oriya seems ambivalent, as in the same breath he claimed it to be both an independent language and a dialect of Oriya (see Pujari 1951b, 1952). He was willing to consider Sambalpuri a dialect or variety of Oriya provided a good number of lexical items were accepted into standard Oriya. Golok Bihari Dhall, who was trained in modern linguistics at London University, debated the nature and concept of standard Oriya with Pujari (and also with Gangadhar Guru). See Dhall, G.B. 1951, 1952. I have not seen Pujari's 1953a and 1953b papers of this

Satyanarayan Bahidar (1913-80) wrote the first grammar of Sambalpuri (consisting of forty-one pages) to add to his creative writings in Sambalpuri. He simply referred to Sambalpuri as a *bhasa* in the title and the first page of his book,[62] without attempting to explain or justify it. Therefore it is not clear whether he was using the term *bhasa* to mean a speech (a language variety or dialect) or a language. It may be mentioned here that Pujari's papers and Bahidar's grammar were written in the standard variety of Oriya and not in Khosli/Sambalpuri. It appears that the first person to claim clearly an independent status for Sambalpuri was Pandit Prayagadatta Joshi (1913-2001) from the princely state of Khariar, which belonged to the Central Provinces till 1936. As his surname 'Joshi' indicates, he was a Brahmin from the Hindi-speaking area who settled in Khariar under the patronage of the ruling chief.[63] He represents the Hindi-speaking immigrants from the north and north-west to the Oriya-speaking tracts, especially those who came to be associated with the courts of the princely states of western Orissa. Tiwari and Dube are the surnames of other such Brahman immigrants. Naturally his attachment was to a variety of Hindi. He did not have much to complain about till 1936, as Khariar was in the Hindi-speaking Central Provinces till then. But after 1936, when Khariar was merged into Orissa, it is likely that he did not feel comfortable either with Orissa or with the Oriyas for quite understandable reasons. Although he knew Oriya well and wrote articles and booklets in standard Oriya, he was not at all prepared to identify himself as an Oriya. For linguistic reasons, however, it was also not possible for him to claim that the speech of the people of western Orissa was just another variety of Hindi. Therefore he tried to do the same thing in a rather roundabout way, taking the rather bold step of claiming the status of a separate and independent language for the speech of western Orissa by trying to establish its close genealogical affinity with Awadhi, Bagheli, and Chattisgarhi, which are considered different varieties of Hindi. In order to show that this so-called language was in no way related to Oriya or

debate. Chand (1996) is of Pujari's opinion that Sambalpuri is, at the same time, both a dialect of Oriya and an independent language.

[62] See Bahidar 1977.

[63] However, Pandit Joshi himself claims descent from one Sanatana Panda, who lined thirty-five generations ago during the reign of Ramai Deva, the founder of the Chauhan dynasties of Patna and Sambalpur. He also claims that he is different from other Brahmins with the Joshi surname who settled in western Orissa. Panda, of course, is an Oriya surname. But his claims are extremely doubtful.

Orissa, he not only rejected its structural or lexical similarities with Oriya, but also named it Koshli, thus linking it with the historical and *puranic* land of Koshala or South Koshala. The Koshala movement of the pre-independence period must have appealed to him, as he published several articles and booklets in support of his claim and debated the issue with those who were not prepared to accept his controversial theories.[64] Others, such as Nilamadhab Panigrahi, P.K. Tripathy, B.K. Tripathy, A.K. Dash, Hrudamani Pradhan, P.K. Padhi, and D.G. Bishi, were to follow suit. Intellectuals from western Orissa who resented the fact that their speech was not accepted as a standard language but was assigned an inferior status as an *upabhasa* were attracted by Pandit Joshi's assertions, which appeared to them to be an excellent way out of their dilemma. Others, who were alienated for administrative and political reasons, as well as members of the former elites, also came forward in support of Pandit Joshi's claims.

However, it should also be stressed that not all the educated people and intellectuals of western Orissa support this claim. Those who retain their Oriya identity oppose it openly. Moreover, there is a division among the proponents of Koshli/Sambalpuri themselves. Some of those from the Sambalpur area do not accept the name Koshli for the speech of western Orissa but instead prefer to call it Sambalpuri. But others, while loudly proclaiming their Sambalpuri identity, silently ignore the call of their leaders to produce creative writing in Koshli/Sambalpuri. Instead they continue to write in standard Oriya, as they want a wider readership for their writing. And finally, people from Bolangir, Kalahandi, and Khariar maintain that their speech is different not only from standard Oriya but also from Sambalpuri.

This is how educated people and intellectuals in western Orissa are making efforts to elevate a subregional tradition into a regional tradition as the basis of a new Koshli/Sambalpuri identity to replace their earlier Oriya identity, a process in which again it is the speech of the region, this time Koshli/Sambalpuri, which is playing the pivotal role.

---

[64] See Joshi 1982, 1985, 1987, 1991, 1993, 1995, etc.

Postscript

In early 2004, just before the general election and the elections to the State Legislative Assembly, which were held simultaneously in Orissa, a demand for a separate Koshal state, comprising the western districts of Orissa, was raised publicly. The Koshal Rath travelled throughout the western districts of Orissa in order to stimulate public support for this demand. Major political parties such as the Indian National Congress, the BJP, and the regional party, the BJD distanced themselves from it, neither supporting nor opposing it, at least not unambiguously. At the same time their leadership disregarded the fact that individual members were taking part in these activities. But, since the elections this demand has no longer been heard.

References

Bahidar, S. 1977. *Sambalpuri Bhasara Sabda-Vibhava ba Samkshipta Sambalpuri Vyakarana O' Rachana*, Sambalpur: Chinmaya Sahitya Sansada.

Chand, J.K. 1996. 'Sambalpuri Banam ... ebam Odia Bhasa: Baisistya, Yogasutra O Anchalikata', in P. Bala, B. Nayak and D. Dash (eds.), *Odia O Odisa. Samiksha* '95, Bhubaneswar: Bikalpa Sandhani Mancha.

Census of India 1971, ed. by B. Tripathi, A Portrait of Population, Orissa.

Census of India 1981, ed. by S.K. Swain, A Portrait of Population, Orissa.

Census of India 1991, ed. by M. Vijayanunni, Orissa State, District Profile 1991.

Cobden Ramsay, L.E.B. 1982. *Feudatory States of Orissa*, Calcutta: Firma KLM (1st printing 1910).

Cronin, R.P. 1981. 'Language and Nationalism in Late Nineteenth and Early Twentieth Century India', in R.I. Crane and B. Spangenberg (eds.), *Language Society in Modern India,* Delhi: Heritage Publishers, 24-38.

Das, C. 1981. *Oriya Sahityara Sanskrutika Vikasadhara*, Bhubaneswar: The Orissa Bureau of Text Book Preparation and Production.

Das, S. 1931 (1338). *Baudara Bhasa,* in *Sahakar* 11 (11), 524-6.

— 1996 (?). *Sua Mumhara Patara*, Bhubaneswar: Sridhar Das Smaraki Pratisthan.

Dash, G.N. 1978. 'Jagannath and Oriya Nationalism', in A. Eschmann, H. Kulke and G.C. Tripathi (eds.), *The Cult of Jagannatha and the Regional Tradition of Orissa*, Delhi: Manohar, 359-74.

— 1993. *Odia Bhasha Suraksha Andolana*, Cuttack: Cuttack Students' Store.

— 1996. 'Anchalika Baisistya, Anchalikata O' Odisa (Bhashagata Anchalikata)', in P. Bala, B. Nayak and D. Dash (eds.), *Odia O' Odisa*. Samiksha' 95, Bhubaneswar: Bikalpa Sandhani Mancha, 33-42.

Dash, S.P. 1969. *Sambalpur Itihasa*, Sambalpur: Akshaya Kumar Dash.

Dhall, Golok Bihari. 1951. 'Standard Likhita Odia Bhasa', in *The Jhankar* 3 (1), 81-2.

— 1952. 'Standard Odia Bhasara Uttara', in *The Jhankar* 3 (12), 1020-4.

Gangadhara Granthabali. 1977, ed. by H.K. Das. Berhampur: Pustaka Bhandar.

Gangadhar Patrabali. 1955. Compiled by S.P. Das. Cuttack.

Ghose, S. 1991. *Orissa in Turmoil (A Study in Political Developments)*, Bhubaneswar: Bookland International.

Hobsbawm, E. 1995. *Nations and Nationalism since 1780*, Cambridge: Cambridge University Press.

Joshi, P.P. 1982. 'Kosali Bhasa', in *Saptrsi* 11 (11), 1-27.

— 1985. 'Swatantra Koshli Bhasha', in *Visva-Bharati Dipika* 6, 23-43

— 1987. 'Hay, Hosli Bhasa', in *Koshal Bharati* 1, 1-10

— 1991. *Kosali Bhasara Samksipta Parichaya,* Titilagarh: Kosalayana.

— 1993. 'Paschima Odisara Kathita Bhasa: Odia na Kosali ?', in *Esana* 27, 27-47.

— 1995. 'An Interview', in *Bikalpa Bichara* 3 (2), 79-81.

Mahapatra, K.N. 1969. *Khurudha Itihasa*, Bhubaneswar.

Mahatab, H.K. 1972. *Beginnings of the End,* Cuttack: Cuttack Students' Store.

Misra, C. 1983. *Arddha Satabdira Anubhuti (Pratham Bhag)*, Cuttack: Nabajiban Pustakalaya.

Mohanty, B. 1989. *Odia Bhasha Andolana*, Cuttack: Friends Publishers.

Mohanty, N. 1982. *Oriya Nationalism: Quest for United Orissa*, Delhi: Manohar.

Mohanty, P. 1992. 'Paschima Odisara Kathita Bhasha: Odia na Kosali?' in *Esana* 25, 49-67.

— 1993. 'Paschima Odisara Kathita Bhasha: Odia na Kosali?', in *Esana* 27, 47-54.

Mohapatra, B.P. 1995. *Odia Bhasa Vibrava*, Cuttack: Vidyapuri.

Nanda, P.B. 1993. 'Sambalpur Hiteisini: Eka Adhyaana', in *Konark* 89, 32-9.

Orissa District Gazetteers. Sambalpur. 1971. By N. Senapati and B. Mahanti, Cuttack: Government Printing.

O'Malley, L.S.S. 1909. *Bihar and Orissa District Gazetteers*, Sambalpur. (2nd edn. 1932).

Padhi, S.P.; Supakar, S. 1996. *Sambalapurare Bhasa Andolana*, Sambalpur.

Panigrahi, K.C. 1981. *History of Orissa (Hindu Period)*, Cuttack: Kitab Mahal.

Panigrahi, N. and P.K. Tripathy. 2001. *Sambalpuri-Kosali Byakarana*, Sambalpur: Sambalpur University.

Patel, P. 2002. 'Sambalpuri Sahitya', in *Esana* 45, 33-53.

Pujari, A.K. 1951a. 'Standard Likhita Odia Bhasa', in *The Jhankar* 2 (11), 1012-14.

— 1951b. 'Standard Odia Bhasa', in *The Jhankar* 3 (9), 764-73.

— 1952. 'Sambalpuri Bhasa O Sarbajanina Utkaliya Bhasa', in *The Jhankar* 3 (11), 887-94.

— 1953. 'Sarbajanina Utkaliya Bhasa', in *The Jhankar* 5 (6 & 7), 531-8.

— 1953b. 'Utkaliya Bhasa O Sahitya', in *The Jhankar* 5 (8), 657-69.

Routray, N. 2001. *Smruti O Anubhuti*, Cuttack: Grantha Mandir.

Sahu, N.K. 1985. *Veer Surendra Sai*, Department of Culture, Govt. of Orissa.

Sarma, B.K. 1983. *The History of Somavamsi Rule in Orissa*, Calcutta: Punthi Pustak

Sengupta, J. 2002. 'Princes, Prajamandals, and Partition: Congress Politics and the Rajas of Orissa, 1937-1949', in S. Settar and I.B. Gupta (eds.), Pangs of Partition, vol. 1: *The Parting of Ways*, Delhi: Manohar, 213-41.

Supakar, S. 1993. *Astaraga,* Berhampur: Asha Pustakalaya.

Udgata, G. 1997. 'Bhasha Prasanga – Odia O' Sambalapuri', in *The Jhankar* 48 (11), 159-70.

13

Imagined Chronologies: Perceptions of 'Development' as a Tool in Mapping Oriya Identity

Jayanta Sengupta

Although this paper does not deal with high social-science theories or abstractions regarding time or the consciousness of time, there is an overarching engagement here with the concept of time, which is present or even conspicuous *only in its absence*. More explicitly, the paper deals with the eternity – or timelessness – of a particular kind of discourse that defines identity politics in one of India's most disadvantaged states, namely, Orissa. It goes without saying that this identity of being disadvantaged, of occupying a space at the margins, is solidly grounded in reality: indeed, serious work of high quality has already been conducted on the material contours of Orissa's 'problems', including poverty.[1] This paper makes no attempt to build on this scholarship, though it does draw on many of its principal conclusions. It is essentially a preliminary exploration not into the *materiality* but into the *perception* of the themes of 'marginalization' and 'development', as well as the importance of such perceptions in constructions of Oriya identity. It examines how such themes serve as abiding points or frameworks of reference in constructions of identity, informing discourses of regional development in both the past and the present.

The principal argument here is that the way in which Oriya themes of 'marginalization' and 'development' are constructed and projected imbues them with a certain quality of timelessness. The relationship between the concept of time and the construction of Oriya political identity is defined by the construction of a certain notion, 'backwardness' or 'deprivation', that ingrains itself in the self-perception of the Oriya elite and which they define or claim as 'timeless' or unchanged. This results in constructions of history – contemporary as well as past – that remain unchanged, because this serves both a specific function and certain

---

[1] See, for instance, Nair 1984; Mohanty 1990. For a recent study of the various issues of poverty and iniquity in Orissa, see Jayal 1999.

interests in claiming and demanding resources and a 'special status' from the colonial as well as the postcolonial Indian state. Since the interests and functions of such a construction have remained unchanged for certain social groups, especially the regional elite, the construction itself has acquired something of an enduring quality.

The Material Basis of Oriya Marginality

It needs emphasizing at the very outset that such perceptions are not typical of Oriyas alone but reverberate through depictions by 'outsiders'. Indeed, it is instructive to note that Orissa has been largely neglected in the highly productive field of modern Indian historiography. For a long time, Orissa's political quiescence led historians to conclude that its politics were dull and uneventful. Its failure to catch the scholar's imagination has, in fact, a long history. Even in the nineteenth century, Oriyas were considered too unremarkable to be of interest to the historian. W.W. Hunter, whose two-volume *Orissa* (1872) was a pioneering work, set out to do nothing more ambitious than chart the history of a nondescript 'race'. His book, he confessed, was

> embellished by no splendid historical characters.... To the world's call-roll of heroes it will not add one name. The people of whom it treats have fought no great battle for human liberty, nor have they succeeded even in the more primary task of subduing the forces of nature to the control of man. To them the world stands indebted for not a single discovery which augments the comforts or mitigates the calamities of life. Even in literature – the peculiar glory of the Indian race – they have won no conspicuous triumph. They have written no famous epic; they have struck out no separate school of philosophy; they have elaborated no new school of law.[2]

Hunter therefore found it hardly surprising that 'no part of India has attracted less notice from the historian or from the scholar'.[3] Nearly half a century later, this observation still held good. In May 1920, on the eve of non-cooperation, Mahatma Gandhi gave himself a moment of self-reflection on a people who had always escaped national attention:

---

[2] Hunter 1956, 1.
[3] Ibid., 48.

> Most of us perhaps do not even know where Orissa is.... Orissa is a part of one of the poorest regions in India. We do not hear much about the suffering there because the people are backward in every way.[4]

> For most of us, it [Orissa] is a mere geographical expression [...] nobody knows whether the people of Orissa are happy or unhappy.[5]

Gandhi's observation succinctly summed up the situation of the Oriyas in the early twentieth century: Oriyas were 'poor' and 'backward', and their 'suffering' was unnoticed, even uncared for. It was thus obvious that such epithets had come to stick to the Oriya people between the 1870s and the 1920s. It is also not at all difficult to see that they arose out of the social and economic realities that affected the Oriyas in the colonial period. The piecemeal nature of the British annexation of Indian territories meant that provincial boundaries cut across linguistic ones, and the Oriya-speaking population was scattered over several different provinces. Economically too, colonial Orissa was one of the poorest and most backward of Indian states, with very few towns and virtually no industrial production. A great number of Oriyas migrated from Orissa to serve as labourers in the factories of Calcutta and its neighbouring jute mills. Simultaneously, a considerable number of the Bengali literati swarmed over the coastal districts of Orissa to take up jobs in the administration and the literate professions. This led many Oriyas to complain that their land had been turned virtually into a colony of Bengal. Since educational opportunities were severely restricted in Orissa, the size of the *bhadralok*, which provided the Congress party with its leadership in the Presidency capitals, was here very small. Due to the relatively limited size of the structure of opportunities created by colonial rule, this small Oriya regional elite found itself competing with those who had easier access to English education and the *bhadralok* professions.

It is out of this struggle that the movement for an Oriya regional identity developed. In actual material terms, this identity was rooted in the Oriya elite's self-perception of marginalization, itself born out of their low level of access to the administrative, legislative, and economic resources of the British Raj. Linguistic nationalism, which aimed to unite all Oriya-speaking areas initially under a single administration and later a separate province, was thus not only an affirmation of the 'primordial' ties of

---

[4] Gandhi 1920a, 396.

[5] Gandhi 1920b, 403-4.

cultural affinity, but also a means of appropriating a larger share for the Oriya elite in the 'opportunity structure' of British India.

To a considerable extent, the Oriya movement drew its inspiration from the colonial constitutional initiative of the early twentieth century, which acknowledged the desirability of the redistribution of provinces on a linguistic basis. The conceding of this principle grew out of a new British sociological discourse regarding India that developed in the late nineteenth century, in which Indian society was seen to consist of a vast plurality of culturally distinct communities demarcated along lines of caste, religion, and language. This immense heterogeneity helped to keep alive a colonial sociology of India that was fixated on the latter's social divisions and cleavages. In this discourse, the perception of India's myriad communities as mutually antagonistic and 'naturally conflicting' necessitated the presence of the British as 'umpires', as it were, mediating such conflicts as 'fair', 'independent arbiters',[6] thus legitimizing imperialism by couching it in the language of paternalism. The Oriya elite, like their counterparts in many other parts of India, were not slow to see the advantages of this discourse for their purposes of securing greater access to official patronage.

The Politics of the Oriya Past: Discourses of Regional Nationalism

It is extremely interesting to note the extent to which the construction of a political identity among Oriyas was closely related to the construction of a very distinctive trajectory of the Oriya political past. In the writings of the Oriya publicist class in the late nineteenth and early twentieth centuries, the political past of the Oriyas was plotted along a narrative with deep breaks in continuity. The chronological landmarks that these breaks came to represent were invariably linked to the Oriyas' construction of their experience of marginalization. Indeed, the rhetoric of Oriya political identity in the formative period of its construction reverberates with numerous references to the abrupt end of a golden age and past glories,

[6] In a perceptive analysis of how these theories of ethnicity and race served the hegemonic ideology of the Raj, David Washbrook has delineated 'a sociology of multiple ethnicity [which] sustained imperialism on the "umpire" analogy, positing the need for an independent arbiter to regulate the affairs of these naturally conflicting communities'. See Washbrook 1982, 155. For another recent and incisive study, see Metcalf 1994.

the beginning of the 'dark ages', a fall from grace, or millenarian anticipations of a new dispensation.

The contours of this rhetoric were formed fairly early. Threatened by the subjugation of their language in the 1860s and perceiving their collective predicament as a community as emanating from their 'administrative dismemberment', the Oriya elite evolved a distinctive style of political bargaining with the British Raj. Their rhetoric placed a heavy premium on the past traditions of the 'Oriya race', constructing a time frame that arranged these traditions along a historical trajectory that represented a progressively downward curve from glory to doom. The Oriya publicist class claimed that their hallowed cultural tradition was being laid low by successive centuries of 'territorial vivisection' and 'official apathy'. This rhetoric marked out specific 'watersheds' or landmarks in the evolution of the Oriya political past as constructed by this elite. It also set much store by Orissa's 'glorious ancient past', when her territories straddled India's entire eastern seaboard.[7] Further, it located the genesis of Orissa's troubles in the Muslim annexation in 1568, an event which is seen as having started the 'territorial vivisection' and 'political dismemberment' of what was 'once a much famed and powerful centre of the Hindus ....'[8] In this rhetoric, successive periods of 'foreign' domination in the form of Mughal, Maratha, and British rule were claimed to have deprived the Oriyas of any experience of indigenous political rule, arrested their economic development and reduced their 'once mighty Empire' to a 'terra incognita',[9] thus threatening Oriyas with their extinction as a 'race'.

Thus, from a relatively early point in its career, the Oriya nationalist rhetoric came to focus on the notion of changing times and fortunes. It also came to engage the colonial authorities in a dialogue that sought to historicize Orissa's marginalization and to induce the Raj to introduce measures that would make good the 'injustices' or 'wrongs' perpetrated by such historical 'misfortunes'. Simply put, this meant that the Oriya

---

[7] Such territorial integration occurred under the Suryavamsi Dynasty (*c.* 1435-1540), whose rulers, referred to as Gajapatis, held sway over the entire territory from Midnapur in Bengal all the way down to Tanjore and south Arcot on the Coromandel coast.

[8] Mohanty 1982, xi. Similar statements abound in other works too; see, for example, Patra 1979, Chapter 1. A rather extreme case is the officially compiled Mahtab 1957, which takes 1568 as the starting point of the 'freedom movement'!

[9] Ibid.

nationalist elite sought to project the image that the Oriyas had fallen on 'bad times', in contradistinction to the better times that they claimed to have experienced before. The juxtaposition of 'good' and 'bad' times was especially important, given the fact that this rhetoric sought to appeal to the Raj at a time when it was introducing an increasing dose of constitutional reform in India.

It was only after the language controversy of the 1860s that, under the three different governments of Bengal, Madras, and the Central Provinces, the Oriyas began to wake up to the adverse consequences of the dismemberment of the Oriya-speaking areas.[10] The administrative amalgamation of these areas therefore became a prominent political issue in the last third of the nineteenth century. Amalgamation was not only an avenue to a brighter future but also a throwback to a golden past, because it called for the restoration of a historical region that had once been the cradle of large and strong Oriya empires. In an archaizing vein, Oriyas now turned to history to refresh ancient imperial memories and thus evoke an image of themselves as an endangered people. The emerging field of colonial sociology readily lent itself to indigenous adaptations. The coming of the census – the epitome of the colonial attempt to catalogue the 'native Indian races' – brought home to the Oriya elite the potential power of 'race' to serve as a cultural referent of the new regional identity that they were seeking to create. The rediscovery of the 'Oriya language' thus brought into being various other corollaries, for instance, the 'Oriya race', 'Oriya culture', and the 'Oriya-speaking country'. The census gave Oriyas an opportunity to register themselves in colonial minds as a distinctive ethnic group, entitled to a voice in its own right. The seeds of minority politics, nursed in the twentieth century by the progressively increasing concessions doled out by colonial constitutional reform, were thus sown.

For Oriyas, their disadvantaged position was the reversal of a golden past, the result of the unkind course of a history that placed them at the mercy of 'foreign' rulers and fragmented their cultural community. The shared sense of this past lay at the core of an emergent regional identity. While the 'cultural' content of this identity derived from the invention of an ancient tradition, its politicization owed itself to more contemporary problems blighting Orissa's 'progress'. Much fervour went

---

[10] For more detailed treatments of the language controversy and its role in the formation of an Oriya rhetoric of marginalization, see Sengupta 1994; Mohanty 1982, Mohapatra 1990; Mahapatra 1997; Chandra 1994.

into the allegation that the Oriyas were the 'victims' not only of colonial rule, but also of various 'sub-colonial' regimes perpetuated by the latter. The theme of official 'apathy', which later became one of the main planks of Oriya nationalist politics, had its genesis in emergent colonial perceptions of Orissa as a resource-strapped region, which stood in sharp contradistinction to Bengal's image as a 'golden goose', i.e. an area that the British could exploit at will and with success. At the core of this colonial perception lay the idea that Orissa did not earn its British rulers enough revenue to pay for its own development. Since Orissa could not 'pay its way' to enlightenment and progress, development in that particular part of the world was expendable.

In the context of an evolving colonial discourse on 'race', 'language', and 'nation-building' in the early twentieth century,[11] the Oriya movement was driven by its own volition towards provincialism, its rhetoric being guided by reasons of expediency towards a historicization of Oriya marginalization. The interesting feature of this 'rhetoric of deprivation' was the manner in which it divorced identity from any specific class context and defined the ethnolinguistic community in terms of historical ancestry and common culture that made class irrelevant. The plight of immiserized Oriya peasants and labourers and the aspirations of a distraught regional elite were thus fashioned together into a collective, imagined community of 'suffering Oriyas'. The time-frame to which this rhetoric made reference gave meaning to a sense of the political past that was shared by this entire community. The myth of a glorious Oriya past encompassed all segments of Oriya society, glossing over its myriad cleavages in a homogenizing sweep. Indeed, such homogenization made sociological explanations of the class divisions of Oriya society virtually unnecessary. It enabled the educated, upper-caste Oriya regional elite to speak for all social constituencies and severely limited the ability of internal class contradictions to pose a challenge to the hegemonic representative claims of this rhetoric.

Opposing Reform, Pursuing Patronage: Oriya Nationalist Perceptions of 'Domineering Neighbours'

Hopes of amalgamation led the Oriya elite in the early decades of the twentieth century to address the new, paternalistic face of the Raj and to

[11] For more in-depth treatments of this discourse, see Metcalf 1994, Moore 1966. For a brief survey, see Brown 1999, 421-46.

play up the theme of their plight, as engendered by the presence of domineering neighbours like the Bengalis and Biharis in the north and the Tamil-speaking communities of Ganjam district in the south. In late 1917, the visit to India of the Secretary of State for India, Edwin S. Montagu, became an opportune moment for the proponents of constitutional reform. Moderate Oriya politicians, keen to use this opportunity called for the mobilization of regional public opinion and demanded the union of scattered Oriya-speaking tracts as a prelude to 'provincial autonomy'.[12] A delegation of the foremost Oriya regional political association, the Utkal Union Conference (UUC), waited in deputation upon Montagu and the Viceroy, Lord Chelmsford, in Calcutta in December 1917 and presented a memorandum arguing for special privileges for the Oriyas.[13] The 'Oriya nation', the memorandum claimed, constituted 'an ancient race with a genius all their own'. But it was locked in an unequal struggle with its 'neighbouring races' which – helped by their early exposure to English education – had cornered 'unique opportunities for posts and preferments and representation in the Councils', and thus assumed 'positions of influence similar to those of an intermediary ruling race'. The memorandum also complained that 'the indifference of the authorities to the continuous prayers of the Oriyas for their administrative reunion ... have [*sic*] raised serious doubts in the minds of eleven millions of [Oriya] people with regard to the pronounced policy of the British Government to give equal opportunities to all classes of people to reap the benefits of British rule'.[14]

Two possible ways forward were then suggested. The first was the union of the Oriya-speaking tracts, outlined in 1903 by the linguist George Grierson in his monumental *Linguistic Survey of India*, into 'one separate administration of the type which Bihar and Orissa now has'.[15] The second suggested, in a more pragmatic vein, that if such an arrangement was 'not feasible under the present circumstances [then] the proposed united Orissa [should] be placed under the Government of Bihar and Orissa for the present with a view that it may at a future time develop into a separate administration'.[16] The memorandum clearly indicated how the Oriya regional elite's hopes had been raised to a high pitch on the eve of the

[12] *UD* 1917.

[13] See EICR 1918. For the text of the memorandum, see Report 1930b.

[14] All these quotations are from Report 1930b, 557–8.

[15] Ibid., 558.

[16] Ibid.

Montagu-Chelmsford reforms, as well as demonstrating the Oriya elite's readiness to make a pragmatic tactical compromise, to meet the Raj's reformist 'nation-building' rhetoric halfway. The Oriya nationalist thesis of unfair colonial rule contended that the latter had done Orissa a great disservice by engendering and perpetuating obnoxious systems of sub-colonialism in its neighbourhood, and then turning a deaf ear to the Oriyas' protestations of the need for a remedy. Written into this abhorrence of sub-colonial dominance being perpetrated by stronger neighbours like Bengalis, Biharis and Tamils were the Oriya elite's ever-present anxieties about shrinking resources, opportunities and patronage. This was brought out clearly in an appendix to the UUC memorandum that dwelt on the manifold 'disabilities' and 'disadvantages' of the Oriyas in the following manner:

> The economic, educational and other disadvantages due to the administrative dismemberment of the Oriyas have all along been the opportunities of the advanced races developing vested interests in the Oriya-speaking districts. All the high posts of trust and responsibility are theirs. They command the majority in all public bodies, local and municipal, Oriyas forming therein only an insignificant minority and that in their own districts.[17]

This passage demonstrates the eagerness of Oriya nationalists to participate in the public institutions created by colonial reform, like those of local self-government. Administrative amalgamation or provincial autonomy, which were envisaged as potential panaceas for the ills affecting the Oriya 'race', held out the prospect of much greater access to such institutions.

Published in July 1918, the Montagu-Chelmsford report ruled out an immediate reorganization of Indian provinces on the basis of language and 'race', but noted 'the artificial and often inconvenient character of existing administrative units', including the Bihar and Orissa province.[18] Along with Berar, the Marathi-speaking region in central India that was annexed to the Central Provinces in 1903, Orissa was specifically mentioned as an area in which the idea of a sub-province could be given consideration. The immediate future, however, held out little hope of this, for the report asserted that provincial redistribution was not to be 'imposed upon the people by official action'. Instead, such a process was

[17] Ibid., 'Appendix B', 561.

[18] Report 1918, paragraph 159.

'to follow, and neither to precede nor accompany, constitutional reform, and was to be effected by a process of consent of the reformed provincial Governments.'[19] However, in the absence of any Oriya representation in the provincial legislatures of Bengal and the Central Provinces, the 'process of consent' in favour of a union of the Oriya tracts lying within the territories of these provinces was doomed to be reduced to just a pious wish. Similarly, there was little chance of realizing this desired consent in the legislative councils of Bihar and Orissa and of Madras, where the Oriya members formed an insignificant minority. Thus, for all the rhetoric expended by a supposedly reformist government during 1917-18 on a federated India consisting of 'self-governing provinces and principalities', the Oriyas – as one historian puts it – 'were condemned to wallow in the backwater of administrative apathy and negligence'.[20] Indeed, it was alleged in subsequent Oriya representations that the 1919 Act, 'far from helping the Oriyas by the introduction of an extended franchise, deprived them of what little patronage they were getting in pre-Reform days',[21] led to 'the growth of an aggressive spirit and monopoly of power by the majority communities',[22] and consequently made the Oriyas unable 'to influence any decision in their favour against contending forces'.[23]

Never was this self-perception of marginality articulated more strongly than in the period between the respective publications of the reports of Montagu and Chelmsford and the Indian Statutory Commission – the so-called reform period of the 1920s, when the themes of Indianization and representative politics attracted a fair amount of attention in the discourses of the Raj. It was now that 'administrative vivisection' and the resultant inability to 'reap the benefits of the British Rule' became closely tied to the theme of 'financial insolvency' in the Oriya political discourse. Throughout the period of the working of the colonial constitutional reforms, Oriya leaders clung to the theme of 'backwardness' or 'deprivation' in order to maintain the image of a wronged race. In course of time it became a sophisticated tool of bargaining for additional funds and other kinds of state patronage. Indeed, central financial intransigence hindering regional development – the crux of post-colonial centre-state relations – emerged as a theme in this period.

[19] Ibid.
[20] Mishra 1979, 96.
[21] See IOR 1932.
[22] Ibid.
[23] IOR 1931.

'The development of the province [of Bihar and Orissa] was ... seriously hampered', it was typically claimed in 1921, 'by its past attachment to Bengal, which tended not unnaturally to devote a larger share of its resources to the neighbourhood of its capital city than to its outlying districts ....'[24]

The scheme of provincial finance devised under the Montagu-Chelmsford reforms further exacerbated their general unpopularity in Orissa. In 1919 a special committee was appointed under the chairmanship of Lord Meston to enquire into the whole question of the financial relations between the central government and the provinces in the light of the Government of India Act of that year. The Meston Committee recognized that the Bihar and Orissa province was 'quite the poorest in India' and noted that 'very special skills will be required in developing its resources'.[25] However, in a move that considerably irked the regional elite, Meston's financial settlement gave the province of Bihar and Orissa only a moderately increased spending power. A decade later, in 1930, the report of the Indian Statutory Commission observed that the history of financial administration in the British Indian provinces in the immediate wake of the reforms was 'largely that of the struggles of the central and provincial Governments to establish financial equilibrium by drastic economy and recourse to additional taxation'.[26] Such stringency undermined, among other things, the Oriya politicians' 'nation-building activities', by which the colonial constitutional reforms set much store. Nowhere was this more strikingly apparent than in the field of local self-government. In the 1920s Orissa's municipalities and district boards frequently clamoured for more provincial resources to spend on local development, but were regularly reminded of the paucity of the provincial finances. This resource-crunch influenced provincial politics at all levels and circumscribed the effectiveness of Oriya politicians' quest for a separate province. In fact, the Oriya political elite in the 1920s were faced with one of the trickiest of political dilemmas. Without provincial autonomy they had little chance of increasing their access to colonial resources, yet at the same time they did not have enough resources to convince the government that the proposed province could 'pay its way', i.e. it was economically feasible.

---

[24] Owen 1922, 38.

[25] Report 1920, 8.

[26] Report 1930a, 353.

When in 1924-5 the Government of Madras appointed a committee of enquiry to ascertain the attitude of the Oriyas of the Madras Presidency towards the question of amalgamation, the committee was deluged with representations from various local as well as supra-local Oriya bodies. These representations harped on the same old themes that had preoccupied the Oriya educated elite for a long time in the outlying areas: inadequate representation in official employment, the use of the Telugu language in official transactions, the predominance of Telugu in local bodies, the lack of proper educational facilities in the Oriya language, and the general decline of the Oriya language and culture due to the rapid spread of Telugu influence.[27] These representations referred to the enormous unpopularity that the reforms had attracted from Oriyas, who feared that it would do away with the modicum of sympathetic patronage that British officials had previously granted to the minority communities. In his evidence to this enquiry committee, a prominent political leader of Ganjam gave vent to his fear that 'Oriyas as a separate race will disappear in Madras in course of time, and the more the Indianization of administration the more will be the sufferings of the minority'. Looking back at what he perceived as the root cause of this misfortune, he concluded that 'the so-called Reform scheme has killed our aspirations and damped [*sic*] our hopes'.[28]

The discourse of Oriya nationalism in the first half of the twentieth century is replete with such protestations of marginality, of 'backwardness' – of the same kind that would subsequently be called 'underdevelopment' – being foisted on the state by the negligence of the central government. In the early 1930s, the representations in favour of an Oriya province deployed the moral rhetoric of the 'Orissa wrong' – made so familiar by Oriya nationalists of UUC ancestry – with a degree of arrogant impatience seldom encountered in their pre-1920 incarnations. In one of these the colonial government was castigated for its role in perpetrating a 'criminal injustice' with 'characteristic callousness', and the Orissa Boundary Committee was called upon to 'redress the wrong perpetrated

[27] Report 1930c, 596-9.

[28] The evidence of Harihar Panda of Aska, Ganjam, to the Philip-Duff Committee, cited in ibid., 599. Panda, the Secretary of the Ganjam Oriya Samaj around 1910 and the author of the pro-amalgamationist tract *United Orissa: a plea* (Berhampur, 1915), had sent a memorandum to Viceroy Lord Hardinge in late-1911 detailing the plight of the Madras Oriyas. Around 1910 he was the foremost Ganjam representative in the Utkal Union Conference.

accidentally or through callous indifference'. Scoffing at British official foot dragging, it asserted that the question of provincial autonomy 'should now be considered as a settled fact and should no longer be qualified with suspicious "ifs" and "buts", nor need it be hedged in by hitherto unworked financial or other improvised barriers'.[29] Finally, it lambasted the constitutional reforms of the 1910s as something that, for all their democratic intent, had deprived the Oriya 'race' of official patronage and reduced them to the position of a hopeless minority:

> Under the regime when the provinces were dependent entirely upon the Central Government in all matters, uncontrolled by the vote of the Provincial Legislatures, the minority race had some chance of getting a hearing if it could manage to find an opportunity behind the screen of official support, in spite of the intermediary ruling power. Now, with the transfer of power from centre to the provinces and from bureaucracy to the people, it is certain that the minor partners will go to the wall.[30]

Through such emergent language of minority politics, the Oriyas were essentially reacting against the unequal distribution of colonial legislative resources among various linguistic communities. Since the legislative resources at their disposal were not adequate for effective bargaining, the Raj's experiments in 'responsible government' merely increased their sense of marginalization, hence the indignant protests against 'the transfer of power ... from bureaucracy to the people'. Oriya nationalism therefore had to distance itself from the limited enclaves of 'representative' politics that were emerging in the provincial legislatures. It was forced, by virtue of its very situation, always to look towards the 'centre' and to appeal to the paternalistic and mediating roles of the Raj.

There was, however, one disadvantage to this form of politics. In the language of such minority politics, there was the danger of Oriya nationalism being perceived as something going against the grain of the politics of the Indian nationalist movement. If the Oriya nationalists were essentially devoting themselves to seeking the continued patronage of the British Raj, how could they contribute to the Indian freedom struggle, which of necessity was directed against British colonialism? In postcolonial India, it was sought to resolve this paradox by wrapping the 'official history' of Orissa's freedom struggle around a new, carefully

[29] Report 1932e, 72.
[30] Ibid., 72-3.

crafted consciousness of time that situated Orissa firmly in a pan-Indian grand narrative of struggle. As Vinay Lal has commented:

> More belaboured still was the attempt of the author of the official history of the nationalist movement in Orissa, who was to note that the 'freedom struggle' in Orissa began as far back as 3rd century BC when the Maurya Emperor Asoka invaded Kalinga in 261 BC. The Kalingan army faced the invader with grim determination and laid down their lives in thousands to save the freedom of their motherland.[31]

It was scarcely necessary, on this logic, to examine what freedom could have meant in third-century Kalinga, what (if any) place the idea occupied in India[n] political philosophy, and whether the political structures were hospitable to the idea of freedom. Nor did the notion of an unbroken history of 'Oriya nationality' over three millennia appear to pose any problems for the author. Much like the English, who were prone to represent themselves as a people naturally imbued with the spirit of freedom, the Oriyas thought of 'being free' as their 'very life blood'; and the history of Orissa was, consequently, none other than the Oriyas' continuing attempts, in true Enlightenment fashion, to retain their freedom:

> That sense of freedom has been all along with the Oriyas and Orissa was the last province in the country to come under the Mughal subjugation. It was, therefore, not unusual that these people should be fighting hand in hand and shoulder to shoulder with their brothers in other parts of the Country to free India from the British.[32]

Placing 'Development' in a Restorative Narrative

The texts of most memoranda submitted in the early 1930s to the Orissa Boundary Committee resorted to what can loosely be described as a 'restorative narrative'. Their territorial claims evoked the image of ancient Oriya empires that straddled almost the whole of India's eastern seaboard. But they were quick to reassure the reader that these claims originated from considerations of 'homogeneity of administrative area', and that they by no means intended 'to grab territories, merely because they are

---

[31] Lal 2003, 86. The citation refers to De 1990, 1. See also Lal 1999, 207-8.

[32] Ibid., 87. The citation refers to De 1990, introductory note by Surendranath Satapathy, i-ii. See also Lal 1999, 207-8.

contiguous to us and would augment the size of the Oriya Province'.[33] However, the claimed 'Oriya-ness' of the territories that *were* demanded often derived from a political ambition inadequately backed up by census statistics. The arguments forwarded in favour of the inclusion of these territories in the proposed Orissa province were, mainly, (a) ancient historical connections, disrupted by 'a break, violent but only geographical, with the conquest of the Oriya country by foreigners – the Mussalmans, the Mahrattas and the British',[34] and (b) 'racial' and linguistic affinities. In some of the outlying Oriya areas, the majority of the population were tribals who spoke dialects and were enumerated in the censuses as non-Oriya 'animists'. Many of the representations claimed that, since the Oriya language was the principal 'civilising medium' for these tribes, the inclusion of such backward tracts in the Oriya province would provide for their social and economic 'development'.[35]

Oriya nationalist leaders did not hesitate to question the validity of census findings when these conflicted with their territorial claims. Thus it was held that the great majority of the people of south-west Midnapur 'are Oriyas ethnologically, culturally, socially and, *if the census figures are not taken as unassailable*, even linguistically' [emphasis added].[36] The memorandum from Singhbhum directly accused the censuses of having failed to achieve a correct enumeration of Oriyas because 'such persons as would not consider an increase in Oriya population to their interest were at the helm of affairs'.[37] The overriding concern with economic viability also led some Oriya nationalists to lay claim to resource-rich areas that

---

[33] Ibid., 26.

[34] Report 1932d, 56.

[35] For instance, the memorandum from Singhbhum claimed that the Hos – the largest ethnic group in the district, forming almost 34 per cent of its population – 'can freely talk in Oriya and they know it familiarly as a medium of conversation'. See Report 1932b, 22. Similarly, the Ganjam memorandum argued that 'centuries ago the aboriginal tribes in the aforesaid [Ganjam and Vizagapatam] Agency tracts came into contact with Oriyas who ruled them, educated them, and gave them such civilization as they possessed before the advent of the British rule' (Report 1932c, 52). The representation from Parlakimedi held that the area's numerous Savara tribals 'should, for historical reasons, adopt the Oriya language as the medium of instruction', also arguing that 'all the aborigines of central India' should be brought together under the proposed Oriya province (Report 1932d, 64).

[36] Report 1932a, 7.

[37] Report 1932b, 30.

could make good at least some of the deficit to which the proposed province seemed inevitably to be doomed. Nothing illustrated this more forcefully than the eagerness with which Oriya nationalists sought to prove their right to acquire Jamshedpur, Singhbhum's new and flourishing industrial centre and the home of the Tata Iron and Steel Works. It was argued that 'the very existence and improvement of Jamshedpur as an industrial centre is due to the iron and manganese mines from Mayurbhanj and Gangpur as also to the immense supply of labour from the neighbouring states of Orissa'. Therefore, the argument ran, 'in all fairness and equity Orissa should have the foremost claim to any contribution made by Jamshedpur towards provincial revenue'.[38] The Utkal Union Committee's memorandum went one better, seeking to forward an essentially economic interest by tickling the Raj's benevolent face:

> The new Province which is always threatened with floods and famines will get an industrial centre where the people may find work when their lands are devastated by floods.... The ancient monuments of the Oriya people...indicate the inherent industrial genius of the people who should be given a chance for proving their genius by allowing them an opening to an industrial centre.[39]

Following the third Round Table Conference in November 1932, the contours of the proposed Orissa province began to take shape, though there was a distinct possibility of its eventual emergence as a truncated state, not including the so-called 'deficit' areas in the Ganjam and Vizagapatam Agency tracts. The appearance of this possibility led to the start of a period of intense political activity on the part of Oriya leaders, outside the fold of the Congress party, who now launched a vigorous drive to achieve a more favourable official decision on boundaries and finances. Some of these leaders had already started trying to make some political and economic capital out of the backward tracts that were to account for 45 per cent of the area of the new province. They visualized a separated Orissa as a 'trustee', burdened with 'the sacred responsibility of uplifting so many of the submerged people, tribes and castes', and advancing them 'in the path of civilisation and prosperity'. This responsibility was, naturally, beyond the new province's capability unless it received 'a share of the provincial balances of Bihar and Madras', as well as a

---

[38] Ibid., 30-1.

[39] Report 1932e, 78.

'proportionate share of famine fund and other trust funds ....'[40] These arguments were repeated by the Raja of Parlakimedi when he led an Oriya delegation to London in 1933 to meet the Secretary of State. The memorandum that he presented on behalf of the delegation also reflected a growing anxiety at the prospect of losing areas rich in economic assets. It was argued that the exclusion of the Madras tracts, which were 'rich with undeveloped forest and mineral resources ... will permanently deprive the Orissa Province of the chance of future development and expansion'. This recurring theme of 'development' now provided an overarching link for many of the areas that the Oriya elite had previously claimed on the grounds of historical and cultural association alone.[41]

Generally speaking, the memoranda and representations that Orissa's champions of provincial autonomy sent to British officials and reform committees in the early twentieth century revealed the regional elite's self-perception of backwardness, as well as their new-found and rapidly growing concern with the idea of 'progress'. What is interesting for us is the fact that this formulation of Oriya identity was based on a conception of Oriya history in which the principal chronological landmarks denoted specific stages in the loss of Oriya political power or in what was perceived as the gradual dissociation of the Oriyas from the mainstream of 'development'. Like the Oriya nationalist elite, the Congress too made it into a highly developed tool of political bargaining after having swept into power in the elections of 1936 in the newly formed province of Orissa. Immediately after the formation of the new province, the financial settlement of the Government of India Act of 1935 – the so-called Niemeyer Award – was denounced by the Orissa Governor's Advisory Council for its 'highly inadequate financial aid'.[42] There was much criticism by the Congress ministry during 1937-9 of the government's decision to designate the Sambalpur and Koraput districts, a large extent of Ganjam and the Angul subdivision of Cuttack district as 'partially-excluded' areas. These tracts covered a total area of 21,000 square miles and had a population of 2.6 million, the majority of them tribals. The designation 'partially-excluded' was unsatisfactory because the Government of India did not make any specific grant or contribution for the development of these areas. The aspiration, much in evidence

[40] The citations are taken from a printed copy of an address made by Bhubanananda Das on 12 February 1933. For the full text, see OSA 1933.
[41] IOR 1933, 512 *passim.*
[42] OAC 1936, 34.

throughout the early 1930s, of the coastal Oriya political elite to act as agents in the 'development' of backward areas and to be subsidized by the Government of India in this effort, thus fell through. It was held that the subvention of Rs. 5 million was too meagre in view of the 'special problems in Orissa [which] relate to the "partially-excluded areas" in which large sums of money will be required and also floods for which adequate safeguards will have to be provided'. A member of the Council cried, in a tone resonating with nationalist moral fervour, that 'justice has not been done to Orissa' and that the province 'has not got its proper share'.[43] This proved disappointing to the Congress cabinet, whose work during its two years in office was dogged by fiscal restrictions.

An official summary of the Governors' reports on the performance of the provincial Congress ministries during 1937-9 alleged that the Orissa ministry's policy was 'coloured by a political bias against the Financial Settlement under the 1935 Act', which they felt was unfair to the Provinces generally and to Orissa in particular.[44] This reveals how the rhetoric of financial deprivation had spilled over from the vocabulary of the early-twentieth-century Oriya nationalists into even the Congress discourse of governance in the new province after 1936. It was the party's experience of government that initiated it into a discourse that had been the cornerstone of the politics of Oriya nationalism.

The province of Orissa thus emerged deeply scarred by its financial travails. Premised on the theme of 'racial' and linguistic affinity, the

---

[43] Ibid., 35. The particular statement referred to here was made by Godavaris Misra, a member of the Swarajya Party and a prominent exponent of the movement for provincial autonomy. His allegations sprang from the fact that although Orissa had nearly double the population of Sind and nearly 3.5 times the population of the North-West Frontier Province, its revenues, even when supplemented by the central subvention, were the smallest of any province in India. In determining the size of the subvention, Niemeyer, who headed the Financial Enquiry Committee of 1936, took the provincial budgets of 1936-7 as his basis. However, unfortunately for Orissa, the Governments of Madras, Bihar and Orissa, and the Central Provinces had prepared the estimates of revenue and expenditure 'in the light of the available actuals of the preceding depression period when strict economy in expenditure was being observed'. Thus Niemeyer, depending on a budget prepared by governments who had no responsibility for the administration of the new province and warned by the heavy pruning of that budget by the Central Government, was moved to make his estimate along extremely conservative lines. See Mahapatra 1941, 25-30 *passim*.

[44] IOR 1942, 36.

Oriya movement attached great importance in its rhetoric to its representative claims. It claimed to speak for the 'Oriya people', a category of abstraction that glossed over the multiple class and ethnic divisions within it and attempted to situate 'people' in a space defined by a common experience of 'backwardness' and 'disadvantage'. This construction lent legitimacy to the claim of the small, educated elite to be the 'natural leaders' of the Oriya people. This leadership could discount the 'masses' even as it learnt the rules of the politics of 'backwardness' and 'development', of 'scarcity' and 'subsidies'. Slogans of 'administrative apathy' and 'central negligence', so frequently raised by Oriya politicians after 1947, were hardly novelties of electoral politics but rather colonial legacies that spilled over into the domain of post-colonial politics, being given new meanings by universal adult suffrage. By way of extending this argument, it may even be said that this same rhetoric has continued to determine the relationship between government and local society, since independence as before it. The Oriya nationalists of the 1920s and 1930s complained of 'administrative apathy', 'hostile neighbours' and 'extreme poverty', and clamoured for a 'fair deal' in the form of provincial autonomy and central subsidies. But the government's coffers were not opened to them as much as they would have wished, and their visions of 'progress' continued to be clouded by an acute sense of marginalization. The Oriya politicians of the 1950s and 1960s thus kept up the time-tested tradition of protesting against 'central neglect' and demanding a greater allocation of resources, a greater share in centrally funded development projects and an 'Orissa for the Oriyas'. The image of the Oriyas as a 'wronged' community, perpetually denied a 'fair deal', thus proved to be an enduring one.

Epilogue: Contemporary Discourses of Development

Perhaps it would not be too much of an exaggeration to suggest that this late-colonial political discourse on development, equity and democracy, by which the leaders of the Oriya provincial nationalist movement set much store, has left very prominent traces on the political parlance of the present, and most importantly on the discourse of liberalization. Liberalization, and the enthusiastic courting of it by state governments of all political hues, gives the Oriyas for the first time an opportunity to look beyond the state and, in a sense, to globalize the question of their development. But even as the Oriya elite warms to the seductive charms of the market, and even as the Orissa state goes on unabashedly courting international capital, the discourse of state-aided development also carries on as merrily as ever. If anything, this discourse has become stronger, as the question of development fragments the Oriya polity and places increasingly vocal demands on the state for funds, subsidies, benefit packages, and the recognition of special statuses.

There is something curiously paradoxical in the language of development and its projection or dissemination under the auspices of the state. On the other hand, there has been a consistent attempt on the part of the Orissa state to woo international capital by projecting itself as a dynamically enterprising, liberalizing and privatizing state. In the mid-1990s especially, Orissa increasingly usurped corporate lore about the putative industry-friendliness of states in western and southern India. According to a study conducted by the Centre for Monitoring Indian Economy (CMIE), Orissa attracted the largest amount of private-sector investment in 1995-6, followed by Gujarat, Karnataka, and Maharashtra.[45] International accolades for the state's new-found dynamism were quickly forthcoming. In January 1996 Janaki Ballabh Patnaik's Congress administration invited the reputed international business consultant, Partha S. Ghosh, to prepare a blueprint for the development of the state's infrastructure. Ghosh came up with an optimistic blueprint, in which he emphasized the 'vigorous but balanced' development of new industries to leverage emerging global trends like environmentally friendly products, resource conservation and agro-based industrialisation.[46] Following on Ghosh's heels, the well-known UK-based management and financial consultancy firm, Coopers and Lybrand, identified Orissa as a major emerging economic power in the Asia-Pacific region. A report prepared by the firm on behalf of the FICCI predicted that by the year 2000, Orissa would have surplus power after meeting its present and future needs, and the largest network of ports in eastern India to facilitate the considerable volume of trade between India, Myanmar, Thailand, and other ASEAN countries. Other forecasts included Orissa's emergence as one of the top five contributors to the country's export earnings.[47] Such predictions of an imminent industrial bounty contrast sharply with oft-quoted colonial

[45] *Outlook* 1996.
[46] *ET* 1996.
[47] *TT* 1996.

musings about the industrial backwardness of Orissa.[48] For a state that was traditionally one of the least industrialized in India, being talked about in the same breath as the so-called 'Asian tigers involved quite a dramatic reversal of identities.' Indeed, during 1995-6 alone, the state firmed up concrete proposals for investment of over Rs. 600 billion in industrial projects alone, excluding sectors like power and mining.

Never was this 'progressive' dynamism more strikingly apparent than when Chief Minister Janaki Ballabh Patnaik made a strong case in favour of Orissa's attractiveness to potential foreign investors to World Bank President James Wolfenson in 1995 and US Secretary of Commerce William Daley in 1997. The success of his propaganda can be measured from the fact that Daley, who headed a large delegation of American corporate investors, announced that Orissa was the best-suited state in eastern India to emerge as the so-called 'gateway of the east'. And, in a curious reversal of historical self-images, the market-friendly, pro-liberalization vernacular newspaper in West Bengal, the *Ananda Bazar Patrika* (incidentally, with the largest circulation figure in the state), wondered why the then Bengal chief minister, Jyoti Basu, could not be an aggressive liberalizer in the mould of his more energetic counterparts, like Chandrababu Naidu of Andhra Pradesh or Janaki Ballabh Patnaik.[49]

However, it is interesting to note that this self-congratulatory tone in Orissa's liberalizing rhetoric has coexisted with what can be seen as its exact opposite, namely, the state's attempt to project itself as backward and poverty-stricken and in dire need of development. This latter image is also kept alive as a means of making new demands on the Union government. For instance, the so-called 'partially excluded areas' have become a point of reference for the province's backwardness, as well as a plank from which to launch a sustained campaign of financial bargaining with the centre. The Partially Excluded Areas Enquiry Committee (called

[48] The non-agrarian sector of colonial Orissa's regional economy remained weak in the absence of a significant growth of manufactures. Colonial observers, struck by this absence, often sought to explain it by falling back, typically, upon what they perceived as intractable drawbacks of 'the Oriya character'. Commenting on the latter, J.F.W. James said in that 'its main characteristics, though marked by many amiable features, are not those which make for industrial progress' (James 1913, 21). 'The only manufacture for which this division has any reputation', commented another colonial official in 1913, 'is that of filigree silver work' (Report 1913, 26).

[49] *ABP* 1997.

the Thakkar Committee, after the name of its Chairman, A.V. Thakkar), instituted by the Orissa administration in 1940, expressed the hope that the Government of India would increase the amount of the annual subvention and special initial grants made to the Orissa Government for tribal welfare in the state. This presently takes the form of a claim, articulated loudly and frequently by the Orissa government, to be declared a 'special category' state in view of its high tribal population and extremely low literacy level.[50] This was demanded, for instance, in a memorandum presented by the state government to the 10th Finance Commission in 1993. Parties like the Congress, which cajoled the United Front administration on this issue between 1996 and 1998, and the Biju Janata Dal (BJD), which broke away with the Janata Dal to make an alliance with the Bharatiya Janata Party (BJP) at the centre in 1998, have made this demand individually and across the board, as witnessed in a unanimous resolution adopted by the state assembly in November 1997 urging the centre to declare Orissa a 'special category' state. In May 1998 there were rumblings of discontent within the BJD that their constant demands had fallen flat with the ruling BJP, while the latter's other regional allies, notably the AIADMK in Tamil Nadu, the Trinamul Congress in West Bengal and the Samata Party in Bihar had already managed to extract their pounds of flesh from the centre for the development of their respective states. Since then, differences of opinion on the 'special category' issue have kept the BJP–BJD alliance tenuous, often threatening to develop into a full-fledged rift.

The clamour for recognition as a 'special category' state has been accompanied by a demand for a restructuring of centre–state financial relations in the state's favour. This takes the specific form of a proposal to replace the so-called 'Gadgil Formula' (70 per cent of central assistance in loans, 30 per cent as a grant) by a 'special category' scheme (90 per cent grant, 10 per cent loan, as in Kashmir and the north-eastern states). A number of reasons are cited in support of this proposal. The huge debt burden of the state (estimated at nearly Rs.7 billion) eats up almost 60 per cent of the state's income through repayments and has prompted the government to make a demand for easier instalments. The administration of Biju Patnaik demanded frequently that the state's share of the central

[50] The large tribal population has been traditionally held up as a demographic factor disadvantageous to the state's potential for growth. Scheduled castes and tribes presently account for around 37.1 per cent of the state's population, compared to the national average of 23.6 per cent (*ET* 1993).

taxes be raised and that Delhi write off the Orissa government's outstanding loans of more than Rs. 2,100 crores to make up for the 'raw deal' that the latter had received in the recommendations of the 10th Financial Commission. It was also contended, indignantly, that even after forty-five years of independence, Orissa grossly lacked infrastructure, largely due to the centre's apathy to its development. The meagre amount of railroad and surface road expansion in Orissa was held up as an indication of this apathy. Indeed, only 38 km of railway track have been added to the state in the course of the last three decades. This has checked both the intrusion of the globalizing forces of the market and the reach of the welfare state. Similarly, the length of surface road per 1,000 sq. km of area is only 122 km in Orissa, which is less than half the national average of 269 km.[51] Orissa's development programme, nearly entirely hegemonized by the rhetoric of liberalization, has thus clearly failed to act as a dynamic for more rapid infrastructural growth. Nonetheless, such stagnation continues to provide the state administration with a perpetual reason to clamour for more development funds from the centre.

The identity of Orissa as a state that has constantly been short-changed in the national distribution of resources, and has therefore been unable to proceed smoothly along the path of economic development, thus appropriates and subsumes all other identities and interests in the lower social substrata. These identities and interests go on making localized demands on the state for funds, resources or attention. Not all such demands are focused on the question of development – indeed, there are significant local environmentalist groups who subscribe to an anti-developmentalist rhetoric and who question the market-friendly, liberal economic policies of both the central the state administrations. But these grievances, and the agitations resulting from them, fail in general to dramatize themselves, to stamp their own voices on the generally popular image of Orissa as a marginal state. In the state's political discourse, the notion of redistributive justice has thus been appropriated by ministerial and bureaucratic talk of the need to democratize the distribution of national resources among the states. This amounts in reality to a demand for per capita equalization of surplus revenues among the states. In other words, the Oriya elite's self-image of peripherality – a well-known legacy of the colonial period – continues to be recycled over and over again in the discourse of democracy and development in the contemporary period, overlaying both centre-state and state-society relationships in the process.

---

[51] *TOI* 1993.

References

Ananda Bazar Patrika (ABP) 1997. Editorial dated 13 December, entitled 'Jyoti Basu banam Janaki Ballabh' [Jyoti Basu vs. Janaki Ballabh].

Brown, J.M. 1999. 'India', in J.M. Brown and Wm. R. Louis (eds.), *The Oxford History of the British Empire,* Vol. IV: *The Twentieth Century*, Oxford and New York: Oxford University Press, 421-46.

Chandra, S. 1994. *The Oppressive Present: Literature and Social Consciousness in Colonial India*, Delhi: Oxford University Press.

De, S.C. 1990. *Story of Freedom Struggle in Orissa*, Bhubaneswar: Orissa Sahitya Akademi.

EICR 1918. East India Constitutional Reforms: Addresses presented in India to His Excellency the Viceroy and the Right Hon'ble the Secretary of State of India, *Parliamentary Papers*, 4: XVIII (1918), no. 61: 'Representation by the Utkal Union Conference'.

The Economic Times (ET), 6 July 1993, 31 January 1996.

Gandhi, M.K. 1920a. 'Famine in Orissa', in *Navajivan*, 9 May 1920, reprinted in *The Collected Works of Mahatma Gandhi* [henceforth, *CWMG*], Vol. XVII (February-June 1920), New Delhi: Publications Division, Ministry of Information and Broadcasting, Govt. of India, 1965.

— 1920b. 'Distress in Orissa', in *Young India*, 12 May 1920, reprinted in *CWMG*, vol. XVII.

Hunter, W.W. 1956. 'Orissa, or the vicissitudes of an Indian province under native and British rule' (originally published from Calcutta in 1872), in N.K. Sahu (ed.), *A history of Orissa*, Vol. 1, Calcutta: Susil Gupta Publishers.

India Office Library and Records (IOR), 1931. London: Round Table Conference files, Q/RTC/31 ['Miscellaneous papers relating to the Round Table Conference'], memorandum presented by the Raja of Parlakimedi to the Round Table Conference, dated 3 January 1931, entitled 'The Oriyas, their need, and reasons for a separate province'.

India Office Library and Records (IOR), 1932. London: L/P & J/9/54, Public and Judicial Department file no. P & J(C) 656, Part II ['Orissa: Question of its constitution as a separate province'], enclosure 5: Memorial submitted by the Oriya Deputation, appointed by the Utkal Union Conference, to Viceroy Lord Willingdon, 17 September 1932.

India Office Library and Records (IOR), 1933. London: Private Office papers, L/PO/6/86: 'Note on the boundaries of Orissa Province', submitted to the Secretary of State for India by the Oriya Delegation in London on 3 July 1933.

India Office Library and Records (IOR), 1942. London: Public and Judicial files, L/P & J/8/588 ['Work of Congress Ministries in the Provinces - Reports by Governors'], file Pol. 4043 of 1942: 'Performance of the Congress Ministries, 1937-1939'.

James, J.F.W. 1913. *Final Report on the Revision Settlement of Orissa, 1906-1912*, Patna: Superintendent, Government Printing, Bihar and Orissa.

Jayal, N.G. 1999. *Democracy and the State: Welfare, Secularism and Development in Contemporary India*, Delhi: Oxford University Press.

Lal, V. 1999. 'History and Politics', in M. Bouton and P. Oldenburg (eds.), *India Briefing: A Transformative Fifty Years*, Armonk, NY, and London: M.E. Sharpe.

— 2003. 'Contours of the Past, Shape of the Future: The Politics of History in Independent India', in idem *The History of History: Politics and Scholarship in Modern India*, Delhi: Oxford University Press, 79-140.

Mahapatra, J.N. 1941. *Orissa in 1936–37 to 1938–39*, Cuttack: Superintendent, Government Press.

Mahapatra, P. 1997. *The Making of a Cultural Identity: Language, Literature and Gender in Orissa in Late Nineteenth and Early Twentieth Centuries*, London: School of Oriental and African Studies, unpublished Ph.D. thesis.

Mahtab, H.K. 1957. (with Sushil Chandra De) eds., *History of Freedom Movement in Orissa*, 5 vols. Bhubaneswar: State Committee for the Compilation of the History of Freedom Movement.

Metcalf, T.R. 1994. *Ideologies of the Raj*, Cambridge: Cambridge University Press.

Mishra, P.K. 1979. *The Political History of Orissa: 1900-1936*, Delhi: Oriental Publishers and Distributors.

Mohanty, M. 1990. 'Class, Caste and Dominance in a Backward State: Orissa', in F. Frankel and M.S.A. Rao (eds.), *Dominance and State Power in Modern India: Decline of a Social Order*, Vol. 2, Delhi: Oxford University Press, 321–66.

Mohanty, N. 1982. *Oriya Nationalism: Quest for a United Orissa*, 1866-1936, Delhi: Manohar.

Mohapatra, B. 1990. *The Politics of Oriya Nationalism, 1903-1936*, Oxford: University of Oxford, unpublished Ph.D. thesis.

Moore, R.J. 1966. *Liberalism and Indian Politics, 1872-1922*, London: Edwin Arnold.

Nair, K.R.G. 1984. *Lagging Regions in a Developing Economy: A Case Study of Orissa*, New Delhi: Indian Council of Social Science Research.

OAC 1936. *Orissa Advisory Council: Official Report of the Summary of Proceedings* (11 May 1936), Cuttack: Superintendent, Government Press.

Orissa State Archives (OSA). 1933. Bhubaneswar: The S.N. Rajguru (Parlakimedi, Ganjam) Collection, Accession no. 1393.

Outlook 1996. 'The Investor's Paradise', in *Outlook*, 18 September 1996.

Owen, G.E. 1922. *Bihar and Orissa in 1921*, Patna: Superintendent, Government Printing, Bihar and Orissa.

Patra, S.C. 1979. *Formation of the Province of Orissa: The Success of the First Linguistic Movement in India*, Calcutta: Punthi Pustak.

Report 1913. *Report on the Administration of the Territories now included in the Province of Bihar and Orissa, 1911-12*. Patna: Superintendent, Government Printing, Bihar and Orissa.

Report 1918. *Report on Indian Constitutional Reforms* [Montagu-Chelmsford report]. Calcutta: Superintendent, Government Printing, India.

Report 1920. *Report of the committee appointed by the Secretary of State for India to advise on the question of the financial relations between the central and provincial governments in India* [British Parliamentary Paper on East India: Constitutional Reforms - Financial Relations], London: His Majesty's Stationery Office.

Report 1930a. *Report of the Indian Statutory Commission*, Vol. I, *Survey*, London: His Majesty's Stationery Office.

Report 1930b. *Report of the Indian Statutory Commission*, Vol. IV, 'Memorandum by the Government of India', Appendix II ['Address presented to His Excellency the Viceroy and the Secretary of State by Representatives of the Utkal Union Conference in 1917'], London: His Majesty's Stationery Office, 557-65.

Report 1930c. *Report on Enquiry into Attitude of Oriya-Speaking Population of the Madras Presidency Towards Amalgamation with other Oriya-Speaking Tracts* (often referred to as the Philip-Duff Enquiry Report), in *Report of the Indian Statutory Commission*, Vol. IV, 'Memorandum, by the Government of India', Appendix V, London: His Majesty's Stationery Office.

Report 1932a. *Report of the Orissa Committee*, Vol. II, *Non-financial appendices*, Appendix 3.A(1): 'Memorandum for south-west Midnapur', Calcutta: Govt. of India, Central Publication Branch.

Report 1932b. *Report of the Orissa Committee*, Vol. II, Appendix 3.A(2): 'Memorandum of Singhbhum'.

Report 1932c. *Report of the Orissa Committee*, Vol. II, Appendix 3.A(4): 'Memorandum for Ganjam'.

Report 1932d. *Report of the Orissa Committee*, Vol. II, Appendix 3.A(6): 'Memorandum of Parlakimedi'.

Report 1932e. *Report of the Orissa Committee*, Vol. II, Appendix 3.A(8): 'Memorandum on the Utkal province submitted by the Utkal Union Committee'.

Sengupta, J. 1994. *Political Change in Orissa: Regional Identity and Popular Movements, 1900-1956*, University of Cambridge (unpublished Ph.D. thesis).

The Times of India (*TOI*), 8 July 1993.

The Telegraph (*TT*), 27 April 1996.
Utkala Dipika (UD), 20 October 1917.
Washbrook, D.A. 1982. 'Ethnicity and Racialism in Colonial Indian Society', in R. Ross (ed.), *Racialism and Colonialism: Essays on Ideology and Social Structure*, The Hague: Nijhoff.

Index